HOLLYWOOD IN SAN FRANCISCO

HOLLYWOOD IN

TEXAS FILM AND MEDIA STUDIES SERIES
Thomas Schatz, *Editor*

LOCATION SHOOTING
AND THE AESTHETICS
OF URBAN DECLINE

—

SAN FRANCISCO

—

JOSHUA GLEICH

UNIVERSITY OF TEXAS PRESS AUSTIN

Printed in the United States of America
First edition, 2018

Requests for permission to reproduce material
from this work should be sent to:
Permissions
University of Texas Press
P.O. Box 7819
Austin, TX 78713–7819
utpress.utexas.edu/rp-form

♾ The paper used in this book meets the minimum requirements
of ANSI/NISO Z39.48–1992 (R1997) (Permanence of Paper).

Library of Congress Cataloging-in-Publication Data

Names: Gleich, Joshua, author.
Title: Hollywood in San Francisco : location shooting and the aesthetics of urban decline / Joshua Gleich.
Other titles: Texas film and media studies series.
Description: First edition. | Austin : University of Texas Press, 2018.
Series: Texas film and media studies series | Includes bibliographical references and index.
Identifiers: LCCN 2018001198 | ISBN 978-1-4773-1645-0 (cloth : alk. paper) | ISBN 978-1-4773-1755-6 (pbk. : alk. paper) | ISBN 978-1-4773-1756-3 (library e-book) | ISBN 978-1-4773-1757-0 (non-library e-book)
Subjects: LCSH: Motion picture locations—California—San Francisco. | Motion pictures—California—San Francisco—History. | Motion picture industry—California—San Francisco—History. | Cities and towns in motion pictures. | San Francisco (Calif.)—In motion pictures.
Classification: LCC PN1995.67.S36 G54 2018 | DDC 791.4309794/61—dc23
LC record available at https://lccn.loc.gov/2018001198

doi:10.7560/316450

CONTENTS

ACKNOWLEDGMENTS

THE KERNEL OF THE IDEA FOR THIS BOOK emerged almost a decade ago when I was working on a master's degree at Emory University. I suggested it in a paper proposal for James Steffen's historiography class. He thought it sounded more like a book proposal, and clearly he was right. This book had a long way to grow though, and reflects generous, thoughtful attention from so many people before and throughout its development.

I would like to thank Jeanine Basinger, my undergraduate mentor at Wesleyan University, as well as Lisa Dombrowski and Scott Higgins. At Emory, Matthew Bernstein was a role model as a professor and has been wonderfully supportive well beyond my two years in Atlanta. I would also like to thank David Pratt, James Steffen, Michelle Schreiber, and Eddy Von Mueller. I am grateful to the late Dana White for introducing me to the field of urban studies.

Tom Schatz has probably read more versions of this book than I have. He has been instrumental as a professor, then a mentor, then a dissertation supervisor, and finally as an editor at the University of Texas Press. Janet Staiger was an exceptional teacher, mentor, reader, and committee member during my time in Austin. Thank you also to committee members Kathryn Fuller-Seeley, Mark Shiel, Allan Shearer, and Joe Straubhaar, as well as Lalitha Gopalan for her unofficial input.

I would also like to thank the archivists and archival staff that supported this project. These include Sandra Joy Aguilar, Jonathan Auxier, and Jeremy Tipton at the Warner Bros. Archives, USC; Jenny Romero at the Margaret

Herrick Library; Julie Graham at UCLA Special Collections; and the staff at the San Francisco History Center. Thanks are also due to the friends who supported me during research trips. Noah Mark and Jon Moshman graciously provided a place to stay, a spare car, and welcome company during a frenzied archival trip to Los Angeles. Eric Gladstone offered housing and occasional research assistance in San Francisco.

I have enjoyed the opportunity to present sections of this project at various conferences, most often at the Society for Cinema and Media Studies Conference, where I've learned a great deal from my fellow participants. In particular, Joshua Glick, Erica Stein, Mark Shiel, Merrill Schleier, Julie Turnock, Brendan Kredell, Pam Wojcik, Nathan Holmes, Stan Corkin, Sabine Haenni, Jennifer Peterson, Lawrence Webb, and Noelle Griffis have been fixtures as panel or audience members, providing invaluable feedback and context for my work. The Urban Studies/Geography/Architecture Scholarly Interest Group deserves recognition for their ongoing support for my research.

Special thanks to members of my PhD cohort, in particular, Paul Monticone and Stuart Davis. Dave Fresko and Ross Melnick have provided much needed advice and support as well. Thank you to my colleagues at Arizona, Mary Beth Haralovich, Barbara Selznick, Brad Schauer, Shane Riches, and Anna Cooper, for helping me balance the completion of this book with teaching and other responsibilities. And thank you to Jim Burr at the University of Texas Press for guiding this project through publication.

Thank you to my parents, Charlie and Sheryl, and my sister, Sarah, for their support and enthusiasm throughout the long process of writing a book while beginning an academic career. My greatest thanks and love to Ariel, who's been there for me across several state lines during the course of this project. And thank you to my daughter, Violet, whose unbridled energy is a daily inspiration.

HOLLYWOOD IN SAN FRANCISCO

INTRODUCTION

GOLDEN GATEWAY

The Golden Gate Bridge is the iconic symbol of San Francisco, captured innumerable times on film and television. It is also a filmmaking location with specific demands. In 1947, *Dark Passage* tried to shoot at the Presidio with the bridge in the background, but couldn't because the park was closed on Sundays, one of many incidents that reflected Hollywood filmmakers' limited experience with extensive location shooting in the immediate postwar era.[1] A decade later, Alfred Hitchcock captured the bridge in its Technicolor postcard beauty for *Vertigo* (1958) in a style similar to the touristic footage featured in popular Cinerama travelogues. *Bullitt* (1968) hoped to take its famous car chase across the bridge, but the traffic problem proved insurmountable; new San Francisco mayor Joseph Alioto, an avid booster of location filmmaking in the city, negotiated an alternative location with the Bridge Authority.[2] In *Dirty Harry* (1971), the bridge looms over a group of medical workers in dim, predawn light as they pull a nude fourteen-year-old girl's body out of a drainage ditch. The scene would have been impossible to shoot a few years earlier, not only for its macabre imagery but also because earlier film stocks would have required far more light.

These production details and screen depictions point to many of the factors that shaped the major studios' development of location shooting practices in the three decades following World War II. Changing economics, technologies, production values, and logistics not only allowed crews to shoot more efficiently and effectively on location, but also guided their choice of locations and style of location filmmaking. The Golden Gate Bridge is as picturesque today as it was during the filming of *Dirty Harry* or *Vertigo*. But Hollywood's approach to capturing San Francisco as a setting underwent fundamental changes during the rocky restructuring of the American film industry between the studio crises of the late 1940s and the rise of the blockbuster in the mid-1970s.

How did the dreamy San Francisco of *Vertigo* become the nightmarish wasteland of *Dirty Harry*? The simplest explanation might be that it suffered a massive downturn akin to postwar Detroit's, but San Francisco was one of the most prosperous American cities during the turbulent 1960s and early 1970s.[3] Perhaps the different styles of directors Alfred Hitchcock and Don Siegel account for the disparate images of the city? Yet Hitchcock's *Frenzy* (1972) provides nearly as bleak a picture of London as Siegel's depiction of San Francisco. It is a unique American city architecturally, topographically, and culturally. However, with rare exceptions, San Francisco appeared onscreen with the same style and narrative function as other popular urban locations of the period.

A primary but underexamined causal factor in Hollywood's shifting postclassical style is location shooting.[4] A minority practice in the immediate postwar era, shooting on location became Hollywood's dominant mode of filmmaking by the 1970s. Dense, active cities like New York and San Francisco offered exceptional production values but also posed extensive logistical challenges for filmmakers and producers. While Westerns shooting on location in the 1950s and 1960s might have faced harsh environments, those rural landscapes lacked the cramped interiors and large crowds that plagued urban location shoots. Yet the actual city offered a spectacle of people and structures impossible to replicate on the backlot, an attraction that filmmakers and producers regularly sought to capture. Improved location technologies and a boom in films set in cities like San Francisco pushed filmmakers to seek out less photographed locations outside of downtown, beyond familiar sites like the Golden Gate Bridge and, after 1968, Haight-Ashbury. Urban location shooting not only provided some of the most influential films of New American cinema but remained at the forefront of new production practices throughout the postwar era. While never becoming a film or television production center on a par with Los Angeles or New York, San Francisco remained the third most popular city setting for decades. At its peak in the early 1970s, the volume of major productions shooting in San Francisco threatened to overshadow that of Los Angeles.[5]

But something strange happened on the way to the city. As filming on location in American cities became routine, filmmakers began to seek out their roughest corners. San Francisco remained a prominent site for Hollywood's growing exploitation of urban location shooting. Yet the rising prevalence of filming in San Francisco during the 1960s and 1970s often degraded the city's most attractive vistas while exploring its ugly recesses. A grimy urban aesthetic emerged and deepened over time in films like *Bullitt*, *Dirty Harry*, and *The Conversation* (1974). On film, the local image of San Francisco soon matched the emergent national image of the American city as a blighted battleground.

Although the problem of urban decline was a prominent issue in the 1940s, cities persisted as cultural centers, providing office jobs and entertainment districts, including the top movie theaters, for a burgeoning suburban population. As the suburbs continued to grow, downtowns became less central to the daily lives of many Americans. The protests and race riots of the mid-1960s indelibly marked cities as crisis centers, inverting the cultural paradigm exemplified by the Hollywood Western. Now civilization existed on the suburban periphery surrounding a core, impoverished wilderness (with African Americans cast in the role of Native Americans). As urban location shooting approached its zenith, the filmic image of San Francisco, along with those of most American cities, grew increasingly dire.

This book traces the intersecting postwar phenomena of location shooting and urban decline, examining films shot partially or entirely in San Francisco between 1945 and 1975. A set of industry crises in the immediate postwar years not only fundamentally changed the American studio system but also precipitated a boom in location shooting in the form of the semi-documentary. While the shift to location shooting was not a clean, linear progression, by the early 1970s it had overtaken soundstage production as the primary method of feature filmmaking. By 1975, high-concept blockbusters like *The Towering Inferno*, whose set pieces and special effects relied on production and post-production facilities largely based in Los Angeles, heralded a significant retreat from location shooting. I end my study there, as the decades-long growth of location filmmaking finally ebbed.

Changing production practices and changing perceptions of the American city combined to indelibly alter Hollywood's and America's images of urban space. Several historical modes of urban cinematic representation suggest interrelated paradigm shifts. The practice of urban location shooting had to develop economically, technologically, and aesthetically to offset the greater control and efficiency offered by the physical studio. Similarly, location shooting had to meet or redefine professional standards of realism established by soundstage production wherein cinematographers favored realistically lit sets over poorly lit real locations. Finally, changes in how Hollywood shot the city and how America saw the city came together onscreen. Just as new tools and approaches for location shooting favored new locations, so did dramatic shifts in popular perceptions of central cities, imagined as tourist paradises in the 1950s, but as lawless ruins by the 1970s. The choice of a given city, the choice of locations within that city, and the organization of urban space through editing were dictated by preconceived urban narratives, while bounded by the physical and economic limitations of location shooting.

One constant among these many variables affecting location film production was the city of San Francisco, which attracted significantly more film and television productions than any other American cities except for New York and Los Angeles during the thirty-year period of this study. Unlike those cities, San Francisco was overwhelmingly a location, not a production center. And whereas New York and Hollywood locations served resident filmmakers, feature filmmakers in San Francisco were primarily visitors. This single urban center provided a number of visually arresting landmarks and vistas whose recurrence helps identify subtle shifts in Hollywood style.

San Francisco's distinct urban form and culture underscore a critical argument of this book. Real locations, no matter how exceptional, are extremely malleable on film and in the imagination. Each of the following chapters explores competing strategies for capturing San Francisco, but together they point toward a prevailing Hollywood urban aesthetic that can be traced and analyzed across specific historical periods. Feature films rarely offer more than a cursory exploration of San Francisco's local culture. More often, the city is a background setting and a location set, a physical environment used to stage urban fantasies that reveal far more about Hollywood filmmaking and American culture than they do about San Francisco.

HOLLYWOOD FILMMAKING IN SAN FRANCISCO

Beginning in 1945, this book covers three decades of Hollywood filmmaking in San Francisco, but American filmmakers' interest in the city began far earlier. In 1906, for instance, Thomas Edison filmed the destruction wrought by the San Francisco earthquake. The rise of the Hollywood studio system increased the capacity and economic incentive to shoot most films in studios or on backlots. A handful of film companies continued operating in San Francisco through the 1920s, but none could compete with the Los Angeles studios after the coming of sound and the onset of the Depression.[6] With rare exception, classical era Hollywood relied on second-unit footage or, preferably, existing stock footage to suggest San Francisco settings while working almost exclusively on soundstages and studio lots and ranches.

For *Greed* (1924), Erich Von Stroheim shot for months on location in San Francisco in a fastidious attempt to capture the real settings of the novel *McTeague*. The expense of such exhaustive location shooting, among other production excesses, ruined Von Stroheim's career and provided a powerful argument for building San Francisco settings on the studio lot.[7] By the 1930s, films like *After the Thin Man* (1936) judiciously created a San Francisco setting through a handful of establishing shots, including one of Nick and Nora (William Powell and Myrna Loy) driving beside a cable car. San Francisco befit the wealthy and urbane characters, while prompting studio sets such as a Chinatown nightclub and a foggy street. Location shooting proved an unnecessary expense, as it did for *The Maltese Falcon* (1942), which avoided a trip to San Francisco by relying on Warners' stock footage library and a handful of scenes shot on location in Los Angeles.[8] Large standing sets on studio backlots readily stood in for San Francisco exteriors. For *San Francisco* (1937), MGM captured all of the principal photography of the city on the New York Streets standing sets on one of several backlots, including a twenty-minute earthquake sequence with full-scale building sets rigged to collapse.[9] B-film crews occasionally shot sequences in San Francisco owing to economic factors such as their inability to build expensive sets, lack of studio space, and a willingness to compromise aesthetics by shooting quickly with available daylight. But after the United States entered World War II, gas rationing further mitigated location shooting outside of Los Angeles.[10]

Filmmakers returned from the war with a newfound experience: working on location for combat cinematography. The war effort also prompted the development of more portable cameras. That, along with labor unrest and a shortage of available studio space in the immediate postwar years, led to a boom in urban location filmmaking.[11] *Dark Passage*, shot extensively in San Francisco, exemplifies postwar approaches to location shooting and their limitations, adapting more rugged semi-documentary techniques from *The House on 92nd Street* (1945) and *The Naked City* (1948) to classical Hollywood form. The style of these semi-documentary films would have a profound effect on realist aesthetics, but the expense and unpredictability of shooting on location would convince Hollywood to rein in domestic location shooting by the early 1950s.

Throughout the 1950s and much of 1960s, technological and economic incentives favored a hybrid approach that combined location shooting and soundstage production for the vast majority of Hollywood films. For instance, scenic locations gained production value with the advent of widescreen and the prevalence of color filmmaking in the mid-1950s. But both widescreen and color demanded far more light, making it less expensive and more effective to combine location footage with studio-lit shots of the leading actors. Meanwhile, the speed of black-and-white film continued to increase, facilitating more extensive location shooting, including night exteriors and location interiors that proved impractical on color film.

The year 1968 marked a turning point, exemplified by *Bullitt*, one of the first major studio color films to be shot entirely on location. By the early 1970s, such a practice was commonplace, and even television shows like *The Streets of San Francisco* (1972–1977) began shooting primarily on location. Local filmmaking facilities, such as labs and post-production houses, emerged in San Francisco, further encouraging location shooting. Francis Ford Coppola, who founded American Zoetrope in San Francisco in the late 1960s, completed all production and post-production for *The Conversation* without leaving the city, an impossible feat for a major motion picture before the 1970s.

What appeared to industry observers to be an inevitable shift from soundstage filmmaking to location shooting in the early 1970s began to change direction by 1975. The rise of special effects–laden blockbusters such as *The Towering Inferno* (1974), *Star Wars* (1977), and *Close Encounters of the Third Kind* (1977) required mechanical and optical effects impossible to achieve on location. Meanwhile, the unprecedented box office return on *Jaws* helped inflate production and advertising budgets for major pictures, making the potential below-the-line costs saved by shooting on location less significant. While location shooting remained a core component of feature filmmaking, by the end of the 1970s, Hollywood illusions provided far greater production value than real locations. I end this study in 1975, when the rise of the blockbuster era marked a paradigm shift for the Hollywood industry akin to the shift in 1945.

Like Hollywood filmmaking, the popular image of the American city underwent drastic changes between 1945 and 1975. The prolonged Depression and the onset of the war both stunted urban construction in the 1930s and early 1940s. Postwar America faced an immediate housing shortage, as well as aging downtowns in need of reconstruction. For the next two decades, cities were transformed by the urban phenomena of suburbanization, highway construction, white flight, and federally funded urban redevelopment. Population declines in major cities led to a sense of urban decline, but the race riots of the second half of the 1960s led to a widening national perception of an urban crisis.[12] As modern architecture and urban planning failed to anticipate or alleviate civic disorder, the dominant urban paradigm of the twentieth century fell to pieces, symbolized by the 1972 demolition of the crime-ridden modernist housing complex Pruitt-Igoe in St. Louis.[13] By the late 1970s, urban gentrification and postmodern skyscrapers began to reestablish shiny, elite business and residential districts in central cities.

Hollywood location shooting and the urban crisis profoundly reinforced one another and, indeed, created a persistent aesthetic paradigm for the city. Films like *Bullitt* and *Dirty Harry* reinvigorated the police genre, but also moved toward a bleaker portrait of the city, one that is still evident in films like *Training Day* (Antoine Fuqua, 2001) and *Nightcrawler* (Dan Gilroy, 2014), or contemporary cop shows like *Southland* (2009–2013) and *Bosch* (2014–). Location production was crossing key technological and economic thresholds just as American fears over the central city were peaking in the late 1960s and early 1970s. Yet like the cine-tourism of the 1950s, the gritty urban cinema of the 1970s was also a fantasy, a preconceived narrative that dictated the choice of locations and style of depiction. Nowhere was this more evident than in San Francisco, whose appearance changed far more drastically on-screen than off-screen.

SAN FRANCISCO EXCEPTIONALISM

Why San Francisco? This question shaped not only the path and argument of this book, but also Hollywood filmmakers' approaches to the city as a location. The simplest answer is that San Francisco is exceptional in a variety of ways that make it particularly attractive to film. As a site with unique scenic qualities and economic advantages, it provides a wealth of case studies for new developments in urban location shooting. As a relatively small city with identifiable landmarks, it offers a more cohesive set of images than the myriad neighborhoods and overwhelming filmographies of cities like New York and Los Angeles. San Francisco films almost always feature the Bay Bridge, the Golden Gate Bridge, the Ferry Building, and trolley cars. Sites like Coit Tower, the Legion of Honor, Fisherman's Wharf, Pacific Heights, and, by the late 1960s, Haight-Ashbury remain prevalent. Analyzing San Francisco's screen image requires fewer exceptions and omissions than those of New York and Los Angeles, but encompasses a larger and more influential body of films than those set in Chicago, Boston, or Philadelphia.

Quantitative data show that San Francisco had a significantly greater screen presence than several more populous American cities. Mark Shiel compiled a list of 518 film noir titles from 1940 to 1959 and delineated the urban setting for each film. Not surprisingly, Los Angeles and New York appeared most frequently, accounting for more than 110 films each. However, San Francisco was the setting for 36 films, three times as many as Chicago, a city with a far larger population and a rather famous history of crime.[14] Such a discrepancy cannot be solely attributed to Dashiell Hammet's *The Maltese Falcon.* San Francisco settings also appeared in *This Gun for Hire* (1942), *The Lady from Shanghai* (1947), *Dark Passage* (1947), *D.O.A.* (1950), *The House on Telegraph Hill* (1951), and *The Lineup* (1958). Between 1945 and 1975, 118 American movies featured San Francisco locations; only 27 were shot in Chicago, the second or third largest city in the country for those three decades.[15] As for critically acclaimed films, 36 Oscar-nominated films featured San Francisco, while only 10 featured Chicago.[16] Simply put, San Francisco has had an impact on cinema quite disproportionate to its population size. Although extensive scholarship exists on film depictions of

Los Angeles and New York, this is the first detailed study of San Francisco's postwar screen image.[17]

San Francisco remained a prominent location throughout the postwar Hollywood era despite greater economic incentives to shoot in other world cities. It never offered the substantial financial benefits that lured Hollywood filmmakers to Europe, such as the expenditure of frozen funds, lucrative coproduction deals, and cheaper labor.[18] As a California city, it could not even offer state-level incentives to entice Angeleno filmmakers to travel north. San Francisco also had far more unpredictable and inhospitable weather for filmmaking than Los Angeles. But the city offered two powerful enticements: one tangible, one intangible. First, San Francisco was the largest major city within a half day's drive of Los Angeles; second, San Francisco looked like it was a continent away from Hollywood.

Both Americans and Europeans have described San Francisco as a European city transplanted onto the Pacific Coast.[19] Los Angeles, the harbinger of sprawling postmodern urban space, seems antithetical to San Francisco, whose density and architecture remain persistently premodern. As Los Angeles pushed east and south across vast plains, the city center shrank in importance; it eventually became commonplace for Los Angeles residents to never set foot in downtown. Meanwhile, San Francisco's peninsular site has preserved a dense, active urban core. The bay and its two elegant bridges provide a spectrum of vistas for the camera. As Los Angeles made and remade itself through road and roadside construction, San Francisco residents fought to successfully preserve urban districts and sights, right down to the iconic trolley cars. The most jarring change in San Francisco's urban environment from the 1920s through the 1970s was a 1960s skyscraper boom.[20] Yet this vertical rather than horizontal growth preserved the most cherished districts and added more sites to San Francisco's embarrassment of visual riches.

Aesthetics alone could never convince Hollywood producers to blithely dispatch filmmakers northward. If the studio system could produce *An American in Paris* (1951) without traveling to Paris, why bother to trek up the coast to shoot in San Francisco with more than a second unit? The decision largely depended on how much a given production could benefit from location shooting. *The Maltese Falcon* (1941) suffered little from a lack of San Francisco location work, but shooting *Vertigo* (1958) without real locations would be inconceivable. San Francisco's unique proximity to Hollywood often made it the most economical city to film in outside of Los Angeles. A trip to San Francisco involved more trucking than flying, and producers could quickly return to meet with Hollywood executives if shooting went over budget or schedule. Second-unit crews could easily return for pickup shots. These reduced costs helped put San Francisco at the forefront of location shooting practice.

San Francisco offers another important exception to other cities. As urban scholar Susan Fainstein suggested in 1986, "Amidst the sorry picture of decline in America's old, ethnically heterogeneous cities, San Francisco appears to offer a stunning example of success."[21] The postwar urban crisis had an incredible impact on America's tenuous attitude toward the city. Urban decline appeared to illustrate and exacerbate the worst socioeconomic and racial tensions of the era, culminating in the violent media spectacles of urban riots and protests in the second half of the 1960s. San Francisco offered a rare picture of urban vibrancy and harmony against a national image of urban blight and chaos. As urban renewal associated New York and other cities with the wrecking ball, San Francisco raised construction cranes. San Francisco's so-called Manhattanization produced a new skyline to announce its emergence as a West Coast hub of business and technology.[22]

San Francisco's relative prosperity during an era dominated by national stories of urban decline offered another advantage. This distinction helps separate San Francisco's specific urban experience from its cinematic history. Changes on-screen, largely captured by nonresident filmmakers, reflected national concerns and Hollywood trends far more than local realities. Films such as *Dirty Harry* and *The Conversation* modeled San Francisco on the desolate New York of *The French Connection* (1971) and *Taxi Driver* (1976), not the city of *Vertigo* or *Guess Who's Coming to Dinner* (1967). This cinematic degradation of the urban exception suggests that filmmaking overpowered the local complexities of physical place far more readily than scholars have acknowledged—let alone closely examined. While filmmakers always exploited San Francisco's unique production value as a location, the chosen sites varied with larger trends in filmmaking. In the 1950s and 1960s, tourist attractions were choice locations, but vice districts and redevelopment zones became just as prevalent in the bleak urban crime dramas of the 1970s.

The near total omission from Hollywood films of key parts of San Francisco's geography and history further distinguishes the city from its screen image. Prior to the late 1960s, Hollywood filmmakers overwhelmingly focused on downtown San Francisco, all but ignoring neighborhoods beyond the city center. For instance, *Petulia* was the only film to shoot a major scene in Daly City, an area just south of San Francisco. Aside from *The*

Graduate (1967), which shot scenes in Berkeley, and *The Laughing Policeman* (1973), which ventured into Oakland, the larger Bay Area rarely figured into films shot in San Francisco. The Summer of Love precipitated the location-shooting boom in the city, but other aspects of San Francisco's cultural history were largely overlooked. For instance, *The Subterraneans* (1960), based on Jack Kerouac's novel, was perhaps the only studio film of its period to depict San Francisco's Beat culture, one of the city's most distinctive and influential movements; instead of shooting in North Beach, producers staged the film almost entirely on the MGM lot.[23] Hollywood's image of San Francisco was narrowly focused, targeting specific landmarks and exploitable cultural icons, like hippies, that reinforced popular conceptions of the city. Rather than revealing the cultural values of San Francisco, films shot there reflect the production values that Hollywood sought to extract from the city.

LOCATION SHOOTING AS PRACTICE

Shooting on location versus the studio lot has always involved a cost-benefit analysis. Production values, economic incentives, and relative risk are critical factors, and in the classical Hollywood era, this analysis largely favored shooting on soundstages and the backlot. Filming on location was thus the exception, and producers had to justify their departure from the control and predictability provided by the studio infrastructure, either by capturing something that could not be adequately recreated on the lot or by finding creative ways to reduce location expenses, either with new technologies or new shooting methods. Studios' tolerance for location shooting depended on the scale and complexity of a given production. For example, filming second-unit footage of the Golden Gate Bridge was a standard practice, but shooting lead actors driving across the bridge in *Dark Passage* or racing through the streets of San Francisco in *Bullitt* entailed far greater risks for delays and cost overruns.

The key factors informing any production decision are economics, technology, aesthetics, and logistics. In the case of location shooting, crews are constrained by budget, photographic requirements, the desired look of the film, and the difficulty of staging scenes in actual places. Furthermore, the relative impact of each of these factors changes over time. For instance, a technological development, like faster film stock, reduced the need for larger lights, thus saving money, providing greater stylistic flexibility, and allowing access to smaller interior locations. Conversely, a beautiful site captured in widescreen Technicolor could offer production value well worth the added expense and difficulty of location shooting. While solutions to best balance these factors are specific to each scene and each film, Hollywood filmmakers adopted similar strategies that well suited historical limitations and opportunities. Industry-wide practices in location shooting not only motivated the choice of San Francisco as a location, but also guided filmmakers looking to capture parts of the city in a certain light.

Technological limitations were particularly relevant to the development of location shooting because, unlike budgets, there was no room for negotiation. Certain scenes were, for practical purposes, unfilmable without major innovations. In the 1940s and much of the 1950s, the vast majority of location scenes were daylight exteriors. Film stock was too slow to shoot at night without setting up an array of massive lights, and the requisite equipment was often too large to fit into residential locations and still leave room for the actors. Black-and-white film had surpassed these limitations by the late 1950s, but color film lagged behind by a decade. Sound equipment designed for studio production was largely immobile, and locations could not be soundproofed like Hollywood stages. By the early 1970s, the camera, grip, lighting, and sound equipment required for most scenes were all small enough to fit into a single vehicle, the popular Cinemobile. Prior to that, an expensive caravan of equipment and crew members had to be transported to a given site. Hollywood's ability to recreate almost any place on-screen masked the fact that many locations were off limits, or exorbitantly expensive or impossible to capture with existing technology.

In *Widescreen Cinema*, John Belton provides a valuable model for analyzing the complicated transition of a minority practice in Hollywood, large-format cinema, into an industry standard. Rather than following a linear development, widescreen cinema emerged when economic forces, technological developments, and the culture of movie-going created the right circumstances for experimentation and rapid conversion to widescreen cinema. The mutual reinforcement of these contributing factors promoted a change in filmmaking practice by removing previous obstacles to adoption.[24] Similarly, location shooting predated soundstage filmmaking, but the Hollywood studio system of mass production realized greater efficiency and aesthetic achievement working under the carefully controlled setting of the physical studio. Location shooting reemerged as a viable alternative in the postwar era as studios coped with the three decades of industry instability between the postwar decline of the classical studio system and the relative stability of the blockbuster era. Meanwhile, improvements in technology, changing aesthetics, and refinements in production methods allowed location shooting to replace soundstage production as the primary Hollywood filmmaking practice by the early 1970s. In the process, San Francisco would be transformed from an occasional scenic backdrop to a living backlot for Hollywood filmmakers and television producers.

CINEMA AND THE CITY

This study of San Francisco's screen image contributes to a growing body of work on the relationship between cinema and the city. Since the mid-1990s, the analysis of cinema and urban space has produced a major concentration of interdisciplinary scholarship.[25] With the exception of Sean Cunningham's edited collection on *Vertigo*, only a handful of authors have emphasized urban space in analyzing films set in San Francisco.[26] Although this may appear to be a flagrant omission, the same could be said for most cities except New York, Los Angeles, Paris, Rome, and Berlin. Not surprisingly, these are all film production centers for major Western cinemas and sites for canonical film movements such as German Expressionism, Italian Neorealism, and the French New Wave. Unlike those cities, San Francisco never developed a local feature filmmaking industry. By the late 1960s, it housed quite a number of filmmakers, but they largely concentrated on television commercials and underground filmmaking. Only in the early 1970s could filmmakers based in Northern California actually shoot and edit feature films in San Francisco, among them Francis Ford Coppola, George Lucas, and Michael Ritchie. Filmmakers shooting on location in Los Angeles were by and large capturing their home city. Many filmmakers working in New York had the same local experience, particularly directors who had emerged from New York's live television industry, such as John Frankenheimer and Sidney Lumet. In Hollywood films, San Francisco largely appeared through the eyes of visiting filmmakers, not resident artists. It was primarily a location, not a production center, and thus its screen depiction often reveals more about Hollywood's approach to cities than San Francisco's specific urban culture.

Scholarship on the cinematic depiction of cities always faces a question of causation: to what extent do filmmakers shape the image of a city, and to what extent does the actual city shape the films? Many scholars have explored how films shot on location in cities lend poetic meaning and criticism to the real changes in a city's urban history.[27] Yet the conflation of film realism and real locations can mask the fact that filmmakers are more than capable of constructing urban fantasies while shooting on location. For example, *Bullitt* and *Petulia* were shot in San Francisco almost simultaneously but suggest two remarkably different cities. Even local filmmaker Clint Eastwood fashioned a San Francisco in *Dirty Harry* that more closely resembles a declining downtown Manhattan than the actual city.

With rare exception, the local realities of San Francisco's unique urban culture were subsumed by Hollywood's prevailing methods for depicting cities. While acknowledging misrepresentation, this book is not concerned with a colloquial debate over real versus "reel" cities. Hollywood films that adhere faithfully to local geographies are rare exceptions. Hollywood's creative geography largely follows decisions based on economic efficiency. Attention to the real versus reel issue masks another assumption: that a real city can be fully captured on film. This is the myth of total cinema magnified to an urban scale.[28]

SAN FRANCISCO THROUGH A HOLLYWOOD LENS

This book is a history of Hollywood's remarkable transition from studio production to location shooting and, specifically, its impact on San Francisco as a film location and narrative setting. San Francisco is as much the object as the subject of this history, as changes in Hollywood production methods and urban aesthetics fundamentally reshaped the city's screen image. Accordingly, each chapter begins by analyzing industry-wide changes in Hollywood, looking at the economic forces that either promoted or restricted location shooting, the technological developments that made location shooting more or less expensive, and the aesthetic trends that promoted new location production strategies. Following this broader context are detailed production histories of key films and television series set in San Francisco. These case studies reveal how Hollywood filmmakers crafted an image of the city within the boundaries of current location production practices and popular preconceptions of urban settings.

Many of the films and series covered in depth are indelibly associated with San Francisco, such as *Vertigo*, *Bullitt*, *Dirty Harry*, and *The Streets of San Francisco*. Others are well known but less clearly associated with the city, such as *Dark Passage*, *Days of Wine and Roses*, *The Conversation*, and *The Towering Inferno*. Finally, I include some lesser-known studio films that offer unique explorations of San Francisco, such as *The Lineup* and *Petulia*. I have excluded films and series set in the past, such as *I Remember Mama* and *Have Gun, Will Travel*, instead focusing on contemporaneous visions of the city.

All of the film and television case studies in this book feature crimes, and for most of them, crime is the central plotline. This is not an arbitrary decision but rather an indication of the strong tie between Hollywood urban realism, location shooting, and crime genres, including semi-documentaries, film noirs, detective dramas, and police films. Over half of the 118 films produced between 1945 and 1975 that were set partially or entirely in San Francisco are crime stories.[29] These include many of the most influential films shot in the city, such as *Vertigo*, *Bullitt*, and *Dirty Harry*. As a point of comparison, the most popular comedies set in San Francisco, *Guess Who's Coming to Dinner* and *What's Up, Doc?* (1972), were described by critics and filmmakers as unrealistic Old Hollywood depictions of the city.[30] Genre analysis is not the major focus of my study, but genre conventions clearly shaped the types of films that were shot in San Francisco in a given period.

In many ways, this book can be divided into two major phases of location shooting in San Francisco. The first three chapters cover the twenty-three years prior to 1968 during which location shooting grew as a component of feature filmmaking, but most productions invariably returned to the soundstage for much of the principal photography. *Bullitt*, shot entirely in San Francisco, heralded a rapid shift away from the backlot. Through the mid-1970s, filmmakers all but abandoned the physical studio, shooting primarily on location and only sporadically relying on studio facilities. This changeover had an enormous impact on San Francisco. From the mid-1940s to the mid-1960s, the city had served as a feature location only a handful of times a year; from 1968 through the mid-1970s, dozens of film and television productions flooded San Francisco, threatening to overshadow Los Angeles as a production hub.

The year 1968 is also a fulcrum for Hollywood's urban aesthetics. San Francisco's rising popularity as a location in the late 1960s coincided not only with a boom in location shooting, but also with a darker current of urban fear. Certainly, elements of urban pessimism and paranoia had appeared earlier: in the film noir style of the 1940s and 1950s, in the melancholy of *Vertigo*, and in the bleak depiction of alcoholics in *Days of Wine and Roses*. But the city still looked glamorous on film, and its problems seemed isolated to characters on the margins of society, particularly criminals, who were effectively captured or eliminated by the police by the end of the film. The riots, protests, and economic woes that befell so many American cities in the late 1960s indelibly altered this screen image; the deterioration of San Francisco's picturesque cityscape was a bitter irony for a place widely considered the exception to urban decay. Chapters 4 through 6 cover films including *Bullitt*, *Dirty Harry*, and *The Conversation*, along with the popular television series *The Streets of San Francisco*, all of which tarnished the city's postcard image. Producers increasingly favored locations and camera techniques that determinedly chipped away at or simply avoided the city's extant visual charms. On-screen, San Francisco came to resemble a New York in crisis, befitting the popular narrative of the grimy, crime-ridden city typified in the resurgent police genre.

Chapter 1 details postwar location shooting during the 1940s and early 1950s, analyzing the industry crisis that promoted semi-documentary location shooting and the technological limitations that quickly discouraged such a practice. A case study of *Dark Passage* reveals how rudimentary Hollywood location shooting remained in an era dominated by soundstage production. Meanwhile the demands of classical Hollywood aesthetics muted the distinction between location shooting and studio-bound production.

Chapter 2 examines the cine-tourist aesthetic, developed to exploit tourist locations as renewed attractions for color widescreen exhibition. At the same time, producers of lower budget black-and-white films took advantage of urban locations as set pieces they could not afford to build. A tourist center with postcard views, San Francisco attracted both types of location production, as demonstrated by case studies of *Vertigo* and *The Lineup*.

Chapter 3 focuses on a pair of 1962 Blake Edwards films set in San Francisco and shot partially on location: *Days of Wine and Roses* and *Experiment in Terror*. A laxer Production Code enforcement combined with technological improvements in black-and-white filmmaking shaped a wave of dark realist dramas extensively shot on location. Edwards and other television-trained filmmakers found more efficient ways to shoot in urban locations—and showed how effectively San Francisco locations could be transformed into low-key nightmare landscapes for desperate characters.

Chapter 4 looks at the onset of San Francisco's production boom as Hollywood filmmakers rushed to exploit the city's locations during its countercultural heyday in the late 1960s. New location shooting practices and technologies shared by European art cinema, television, and documentary production further opened the city to filmmaking. A new mayor, Joseph Alioto, engaged directly with Hollywood producers, hoping to draw more of them to the city. *Petulia* and *Bullitt*, the first two major studio films shot entirely on location there, both sought to authentically capture San Francisco, yet they essentially depict two different cities, an indication of Hollywood's ability to effectively transform locations to suit different production strategies.

Chapter 5 centers on *Dirty Harry*, a defining film that, like the myriad police films that followed it, staged San Francisco as a bleak, chaotic city modeled on a declining New York. By the early 1970s, location filmmaking was the dominant mode of Hollywood production, facilitated by portable equipment designed specifically for location work. At the same time, filmmakers purposefully degraded their cinematography, developing a new semi-documentary aesthetic that gravitated toward the ugly corners of cities like San Francisco. The sleazy, crime-ridden world of *Dirty Harry* fit the popular imagination of the urban crisis and created an enduring image of urban blight, serialized in *The Streets of San Francisco*.

Chapter 6 details San Francisco's struggle with the glut of Hollywood location production in the mid-1970s, which spurred residents to question whether the economic benefits of location shooting outweighed the city's increasingly negative screen image and the regular inconveniences caused by production crews. Two 1974 films set and shot in San Francisco, *The Conversation* and *The Towering Inferno*, alternatively represent the peak of location production in San Francisco and the nascent blockbuster aesthetic that pulled filmmakers back to the Hollywood lots. Francis Ford Coppola conceived, shot, and edited *The Conversation* entirely in San Francisco, home of his American Zoetrope production facility, but offered a despairing picture of urban alienation. By contrast, *The Towering Inferno* built an expensive, escapist disaster too dangerous and expansive to capture on location, with little emphasis on its San Francisco setting.

The book's conclusion summarizes how changes in location shooting transformed San Francisco's screen image and its status as a site for Hollywood filmmaking. Unlike contemporary centers of location shooting that primarily rely on tax incentives, such as Louisiana, San Francisco attracted filmmakers with its visual qualities, convenience, and the cooperation of its local government. Despite aspiring to become a film industry hub, the city remained primarily a location, malleable to Hollywood narratives, production practices, and aesthetics. San Francisco's role on-screen reveals more about Hollywood's developing practice of location shooting than it does about San Francisco's unique urban form and culture.

San Francisco's three postwar decades as a film location offer a unique perspective on how extensively the growth of location shooting altered Hollywood production strategies, shooting methods, and in the end, popular conceptions of the city. It was a proving ground for new location shooting practices and a barometer for America's growing estrangement from urban life. San Francisco continued to thrive as a tourist site and cultural center, but its screen image deteriorated to fit the nation's deepening sense of urban decay. Its carefully cultivated image was no match for Hollywood's expanding ability to capture and transform locations to suit new production methods and urban fantasies.

1

POSTWAR LOCATION SHOOTING, THE SEMI-DOCUMENTARY, AND *DARK PASSAGE*

BETWEEN 1945 AND 1948, Hollywood launched a new subgenre, the semi-documentary, whose primary stylistic distinction was location shooting in various American cities. The boom in semi-documentaries represented the first extensive use of location shooting for Hollywood features since the silent era.[1] By using portable technologies along with production methods developed for combat documentaries, filmmakers sought to bring documentary realism to a series of crime and espionage stories. Despite the box office appeal of several semi-documentaries, including *The House on 92nd Street* (1945) and *Call Northside 777* (1948), this subgenre all but disappeared following its most ambitious production, Mark Hellinger's *The Naked City* (1948). Although spiraling production costs and studio overhead had prompted experiments in shooting on location to avoid the expense of building major sets, the production of films such as *The Naked City* and *Dark Passage* (1947) revealed that Hollywood filmmakers' inexperience working extensively away from the soundstage, with often challenging logistical and technological barriers, made location shooting a false economy. Hollywood crews often fell behind schedule due to the unpredictability of actual urban spaces, causing location expenses to climb, rivaling set-building costs. As major studios slashed production budgets in the late 1940s, the semi-documentary proved less efficient than carefully supervised productions primarily shot on the soundstage.

By the 1950s, the term *semi-documentary* was being used to describe a style rather than a subgenre, showing the impact of the 1940s boom in urban location thrillers on Hollywood's realist aesthetics and location production methods that would last for decades to come. But semi-documentaries illustrated the formidable obstacles that Hollywood needed to overcome to efficiently shoot on location, a practical reality that limited the extent of location shooting whenever financial incentives, such as those offered by European countries in the early 1950s, did not exist. Between 1945 and 1954, at least forty-four Hollywood films featured a contemporary San Francisco setting; *Dark Passage* and *The House on Telegraph Hill* (1951) were the rare exceptions that stayed longer than a week. *Dark Passage* shot first-unit footage throughout the city and surrounding areas, but *The House on Telegraph Hill* limited most of its location work to a single site on Telegraph Hill, indicative of a more conservative approach to location shooting following the end of the semi-documentary boom in 1948.

Dark Passage, which shot in San Francisco for nearly a month, presents a limit case for location shooting in the city during the decline of classical Hollywood. Despite its prolonged urban shooting schedule, the finished film's image of San Francisco rarely differentiates itself from those of other 1940s and 1950s films. Production difficulties were partly to blame for the film's struggle to capture stars on location, as well as the false economy of location shooting. Yet production correspondence and the film itself reveal how readily the norms of classical Hollywood filmmaking could transform unique locations into dramatically limited settings. Whether in background projection or first-unit location footage, the image of San Francisco was circumscribed not only by the demands of the story and stars, but also by a cinematic logic that carefully bound the role and appearance of urban settings.

LOCATION TECHNOLOGIES

A variety of technologies that facilitated location shooting had gained industry acceptance in Hollywood by the end of the 1940s. The rapid adoption of these new tools not only suggested the growing importance of location shooting in postwar Hollywood filmmaking, but also revealed how poorly equipped Hollywood was for extensive location shooting. The economic and logistical difficulty of capturing San Francisco and other cities on film became readily apparent to production executives overseeing a wave of postwar semi-documentaries. Existing equipment designed for the soundstage often limited the effectiveness of new, more portable cameras and lights. As in later eras, technologies that reduced overall lighting requirements had the most substantial impact on location shooting, simultaneously adding time, money, and stylistic latitude to productions through quicker lighting setups and smaller crews. Nonetheless, by the end of the semi-documentary boom in the late 1940s, rear-projected backgrounds still proved far more cost-effective than location shooting for the great majority of studio productions.

Not surprisingly, World War II played a decisive factor in promoting location shooting outside of Hollywood. Several major producers and directors—including Darryl Zanuck, William Wyler, and John Huston—served in the Army Signal Corps, adapting their studio experience to shooting combat documentaries. One of the fundamental challenges of representing warfare was developing production tools that functioned efficiently and effectively in not only dangerous but poorly lit locations. Unlike soundstage production, which facilitated precise lighting, set design, and repeated takes, combat cinematography needed to capture events as they unfolded with limited control over the settings or lighting.[2] Engineers responded with the Eyemo, a 16 mm camera that was portable, durable, and could be operated handheld. The camera's ability to capture real locations would have a clear application in realist Hollywood dramas shooting on location in the postwar era.

In mid-1945, as the war reached its end, cinematographer James Wong Howe argued that this new camera could extensively alter Hollywood production practices in an *American Cinematographer* article broadly titled "Post-war Motion Pictures." Showing the pragmatism of a Hollywood veteran, he led with the economic advantages of the combat camera, as noted by Ezra Goodman: "The 16mm camera, according to Jimmy [Wong Howe], has more maneuverability, costs less to operate and necessitates lower production costs. As a result, its adoption by professional picture producers will bring greater flexibility to Hollywood movie methods and help accentuate the film as an art by eliminating many of its costlier practices which have in the past tended to reduce the screen's area of experimentation."[3] In Howe's interview, he neatly expressed how an interplay between technology and economics could change production practices, as it would with each innovation that facilitated location shooting. While new technologies such as handheld cameras and portable lights created new aesthetic possibilities, their increased efficiency created room in the budget and schedule to develop new production methods.

For Howe, economy was the mother of invention. He cited Karl Freund's mobile camerawork for *Variety* (1925) and *The Last Laugh* (1924) to support his claim. Another advantage of the smaller camera evident in *The Last Laugh* was the ability to better match camera movement to actor movement. By retaining smaller-gauge film, which reduced the need for powerful lighting units, Hollywood could shoot more frequently with natural light. The portable camera might also recreate the vivid realism of combat newsreels for narrative features, perhaps a necessary reaction to a documentary style that "put Hollywood professional 'realism' to shame."[4] Howe doubted Hollywood cameramen returning from war service would simply abandon their experience, and he assumed that audiences would retain a similar attention to realism.[5]

MGM's *Lady in the Lake* (1946) seemed to confirm Howe's predictions (aside from the adoption of 16 mm). Cinematographer Paul Vogel had served as a cameraman in Europe with the Signal Corps. He particularly appreciated the combat camera's ability to capture the point of view of soldiers on the front, creating a visceral, embodied experience for home-front audiences. *Lady in the Lake* would famously capture almost the entire action of the film from the optical perspective of the protagonist, played by director Robert Montgomery. Vogel shot extensively with an Eyemo camera specifically designed for shooting combat footage in tight spaces with available light; Bell and Howell frequently advertised this application of the Eyemo in *American Cinematographer*. The unique style gained industry attention, although critics and audiences found the film's point-of-view (POV) experiment "gimmicky." The Warner Bros. film *Dark Passage*, which began shooting soon after *Lady*'s release in November 1946, attempted a more limited application of the technique, hoping to add a thrilling sense of presence within real locations in San Francisco.[6]

The French Éclair and German Arriflex were further improvements on the handheld camera in the late 1940s. Unlike the Eyemo, these cameras offered direct reflex viewing, allowing the cameraman to see a reflection of the image captured by the camera lens.[7] For the first time, professional cinematographers could see an accurate image while they filmed, which proved particularly useful for maintaining proper framing during ad hoc camera movement. The new handheld cameras were specifically designed for 35 mm Hollywood filmmaking, eliminating the need for studio camera departments to retrofit combat cameras to shoot dramatic features.[8] The Arriflex camera was periodically redesigned and remained a staple of location filmmaking through the 1970s, facilitating camera movement in cramped interiors, on uneven ground, and in other locations that prevented laying dolly track. However, in the 1940s, the promise of shooting on location with a light, portable camera quickly met the weighty reality of existing lighting and sound technology.

Louis De Rochemont, who produced and directed the *March of Time* newsreel series, pioneered the semi-documentary with *The House on 92nd Street*, followed by *13 Rue Madeleine* (1947), both shot by Norman Brodine. When shooting both exteriors and interiors on location, camerawork was largely constrained by big lights and other rigs. Setting up equipment in actual interiors for *13 Rue Madeleine* left barely enough room for the actors and cameramen. Meanwhile, each location required generators since professional lights demanded more power than household electricity could provide.[9] Sound equipment designed for large soundstages proved just as cumbersome. Thus the efficiency of the portable camera could be quickly subsumed by the additional equipment and crew members required for adequate lighting and sound.

An incident from the production of *The Steel Trap* (1952) illustrates the challenge of fitting equipment, crews, and actors into restrictive locations. Cinematographer Ernest Laszlo shot most of the film in downtown Los Angeles. Capturing two actors speaking in the backseat of a taxi required the following procedure: "Two taxis were securely tied together in tandem. . . . The players, Laszlo, the director, camera, and camera crew were crowded into the second taxi; the sound recording equipment and power supply batteries were in the first taxi along with the driver, a gaffer, and sound recording engineer."[10] Rather than attempt such a complicated location shot, most 1950s filmmakers performed similar shots on the backlot. In *On the Waterfront* (1954), a film renowned for its location photography, Terry (Marlon Brando) makes a famous speech in the backseat of a taxi. Producers wisely chose a studio reproduction with an improbable set of venetian blinds covering the taxi's rear window. Even the lightest camera could not outmaneuver the other massive pieces of equipment needed to shoot on location.

Location difficulties helped spur more efficient lighting units. By 1948, Universal had developed the quad-light, a rectangular metal pan that accommodated four photoflood bulbs. These lights, primarily used by amateur photographers, helped light small location interiors for *The Naked City*. The new lighting units could be powered by utility lines, reducing the need for generators. When William Daniels won the Oscar for Best Cinematography, he helped legitimize the application of photofloods for Hollywood location shooting. The potential savings were obvious when Daniels shot *Deported* (1950) in Italy. The lights, packed into two trunks, arrived in Italy via air in thirty-two hours; Daniels contrasted this with the fourteen days it took to transport lights to Italy via ship for *Ben Hur* (1925).[11] Photofloods were particularly handy for shooting night exteriors; Robert Surtees attached them to streetlights to capture night-for-night scenes in the film noir *Act of Violence* (1948).[12]

More-photosensitive film stock held the greatest potential for both lowering the cost and improving the aesthetics of location shooting by reducing the necessary light levels for every scene. However, Eastman did not offer significantly faster black-and-white stock until Tri-X debuted in 1953, and even this new stock produced a grainer image than the standard Plus-X.[13] Instead, studios experimented with alternative film stocks and development processes, hoping to effectively shoot on location at lower levels of illumination, particularly at night. Universal even tried to economize by shooting day-for-night scenes with infrared film rather than eliminate dark scenes from scripts due to location lighting expenses.[14] Paramount technicians found a more elegant solution, a development process known as latensification, which could intensify lighting on exposed negative film, effectively adding up to two f-stops during development (similar to post-flashing, widely used in the 1970s). Paramount realized the clearest benefits on location: "Production has been able to use many desirable locations which otherwise could not have been considered, either because of prohibitive lighting expense or because of restrictions which would have made it impossible to bring in the necessary lighting."[15]

Latensification played a role in two of Paramount's seminal film noirs of 1950. In *Asphalt Jungle*, John Huston and cinematographer Hal Rosson captured a chase through a dark tunnel using only existing lightbulbs.[16] For *Sunset Boulevard*, Billy Wilder and cinematographer John Seitz used the process on 15 percent of the film to maintain depth of field in low-key lighting.[17] From the urban nightscapes of *Asphalt Jungle* to the shadowy interiors of Norma Desmond's mansion, the ability to use less light not only opened new locations to filmmakers but allowed cinematographers to use more subtle lighting effects, helping distinguish low-key A-noirs from high-contrast B–crime thrillers: *Asphalt Jungle* and *Sunset Boulevard* would both be nominated for Academy Awards for Best Picture and Best Cinematography (in 1951 and 1952, respectively). The success of latensification in these films stemmed from its invisibility; rather than creating a spectacular effect, the process facilitated location shooting by reducing the aesthetic compromise required to shoot a challenging location. Paramount came to use the process for adverse lighting conditions in up to two-thirds of its productions.[18]

As with all new technologies that reduced the illumination levels required to film, the effect of latensification was just as much economic as aesthetic. By the end of 1949, every major studio except MGM had adopted latensification to varying degrees. At Columbia, latensification allowed the studio to overhaul its method of B-film production, relying on "50 foot-candle lighting," roughly 60 percent of standard light levels. Now smaller lights, like photofloods and Colortrans, consumed less power and took far less time to rig. For "comedy shorts and action westerns," Columbia found that, "the arty lighting and photography employed in major features is unnecessary."[19] If lower light levels offered aesthetic benefits for expensive pictures, they offered cost cuts for cheaper features. The same distinction occurred when faster film stocks appeared in the 1950s and 1960s; television series chose to reduce lighting output to save costs, while major Hollywood productions explored new locations and subtler lighting schemes.

In the late 1940s and early 1950s, various technical solutions emerged to address the myriad inefficiencies of location filmmaking. For instance, in 1948, cinematographer Robert Burks devised a mobile film lab that promised to save hours of work for assistant cameramen, who could spend up to three hours after shooting working in makeshift darkrooms and another two hours transporting equipment to and from locations.[20] This production vehicle anticipated the Cinemobile of the early 1970s, which neatly packaged feature production equipment into a single van or truck; by contrast, Burks's 7,000 pound, 22 foot trailer merely held equipment for a single production department. Disney debuted a new mobile generator unit in 1950, while various car-mounted camera lifts for crane shots appeared throughout the early 1950s.[21] Crew members even devised a new system of hand signals for use in noisy outdoor locations such as the windy Malibu beach settings for Goldwyn's *With All My Love*.[22] The range of innovations highlighted how little attention studio departments had previously paid to designing technologies that could function effectively away from the lot.

Although new production technologies could increase the efficiency of location shooting, they competed with improvements in producing location backgrounds on the soundstage. For instance, M. B. Paul won a technical Oscar for his large, translucent photographic backgrounds. Previously, these backgrounds had to be printed in sections and meticulously woven together to create larger backdrops.[23] As an early adopter of this technology, Goldwyn's studio eliminated two days of location shooting on *With All My Love*, and also reduced the lighting costs for background transparencies. Furthermore, cinematographer Lee Garmes could continue to use "small aperture" photography, inspired by Gregg Toland's high depth-of-field cinematography. Such a style would be difficult to achieve with either lower light levels on location or painted backdrops.[24] Unlike Howe, many cinematographers preferred the lighting control of the studio to the inconsistent illumination of location shooting.

While rear projection can appear staged to contemporary viewers, postwar filmmakers closely associated it with location realism. For example, Joseph LaShelle, who won an Oscar for shooting *Laura* (1947), described the practice on *Under My Skin* (1950) as follows: "A majority of studio action was filmed against process plates provided by scenes shot on location, following the usual procedure of staging live action in front of translucent screens on which background scenes are projected by rear projection. Thus the authenticity of backgrounds was maintained throughout."[25] LaShelle suggests that photographic backgrounds of real settings added more realism than staged settings, regardless of the fact that the actors and real settings were never physically co-present. He used the same procedure on gritty noirs like *D.O.A.*, which relied extensively on rear projections of San Francisco. For LaShelle, "closer shots filmed in the studio must match the location quality as closely as possible while at the same time achieving the amount of technical finish one expects from Hollywood major studio cinematography."[26] Rather than adapting Hollywood standards to real locations, Hollywood cinematographers like Garmes and LaShelle largely sought to adapt real locations to Hollywood's photographic standards, typical of their profession's aesthetic balancing act as described by Patrick Keating.[27] Unrefined "documentary" realism would be relegated to lower-budget features; *The Steel Trap* deployed the cumbersome tandem-taxi rig to avoid the greater expense of shooting background plates for rear projection.[28]

Through rear projection, filmmakers could precisely coordinate foreground and background actions that proved difficult to shoot together on location. Although *The Lady from Shanghai* filmed at San Francisco's Steinhart Aquarium, the backgrounds of sea creatures were projected and enlarged by process at the studio. *American Cinematographer* praised the resulting effect, where Welles timed the appearance of eels and octopi to specific lines of dialogue.[29] Hitchcock achieved the same dramatic timing of real location footage with actors on set in *Vertigo*, when Scottie and Madeleine's first kiss coincides with crashing waves in the background. The aquarium scene in *Lady from Shanghai* also simulated the silhouetted backlighting of characters lit by the fish tank lights, an impossible feat for the actual location without moving the fish. Thus rear projection held the potential to perfectly photograph and synchronize a location background and a studio foreground rather than compromise the lighting and timing between these planes of action.

LOCATION PRODUCTION AND THE OVERHEAD PROBLEM

The Hollywood studios thrived on building realistic settings within the confines of soundstages, backlots, and ancillary sites such as the Warner Bros. ranch. Wartime restrictions on gasoline and Los Angeles location shooting did nothing to deter studios from setting most film noirs in American cities like New York and San Francisco.[30] Hence the decision to shoot a wave of semi-documentaries in various cities cannot be solely attributed to realist aesthetics or technological innovations, which proved inadequate in reducing production costs. Rather, as William Lafferty details, the postwar semi-documentary boom directly responded to quickly rising set construction costs and overhead expenses, as well as violent labor unrest. A roughly three-year experiment with extensive location shooting (1945–1948) revealed that semi-documentary style location shooting proved just as expensive as set-building and far more unpredictable. Instead, by the early 1950s, Hollywood was pruning production budgets and schedules, favoring careful planning and cost assessment over new production techniques. As a result, domestic location shooting became primarily a supplement to studio-based filmmaking rather than a viable alternative.

Production of *The Maltese Falcon* (1941) exemplified the efficient process of constructing on-screen cities without leaving Los Angeles. Although it takes place in San Francisco, there is no evidence that any crew member set foot there during the making of the Warner Bros. film. Instead, the San Francisco of *Maltese Falcon* already existed in the studio's stock footage and stills. Leo Kuter of the art department would send regular requests for specific scenes to the research department, which would respond with appropriate footage. For instance, on May 15, 1941, Kuter requested "San Francisco Streets Business—Apt Houses etc.—Hotel Lobby—Mark Hopkins." Research responded with five clips from "US Streets Calif Miscellaneous," eighteen clips of "US Apt Houses Calif SF," and three clips of "US Hotels Cali S.F."[31] When no in-house footage existed, research could find it elsewhere. An order for "ext and int of bus stations San Francisco" ended with a request to a Santa Fe Public Relations firm, with "2 negs being picked up by transportation."[32] Existing footage would also make it easy for the art department to recreate San Francisco sets to match the stock footage.

The Maltese Falcon budget had a small provision for location shooting, but only for three scenes shot in the Los Angeles area. These included "Ext. Bush Street—2 Nights, Ext. Water Front—1 Day, and Ext. Street."[33] These three locations would cover exteriors of Sam Spade's apartment and two others, as well as the docks and backgrounds for the murder sequence. Even this limited location shooting reveals how many additional expenses could quickly accumulate. For example, $600 of the $1,213 budget to shoot at Bush Street went to renting buildings and rigging lights. These were particularly short night shoots because the crew could only work until midnight. The rest of the budget went to 150 hot lunches, six policemen, four watchmen, equipment parking, a location man, and miscellaneous expenses.[34] By doubling Los Angeles for San Francisco, Warner Bros. avoided the lodging, transportation, and extra union fees for distant location shooting.

Less distinctive urban exteriors could be easily reproduced on the lot, where New York Street stood in for the exterior of Spade's apartment at night. The crew shot apartment exteriors and an alley sequence where Spade discusses Archer's murder with detectives on the Brownstone Street set.[35] An additional location expense appeared in a special request from the location department to the special effects department to capture backgrounds in Bronson Canyon.[36] The final use of location shooting was for retakes. After principal photography ended in June, Huston needed another shot to match a process shot of Archer's murder. A crew picked up an exterior shot on a hillside at a controlled location, the Warner Bros. ranch.

The Maltese Falcon illustrates how efficiently classical Hollywood could capture believable settings in real cities with limited location work. Interiors dominate the film, typical for a dialogue-heavy script. Meanwhile, dark city streets add atmosphere for the film's two major action sequences: Archer's murder and Wilmer's fight with Spade in the alleyway. In both scenes, stylish low-key lighting has a secondary function, masking the background details and architecture that might distinguish San Francisco from Los Angeles or a studio mock-up of New York. Meanwhile, stock footage covers the wider vistas that establish San Francisco as a distinct place. The art department specifically requested images of the Embarcadero and the Bay Bridge, scenic waterfront locations that establish the photographic reality of San Francisco. Excluding the stock footage and the occasional prop sign, *The Maltese Falcon* leaves no trace of any specific city.

Just three years later another Bogart film, *To Have and Have Not* (1944), shot just as extensively on the studio lot despite a farther-flung story. In late 1943, director Howard Hawks hoped to shoot backgrounds for the picture, about a boat captain in the Florida Keys and Cuba, on location in Cuba if he could sort out the island's political uncertainty.[37] Instead, the already over-budget picture shot exteriors on the Balboa and Laguna Islands of Southern California. After three days of first-unit work, the second unit covered the remainder of this nearby location with doubles instead of stars.[38] The Warner Bros. research department detailed all of the existing stock footage that could be used in the film and supplied a "bible" of relevant images of Cuba and Key West.[39]

The production process mirrored that of *The Maltese Falcon*, but the budget told a different story. The total cost of *Maltese Falcon*, $381,000, paled in comparison to the more than $1.5 million cost of *To Have and Have Not*. While high inflation was a factor, the real cause was the growing cost of set construction. The cost of building sets was $25,000, roughly half of the cast salary on *Maltese*, but for *To Have and Have Not*, set-building expenses ballooned to over $162,000, $20,000 more than the actors were paid (not counting Humphrey Bogart's salary, which was withheld from the budget). Meanwhile, "Trick, Miniature and Glasses" (a budget category including background mattes and rear projection) swelled from $3,560 on *Maltese* to $61,616 on *To Have*. As with every studio, an overhead charge for keeping the facilities staffed and running was applied to each picture. For both pictures, this came in above 40 percent, meaning that each dollar over the budget would incur another 40 cents in expenses after the picture's completion.[40] Thus despite Hawks's proven track record as a director, Jack Warner regularly sent telegrams complaining about the number of takes in the dailies or the two weeks he was behind schedule.[41]

At the war's end, labor strife exacerbated these growing expenses. Not surprisingly, the most aggressive union was the Conference of Studio Unions (CSU), whose largest contingent of members were the carpenters who built the sets. (A violent battle between union members and police had broken out at the Warner Bros. lot in 1946.) What began as a jurisdictional dispute between the CSU and the International Alliance of Theatrical Stage Employees (IATSE) grew into a power play by the studios to replace CSU carpenters with less skilled and lower paid IATSE workers in September 1947. The lockout of CSU workers began in October, a month before *Dark Passage* began principal photography. Meanwhile, sporadic violence, such as union members beating up painters who crossed the picket line, continued at the studio.[42] With skilled carpenters locked out and potential violence at their gates, late 1947 was the perfect time to send Bogart and Lauren Bacall up to San Francisco for a month.

William Lafferty notes how these expenses, as well as limited set space, spurred the semi-documentary boom.[43] Yet another factor was the ongoing involvement of the Civil Protection Administration (CPA), a government agency that limited Hollywood set-building during World War II. In April 1946, nearly a year after the bombing of Hiroshima, the CPA continued to impose a $15,000 limit on set construction. This, coupled with the demand for set space, all but eliminated retakes for most Hollywood productions once principal photography was completed.[44] But while wartime set-building restrictions persisted, travel options were increasing with the postwar growth of commercial flight. David O. Selznick decided to shoot all of his pictures in real locales—including London for *The Paradine Case* (1947) and Concord, Massachusetts, for *Little Women* (1949)—because "airplane travel [is] making Hollywood only a 50-hour trip from any place on the globe."[45]

Extensive location shooting in American cities peaked between April 1946 and August 1947, reflected in *Variety* headlines such as "Studios Broaden Program of Filming Yarns in Real Locale" and "WB Scatters Units to 4 Winds; Locationing Hits Record High."[46] By August 1947, RKO had twelve pictures in production, but only two shooting on the home lot.[47] Although filmmakers and studios continued to cite realism as a reason for shooting on location, *Variety* made the economic incentives explicit in a June 10, 1947, headline: "Studio Is Saving Set Costs Thru Location Lensing." The article begins: "Studios are shopping around for stories which can easily be filmed on actual locations, thus eliminating costs of set construction. During past six months this item has become so major an expense factor that plenty of story properties have been shelved." Prestigious realist films were no exception. For instance, "Mark Hellinger currently is filming 'The Naked City' in New York as direct outgrowth of upped set costs."[48]

While *Naked City* exemplified the economic incentives for location shooting, it also proved that extensive location shooting was often a false economy in the late 1940s. The production incurred $42,688 in travel expenses, including $5,958 for eighteen round-trip air tickets to New York, and $4,455 for eleven round-trip rail tickets. Hotel meals and lodging for cast and crew totaled $22,735. Director Jules Dassin and cinematographer William Daniels needed hotel rooms for seventy-five days. Meanwhile, an additional $3,000 went to feeding New York crews and extras.[49] Mayor William O'Dwyer actively courted Hollywood filmmakers to shoot in New York, promising "full cooperation of city."[50] Yet the *Naked City* expense report lists miscellaneous expenses of $10,000 for the NYPD Athletic Fund and $7,500 for "Gratuities and Entertainment for New York Police," suggesting that "full cooperation" came at a price.[51]

The logistics of shooting *The Naked City* became equally daunting. Hellinger needed to airmail all the dailies to Los Angeles. New York had no procedure for approving so many location shoots at one time, requiring individual permits for each of the 107 locations at least a day in advance. Meanwhile, thirty-four exterior locations drew large crowds.[52] At one point, the crew hired a juggler to draw onlookers away from the set.[53] In order to grab street scenes without alerting pedestrians, Daniels used a camera hidden behind a mirrored glass window of a van. This concealment proved effective, but reduced light by at least two f-stops.[54] Filmmakers working in San Francisco faced similar challenges, with the important exception of lower transportation and shipping costs.

Variety noted Hellinger's flight to New York to begin *Naked City* on the front page of its August 18, 1947, edition. Yet the lead headline, "Slice Film Costs 30%," suggested that location shooting alone could not solve Hollywood's production expense crisis.[55] The imposition of a 75 percent tax in Hollywood's most important foreign market, Great Britain, was the final straw that motivated an industry-wide effort to reduce production costs by 30 to 40 percent. While Hollywood continued its efforts to limit construction costs and, less successfully, star salaries, several studios decided to freeze productions until scripts and budgets could be finalized to ensure continuous shooting. Executives also targeted wastefulness in scripts and shooting practices. In 1947, semi-documentaries appeared to be a cheaper alternative to expensive set-bound pictures. By 1948, expensive productions like the *Naked City* and *Dark Passage* revealed that extensive location shooting added as many new costs as it saved in set construction, including production delays caused by inclement weather and logistical problems that exacerbated "shooting waste."[56]

MGM, the studio with the biggest backlot and thus the least incentive to shoot on location, led the "economy wave" with a strategy of more careful production planning and shorter shooting times, cutting production time 25 to 40 percent. In terms of days, 54-day shoots became 36-day shoots, while for smaller films, 36-day shoots became 20-day shoots. These and other changes, such as negotiations with talent, brought the budget for *Joan of Lorraine* down from $5–$6 million to $4 million.[57] Precise planning and tight schedules ran counter to the unpredictability of late 1940s location shooting, while the success of cost-saving measures reduced the need for alternatives to studio-based production.

Fox's production head, Darryl Zanuck, added specifics to MGM's strategy in a series of late 1940s memos. In May 1947, he addressed Fox's directors—including Elia Kazan, Ernst Lubitsch, Joseph Mankiewicz, Otto Preminger, and John Stahl—with a point-by-point criticism of working methods, made "critically urgent" in light of the industry's economic struggles. First he emphasized preplanning, noting that "Even if *only one* superfluous angle per day is shot, this could easily add six to nine days to a schedule."[58] Other troublesome practices included building sets with four wild walls for flexibility rather than necessity, time-consuming "fluid" crane shots, and long takes.[59] He swept aside possible objections. Directors complained about overly large crews, but an increase in union and guild jurisdictions over the past five years made this an unavoidable reality. Instead, directors were told to eliminate crews through controlling setting: for instance, if shrubs and lights stayed in place, no greens men or electricians would be required to move them. As for high overhead charges, the only solution would be shorter shooting schedules, which would spread the cost of overhead over a higher number of pictures.[60]

In a similar December 1949 memo accompanied by a detailed spreadsheet, Zanuck emphasized the 1,652 feet of footage per film that never reached the screen. Over the course of twenty-three pictures in 1949, this cost $2,226,000, or "the *physical cost* of approximately four feature 'A' productions."[61] By point of comparison, Dassin and Hellinger shot nearly 225,000 feet of film for *Naked City*, nearly equivalent to the first cut of all of Fox's twenty-three features combined![62] Dassin shot a less ambitious semi-documentary for Fox in 1949, *Thieves' Highway*, capturing real location footage in San Francisco's large produce market. Zanuck marked this picture's 2,820 feet of eliminated footage with an asterisk, noting, "These pictures, in respect of added scenes and retakes, are of special interest."[63] The unpredictability of partially controlled actual locations made semi-documentaries particularly prone to overshooting and retakes. As Hollywood studios pursued more careful cost oversight, location shooting offered less predictability than soundstage production.

Mark Shiel has identified a decline in film noirs shot in New York in the 1950s compared to the number shot in Los Angeles.[64] The prevalence of Los Angeles in 1950s noir clearly shaped the genre, and the difficulty of filming in other American cities helped drive this trend. By January 1950, budget paring had stabilized for all studios at roughly 25 percent of 1946 per picture costs, and as *Variety* noted, Warner Bros. exemplified the change. "Story is the same everywhere. Warners took 80 days to lens 'Dark Passage,' Humphrey Bogart starrer, in '46. A year ago his pix were coming under the wire in the low 70's. In 1949 'Chain Lightning' was brought in in 60 days."[65] While studios continued to lament actors' high salaries, they saved money in an area they better controlled: below-the-line costs.

Tighter budgets far from ended location shooting. What they ended was the extensive first-unit location shooting that defined the semi-documentary boom of the postwar era. Urban semi-documentaries like *Panic in the Streets* (1950), shot in New Orleans, became more infrequent. The box office failure of this film, as well as *Asphalt Jungle*, suggested to Zanuck that the market for violent crime films was dying, and Fox largely abandoned the semi-documentary genre that it had pioneered.[66] Meanwhile, location shoots were strictly budgeted, allowing little room to add extra days for production difficulties. William Wellman shot *Across the Wide Missouri* in 1951 for MGM, a studio often synonymous with lavish productions. Amidst rain and snow, Wellman's crew hurriedly switched between multiple alternative setups to match previously shot footage. His comment "No Time For Weather" headlined an *American Cinematographer* article on the production, a clear contrast to *Dark Passage*, where producers waited out several rainy days in San Francisco.[67]

Between 1947 and 1952, roughly thirty films were shot on location in San Francisco,[68] but only Warners' *Dark Passage* shot extensive first-unit footage in the city.[69] RKO, which filmed at least ten features in San Francisco between 1945 and 1952, offered a more typical model for economical, restrained location shooting, particularly in the wake of the industry's overhead crisis. *Born to Kill* (1946), directed by Robert Wise and starring Claire Trevor, captured all of its San Francisco locations with process shots. The final cost was about $450,000 and included a 27 percent overhead cost. In 1947, *Night Song*, directed by John Cromwell and starring Dana Andrews, cost far more: $189,000 with a 29.5 percent overhead cost. A higher location budget provided for three days of second-unit cinematography with two doubles. By 1948, overhead had swelled to 51.9 percent, likely due to the production of fewer pictures, yet budgets were successfully trimmed. *Every Girl Should Be Married*, starring Cary Grant, included the lead actors in a one-day shoot in San Francisco and came in at only about $1,240,000. RKO scaled back its overhead to 43.4 percent in 1949, and 30.2 percent in 1950. Just three pictures—*The Woman on Pier 13* (1949), *Born to Be Bad* (1950), and *Where Danger Lives* (1950)—all cost between $900,000 and $1 million. *Woman on Pier 13* shot first and second unit at the Bethlehem Shipyards for three days, but neither *Born to Be Bad* nor *Where Danger Lives* ever set foot in San Francisco. Nick Ray managed to shoot *Born to Be Bad* in ten days.[70]

As in the case of RKO in San Francisco, location shooting stabilized along with production economies as domestic location shooting supplemented rather than supplanted studio production. Second-unit work, including shooting backgrounds for rear projection, provided authentic backdrops that added production value without the high costs of either set-building or prolonged first-unit location shooting. Second-unit location footage offered an inexpensive, realistic alternative to stock footage or painted backdrops. By contrast, first-unit location work, unless supported by financial incentives such as frozen European funds, was limited to what could not be captured on the lot at a comparable cost. San Francisco appeared regularly in Hollywood films, but largely in process photography for modestly budgeted crime films and melodramas. *Dark Passage*, a semi-documentary A-picture that shot a month of first-unit footage in San Francisco, was a key exception. As a limit case for what Hollywood could accomplish in San Francisco, its production history reveals the inefficiency, inexperience, and at times imperceptible aesthetic value of late 1940s urban location shooting.

THE PRODUCTION OF *DARK PASSAGE*

Urban location shooting presented the antithesis of the controlled, predetermined shooting conditions of soundstage production. Ironically, location shooting could only be cost-effective if locations functioned exactly like sets. *The Naked City* sought to build a style and a story out of New York City itself. Most semi-documentaries attempted to do the opposite: force the city to fit into the constraints of a predetermined story, style, shooting schedule, and budget. The San Francisco of *Dark Passage* fell somewhere between the urban shooting program of *The Naked City* and the modest location strategy of the early 1950s exemplified by *The House on Telegraph Hill.*

Dark Passage combined the popular semi-documentary format with the popular screen couple of Humphrey Bogart and Lauren Bacall. The story of fugitive Vincent Parry, who must change his face through plastic surgery before fighting to clear his name, also provided an opportunity to exploit handheld, POV camerawork on location in order to hide Parry's presurgery face. Premiering during the peak of the semi-documentary boom, the film would go over budget and over schedule before opening to middling reviews and tepid box office returns. The various technical and logistical problems encountered on location demonstrated the inadequacy of Hollywood's location practices compared to soundstage shooting. These challenges not only increased the expense of location production but circumscribed where and how location shooting in San Francisco could proceed. Coupled with a rigorous attention to narrative and spatial clarity, *Dark Passage* often minimized the visible distinction between real locations and studio sets, effectively negating some of the production value gained through first-unit shooting in San Francisco.

Warners' publicity department clippings describe *Dark Passage* as a semi-documentary: "*Dark Passage* is another in a succession of thrillers photographed against authentic locales; in this case, San Francisco."[71] They also aligned the film with producer Jerry Wald's larger body of work: "Like the recent few Jerry Wald productions, this one leans to the semi-documentary in its treatment. It is set in San Francisco, generally, and location shots being the real thing give the plot striking credence."[72] Actually, Wald's previous four pictures—*Mildred Pierce* (1945), *Humoresque* (1946), *The Unfaithful* (1947), and *Possessed* (1947)—bore little resemblance to films like *The House on 92nd Street* or *The Naked City*. All but *The Unfaithful* starred Joan Crawford as a headstrong woman caught up in romantic plots with deadly consequences. They all featured noir aesthetics, but without the police procedural or criminal plots commonly associated with the semi-documentary. At least for publicity purposes, the use of real locations for backdrops, a downbeat plot, and low-key lighting sufficiently fit the broad definition of this trend. *Dark Passage* expanded the use of real locations, but the overall look of the picture was not radically different from the Crawford melodramas.

An important distinction from other topical thrillers was the extensive use of first-person camerawork throughout the opening third of *Dark Passage*.

This "gimmick," as *Variety* called it, followed quickly on the heels of *Lady in the Lake*, released in January 1947. For at least one reviewer, *Dark Passage*'s more limited use of POV camerawork was a virtue: "Unlike 'The Lady in the Lake,' which used the device merely as a novelty and with little imagination, 'Dark Passage' tells the first quarter of its story in the first person for reasons of dramatic necessity."[73] The necessity was the Parry character, who resorts to plastic surgery to hide his identity. Post-operation, he looks like Bogart; pre-operation, the camera takes his place. Even this limited camera effect displeased Richard Coe of the *Washington Post*, who would prefer makeup effects to "the absurd shift of the camera's role."[74]

Although the dramatic value of anthropomorphic camera movement would be debated, this technique fell within the same technological and industrial trends that drove postwar location shooting. The use of mobile, lightweight cameras for POV shots became one method of adapting combat newsreel techniques to dramatic pictures. Hollywood producers sought an analogous sense of embodiment and excitement, drawing viewers closer to the character's experience in the story milieu rather than the soldier's experience at the front. The studio's synopsis clearly suggests this effect: "During the first part of the picture the camera itself is the fugitive, seeing and hearing only what the fugitive himself is able to see from his point of view."[75]

Warner Bros. also had a technical advantage over MGM: a German newsreel camera brought back after the war by Walter Klinger of its foreign department. Commercially released as the Arriflex following its use on *Dark Passage*, this camera proved more portable and steadier than the Eyemo combat camera used on *Lady in the Lake*. Even more important, the Arri was the only professional camera that offered a direct viewfinder; the camera operator could see exactly what the camera saw, creating a seamless optical perspective for Bogart's character.[76] Wald and director Daves requested two days of experimental camerawork to test this first-person effect. The "German camera" was the clear choice, but key challenges remained to simulate the perspective of a moving human.[77]

For instance, a person walking shifts vertically and horizontally as he or she moves from one leg to another, yet such an effect had to be minimized so as not to distract the viewer. Patrick Keating describes a similar conundrum from the early teens. The recreation of a sunset through theatrical lighting threatened to concern the viewer with the realism of the effect over the reality effect of the drama.[78] Camera technicians solved the problem with a shoulder harness. In the future, they hoped to combine this apparatus with a small double gyroscope being developed at Stage 5, Warners' process-shot stage. The studio's camera department had figured out the essential components of a Steadicam thirty years before its debut.[79] That they never completed a prototype speaks to the decline of extensive location shooting, as well as the failure of POV camerawork to improve box office returns for films like *Dark Passage*. Meanwhile, economy measures limited camera experimentation, as indicated by Zanuck's late 1940s screed against unnecessary camera movement.[80]

The goal of the extensive POV camerawork was to identify the audience with Bogart's escaped convict, "sharing, precariously, every action that takes place."[81] However, seeing the world through one character's eyes meant seeing a fraction of the different camera perspectives needed to orient the viewer. The camera department advised that the POV shots include close shots, medium shots, and full shots to provide "the variation on the screen" achieved by cutting. Meanwhile, since cutting would break the effect of a continuous POV, the "camera-character" would need to move to establish new angles. The camera department gave a more general warning:

> Much more emphasis must be given in this picture to foreground objects and props that will immediately establish geography than in the average pictures. In other words, the first object or objects the camera sees as the camera-character enters the scene or moves to a new setting should identify, in the audience's mind, the exact nature of the setting so that the audience will not have to guess where they are.[82]

Before the production crew left for San Francisco, the city's role had already been restricted by the demands of the innovative camera technique. For the first forty pages of the film, the spaces of the city would need to speak directly to the character's position to a greater extent than typical settings. If the image of San Francisco grew too complex, it threatened to disorient the viewer and disembody them from the fugitive.

These complicated camera demands called for a cinematographer with exceptional technical skills. In September 1946, Wald specifically requested Robert Burks, who began his career working at Stage 5.[83] Burks would go on to shoot many of Hitchcock's technically demanding films, including two in the Bay Area, *Vertigo* (1958) and *The Birds* (1962). Wald changed his mind a month later: "Last night Del [Daves] and I had a long talk with Bogart and Bacall. If you could work it out, they would be very happy with Sid Hickox as the cameraman. As you know, Hickox did her last two pictures, and she feels that he could do a good job with her again."[84] Thus Hickox replaced Burks. The POV camera proved less important than the object of its gaze; the stars chose the cameraman who would best light Bacall, replacing the cameraman who might have been better equipped to handle a complicated production on location.

Writer-director Delmer Daves was a native of San Francisco, bringing a knowledge of its less stereotypical locations to the production. However, pre-production had already shaped the geography of San Francisco for *Dark Passage*. As with *The Maltese Falcon* seven years earlier, the research department had searched the stock footage library for useful clips. Some of the requests for footage included several approaches to the Golden Gate Bridge and an exterior of a modern Russian Hill apartment.[85] By staging characters walking or driving through actual locations, Daves minimized the use of stock footage in the finished film. Such moments helped establish the leading characters in actual settings, a continued point of emphasis for location shoots in the 1950s and 1960s.

To avoid potential legal issues, Warners' legal department eliminated all references to real people, places, and local institutions from the script. Benton Street was renamed Benson Street, and since an actual Irene Janney lived in San Francisco, Bacall's character became Irene Jenson. Even the name of the daily newspaper was changed, from *The Chronicle* to the *San Francisco Record*.[86]

Close to thirty crew members traveled from Hollywood to Marin County, near San Francisco, to begin shooting *Dark Passage* on October 29, 1946. In addition, three actors, two doubles, six state motor police, one bus, and a handful of cars and trucks were on hand for the first day of shooting. The studio paid for 120 lunches, the best estimate of the number of people working on location on October 30.[87] The studio also needed to cover dinner and lodging for the more than thirty traveling employees. This included Sundays, when union members could not work unless the production paid steep penalties. On location, each additional day of fully crewed production could raise the budget exponentially compared to an extra studio day. For instance, Frank Capra shot scenes for *Riding High* (1949) at a San Francisco racetrack. By shaving a day and a half off the schedule and avoiding the weekend, he saved $25,000.[88]

Despite these financial imperatives, *Dark Passage* soon fell behind schedule. While the labor lockout provided the ideal time to shoot on location,

November is a far from ideal month to shoot in San Francisco. On just the second day, the crew left the hotel at 7:45 a.m. and was ready to shoot by 10:45, but fog prevented any filming at an unspecified San Francisco bridge location. The crew tried to shoot inserts, but they called it quits at 11:30 as the fog rolled in again. Moving to another location, the crew faced further lighting changes and rigged additional lights, but by 3:30, the fog had returned. Without enough light to shoot, the day was called off. They resolved to find new locations as well as backup locations for the next day. This impromptu planning was a partial success; they lost only half of the following day due to poor light and high winds.[89]

Despite decades of technological development in Hollywood, by the time the first unit returned to the Warner Bros. lot on November 25, poor lighting, rain, or both had interrupted at least fifteen of the twenty-five location shooting days. Los Angeles's ample sunlight and dry climate remained significant advantages. A similar environment helped make Italy a prime location for so-called runaway production in the 1950s. Upon canceling shooting at the Presidio during *Dark Passage*, a cameraman noted that "the bridge and background would look like a poor process shot."[90] Ironically, filmmakers could likely produce a more realistic illusion on a studio set than shooting at a real location on a hazy day.

Failing to adequately plan for inclement weather was one of several indications that the crew lacked experience with extensive location shooting. For instance, the company tried to make up time by shooting at the Presidio on a Sunday only to find out, after nearly an hour setting up their shot, that they did not have permission to do so.[91] On another day the company had to switch locations because the lights they needed were being rigged for a night shoot elsewhere.[92] And even though the studio had secured permissions for locations, one apartment owner appeared unprepared for the schedule and steadily complained about the long days and late shooting hours.[93] Permission to shoot on one location, a field in Marin County, had either not been secured or was never requested. When the property owner approached the crew, they claimed they had permission and rudely shooed her away. After attending the film and seeing her property featured, she sent a complaint letter to Warners' legal department.[94]

The crew appeared unaccustomed to working on location, and San Franciscans were similarly unaccustomed to Hollywood movie stars working in town for an entire month. Herb Caen peppered his *Chronicle* column with

Bacall and Bogart sightings. He also wrote, "So many San Francitizens cluster around the 'Dark Passage' company, on location here, that shooting sometimes is almost impossible."[95] The biggest crowd incident would at least provide an item for the studio's publicity department, which announced, "More than 1,500 San Francisco movie fans tied up traffic at the Golden Gate bridge and brought out a dozen highway patrolmen to disperse the crowds when Humphrey Bogart and Lauren Bacall were working in a toll-gate shot on the San Francisco entrance to the bridge . . . the stars obliged with autographs and posed for photographs until the situation got out of hand."[96] In this case, San Francisco's population density coupled with infrequent Hollywood location shooting had generated enough onlookers to shut down part of the city. Either by fortune or foresight, *Dark Passage* rarely shot in such public locations, but by avoiding the crowds, the film sacrificed a prime asset of location shooting: seeing star actors appear in a city's most popular places.[97]

One method to avoid such problems was to shoot with a hidden camera. Bogart walking through the street would cause far less notice without a large camera crew setting up for hours preceding his arrival. Wald suggested that such a shot for Parry's final escape would add "a natural quality" since cars passing Bogart would provide a sense of documentary realism (Figure 1.1).[98] However, Bogart's unforgettable face and the reduced aesthetic quality of film recorded with a hidden camera limited the use of this technique.

Extensive second-unit cinematography with Bogart's body double, Joe Smith, proved a far more effective and efficient method for capturing the protagonist within the bustling city. While stunt doubles make for exciting anecdotes, body doubles serve a far more practical role, and this was particularly true in the location shooting of the studio era. Smith drew far less attention than Bogart, preventing the starstruck commotion of the Golden Gate Bridge shoot from occurring on a daily basis. Wide shots could mask his identity while allowing the camera crew to use a greater subject distance and be less conspicuous. These wide shots could also capture the spectacle of the crowded urban landscape of pedestrian and motor traffic rather than expensively recreating it with extras and police cordons.

Second-unit work maximized the efficiency of the more valuable first-unit crew. Daves could return to the lot to direct the principal actors rather than tying up the production schedule shooting backgrounds. Finally, a special-effects unit was used to capture technically demanding shots and backgrounds for rear projection. Cinematographers like Hickox specialized in lighting sets and female leads, making it far more efficient to keep him

1.1. A rare shot of Humphrey Bogart on location in *Dark Passage* (Warner Bros., 1947). The trolley car helped isolate him from fans who might have disrupted the shoot.

with the actors and allow technical experts to capture some of the innovative first-person camerawork.

The second unit worked far more efficiently and inconspicuously on location than the first unit. For example, they shot body double Smith at three public locations in a single day—two intersections and inside a cable car—an impossible feat with the crowd attention paid to Bogart. When the first unit returned to the studio, the special-effects unit stayed on location for five more days, saving the studio the cost of keeping a larger cast and crew there. Upon returning, this special-effects crew would employ the backgrounds they shot for rear-projection scenes filmed at Stage 5.[99] The second-unit footage amounted to far more than just establishing shots and transitions. The climax of the film features Parry fleeing on foot, trolley, and bus through downtown San Francisco. Aside from the scene in the interior of the bus station (constructed in the studio), the viewer rarely sees Bogart's face. Instead, it was Smith who was filmed for the action finale that ultimately opened the active San Francisco downtown to the camera.[100]

Producer Wald oversaw the production from the studio, but distance and labor problems made remote supervision more difficult. He wrote to Bogart and Bacall saying, "Because of the labor strike, we've not been able to see too much of the work done, but what we have seen has made the whole trip worthwhile."[101] Meanwhile, Daves could only view dailies without sound in San Francisco. Even after resolution of the labor dispute, productions shooting on location relied on Hollywood labs to develop dailies from locations like San Francisco that lacked a professional motion picture lab. Location productions commonly faced multiday delays in receiving dailies or were simply shot without using them.[102]

Wald remained most encouraged by the "documentary feeling" he saw in the footage.[103] In fact, the ongoing rain spurred Daves to shoot some interiors on location, and Wald loved these improvised setups. He wrote, "The shots you made in the interior of the hotel lobby are as good photographically as anything you could do at the studio. They have more reality and certainly give a documentary feeling you could never capture at the studio."[104] He encouraged Daves to shoot a bus station scene on location if bad weather persisted. Wald highlighted the fundamental contradiction of this period of location shooting. The best location footage looked as good as studio work *and* distinctively more real than studio work. Such an achievement required a rather subtle aesthetic distinction, because the rough edges of even a polished documentary style would fail the first criterion. In the final film, the hotel lobby scene looks indistinguishable from a studio set; a perception of enhanced realism might only come with the knowledge that the scene had been shot on location.

Wald's second major point of emphasis was geographical clarity. Certainly, the camera tests had highlighted the need for spatial clarity for the POV effects, but Wald's focus on geography extended well beyond that. During the POV section, Wald suggested a shot of Parry looking up and down the street. The reason was not to sell the effect, but to establish the surroundings of the apartment for later, conventionally shot scenes. Wald also emphasized the geographical links between shots. For the scene where Parry ascends a staircase on Telegraph Hill following his surgery, Wald specifically asked for closer coverage than a long shot to clarify the connection between background warehouses and the adjacent flight of steps.[105] For the scene when Parry escapes on a bus to catch a flight to South America, Wald suggested a pan from the departing bus to a vista of the city. This apparent scenic indulgence had a precise function: to smooth the dissolve to an establishing shot of a South American café.

San Francisco's unique sights were a production asset that also threatened to perplex viewers unfamiliar with the city. For instance, when the camera follows Irene's car down the exit ramp from the Golden Gate Bridge, the road curves back to reveal a view of the bridge in the foreground. Wald thought most viewers would be confused to see the bridge a second time and suggested further shots to clarify the roadways. A cable car turntable adds suspense by extending Bogart's attempt to flee the city unnoticed. Yet Wald wrote, "We are afraid you might get a laugh from people not living in San Francisco at seeing an entire trolley car pushed around. By getting a long shot shooting down at a cable car arriving at the turn-table and seeing the turn-table, it will clarify the entire geography" (Figure 1.2).[106] Clarifying character movement through a busy urban location required more than basic continuity editing. Preserving the coherent space of Hollywood classicism involved a thoughtful and efficient spatial exposition that reoriented the viewer to the specific locomotive rules of actual places.[107] Wald's plain suggestions imply profound ways that location shooting can both challenge and conform to Hollywood's controlled spatial logic. In *Classical Hollywood Cinema*, David Bordwell writes,

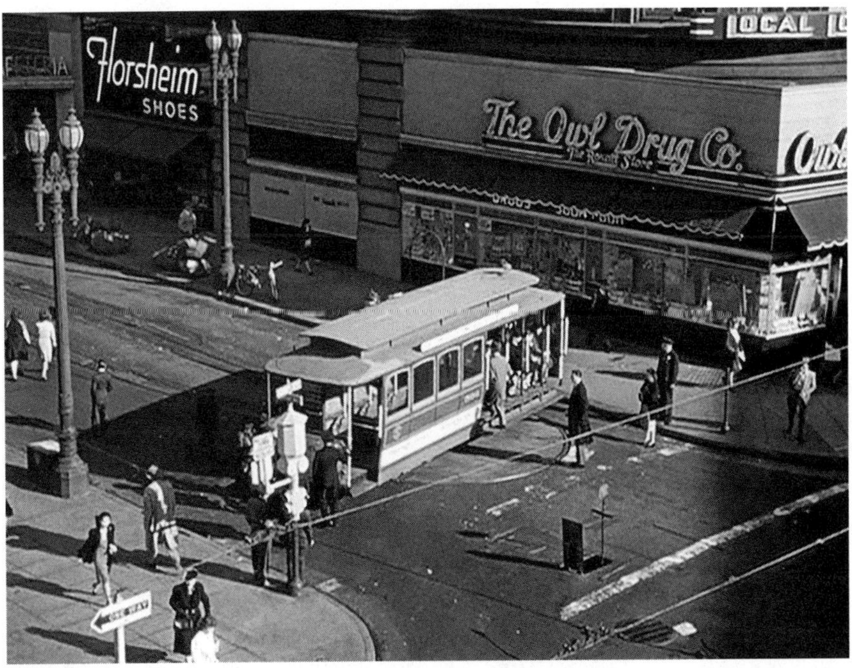

1.2. This establishing shot of a trolley turntable in *Dark Passage* was used to reorient the viewer faced with this local peculiarity.

"Space becomes chiefly a container for character action: the story has appropriated it. That a locale is of little interest in its own right is shown by the fact that typically the exposition of space takes up the least time of any phase of the scene."[108] Yet a common element of any urban location thriller is the protagonist traveling, sneaking, chasing, or being chased through the city. Here the excitement hinges on the continual establishment of space, character navigation of space, and establishment of new space. Wald, like most Hollywood filmmakers, stressed spatial clarity; his strategy for dealing with local eccentricities was to expand spatial exposition with additional shots. Such a strategy preserved the actual geography of San Francisco. Yet no film shot partially on location could totally follow this strategy. Instead, creative geography had to form new chains of shots connecting local spaces to studio sets.

In other words, local geographies had to follow a paradigmatic geography of Hollywood filmmaking. Locations that could not be instantly read into an image required more careful attention. Furthermore, the price for leaving gaps in continuity was far costlier on location. *Dark Passage* provided Warner Bros. with another expensive piece of publicity when Daves flew a door from San Francisco to the studio for a one-day shoot. This was the easiest way to match the apartment exterior, shot on location, with the studio set.[109]

THE SAN FRANCISCO OF *DARK PASSAGE*

Although *Dark Passage* highlights the myriad production difficulties facing Hollywood crews in San Francisco, it also provides the most thorough onscreen representation of the city prior to the 1958 films *Vertigo* and *The Lineup*. With the exception of a few scenes, the resulting image of the city did not depart significantly from those of other films set there. After entering San Francisco, most classical Hollywood narratives remained largely confined to the lavish interiors of hilltop houses overlooking the bay and, most often, the Golden Gate Bridge. While *Dark Passage* features Russian Hill, other scenic districts offer similar topographies. *The Falcon in San Francisco* (1945) and *Born to Be Bad* (1950) center on Nob Hill mansions, while *The House on Telegraph Hill* largely occurs within its titular location. Although the character of Vincent Parry is an escaped convict, he comes from the world of high society, as does Madge Rapf (Agnes Moorhead), and hides out with society girl Irene Jansen (Bacall). Early scenes briefly capture Marin County and San Quentin, but the film overwhelmingly takes place in downtown districts, unlike the sprawling car trips to come in *Vertigo* and *Bullitt*.

Hollywood's image of a wealthy, scenic downtown hub was no different than the image that San Francisco itself successfully projected for much of its postwar history.[110] As the *Chicago Daily Tribune* gushed in 1947, "San Francisco has more color, glamor, style and friendliness than New York will ever have."[111] In 1949, another *Tribune* writer proclaimed, "San Francisco's sheer physical magnificence was breathtaking" and also noted the famed downtown districts such as Nob Hill and sites like Coit Tower that appeared in *Dark Passage*.[112] The film's emphasis on socially and physically elevated central districts provided beautiful scenery. Irene's large apartment windows reveal a postcard view of the bridge and the ships by the bay. Even low-class characters like the criminals in *Born to Kill* (1947) eventually found their way to mansions, as well as Golden Gate and Bay Bridge backdrops. But such stunning views often draw cinematic attention away from the actual city, as the camera gazes outward from the city center rather than toward it. In *Dark Passage* San Francisco largely functions as a structuring absence, with panoramic views establishing the downtown by its edges rather than its center. Such a production strategy also minimized logistical difficulties by setting actors against the scenery rather than among the crowds.

This scenographic vision of urbanism has a rich history in American city building. Perhaps the definitive manifestation of this strategy was Daniel Burnham's Chicago plan of 1909, the culmination of the era's City Beautiful movement. As Peter Hall describes, it was "to restore to the city a lost visual and aesthetic harmony, thereby creating the physical prerequisite for the emergence of a harmonious social order."[113] The City Beautiful movement shaped cities for a privileged class, providing an image of cultural order instead of solutions to the social problems causing urban disorder. Hollywood had a similar prerogative, whereby urban backdrops glamorized central characters and organized plot development. How did the apparently opposing styles of film noir and City Beautiful coexist in *Dark Passage*? San Francisco's small, centralized downtown perfectly suited the centripetal film noir plot identified by Edward Dimendberg, where the city draws characters inward like a beacon. He ties these trajectories to nostalgia for the thriving central cores that had faded away in so many American cities yet still appeared to exist in San Francisco, whose own struggle with suburbanization played out off-screen.[114]

Dimendberg also provides a useful distinction between distant shots of the city, presenting a coherent whole, and ground-level representations, which provide glimpses of the city's seamy underbelly.[115] Certain film noirs, such as *Double Indemnity* (1944), suggest a dialectic between the modern American city and the rising postmodern megalopolis, but Hollywood filmmakers largely avoided such diegetic disruptions. Unlike *Double Indemnity*, in which Phyllis and Walter plot a murder at a supermarket, *Dark Passage* clearly demarcates its shabby and shadowy criminal milieu. For instance, Parry arrives at a dim back alley at night seeking an illegal plastic surgeon. The noir plot reveals a darker side of the city, but never threatens its inherent logic. The elided distance between the panoramic view of the city and the street-level view facilitates an ordered city within the grammar of establishing shots and plot-driven changes in location. Between the scales of the city and the street, a richer geography of the city might come into focus, but these excess details would only impede the classical Hollywood narrative, where character movement and progression only map the locations that serve the plot. Meanwhile, shooting distant shots and street scenes proved relatively easy, but preparing several city blocks for filmmaking was a daunting, expensive task.

With its extensive POV camerawork, *Dark Passage* sought to capture the story through the eyes of a fugitive. The production's location shooting was similarly fugitive, clandestinely capturing the city without drawing too much attention to the stars or crew. Eliminating Bogart's face from the first quarter of the film made this an easier task, but despite this freedom, the POV shots in San Francisco largely occur on dark, empty streets. Daves wrote and directed this story set in his hometown, but he effectively saw it through the eyes of a Hollywood professional. As a location, San Francisco would still only be a stage for the story, not a driving element. Russian Hill offered a visually dramatic setting where, weakened by surgery, a bandaged Parry barely makes it up a steep set of stairs. Although the view from the top is clearly San Francisco, the scene could also have been staged effectively in the hills of Los Angeles.

The scene of Parry's fistfight with a blackmailer beneath the Golden Gate Bridge is emblematic of the production benefits of a well-chosen location. Rather than building an expensive set or relying on rear projection, Daves framed the action against two real dramatic elements: the span of the bridge (Figure 1.3) and the cliff of the Presidio. In various shots the arches of the girders dramatically divide the characters in combat, while camera angles accentuate the height of the bridge and the steep fall below. Here the physical presence of Bogart played against the actual landmark and landscape creates an image that could never be as sharply or effectively

1.3. In *Dark Passage*, the Golden Gate Bridge serves as a location set piece to punctuate a confrontation and fistfight between Parry (Bogart) and a blackmailer.

captured in a studio. And working on a small section of military-owned land with restricted public access gave filmmakers far more latitude than a less secure location.

Despite the extended location shoot, *Dark Passage* still required plenty of rear projection. The benefit of shooting on location was the variety of backdrops and the ability to intercut them with second-unit location footage. For example, when Irene crosses the Golden Gate Bridge, several views trace the car entering a tunnel, approaching the toll booth, and finally exiting the bridge. These are matched with rear-projected images of Irene driving with bridge traffic behind her, as well as wide shots of the car traveling past the bridge and pulling up to the apartment. The extent of this driving footage helps draw out this suspenseful scene and maximize the value of the commotion caused by shooting Bacall at the bridge toll booth. It also demonstrates how effectively second-unit footage could capture a location, making expensive first-unit location production appear to be an unnecessary expense. Other than one wide shot, the shots of Bacall appear readily reproducible on a studio stage.

1.4. Scenic shots reveal San Francisco's beautiful views while also isolating actors from potential crowds of onlookers in *Dark Passage*.

The climactic escape from San Francisco made the most effective and extensive use of downtown San Francisco locations but also relied on a body double and carefully limited crowd exposure. Wide shots show Smith (and occasionally Bogart) running across a rooftop, climbing down a hotel fire escape, and boarding a trolley car, revealing a picturesque city eerily devoid of people and traffic (Figure 1.4). A clever shot from inside the trolley finally captures the protagonist among the people of the city. Bogart sits in the foreground with his back to the camera, and the trolley movement reveals throngs of residents walking the streets. Because it is intercut with wide crowd shots captured from rooftops, the viewer is briefly immersed in the life of the city. But the crowd is far from reassuring company; any pedestrian might recognize Parry from his image in the newspaper and foil his escape to South America. Similarly, anyone might recognize Bogart and ruin the shot. San Francisco's bustling downtown proved just as much a production burden as an asset.

Ironically, Wald's meticulous attention to visual clarity did not extend to the clarity of the film's convoluted script. One reviewer summed up the consensus with the headline "Don't Be Reasonable: Then You'll Like 'Dark Passage.'"[116] Perhaps Daves had paid more attention to the setting than the plot. However, this criticism reveals far less about major changes in postwar Hollywood filmmaking than the film's prolonged production. As an experiment in location filmmaking, facilitated by a labor stoppage, *Dark Passage* failed to justify the expense of shooting extensively in an urban environment outside of Los Angeles. By contrast, *The House on Telegraph Hill* maximized the value of its San Francisco setting through set design, matte work, and carefully planned scenic and action shots in the city.

THE LIMITS OF LOCATION AND THE POWER OF SET DESIGN: *THE HOUSE ON TELEGRAPH HILL*

The House on Telegraph Hill scheduled three weeks of location shooting in San Francisco for August 1950.[117] In *American Cinematographer*, Herb Lightman praises the "authentic mood" of the exteriors shot largely around the city, but "it is inside the mansion itself, where the main body of the action takes place, that the camera functions most directly as an instrument of mood."[118] The film was nominated for Best Art Direction, using the ornate house as a shadowy trap for the heroine, much like *Rebecca* (1940) did. Meanwhile, the interior plot helped mitigate a potential production problem: there was no house on Telegraph Hill.[119]

Telegraph Hill overlooks the Bay Bridge as well as Alcatraz and three other islands, rivaling the Nob Hill and Russian Hill views of the Golden Gate Bridge. However, the only large site offering such a view was a restaurant. Undeterred, set builders constructed the mansion's first floor façade around the restaurant. The rest of the building was added later through matte painting (Figure 1.5). Lightman noted that "needless to say, the match is a perfect one," and watching the film today, it is still almost impossible to see where the façade ends and the matte begins. By limiting San Francisco filming to exteriors, director of photography Lucian Ballard could capture picturesque images of landmarks such as Union Market, the marina, the Embarcadero, Coit Tower, and the Golden Gate Bridge. Despite the fact that the stars were rarely filmed in public locations, crowds still flooded some of the shoots as they had during *Dark Passage*. To capture a busy Market Street, the crew used a sidewalk elevator and a camouflaged camera.[120]

Like *Dark Passage*, *The House on Telegraph Hill* took advantage of San Francisco's topography, but by staging most of the exterior action on the cloistered restaurant grounds (dressed as the mansion back lawn), the setting functioned like a backlot set. And the hilltop afforded not only panoramic views of the city, but also dramatic potential. In one scene, Victoria (Valentina Cortese) falls through a hole in a mysterious backyard clubhouse and then dangles above the rear-projected city. The streets below the hill feature prominently in a major action sequence where a cut brake line sends Victoria's car hurtling down the hill. Shots of the speeding vehicle and POV shots from Victoria's perspective allowed an effective action sequence to be captured by a second-unit crew. Only a handful of scenes set at the waterfront and the Union Street grocery feature actors walking through the city; like *Dark Passage*, the backgrounds of these public spaces were almost deserted. While *Dark Passage* struggled to make San Francisco function like a backlot, later productions like *The House on Telegraph Hill* tailored stories and shooting schedules to the specific challenges of location shooting. Nonetheless, even three weeks of carefully controlled first-unit location shooting in San Francisco remained an exceptional practice.

Lightman noted how well Ballard captured "the specific glamour of that cosmopolitan metropolis."[121] Regardless of the quality of the cinematography, postwar San Francisco consistently appeared as such: specific, glamorous, and cosmopolitan, with distinct landmarks, tony residences, and a variety of districts, including Telegraph Hill, Chinatown, and Fisherman's Wharf. Although it was rarely used for extensive location shooting, the city's

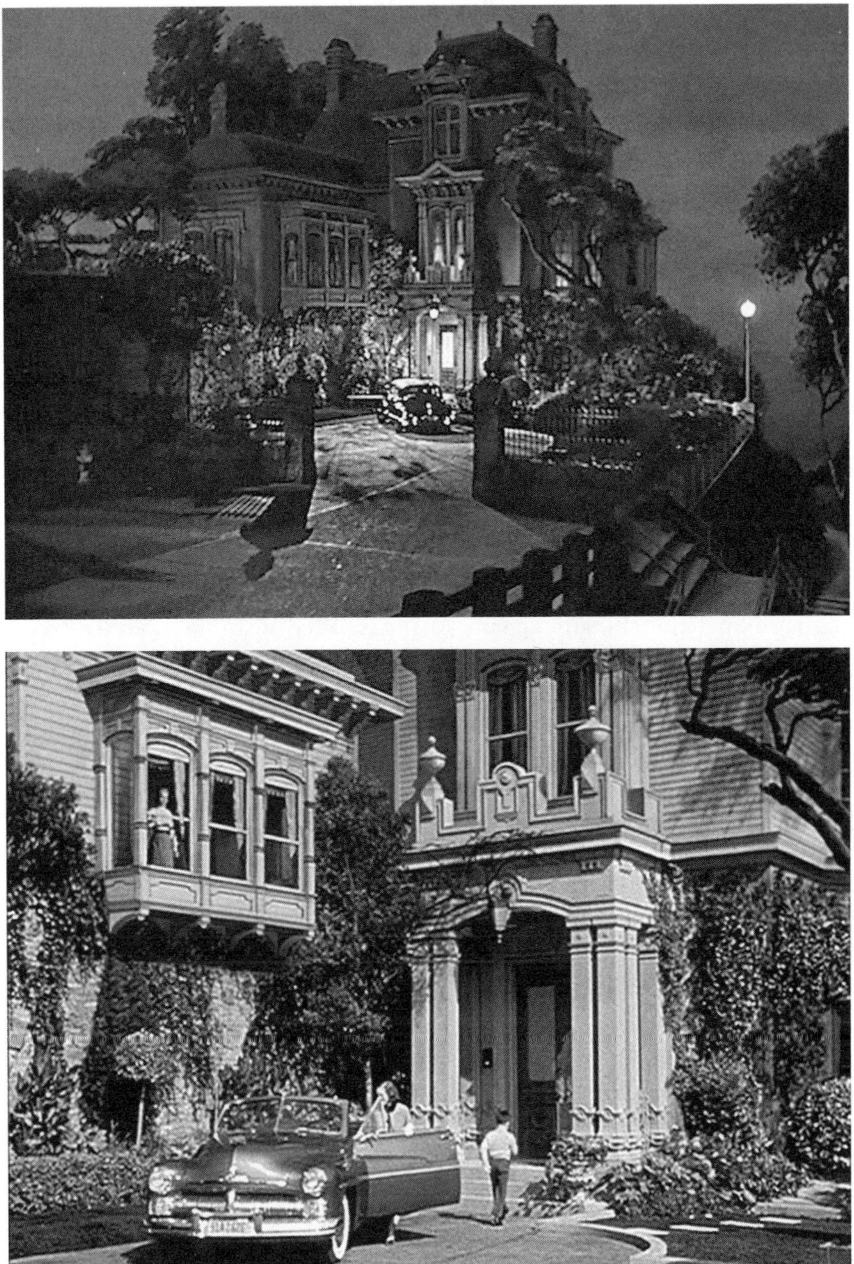

1.5. Establishing shots for *The House on Telegraph Hill* (Twentieth Century-Fox, 1951): *top*, for the night exterior, the upper floors were later matted in; *bottom*, because the only large site offering the desired view was a restaurant, set builders constructed the mansion's first floor façade around it. The rest of the building was added later through matte painting.

popularity as a setting for Hollywood features and documentaries had nearly exhausted its panoply of sights by the early 1950s. Robert Wise compared it to Monument Valley, where "every nook and cranny of the area has been seen on the screen a dozen times."[122] Despite such overexposure, San Francisco remained a popular setting in the 1950s as new production practices and technologies restored the novelty of scenic locations.

The simultaneous development in the 1950s of widescreen cinema and runaway production drew Hollywood further from the constraints of lush interiors and tight narratives. On widescreen color film, San Francisco's familiar locations gained a renewed appeal, while the expansion of tourism raised cinematic visits to cities like San Francisco to spectacles in their own right. Financial incentives opened foreign locations to runaway production, placing a newfound emphasis on authentic backgrounds and location shooting. Television and independent production also developed new location shooting practices that would shape the studios' aesthetic responses to the competition. Finally, the increasing reliance of studios on fewer, costlier A-pictures helped inflate production budgets, allowing them to better accommodate the expense and uncertainty of location shooting. The postcard beauty of San Francisco made it a privileged domestic site for Hollywood production as the functional city of classical Hollywood came to accommodate the scenic digressions of cine-tourism.

2

THE CINE-TOURIST CITY

From Cinerama to *The Lineup* and *Vertigo*

VERTIGO WAS A TYPICAL 1958 HOLLYWOOD FILM: typical of a more stable relationship between independent and studio production; typical of the integration of distant location shooting into the work flow of established production methods; typical of the spectacular locations featured in widescreen color pictures; and, finally, typical of the best and worst practices for weaving picturesque urban travelogues into narrative cinema. *The Lineup* (1958), a seldom seen big screen adaptation of a popular television police procedural, appeared the same year and was also shot in San Francisco.[1] It exemplified another staple of 1950s production, the typical fare that kept theaters from going dark and studios from going idle between major A-picture releases. Shooting black-and-white film on location proved far less expensive than relying largely on process shots on the Columbia lot, where the studio's television subsidiary, Screen Gems, profitably occupied several soundstages previously reserved for feature film production. Director Don Siegel—a veteran of moderately budgeted thrillers such as *Riot in Cell Block 13* (1954) and *Invasion of the Body Snatchers* (1956)—shot more extensively in San Francisco than Alfred Hitchcock, who spent only two first-unit weeks in the Bay Area compared to more than two months on the Paramount lot.[2]

Both films lead the viewer on a tour of San Francisco, but the characters and itineraries are as different as their production histories. In *Vertigo*, Scottie (Jimmy Stewart) is a local detective who falls victim to the voyeurism and nostalgia also imbued in the tourist experience of San Francisco. In *The Lineup*, San Francisco falls victim to Dancer (Eli Wallach), a contract killer on a murderous day trip through the city. The urban spectacle serves as a siren, drawing characters toward danger while drawing dangerous characters to the city.

The appearance in 1958 of two San Francisco films that both exhibit and critique tourism underscores Hollywood's shift in urban aesthetics during the course of the 1950s. New technologies, exhibition practices, and production strategies allowed picturesque locations to increasingly intrude upon the filmic narrative or, in the case of early Cinerama films, to supplant the narrative entirely. As authentic locations became sellable production assets for films, ranging from the escapism of *Roman Holiday* (1953) to the realism of *On the Waterfront* (1954), settings became more than mere backgrounds. San Francisco lacked the financial incentives of foreign cities and the production facilities of New York, but it offered an urban grandeur and distinction lacking in Los Angeles's sprawl. Thus, like tourists, Hollywood crews journeyed north for a week or two, capturing exterior landmarks to embellish studio interiors.

Hollywood studios' cine-tourist aesthetic authenticated color spectacles with the occasional use of semi-documentary techniques. Meanwhile, spartan black-and-white pictures by independent producers reinvigorated the semi-documentary realism of the late 1940s. For well-financed color films, scenic locations added production value akin to the opulent sets of the 1930s; by contrast, a black-and-white realist aesthetic offered production economy, lending style and gravity to lower-budget pictures while cutting major expenses for set-building and soundstage rentals. This created a bifurcation between location shooting as an element of color spectacle and an element of black-and-white realism. *Vertigo* and *The Lineup* largely followed these two trends in location cinematography, and both films exploited San Francisco's famous sites as tourist fantasies masking real threats to urban citizens.

On the 1951 debut broadcast of *See It Now* on CBS, Edward R. Murrow asked for the East Coast and West Coast feeds. The West Coast monitor appeared first, offering images of the Golden Gate Bridge and the San Francisco skyline. The East Coast feed featured the Brooklyn Bridge and the New York skyline. As Thomas Doherty describes in *Cold War / Cool Medium*, it was "America from sea to shining sea seen for the first time over the monitor in the living room."[3] This feat would be repeated, more spectacularly and more literally, at the close of *This Is Cinerama* (1952). As aerial footage traverses the country to the music of "America the Beautiful," the camera soars toward the Golden Gate Bridge, the visual accompaniment to "from sea to shining sea" (Figure 2.1). San Francisco appeared again in *Cinerama Holiday* (1955), featuring images of trolley cars and Chinatown street performers.[4] Although Los Angeles, as a center of population and industry, was New York's West Coast rival, as a city image symbolizing the western edge of the country, San Francisco was New York's Pacific rhyme.

A science-fiction film from 1955, *It Came from Beneath the Sea,* offers the simplest explanation for San Francisco's visual status. What comes from beneath the sea is a giant octopus, the mutant product of nuclear testing, that attacks both the Golden Gate Bridge and downtown San Francisco. Clearly the plot called for a coastal city and a naval presence, which Los Angeles could easily provide. Yet what would the octopus attack? The docks of San Pedro? The Santa Monica Pier? Could it even reach the increasingly neglected downtown?[5] San Francisco was not only a striking city, but also one that could be captured in a single poster image, whether in the synecdoche of the Golden Gate Bridge or in the hilly skyline rising above the marina. In a later science-fiction film, *On The Beach* (1959), the survivors of a nuclear war travel by submarine to investigate a distress beacon in

2.1. The Golden Gate Bridge symbolizes "from sea to shining sea" in the "America the Beautiful" segment of *This Is Cinerama* (Cinerama, 1952).

San Francisco. As they approach the coast, the crew can already see they are too late as the camera tracks across wide shots of a deserted city. In hopeless delirium, a sailor leaps into the water, saying, "I have a date on Market Street, Captain. I'm going home." As he swims to shore, an extreme wide shot captures the haunting spectacle of an entire city emptied of any sign of life.

Edward Dimendberg has observed how the growing sprawl of Los Angeles imbued film noirs with centrifugal movement, where doomed characters in automobiles attempted to flee the bounds of the city. There the dramatic crisis portends an aesthetic crisis of how to represent this new, dispersed form of urban space.[6] Although San Francisco, like all American cities of the 1950s, struggled with automotive sprawl, it preserved its appearance as a centralized city in several ways. The first was natural: San Francisco's peninsular site encapsulates the central business district, displacing the image of sprawl beyond the bay. Second, San Francisco citizens' groups were tenacious preservationists. They saved the trolley cars in the 1940s and became the first American city to halt freeway expansion, leaving the Embarcadero Freeway "literally hanging in mid-air" across from the Ferry Building. *The Lineup* staged its climax on this ready-made set piece.[7]

Finally, and in keeping with its on-screen image for most of the 1950s, San Francisco was well aware of its tourist potential. In 1956, prominent businessman Charles Blyth asked the new mayor, George Christopher, how they might reduce the visual impact of the Embarcadero on the historic Ferry Building. Blyth, who would later form the powerful private redevelopment group the Blyth-Zellerbach Committee, saw the highway as a threat to the city's old-fashioned ambiance and thus a threat to future tourism and waterfront development.[8] In the aftermath of World War II, San Francisco hosted one of the major conventions of the twentieth century as dignitaries flocked to the city to sign the United Nations Charter. The city's Convention and Visitors Bureau described the vision San Francisco would project to the world through the mid-1960s: "Paris, San Francisco, New York, New Orleans—these are story towns . . . you will not leave this city without experiencing the thrill of its mixture of beauty, old and new."[9] A decade removed, this text could serve as a tagline for *Vertigo*.

THE BUSINESS OF CINE-TOURISM

Today's critics universally regard *Vertigo* as a masterpiece of cinematic technique.[10] However, upon the film's release, *Variety* offered a trenchant critique of its execution. The first half was said to be too slow, and Hitchcock's striking location photography of San Francisco was likely why. Location scenes were "absolutely authentic and breathtaking. But these also tended to intrude on storyline too heavily, giving a travelogueish effect at times."[11] In an anthology specifically dedicated to *Vertigo*'s relationship to San Francisco, two scholars address and deflect this criticism, justifying Hitchcock's incessant attention to San Francisco backdrops. Ana Salzberg ties Hitchcock's scenic interludes to his specific approach to the VistaVision format, while Diane Borden relates the emotional pathology of tourism to the traumatic plot.[12] These analyses focus on *Vertigo*'s unique resolution of the tourist impulse in 1950s Hollywood, relying on detailed readings of the film itself. Shifts in Hollywood location shooting practice in the 1950s, as well as the production history of the film, suggest that the travelogue problem was never fully resolved, nor fundamentally unique to *Vertigo*.

While distant location shooting took advantage of new exhibition technologies and financial incentives, it could not simply overhaul established production and storytelling practices. Rather, the spectacle of exotic cities had to find an appropriate place within well-established economic and narrative constraints. In this sense, the *Variety* review is sharply accurate. *Vertigo* unforgettably captured San Francisco. It also went over budget and failed to earn as much as Hitchcock's recent European thrillers, *To Catch a Thief* (1955) and *The Man Who Knew Too Much* (1956).[13] Location shooting simulated the experience of luxurious travel as an ancillary production value to narrative features, but in films like *Vertigo*, this tourist aesthetic threatened to overwhelm the production budget as well as the narrative. Without moderation, location shooting might do as much harm as good, inflating production expenses and disengaging viewers from the on screen drama.

By 1948, the Motion Picture Export Association (MPEA) effectively negotiated trade pacts with England, France, and Italy that overcame strict quota restrictions for distributing American films abroad. The key caveat in each agreement was the withholding of a large share of box office profits in frozen accounts; in Britain, the largest foreign market for Hollywood films, over 70 percent of Hollywood's 1948 box office profits remained frozen. Foreign countries allowed American studios to spend blocked funds on production facilities and expenses since these investments benefited the local economy.[14] Yet Hollywood's limited capability for location shooting and tight production budgets of the early 1950s delayed the full exploitation of this powerful exception to foreign protectionism.

As Robert Shandley details in *Runaway Romances*, the mid-1950s boom in Hollywood production in Europe began as an overt attempt to free frozen box office profits by employing elements of the semi-documentary style. *Roman Holiday* (1953) served as an influential and successful experiment in foreign location shooting. Paramount accepted shooting in Rome as a sacrifice of production values. Director William Wyler employed inexpensive semi-documentary techniques on location, including concealed cameras and post-synchronous sound, to capture his stars against famous Roman landmarks. Production correspondence revealed major difficulties with Italian laborers and technicians, as well as a lack of police assistance. Whether at Cinecittà or on the streets, the conditions were deemed inappropriate for a Hollywood film. This attempt to recoup box office profits being held by the Italian government became a bona fide hit. Meanwhile, critics lauded the use of locations: the excitement of seeing real actors in actual exotic locations outweighed the rough cinematography of ad hoc location shooting.[15] Following early successes like *Roman Holiday*, Hollywood production abroad boomed for much of the 1950s and 1960s.

In a 1956 *Variety* piece on runaway productions, a studio executive emphasized that "the keynote in today's films is realism." Another executive asked, "Can you imagine a 'Three Coins in a Fountain' produced on a back lot?"[16] A perceived audience demand for photographic realism justified runaway production, despite any clear evidence of audience preference. In fact, critics faulted the overabundance of real locations in *Three Coins in the Fountain* (1954), a film that sacrificed its drama for touristic travel in CinemaScope.[17] This intangible realism served the tangible goal of quelling union complaints. In 1953, amid threats of investigations by IATSE and SAG, producers justified runaway production based on the need to capture actual locales and release frozen funds abroad.[18] Although by 1954 unemployment for production workers had grown relatively high, IATSE tentatively accepted Hollywood's financial need to shoot overseas, but only if the story demanded it. For instance, IATSE vice-president Carl Cooper railed against a film set in the Dakotas but shot in Mexico to save on labor.[19] The compromise between IATSE and the studios checked the form of runaway production where a foreign city often doubles for New York to save on expenses, but the implicit agreement always remained fraught. For instance, in 1958 the cameramen's local chapter of IATSE publicly complained that their workers were left home too often on foreign productions.[20]

While shooting in foreign locations increasingly became an integral production strategy for Hollywood, the European honeymoon did not last. In

1956, Darryl Zanuck left the Fox lot to work as an independent producer based in Paris, mounting major foreign productions such as the successful *Island in the Sun* (1957) and the expensive failure *The Roots of Heaven* (1958).[21] At the time, he observed that Hollywood filmmakers hated working with inferior production facilities abroad, potentially driving them back to the Los Angeles studios.[22] Independent producers, largely shooting in the United States, realized similar false economies in the mid-1950s; hoping to save money by avoiding studio soundstages and shooting on location, weather and inadequate facilities often made foreign productions more expensive than films shot in Hollywood.[23]

Shooting abroad did, however, offer the fiscal incentive of unlocking frozen funds, despite being less cost-effective. Production spending on lavish epics effectively transformed blocked currency into surplus production values, including equipment, costumes, and scenery that could be exported back to Hollywood. Such endeavors grew as epic as the films themselves. The sets for *Ben Hur* (1959) took eight months to build at Cinecittà and cost $125,000 just to dismantle. Metro shipped 100 tons of equipment to Italy. Workers razed the galley and pirate ships to prevent Italian producers from exploiting these elaborate set pieces for "lesser productions." They sold the donkeys and camels to European zoos and circuses.[24] The success of *Ben Hur* kept struggling MGM afloat, but also exemplified the complex, expensive productions that eventually sunk the studio.

In the 1950s, New York was the domestic capital of runaway production. Although it lacked the financial incentives offered by foreign cities, it offered a similar combination of arresting urban locations and existing studio facilities. Broadway and the booming television industry also provided fresh talent and trained technicians for location crews. Between 1951 and 1956, feature film production in New York rose from 13 to 63 percent of total film production in the city. Filmmakers such as Hecht-Lancaster and Elia Kazan shot multiple features there, renewing its association with the gritty black-and-white realism of *The Naked City*.[25] As in Europe, however, location shooting proved less cost-effective than anticipated. Despite open encouragement from the mayor's office to shoot in New York, producers faced a slew of payoffs for local businessmen and officials. Robert Altman decried this "Let's take 'em attitude" after shooting an episode of Alfred Hitchcock's hour-long *Suspense* in 1957, where "hold-ups by landlords, city officials and police" doubled production costs.[26] Frequent precipitation from midwinter to May also hurt productions, particularly television series, where one lost day could immediately put an episode over its shoestring budget.[27]

Figures like Mayor Robert Wagner and Kazan fought to keep production booming in New York. Nonetheless, in 1958, the city was still not cooperating with filmmakers and was 25 percent more expensive per episode than Los Angeles, the rising new center for telefilm.[28] Television Westerns shot in the controlled climate of Los Angeles soundstages and backlots were proving to be more cost-effective and popular than the television dramas filmed in New York, which began disappearing from schedules in the late 1950s.[29]

The cost versus the reward of shooting on location largely depended on the scale of the production. In television, budgets were inflexible, and in the late 1950s, negative costs represented nearly two-thirds of total series costs.[30] Thus the increased cost of shooting in a distant location pushed more television series onto Hollywood lots. For a major feature, location costs could be insignificant compared to above-the-line costs for major stars and directors. Semi-independent producers such as Alfred Hitchcock, whose use of the Paramount lot was factored into his multipicture deal with the studio, could choose to shoot certain locations for aesthetic purposes and complete the rest of a film under the technical control of a soundstage.[31] For example, the first-unit shooting schedule for *Vertigo* called for eleven shooting days on location and twenty-nine days in the studio.[32] Independent producers unaffiliated with a studio, who by 1957 were producing 40 percent of Hollywood features, largely preferred shooting on location to the often exorbitant rental rates for studio space.[33]

These per-picture decisions had larger ramifications for each studio's bottom line as the economies of overhead and real estate shifted. *Variety* summarized the dilemma in 1956: "Shooting of product abroad means that only a small charge, if any at all, can be made against the studio upkeep expense, which basically remains constant."[34] The more the studio shot on location, the higher the overhead costs for the pictures shot on the lot, since the cost of running the studio would be largely amortized across this smaller number of productions. Conversely, shooting every picture on the lot was not feasible during an era when the biggest hits, such as *The Ten Commandments* (1956) and *Ben Hur*, featured foreign backdrops. Struggling RKO took a drastic approach, halting soundstage production on the main lot in 1957 in favor of location shooting.[35] Whether this strategy failed or simply masked plans to disband the company, RKO all but disappeared by the end of 1958.[36]

A less drastic solution for studios was to rent their facilities and technicians to television and independent producers. The nascent telefilm industry set off a studio real estate boom in 1952 when most of the independent studios sold their lots or rented out their unused stages for television productions.

Hal Roach, whose soundstages nearly reached capacity with telefilm productions, valued his lot at $4 million that year. Major studios sold or rented their ancillary lots, such as Warners' Gower Studios, valued at close to $1 million. By 1955, Republic was shooting half of its films on location while earning $1 million per year in rent from MCA television shows.[37]

Despite the meteoric growth of television, studios built for mass production often had room to spare as the previous decade's fifty to sixty pictures per year had shrunk to twenty by 1956. *Variety* reported that an unnamed major studio was shooting on only four of its thirty soundstages.[38] However, rising real estate prices in the fast-growing Los Angeles of the 1950s delayed a massive shift to location filming. Despite pressure to streamline overhead, Joe Vogel hesitated to sell off MGM's backlot due to its ever-rising property value, hoping to rent it to independent producers in the meantime.[39] Oil found on the Fox lot made it far more valuable as a property than a production plant. This spurred a creative solution, whereby Fox planned to sell its lot for $25 million and become co-tenants on the Warner Bros. lot, allowing them to split the overhead and fill the lot's vacant stages.[40] Fox instead opted for a more ambitious $50 million plan to build Century City, the still-standing skyscraper hub on the former Fox backlot.[41]

Warner Bros. instead filled its lot with in-house television production. Seen in 1958 as the model for committed studio investment in television, its telefilm business had collapsed by the mid-1960s.[42] Columbia's subsidiary, Screen Gems, had greater long-term success and in 1958 managed to shoot eight of its ten shows on the lot. Robust in-house production attracted more independent television producers, likely because these studios could offer crews with telefilm experience.[43] A full rental (including crew) for a standard thirty-nine episode series brought in roughly $800,000 a year, whereas renting just the space brought in only $150,000. MGM's hesitation to produce independent films and television proved costly; they hosted only one series in 1958 while losing close to $10 million that year. With Hollywood's biggest backlot, MGM proved least adaptable to the new overhead economies.[44]

Increased location shooting, whether domestically or abroad, facilitated the transition of studios from production centers to rental facilities. But the glut of available stages from the mass production era left plenty of room for filmmakers who required the technical advantages of a professional studio, such as the meticulous art direction and camera effects for *Vertigo* and the sprawling sets and casts for MGM musicals. Meanwhile, independent lots fully converted for rental offered cheaper alternatives. Often one studio financed a picture to be shot on another studio's lot, creating far greater flexibility than in the earlier era of star and facility loan-outs. For instance, *The Lineup* was an independently produced feature, adapted from a CBS television series based on the Desilu lot, distributed by Columbia, and shot largely in San Francisco. In this new environment, the need to balance overhead and the expense of location shooting created a hybrid lot funded by in-house and rental productions.

TECHNOLOGIES FOR AND AGAINST LOCATION SHOOTING

The development of widescreen processes in the mid-1950s exacerbated the runaway production trend. As John Belton argues in *Widescreen Cinema*, new technologies can briefly restore the novelty phase of film spectatorship.[45] Cinerama confirmed this thesis, relying on outdoor travelogues of spectacular European and American locations for its earliest hits. Cinerama embodied cine-tourism in two key ways. First, it transformed movie-going into a leisure event analogous to a tourist vacation. Second, the enormous triptych screen offered the embodied sensation of traveling through space, whether as a rider on a rollercoaster or as a sightseer on vacation.[46] Just as location shooting sacrificed production concerns to financial concerns, Cinerama favored exhibition value over production logistics. Shooting in Cinerama created major technical challenges, including lens distortion, high-intensity lighting requirements, and image distortion during camera movements.[47]

Although less cumbersome for filmmakers than Cinerama, CinemaScope similarly favored exhibitors over filmmakers. Fox president Spyros Skouras successfully pushed a process with lower conversion costs to theaters, whose major purchase would be anamorphic projector lenses rather than the three projectors and three screens required for Cinerama.[48] Producers shouldered greater conversion costs, such as the lens distortion problems that plagued Cinemascope films until a new Bausch and Lomb lens debuted in 1954.[49] Existing setups for process photography were incompatible with the new screen dimensions, forcing Fox engineers to develop an entirely new rear-projection system.[50]

The shift to widescreen created additional challenges for independent producers. *American Cinematographer* detailed Cornel Wilde's widescreen decision for *Storm Fear*, a 1955 feature shot on location in Idaho. A cast of seven made for an economical picture, but Wilde and Joseph LaShelle, a veteran Fox cinematographer, worried that such a small cast could barely fill the larger frame. Yet widescreen complemented their greatest production value;

location footage of mountain landscapes. They compromised on a 1:1.85 aspect ratio, offering a wider format without the daunting 1:2.35 width of CinemaScope. The wider frame made location shooting inviting for independent producers but also challenged them to find stories that could adequately and affordably fill the frame.[51]

In a 1956 *Variety* article, one executive noted how widescreen processes "so cruelly show up any artificial note," pushing productions to further rely on location footage.[52] The growing emphasis in the 1950s on realistic backgrounds and runaway production did not limit the use of rear projection and other matte processes; it encouraged them. No evidence suggests that these special-effects processes appeared artificial to viewers, technicians, or producers; backgrounds shot on location and incorporated on special-effects stages replaced sets and backdrops, which had to be bigger and more realistic—thus more expensive—to meet the larger screen dimensions.[53] Generic exteriors were still frequently shot on the lot. In 1953, *American Cinematographer* reprinted a 1946 article on exterior photography without noticeable changes; despite the postwar boom in location shooting, capturing exteriors on the soundstage remained commonplace.[54]

Studio commitments to color and widescreen exposed the limitations of existing rear-projection techniques, but also spurred the development and adoption of new processes.[55] After successfully testing a blue-screen process for CinemaScope in 1954, Fox's R. A. Klune sent a memo to nearly all production personnel with a clear directive: "A vast amount of money has been spent by us on engineering, equipment and testing in order to bring these new processes to the current point of development and everyone should endeavor to make the most valuable use of them."[56] In other words, to offset research and development costs, process photography would be emphasized over other solutions, such as shooting actors on location. Paramount also invested in rear-projection technology that complemented its own large-format process, VistaVision. In 1952, they purchased a 50 percent stake in Vistascope, a process that, unlike blue-screen, could work with black-and-white or color. The new technology offered "huge budget savings" by eliminating matte shots and expensive foreground sets.[57] Paramount won Scientific and Technical Oscars in 1955 and 1956 for a new background projector and a rear-projection screen.[58] Thus *Vertigo* could take advantage of San Francisco backgrounds in the studio more efficiently and precisely than on location.

In 1954, Fox technicians gave a detailed description of state-of-the-art matte photography to the Society of Motion Picture Technicians and

Engineers (SMPTE) (reprinted in *American Cinematographer* in 1957). For each process, they emphasized economics over aesthetics. For instance, stationary mattes saved not only on transportation and housing, but also on building the top floors of buildings. Such a process would come in handy for *Vertigo*'s pivotal bell tower scenes.[59] Composite mattes could turn a crowd of 200 extras into a crowd of 2,000. Meanwhile, the new blue-screen traveling matte process allowed any background to be embedded behind the foreground action, even before that background was shot. Rather than matching set lighting to location lighting, as in *Dark Passage*, cinematographers could capture or recapture backgrounds to better fit the key dramatic action in the foreground.[60]

Postwar Hollywood studios seamlessly integrated new backgrounds into scenes shot on a process stage. For the static sections of the background, matte technicians could superimpose other images, such as ceilings to cover overhead lights or extra stories of a building, as in *The House on Telegraph Hill*. For moving backgrounds, rear projection produced a moving image behind the actors and props on the soundstage and was frequently used to film actors in a car on the soundstage with background footage appearing behind them. For scenes involving a more precise coordination between foreground and background, a traveling matte process combined negative and positive prints of black-and-white film over several phases of development and photography, artfully integrating multiple moving-image planes into a single shot.

In a 1958 *American Cinematographer* article, Joe Henry summarized the advances in process photography: "One of the most highly perfected of cinematic sciences is that of background projection and process photography, which is employed in nearly every major feature film production today."[61] Widescreen and color increased the cost and complexity of location shooting at the same time that new technologies lowered the cost and complexity of process photography. These techniques blurred the line between location and studio photography. Commenting on *Gigi* (1958), Arthur Gavin wrote, "You are scarcely aware that it was photographed for the most part on actual locales in France."[62] The aesthetics of location shooting were not strongly distinguishable from studio process photography. The final sequence of *Pal Joey* (1957) exemplifies just how interchangeable studio and location footage was by the late 1950s. In three successive shots, director George Sidney cuts from a body double of Vera (Kim Novak) on location in San Francisco to a process shot of Joey (Frank Sinatra) to a sweeping crane shot of Joey and Vera captured on a studio set (Figure 2.2).

2.2. Three shots were cut together for the final sequence in *Pal Joey* (Columbia, 1957): *top*, location footage of Vera using Kim Novak's body double; *middle*, a process shot of Joey (Frank Sinatra) using rear projection; *bottom*, a sweeping crane shot of Joey and Vera captured on a studio lot.

Unaffiliated independent producers rarely shared in these technical innovations. Studio process stages and technicians were too expensive to rent, and independent companies lacked the personnel, physical plants, and capital reserves to build or purchase their own. By 1958, independent process specialists such as Bob Hansard had begun to cater to those excluded companies, including independents, television producers, and industrial filmmakers.[63] But independent producers had already found successful ways to profit without process. While Hollywood was shooting color spectacles abroad, independents more often succeeded with realist black-and-white dramas shot on location in the United States.

Black-and-white offered several technical advantages over color for independent producers. Studio lights, particularly outside the set, created fluctuating color temperatures that had to be carefully monitored.[64] The combination of widescreen and color film required significantly higher-intensity lights, limiting which locations could be captured effectively.[65] More light also required more equipment, including generators, whereas smaller lights could run off of household power.[66] The debut of the high-speed Eastman Tri-X black-and-white stock in 1953 further distinguished monochrome stock from color. At twice the speed of Eastman's previous high-speed stock, Tri-X was only slightly grainier than the black-and-white standard, Plus-X.[67] With the introduction in the 1950s of the wide-angle Angénieux lens, which also required less light, black-and-white film could reach exposure under almost any conditions.[68]

Black-and-white film offered "pictorial and economic advantages," according to cinematographer Stanley Cortez, who felt his darkly lit location footage (shot on Tri-X) set the tone for *Black Tuesday* (1954), "a tense melodrama about a killer condemned to die in the chair."[69] Filmmakers who in the 1940s pushed the association between low-key lighting and dark, realistic subject matter now extended this association to black-and-white film as a whole. For instance, cinematographer Joseph LaShelle suggested that "color doesn't lend itself to strong dramatic action," while producers Mike Ripps and Ed Fessler argued that "human conflict is best expressed in terms of subtle shadings of black, gray and white."[70] The new emphasis on black-and-white in contradistinction to color arose during Hollywood's brief color boom of the mid-1950s. Between 1952 and 1954, the number of color releases rose from roughly a third of all films to half. Color fit Hollywood's strategy of selling widescreen processes to exhibitors and widescreen spectacles to audiences. And as RCA trumpeted color television, the potential network conversion to color programming promised to boost the value of color movie sales to television while dropping the price for existing black-and-white movies. This is exactly what happened when the networks switched to color programming in the mid-1960s, and Hollywood responded by virtually ceasing to produce black-and-white films. In the 1950s, the studios' color strategy proved premature as consumers were slow to convert to color television sets, and black-and-white films remained commercially valuable for theatrical and, particularly, network sales. The Hollywood studios' color output dropped to less than a quarter of all films by 1958.[71]

As the major studios produced more color features, independent producers often distinguished their products by promoting dramatic realism and taking full advantage of the economies of black-and-white location shooting. A husband and wife production team, Andrew and Virginia Stone, made headlines when *The Night that Holds Terror*, produced for $76,000, became a sleeper hit in 1955. The Stones shot and recorded sound entirely on location, never building a set or using a process shot. The success of their first film gained the interest of Doris Day and her husband, producer Marty Melcher; Day starred in their next feature, *Julie*, set in San Francisco. The film shows less the dramatic value of locations than the ability to dramatize generic suburban California locations with shadowy black-and-white cinematography. The only visual indicator of San Francisco is a small hotel room and a steep hill, likely captured elsewhere.[72] The next year the Stones produced *Cry Terror* for MGM. A quick style of location filmmaking became common for many low- to medium-budget films, although it was not without jarring disadvantages. Although shooting in the Holland Tunnel showcased the photosensitivity of black-and-white film, the fumes from generators running the lights sent the lead actress, Inger Stevens, and several crew members to the hospital due to exhaust inhalation. Undeterred, the Stones kept shooting with Rod Steiger; as they emerged to a clutter of emergency vehicles attending to the crew, they shot the chaos to use for the film's closing image.[73]

Clearly, the Stone method was not suitable for most productions, but certain lower-budget black-and-white techniques appeared in more prestigious fare. *Blackboard Jungle* (1955) earned four Oscar nominations, including for Best Black-and-White Cinematography and Best Black-and-White Art Direction. Director Richard Brooks chose to shoot almost entirely in Tri-X in order to achieve maximum depth of field without high levels of light. Thus he could keep multiple rows of students in focus, allowing dialogue between front and back rows in a single shot. Meanwhile, night sequences on location could be captured with available streetlights. Less lighting also made for quicker setups. Cinematographer Russell Harlan managed to shoot 600 students in an auditorium in a little over an hour; he estimated that with slower film it would have taken a day or more. Ironically, low-key lighting and fast film stock could create a sense of real place without location shooting. *Blackboard Jungle* was shot almost entirely on the studio lot, yet the stark, low-key cinematography set the tone for the tough inner city. The aesthetic of black-and-white realism, strengthened in comparison to color, could effectively sell sets as actual locations.[74]

Despite a deepening distinction between studio color spectacles and independent black-and-white thrillers, both methods of filmmaking privileged shooting actual places over set-building. Runaway production, widescreen exhibition, and advances in process photography placed greater emphasis on real settings as production assets. Meanwhile, exciting locations offered attractions for independents who lacked the means for process photography or major sets. San Francisco effectively served both aesthetics. Along with its impressive tourist vistas, it also provided a dense urban core whose shadowy hills and rooftops further dramatized crime dramas.

VERTIGO: EVEN BETTER THAN THE REAL CITY

As early as 1950, as Robert Wise struggled to find previously unfilmed locations for *The House on Telegraph Hill*, it seemed San Francisco had been overexposed in Hollywood cinema.[75] But by 1953, widescreen processes, particularly in color, had helped revive the city's well-worn backdrops. As Zanuck shared with his directors in a confidential memo, "CinemaScope demonstrations reveal that familiar monuments such as the Statue of Liberty and the Arc d'Triumph look entirely new and different in CinemaScope than any other medium. We have therefore tried to load these pictures with these plus values."[76] The same could be said of Coit Tower and the Golden Gate Bridge.

As Merrill Schleier details in her essay on *Niagara* (1953), staged at the famous Niagara Falls, touristic Hollywood films of the 1950s faced a conflict between two genres: the simulated travelogue and the noir-influenced melodrama.[77] In his essay "Cities: Real and Imagined," Geoffrey Nowell-Smith uses *Vertigo* as an example of a specific type of city film that offers touristic attraction as "personal dramas are played against attractive backdrops."[78] Such close attention to backgrounds marks a key departure from previous standards for art direction, where the sets and backdrops functioned to enhance the drama rather than draw attention to themselves.[79] The "plus values" of location monuments and vistas always ran the risk of overpowering the drama. In the opinions of many contemporary reviewers, Hitchcock made precisely this error. As one critic put it, *Vertigo* was a "thrillorama," a mix of thriller and panorama, and in the end, the scenery outpaced the thrills.[80]

Vertigo followed several other mid-1950s color films that to varying degrees portrayed San Francisco as a tourist destination. The first two Cinerama films, *This is Cinerama* and *Cinerama Holiday*, were travelogues, with San Francisco appearing as pure visual spectacle without any dramatic interference. *Kiss Them for Me* (1957), set in the recent past of World War II, was a loose remake of *On the Town* (1951). Instead of New York, Crewson (Cary Grant) and two sailors on leave tour San Francisco from the scenic Top of the Mark bar at the Mark Hopkins Hotel to the trolley cars and nightlife districts. *Pal Joey* (1957), the most successful San Francisco film of the 1950s, focused on San Francisco's racier tourist attraction, the Barbary Coast, a waterfront entertainment district famed for burlesque houses. As proven by the successful Broadway play, this risqué setting could be successfully staged rather than shot on location. After shooting a scenic ferry ride to San Francisco, the production largely relied on studio interiors. *Pal Joey* depicts San Francisco's vice district as a brightly colored escapist setting for a musical comedy—a far cry from the dim, seedy depiction of the city's red-light district in *Dirty Harry* (1971).

Hell on Frisco Bay (1955), a crime drama starring Edward G. Robinson and Alan Ladd, whose Jaguar Productions produced the film for Warner Bros., is one of the oddest and most telling location thrillers of this period. At the height of the color film boom, John Seitz shot the film in color CinemaScope, despite a cast and a story that suggested 1930s gangster films and early 1940s noir. The film was an attempt to cash in on the popularity of both the Kefauver crime hearings and *On the Waterfront* (1955), but Warners' legal department struggled to find a plot and a waterfront city where allegations of corruption would not provoke lawsuits. Along with its Academy Awards, *On the Waterfront* (1955) drew a $750,000 libel claim from a Chicago Longshoremen's union.[81] San Francisco was chosen over New Orleans, and a mixture of rear projection, matte paintings, and sporadic location shooting offered several bay views, including a climactic motorboat chase through the bay. These plus values proved worthwhile. *Variety* faulted the film's "routine and contradictory melodramatics," but praised the views of San Francisco.[82]

Vertigo was a less routine picture than the largely forgotten *Hell on Frisco Bay*, but it faced two similar challenges. Unlike a comedy such as *Kiss Them for Me,* which could flit from scenic location to location, letting the upbeat sights complement the comedic episodes, thrillers needed to sustain suspense and character across scenic interludes. Also, by abandoning the association between tense drama and black-and-white, wide-format color thrillers had to recode tourist attractions into sinister objects. The weak association between color travelogue and dark thriller helped Hitchcock mask his intentions from the viewer. In a letter to screenwriter Maxwell Anderson, Hitchcock emphasized that the audience should not be aware that this was a murder story; instead, he sought the tone of "a strange mood love story."[83] At the same time, the socially acceptable pleasure of sightseeing softens Scottie's perverse, voyeuristic pursuit of Madeleine.

In his book *The Tourist*, Dean MacCannell repeatedly references San Francisco, virtually the only US city touched upon in a work devoted to international travel by Americans. In the same sense, the San Francisco of *Vertigo* has much in common with the European travelogue dramas of the 1950s. Even contemporary American urbanists such as Austrian émigré Victor Gruen, writing in the 1960s, found San Francisco more similar to Continental cities than American ones.[84] As MacCannell writes, "Sightseers do not, in any empirical sense, *see* San Francisco. They see Fisherman's Wharf, a cable car, the Golden Gate Bridge, Union Square, Coit Tower, the Presidio. . . ."[85] The same is true of *Vertigo*, which features all of these sites except Fisherman's Wharf. More generally, MacCannell writes, "The act of sightseeing . . . helps the person to construct totalities from his disparate experiences. Thus, his life and his society can appear to him as an orderly series of formal representations. . . ."[86] Hitchcock's formal construction of *Vertigo* provides such a totality. Yet similarly, an overwhelming sense of San Francisco comes with a minimum of location shooting. As with other touristic films, well-placed drives, landmarks, and backgrounds create the tourist's sense of knowing a city through its scenic fragments.

Hitchcock spent eight first-unit days in downtown San Francisco and, like filmmakers in the 1940s, captured almost exclusively exterior shots. The most extensive interior work came in the art gallery scenes shot at the Palace of the Legion of Honor. The only other location interiors were the lobby of the McKittrick Hotel and the interior of the flower shop. As for the exterior shots, they consisted overwhelmingly of entrances and exits. For instance, "EXT Mission Dolores . . . Scottie watches Madeleine enter Mission—Scottie

2.3. Entrances and exits from cars and buildings serve to establish the lead actors in scenic locations in *Vertigo* (Paramount, 1958).

exits car, enters Mission"; similarly, "EXT Brockleback Apt . . . Madeleine exits bldg., drives off in jaguar—Scottie follows in car." These shots establish not only a narrative sense of place, but also a physical sense of place in San Francisco for the leading actors (Figure 2.3). Each entrance and exit can cut away to studio interiors, carrying this sense of real place across the threshold of location and studio work.[87]

Some background plates were shot along with the first-unit work, such as the moving background plate for Scottie walking through the graveyard in the dream sequence and stationary exteriors of cars on the street. These scenes, which perhaps required more specific coordination for the process shot, could be matched on location with principal photography. Infrequently, when the schedule permitted, the filmmakers could capture pure backgrounds, such as a "scenic shot of foggy city," captured at the end of a day filming actors by the Golden Gate Bridge and downtown. Yet overwhelmingly, the location work in San Francisco concentrated on two segments of the film: Scottie's investigative pursuit of Madeleine, and his wandering after her apparent death. Thus the audience's movement through San Francisco is entirely bound to Scottie, a tour guide through the winding streets and scenic buildings.[88]

As in *Pal Joey*, location footage and studio work were regularly combined and intercut. For instance, Madeleine and Scottie's dramatic kiss by the waves was shot only partially at Big Basin State Park. For the scene where the couple pause against a tree, a transparency was filmed on location and the foreground tree was added on the studio set. Wide shots of Scottie chasing Madeleine down the rocky coast used body doubles on location. Finally, for the climactic moment when Scottie and Madeleine kiss, location footage of the waves was shot on transparency, ensuring that the background would be exactly timed to the foreground (Figure 2.4).[89] Even static exterior shots might be filmed on location to be completed later on the lot. The Mission San Juan was the perfect setting except for not having a bell tower. This key architectural element was instead painted on a glass matte for exterior shots, while interiors were shot on a set (see Figure 2.4).[90]

The plan to shoot in San Francisco came well before principal photography began. The first location survey was a five-day trip in October 1956 by Herbert Coleman (second-unit director), Sid Street (location manager), Danny McCauley (assistant director), Henry Bumstead (art director), and Robert Burks (director of photography). In November they made a second trip joined by Hitchcock and Doc Erickson, the unit production manager, as well as the script supervisor and chief electrician. They set off with a list of fifteen locations, including several that would never be shot, such as Sutro Gardens and the Opera House. The result would be pages of notes that specified each shot to be filmed in the city.[91]

The location notes, compiled by Coleman, are meticulous. For instance, for the scene of Scottie pulling up to the flower shop, Coleman notes, "Remove NO PARKING signs on Claude Lane. Scene 42 In Claude Lane—shooting at an angle to building but missing the street (bush) at the end of alley." At the location of Scottie's apartment, the door was to be repainted and a streetlight added. Even state parks would need to be properly adjusted; for the scene in Big Basin, Coleman wrote, "Obtain permission to cut two wax myrtles that now obscure the shot." Finally, for the scene where Scottie finds Judy with two friends, Hitchcock requested Judy's double as well as a Chinese girl with glasses and a second Caucasian girl to be personally selected by Hitchcock himself. This brief street scene would require a camera hidden in a truck, still a necessary device to keep downtown passersby from disrupting the shot.[92]

Although the need to sometimes hide cameras from the public remained, a helpful figure, retired police lieutenant Morrie Reardon, brought some order to ad hoc shooting practices. Over the course of his career, Reardon received only one screen credit, as the technical adviser for *No Escape* (1953), a noir shot in San Francisco.[93] But his name appears elsewhere, including Doc

2.4. Rear projection and matte painting were used to modify San Francisco to suit Hitchcock's image in *Vertigo* (Paramount, 1958): *top*, rear projection allowed the kiss to be perfectly timed with the clashing wave; *bottom*, matte painting was used to add a bell tower to the Mission Dolores outside of San Francisco.

Erickson's oral history of shooting *Vertigo*. Beyond working as the primary police contact, Reardon assisted with finding locations. One night he took Erickson and Burks on a tour of eight or nine restaurants, including Ernie's, which gained national publicity in a 1956 *Life* photo essay on San Francisco nightlife during the Republican convention.[94] Ernie's was exactly the type of "old-world restaurant" that Hitchcock was looking for. The production never shot there, but art director Henry Bumstead replicated the restaurant exactly on the studio lot.[95] Erickson recalled no difficulties on location, and "terrific help from the police and mayor." Experienced location men succeeded through finding local point people like Reardon, particularly since they were often new to the area. Erickson had never even visited San Francisco and claimed Hitchcock hired him so that he could enjoy working in a new city.[96] In fact the Unit Production Managers Guild, which began publishing credit bulletins for the major studios in 1952, earned their reputation working in unfamiliar surroundings. In the prologue to a list of members' credits, they boasted, "These men have pioneered trails into new and colorful territories and have acquired the know-how and practical experience to best serve our industry on foreign locations."[97]

Police contacts like Reardon did not, however, guarantee a smooth shoot, particularly when local citizens felt disenfranchised by location crews. *Pal Joey* drew ire when weather delays pushed production to Easter Sunday. Nearly a thousand cars were turned away, ruining people's holiday excursions to a scenic hilltop. One citizen asked, "Who's paying the taxes on that property up there, us or the movie company?"[98] A week later, Reardon made the front page of *Variety* when *Kiss Them for Me* ran into trouble on its four-day trip to San Francisco. Local station KOBY, possibly incensed when the police department rebuffed its request for an officer to read court headlines, aired an editorial attacking the misuse of police resources for the shoot. Beginning with "Attention taxpayers," the frank editorial featured lines such as "True, San Francisco people were able to view minks and bosoms, but in the meantime, traffic was completely snarled around Nob Hill." The *Variety* article revealed Reardon's role in blocking the streets and guarding property, assisted by off-duty cops for hire. The defense by Fox and the police was, fittingly, the tourist benefits of location shooting for San Francisco.[99] Mayor Alioto would offer a similar refrain when citizens complained about location production in the 1970s.

Animosity between locals and crews underscored not only the typical friction between San Francisco and Los Angeles, but also the potential for negative publicity on location, particularly in a dense city full of media outlets. As *Variety* put it in a 1956 headline, "Location Crews and Casts Good Hollywood Ambassadors Barring Tactlessness or Turpitude."[100] These concerns help explain Paramount's months-long correspondence with Rev. Michael Sullivan, custodian of the Old Mission in San Juan Bautista. In October 1956, Herb Coleman, serving as associate producer, sent a synopsis to Sullivan, as well as an odd assurance that he would contact Leo McCarey. In his reply, Sullivan thanked Coleman for Paramount's $2,000 offer and reserved the right to discuss the sanctimony of any interior scenes shot in the mission. He also revealed his plans for a film about the mission; he likely thought of McCarey, based on his successful film *The Bells of St. Mary's* (1945). By February 1957, Sullivan was corresponding with Farciot Edouart, Paramount's special-effects head, about some type of visual effects display to attract visitors to the mission. Sullivan wrote, "I certainly enjoyed my visit to Paramount. Now I know big corporations have souls—if you meet the right people. You made me feel like the King of Siam."[101] This letter shows the people skills that kept *Vertigo* running smoothly on location, as well as how the key set piece was secured well before the start of production.

Months before principal photography, second-unit crews shot most of the background plates for *Vertigo*. As early as February 1957, a small unit led by Herb Coleman, Dan McCauley, and Doc Erickson captured key backgrounds such as Scottie's window view of Coit Tower and the exterior of the Golden Gate Bridge. Second-unit crews, shooting with doubles, were far more flexible and inexpensive than first-unit crews; by comparison, the forty-person first unit on location for *Pal Joey* was described as a "skeleton crew."[102] Principal photography began on September 30, and the first-unit crew left San Francisco by October 15 after falling four days behind due to the inevitable bad weather. Yet as Hitchcock and Burks worked on interiors in the studio, the second unit remained on location for another week as Coleman directed scenes such as the vertiginous camera effect for Midge's apartment. As first-unit shooting revealed the need for additional pickup shots on location, the second unit traveled four more times between November 1957 and February 1958 to San Francisco, where they captured the haunting drive through the tall trees approaching the mission near the climax of the film.[103]

As in the 1940s, the director's role was to work with the actors, not the scenery, regardless of the increased importance of location shooting as a source of production value. Hitchcock's control of the majority of the San Francisco footage was remote control. Detailed descriptions, from storyboards to written notes, guided trusted second-unit crews while Hitchcock remained in Hollywood. He even suggested weather conditions for each shot, something he could never afford to wait for but the second unit could, within reason. The low cost of second-unit work let Hitchcock regularly dispatch them to San Francisco for additional or improved backgrounds. With Paramount's state-of-the-art rear-projection technology, Hitchcock could change backgrounds before and after principal photography, finalizing images on the process stage at the end of production, mid-December 1957.[104]

The production history of *Vertigo* reveals greater collaboration than Hitchcock typically acknowledged.[105] Yet it also shows how collaboration, particularly with his second unit, allowed him to extend his control of the image beyond his physical presence. In the same regard, Hitchcock's fidelity was not to San Francisco itself but to his sense of the ideal San Francisco for the film. Ernie's would be faithfully reconstructed because it so perfectly fit the desired setting; if the real setting did not match his desired image, it would be altered, as the matted mission tower was. Like Judy, San Francisco had to conform to a mind's image, half imagined and half remembered. MacCannell saw in tourism a "modern form of alienation," where the model is preferred over the life it represents.[106] *Vertigo* devastatingly proves this in the denouement of Scottie and Judy's tortured relationship, yet unlike the characters, San Francisco never loses its mystique.

The production team rarely strayed from the picturesque neighborhoods of downtown, Telegraph Hill, Nob Hill, and Russian Hill. The exceptions are mainly landmarks: the Golden Gate Bridge, the Palace of the Legion of Honor, and the Mission Dolores. Two shabbier locations—the McKittrick Hotel, where Madeleine mysteriously goes during her trances, and the Empire Hotel, where Judy lives—stand farther west of downtown. The McKittrick's faded paint and sign suggest Madeleine's movement into Carlotta's past, while the Empire's cheap veranda suggests how working-class Judy pales in comparison to heiress Madeleine.[107] As in *Dark Passage*, the plot dictates a move to a seedier location that could be readily avoided in less dire straits. The world of the tourist district lies inaccessible due to the characters' downward spiral, not the city's decline.

In this geography, *Vertigo* resembles San Francisco's national image in the 1950s. In 1958, the editors of *Fortune* published a book of essays titled *The Exploding Metropolis* that sought relief from what William Whyte saw as a growing alienation between the city and the American way of life, now largely defined by suburbia. Nearly every contributing author, including soon-to-be famous urbanist Jane Jacobs, cites San Francisco or certain streets in the city as shining examples of urban vitality. Yet as Daniel Seligman mentions, despite being "widely acclaimed as the best place in the country to live," slums persisted in San Francisco, as they did in all other major cities.[108] Nevertheless, San Francisco would maintain an image of wealth and beauty. For example, the two *Life* magazine articles about the city in the 1950s covered a debutante ball and the opening of an opera house.[109] *The Lineup*, released the same year as *Vertigo*, provided a rather different cityscape, one in which criminals navigate between San Francisco's ugly interstices and working-class scenic districts. Like the production itself, this city fell in the shadow of *Vertigo*.

THE LINEUP: EXCEPTIONAL STANDARD FARE

After years of losses, Twentieth Century-Fox finally turned a profit from motion pictures in 1957. Fox's decision to step back from its all-color A-picture policy and finance Regal Films to produce inexpensive ($125,000) black-and-white CinemaScope pictures, mostly Westerns and crime pictures, brought in handsome profits. The sales department backed this policy after suffering from a lack of "standard, routine fare" to supply to theaters.[110] Despite an erratic shift from mass production to package production, Hollywood studios continued to produce a relatively stable number of pictures per year for most of the 1950s. The steepest decline came in 1954, when releases by the eight majors dropped by about 33 percent, but by 1957 they had returned to 83 percent of their highest yearly output for the 1950s. A more precipitous decline in output and profits would begin in 1958, on the heels of RKO's collapse and the closing of over 3,000 movie theaters.[111] In short, although the market for studio B-pictures evaporated in the late 1940s, the market for cheaper A-pictures between more extravagant releases remained vital.

The Lineup exemplified this production strategy, which emphasized a rather different location practice than *Vertigo*. By shooting many scenes in daylight exteriors, filmmakers exploited more San Francisco locations than *Vertigo*, not only for their scenic beauty but for their economic and dramatic potential. Building action and suspense sequences around sites such as freeway structures and tourist centers not only saved days of expensive soundstage work, but also provided dramatic settings that the independent producers could never afford to build on a small budget. Like *Vertigo*, *The Lineup* featured urban sightseeing as both a spectacle and a potential threat. Unlike the dangerous mystification with the image that destroys Scottie, the tourist culture of San Francisco threatens the city itself, making dangerous outsiders nearly indistinguishable from the crowds of tourists.

San Francisco provided a dramatic, accessible city for inexpensive second-unit filming and brief first-unit location jaunts. An independent producer could capture a lot of atmosphere in a short amount of time. For instance, in 1952, Stanley Kramer spent six days there shooting *The Sniper*. On just the first day, the crew captured exteriors for twelve different scenes. The location footage covered nearly all of the action scenes, in which a sniper and the police prowl the rooftops of the city day and night. The verticality of the setting revealed several views of the bay, while vantage points between the roof and hilled streets created dynamic compositions, particularly paired with low-key noir lighting. The footage shot in San Francisco added a sense of real but extraordinary place to the semi-documentary crime story, based on a recent series of shootings in Los Angeles.[112] Yet it also accounted for only 20 percent of the script. The remaining exteriors were economically captured in Los Angeles and at the Columbia ranch, with interiors all shot on the studio lot.[113] Kramer could not afford distinctive sets or process shots under his 1952 Columbia contract, which paid $25 million for thirty pictures over five years.[114]

Other inexpensive black-and-white productions would briefly touch base in San Francisco. *The Rack* (1956) features one exterior scene on the Presidio grounds. *Crime of Passion* (1957) opens with a trolley descent toward the bay and an exterior of the San Francisco Police Department before the story moves into interiors and, soon, to Los Angeles. *The Midnight Story* (1957) made more extensive use of location shooting, taking advantage of San Francisco backgrounds in CinemaScope. The production largely limited itself to one area of the city, North Beach, an ethnic Italian neighborhood that shapes the film's story.

The Lineup was standard fare following a different precedent in San Francisco: the successful CBS police procedural of the same name, which ran from 1954 to 1960. While never as popular as *Dragnet*, *The Lineup* was one of the top twenty shows from October 1954 through April 1958.[115] The show distinguished itself from the largely set-bound *Dragnet* by shooting extensively on location in San Francisco, becoming one of only a handful of Hollywood-produced series shooting outside of Los Angeles in the 1950s. By 1958, Nick Musuraca, the cinematographer for the series, had captured more footage in San Francisco than any Hollywood cameraman before him.[116] While shooting almost every exterior shot in San Francisco, all the interiors were shot on a soundstage at Desilu Studios.[117]

The crew captured footage for up to four different episodes in a single day. Working six-day weeks, they typically finished exteriors for eight half-hour episodes in eleven days. Such a schedule left no time for weather delays.

Despite an entire week of rain, regular fog, and high winds, production continued using a mixture of filters, camera angles, and exposure changes to compensate for shifting light and weather patterns. Musuraca would adjust the variable shutter with one hand while checking the light meter in his other hand. The tight budget and schedule precluded any process shots or the use of dailies. As Musuraca said, "By the time rushes reached us from the lab we would already be shooting scenes on a new script."[118]

Early in his career, in the late 1920s, Musuraca shot nine-day Westerns for FBO Studios and its eventual buyer, RKO. The pace and adaptability of B-production set the tone for shooting the series. Smart improvisation with existing conditions could add production value in place of poor cinematography. Rather than waiting for scattered fog to clear, Musuraca once sent an actress wandering through the fog banks, heightening the suspense of a foot chase by an assailant. Overcast days provided a sinister mood for crime stories. Similarly, location sound might be incorporated into the script on the spot. The fast schedule prevented the use of a sound blimp on the camera, since its cumbersome size and installation between reels might slow down production. Beyond the noise of the camera, actual urban locations were rarely quiet. It proved quicker and more effective to write a siren or a pile driver into the script than to negotiate with the workers or officers making the noise.[119]

In sharp contrast to *Vertigo*, in which Hitchcock could afford to shape San Francisco sites into his predetermined images, local conditions actively shaped the look of *The Lineup*. Musuraca rarely shot close-ups on location. Tighter shots of actors could be easily captured in the studio and left little room in the frame to exploit the location backgrounds. Whenever a landmark or architectural element was available on location, the crew worked it into a medium or two-shot of the cast members.[120] Throughout the series, cars almost exclusively parked uphill rather than downhill, allowing the camera to capture the city receding deeply into the background toward the scenic bay. The climax of many episodes featured distinctive, dramatic places such as the Cliff House, where a woman attempts suicide on the wave-battered rocks. In syndication, the show further exploited its location with a new title, *San Francisco Beat*. A two-page *Variety* ad for syndication sales touted San Francisco places that Los Angeles could not replicate, such as Chinatown and the urban waterfront. The image, which covered the top two-thirds of the ad, placed the lead detectives at the top of a hill, flanked by Victorian row houses and a picturesque view of the water.[121]

If San Francisco's sites had already seemed exhausted by the time *The House on Telegraph Hill* was made (1951), *The Lineup*'s thirty-five new episodes a year left even fewer unexploited sites for the 1958 feature film. Series producers Frank Cooper and Jaime Del Valle hired Don Siegel, who had shot the series pilot, to direct. In his autobiography, Siegel claims he and writer Stirling Silliphant hated keeping the same title as the series, a strategy that had already failed for *Dragnet*'s 1954 feature film.[122] He summarized the script as a chilling story of two criminals, and in the finished film, the television detectives are largely superfluous to the criminals, Dancer (Eli Wallach) and Julian (Robert Keith), who overtake the police story once they arrive via airplane. Siegel and Silliphant's suggested title, *The Chase*, points to the "impossibly scary chase" at the climax of the film.[123] Here the filmmakers found the rare exception, an ignored downtown San Francisco sight: the newly constructed Embarcadero Freeway. Rising unfinished above the waterfront, this road to nowhere was tailor-made for the criminals' failed escape. This location previously had remained off-screen for one good reason: it was San Francisco's most famous eyesore.[124]

The Embarcadero Freeway was a structure not even an engineer could love, described by San Francisco consulting engineer William Lathrop Jr. as "so unnecessarily ugly that its appearance has been almost universally condemned."[125] Builders attempted to minimize the freeway's footprint with a double-decker structure that could fit sufficient traffic lanes within the limits of the industrial zones of the waterfront.[126] The result was a far greater visual impact, ruining downtown views of the Ferry Building, the historic entrance to San Francisco by water and rail. This particularly enraged wealthy neighborhood groups such as the Telegraph Hill Dwellers' Association, whose scenic views and property values were threatened by any further highway expansion.[127] Joined by civic clubs and merchant groups, they helped push the Board of Supervisors to all but cease downtown freeway construction.[128]

Impassioned protests against the construction of San Francisco's freeways echoed the fears of Don Siegel's earlier film, *Invasion of the Body Snatchers*. As Joseph Rodriguez describes, "Critics portrayed the attempt to build freeways in the city as the invasion of an alien suburban culture that conflicted with the urbanism of San Francisco."[129] And by connecting San Francisco more explicitly to the booming suburbs surrounding it, the freeways challenged the centrality of the city, as if "the city had become a throughway and not a destination."[130] Nothing could have punctured the dreamy landscape of *Vertigo* quicker than if Scottie had turned onto Market Street and confronted this concrete monolith. Hitchcock harnessed San Francisco's touristic beauty to Scottie's fatal enchantment with the past, keeping modern structures out of the frame. Instead of this fatal tourism, *The Lineup* focuses on a pair of fatal tourists, killers searching the city for missing narcotics. Like the freeway, they are an ugly consequence of a changing city, outsiders who infiltrate the city and lurk beneath its tourist façade.

The Lineup opens with a taxi racing across the cable car–tracked streets near Pier 43, as quick camera pans heighten the sense of speed for the police cars and bikes in pursuit. The cab driver crashes to his death after stealing a Chinese statue from a businessman that contained enough heroin "to fix every addict in San Francisco for two weeks." Police soon realize that an international network of drug dealers has sold souvenirs loaded with heroin to tourists who then unsuspectingly carried these items into San Francisco. Within the first twenty minutes of the film, the city's vitality as an urban center marks it as uniquely vulnerable to crime. The film suggests that as "the busiest port on the coast," the glut of visitors makes it impossible to catch every shipment of narcotics. Criminals such as the corrupt cab driver appear indistinguishable from ordinary residents. While automobiles serve as the primary mode of transportation and policing, the waterfront, where recreational and cargo ships both land, provides a front and back entrance to the city, available to disembarking tourists and criminals alike.

In contrast to these older forms of transportation, Dancer and Julian arrive in modern comfort via a commercial airline. Dancer is reading a grammar book in his first screen appearance, a tool to blend in with local residents by abandoning his street vernacular under Julian's instruction. Like the cab driver, these well-dressed criminals seek cover among the crowd, a theme that will play out the entire film. Julian and Dancer criticize their local accomplice, Sandy McLain (Richard Jaeckel), for a flashy car that might draw extra attention. Later Julian crows, "We can walk down the streets . . . stand on heavy intersections at high noon." But like all tourists, the criminals cannot help but stand out from the locals, and eventually their Miami tans alert police to their nonresident status.

A related theme, the power to see without being seen, is central to the film's narrative, mise-en-scène, and urban topography. The criminals move to a secluded hotel high on the hilly outskirts of San Francisco, revealing a panoramic view that suggests a covert mastery of the city. Observing it from a high vantage point served as both a method of shooting crowds unaware on location and a persistent motif of urban anxiety. Disguised surveillance of San Francisco would define later screen villains such as Red Lynch in *Experiment in Terror* (1962) and Scorpio in *Dirty Harry* (1971), as well as protagonists like Harry Caul in *The Conversation* (1974). In *The Lineup,* public surveillance by police, including the mounted officer who peers into a car to identify the villains, counters the criminals' efforts to anonymously navigate and observe the city. The fact that Dancer is a killer is finally revealed in a scene shot at Sutro's, a popular tourist destination where the practice of sightseeing unites clandestine killers and innocent spectators (Figure 2.5).

2.5. San Francisco appears under surveillance in *The Lineup* (Columbia, 1958): *top,* through binoculars at Sutro's; *bottom,* by a mounted police officer.

As Dancer enters the tourist entertainment complex, a sign reads, "You haven't seen Sutro's . . . you haven't seen San Francisco." Sutro's offers an ice skating rink, nautical exhibits, and oversized binoculars and telescopes to look out at the ocean. Unlike the stately museums and enchanting missions of *Vertigo*, it is a mass attraction, coupling nautical vistas with Coney Island amusements. Schoolgirls gleefully run through the arcade on a class trip while Dancer waits for his boss (Vaughn Taylor), infamous for never allowing himself to be seen by his accomplices. A schoolgirl innocently asks Dancer to help her work the binoculars, a disturbing interaction for viewers who have already seen him murder without hesitation. Rotating the binoculars from the ocean view toward the boss, appearing in a wheelchair, Dancer subverts sightseeing into surveillance. Yet when Dancer confronts his boss, seeing him in person seals his fate. The boss says, "You're dead," takes an excruciatingly long pause, and then explains, "Nobody ever sees me." The ability to see and not be seen, reinforced by the presence of telescopes and binoculars, serves as the fatal logic of the criminal hidden in the crowd. A frustrated Dancer pushes the boss off the balcony onto the ice below, revealing his own criminality to the surrounding public, and flees for the car. Vision plays a key role in *Vertigo*, where Judy pales in comparison to Scottie's image of Madeleine in enchanted San Francisco. Dancer faces the opposite problem, a small reassurance to the audience. Despite nearly blending into the tourist spectacle of San Francisco, a moment of public violence immediately exposes the criminals to the authorities.

Sutro's is the culmination of a murderous tourist trip for Julian and Dancer during which they infiltrate both high and low, public and private places of the city. They visit the Steinhart Aquarium, where a symbolic pan from a shark to the approaching Dancer recalls the scene set there in *The Lady from Shanghai*. Here Dancer convinces a woman and child that he is a fellow tourist in a ploy to find the missing heroin. Dancer kills a man in the steam room of the Sailor's Club, where no one locks their doors. Between Julian and Dancer's intimate relationship and a murder in a seminude steam room, homosexuality appears as a vaguely implied threat to a changing San Francisco. Dancer also kills a Chinese servant at a hilltop estate, showing an ability to talk his way into any social echelon. McLain drives Dancer and Julian from murder scene to murder scene on an automotive tour of the city. After each killing, Dancer tells Julian the victim's last words; Julian treasures each line before writing them in his diary, building a morbid travelogue of a savage excursion.

For urban designer Victor Gruen, one of the great pleasures of the city threatened by urban sprawl was the chance encounter between pedestrians in "more concentrated and urbane cities."[131] *The Lineup* adds a tourist dimension to the anxiety lingering beneath the pleasure of the chance encounter, dramatized in earlier film noirs like *Scarlet Street* (1945). Here tourist attractions like Sutro's and the aquarium draw distracted strangers from distant points of origin together; like the port, the sights of San Francisco draw both sightseers and criminals. Dancer's ability to alternatively act like a local or a tourist casts a pall on the city and the faceless tourists who stream into the city's popular entertainment districts. Another external threat appears in the film's climax in the form of the newly constructed section of the Embarcadero Freeway ramp, linking the booming Bay Area suburbs to downtown. This new infrastructure defeats the criminals but suggests another monumental challenge to San Francisco's urban form that dangles over the city.

Once Dancer flees Sutro's, the climax of the film is a high-speed car chase where the twisting curves of the San Francisco coast provide the dramatic setting that *Bullitt* (1968) would famously exploit a decade later. Unlike *Bullitt* the sequence had to rely on rear projection for the lead actors, a technique unavailable to the television version of *The Lineup*. While Hitchcock used rear projection in *Vertigo* to carefully control the background, *The Lineup* uses it largely as a logistical and safety measure, allowing the lead actors to safely appear in the fleeing car. By intercutting these process shots with location footage of stunt drivers swerving around the hills of the city, the film efficiently exploits the exciting location without losing track of the central characters. Local police supervised the final stunt, where the villains' car skids to the edge of the unfinished freeway ramp, but there was no room for error, with no obstacle to prevent the stunt driver from plummeting off the highway.[132] The result is a thrilling image at little expense that also suggests lax supervision of location shooting in 1950s San Francisco. This laissez-faire attitude toward filmmaking caused few problems for the city for the short, infrequent location shoots of the 1950s but became a major concern in the 1970s, when scores of Hollywood filmmakers seemed to be running rampant in San Francisco.

The villains and their hostages, the woman and child from the aquarium, careen up the ramp of the Embarcadero Freeway after a roadblock cuts off access to the Golden Gate Bridge. A long overhead shot shows the car skidding to a stop just short of the precipice (Figure 2.6). Panoramic views show the car hovering above the center of the city but completely

2.6. The Embarcadero Freeway, San Francisco's most infamous eyesore, serves as a climactic set piece in *The Lineup*.

disconnected from the grid below. Sandy speeds backward but chooses the wrong lane, wedging the car between two narrowing guardrails. Frustrated by his conspirators and the failure of the automobile, Dancer walks onto the highway, shoots Julian, and takes the child hostage. Wide shots reveal the gnarled concrete ramps of the highway juxtaposed with the Bay Bridge majestically receding into the hills. A pedestrian on an empty highway, Dancer stands trapped between the walking city below and the aerial highway. Dancer releases the child and climbs astride two ramps, peering down the narrow corridor between them at a car below. Before he can make a desperate leap, the police shoot him, and his body tumbles down between the lanes.

As the police survey the scene of the crime, the camera pans right from the police walking down the jumbled freeway toward an unimpeded view of the bridge and the bay; a waving flag and words thanking the San Francisco Police Department half dissolve over the image. The death of the villain allows the camera to abandon the disjunctive image of the highway slashing across the city for the postcard beauty denied by the criminal presence. Siegel would employ similar lateral pans toward and away from urban concentration and criminality in *Coogan's Bluff* (1968) and *Dirty Harry* (1971). In *The Lineup*, the police honorarium, notorious in *Dirty Harry*, combines with the reclaimed pastoral view of the bridge spanning the bay. Yet this nod to police authority is not redundant with the plot; instead, it pragmatically acknowledges police assisting on location who allowed the producers to mount a dangerous series of driving stunts.

The Lineup depicts the most frightening tourists possible: a pair of amoral killers passing as ordinary citizens. Yet as in Scottie's pathological behavior, the viewer can identify with their struggle as tourists. They provide not only the vicarious thrill of sightseeing, but another powerful fantasy of travel: the ability to blend in with new surroundings and leave one's identity behind. But there is also a hint of contemporary tragedy in the killers' inability to navigate the highway system. The logic of modern urban form breaks down on the ramp, as the city appears all around them but entirely inaccessible. Forced to walk in a space designed only for driving, the terrain becomes perilous and confounding. The elevated freeway appears as foreign and incomprehensible as the villains, denying San Francisco its splendid isolation from the key urban anxiety of the time, the highway sprawl into and out of the city.

Vertigo and *The Lineup* suggest two critical poles of location production in late 1950s Hollywood. The star-driven A-picture could afford lavish color cinematography in the city but required far more studio work to ensure its professional polish. Black-and-white standard fare like *The Lineup* instead grabbed every possible location asset as a cheaper alternative to elaborate sets. While *Vertigo* adapted San Francisco to the demands of its story, *The Lineup* wisely tailored its narrative to San Francisco locations. The semi-documentary style of the procedural offered an economical strategy to exploit locations but ceded the meticulous, total control of the image that Hitchcock wielded during the production of *Vertigo*.

The cine-tourist image of San Francisco extended well beyond the 1950s. So did debates over runaway production, which sharpened in the first half of the 1960s. The pure spectacle of San Francisco's cityscape inevitably faded, and even Cinerama had shifted to narrative films by the late 1950s. But the escapist image of a wealthy, buoyant city persisted, particularly in color film comedies of the 1960s.

Although on-screen San Francisco remained a scenic playground, it fell under a critical new black-and-white urban aesthetic, exemplified by Blake Edwards's stark depiction of the city in two 1962 films, *Experiment in Terror* and *Days of Wine and Roses*. *The Lineup* could only effectively shoot daylight scenes on location, but improvements in black-and-white film stock and location production allowed Edwards and his cinematographer, Philip Lathrop, to capture San Francisco at night with subtle low-key lighting that in the 1950s could only be achieved on the studio lot. Like other black-and-white films shot domestically throughout the United States in the first half of the 1960s, incisive depictions of American social decay reached beyond the criminal world of 1950s film noir. A loosening Production Code and the growth of domestic location shooting brought a wave of tortured characters to the screen, with bleak, distinctly American settings underscoring their plights. Black-and-white location shooting became a critical component of a production trend for sordid realist dramas, and in Edwards's films, San Francisco's scenic beauty took on a tragic tone.

3

"SICK TALES OF A HEALTHY LAND"

Blake Edwards in San Francisco

"SICK" HAD BECOME A MULTIVALENT description of Hollywood by the early 1960s. The most visible malady appeared on-screen. In a 1961 article titled "Sick Tales of a Healthy Land," *Variety* criticized "a rash of diseased characters, bankrupts, weaklings with rampant vices," whose sordid behavior prompted a stinging critique of Hollywood in *Reader's Digest*.[1] These characters ranged from disturbed killers such as Norman Bates in *Psycho* (1960), addicts like Mary Tyrone in *Long Day's Journey Into Night* (1962), and the corrupt religious and secular leaders in *Elmer Gantry* (1960) and *Advise and Consent* (1963) to any number of depraved Southerners from Tennessee Williams and his imitators. Blake Edwards followed the trend with two 1962 films set in San Francisco: *Experiment in Terror*, which features a perverse killer manipulating a pair of sisters (Figure 3.1), and *Days of Wine and Roses*, a bleak depiction of the depths of alcoholism. Hollywood's weakened

3.1. This poster ad for *Experiment in Terror* (Columbia, 1962) emphasizes the film's risqué content and dark tone.

enforcement of the Production Code enabled such films, but this was only one symptom of an increasingly fragmented Hollywood production system.

Runaway production had cast a sickly pall across the Los Angeles film industry. The major companies had survived the postwar transition out of vertical integration and mass production, but as middlemen increasingly dependent on Wall Street capital, high-priced stars, and producers. As top talent found financial incentives to shoot independent productions away from the studio, the major companies sold unused lots to real estate developers. The remaining lots remained half full, with television series occupying most of the active soundstages. As backlot employment dwindled, several observers felt a creeping malaise. In "Hollywood Come Home," a public affairs special for Los Angeles television station KNXT, narrator Ray Milland compared runaway production to "moving the Vatican out of Rome."[2] *Variety* covered the special under the headline "Hollywood's Self-Diagnosis: 'Doc, Why Do We Feel So Weak?'"[3] The vacant, fading movie workshops bred nostalgia; as Milland lamented, "[F]ewer stars, fewer Rolls Royces and fewer camera-calls . . . the dream factories of the motion picture business are oddly quiet."[4] The decentralization of production across the globe had eroded Hollywood's ability to self-regulate not only its content, but also its production process, labor practices, and creative workers.

These ailments both masked and facilitated a tremendous surge of creativity and innovation in American filmmaking. A wellspring of new talent migrated from television to feature filmmaking in the late 1950s and early 1960s, including directors Blake Edwards, Sidney Lumet, John Frankenheimer, Sam Peckinpah, and Martin Ritt. As television's golden age of live drama quickly faded, these filmmakers transplanted stark social dramas of the American landscape from television onto the bigger screen. Television taught them how to shoot quickly and cheaply, often with limited production facilities or on location. With greater production efficiency, more extensive location shooting could now viably compete with the cost and aesthetics of soundstage production.

Technological improvements, from faster film stocks and lenses to portable lighting and camera equipment, responded to the higher demand for location shooting by independent producers and runaway production. While color filmmaking still required a flood of high-intensity lighting, black-and-white film no longer had to sacrifice image quality shooting on location, even in places lacking the perpetual sunshine of Los Angeles. These changes set off another boom in New York filmmaking, while promoting location shooting for stories set in cities such as Washington, DC, and San Francisco. However, although the photographic challenges of filming in American cities had decreased, major logistical challenges still remained.

Film depictions of social problems largely focused on rural and inner-city locations, aberrations from the growing concentration of suburban commuters. In 1961, *Variety* cautioned against the overuse of "sick-sick-sick-types out of the Southern swamplands or the city slums."[5] Both the central city and the rural hinterlands suggested isolated pockets of cultural deviance existing in dubious opposition to suburban culture. Blake Edwards's depictions of San Francisco offered sharp glimpses of urban decadence falling into urban decay, although like earlier film noirs, his films delineated crime and depravity into districts rather than indicting the city itself. From the quasi–San Francisco of *Peter Gunn* (1958–1961), to the lurid noir of *Experiment in Terror*, to the human tragedy of *Days of Wine and Roses*, Edwards darkened but never dispelled San Francisco's beautiful image.

Changes in Production Code enforcement, runaway production, filmmaking technology, and an influx of television talent contributed to an early 1960s trend for stark black-and-white realism. Dark films such as *Birdman of Alcatraz* (1962), *Hud* (1963), and *Days of Wine and Roses*, which exploited salacious content and were all directed by television veterans, won Oscar nominations. Edwards transformed San Francisco's vibrant urban scenery into a sordid, even nightmarish realm to suit his bleaker narratives. The city appears like an inky shadow of the melancholic but exhilarating New York of his more famous film, *Breakfast at Tiffany's* (1961). Edwards, who worked almost exclusively as a comedy director before and after 1962, launched his career as an independent producer-director with a pair of dark, challenging films, indicative of the tremendous impact this wave of disturbing black-and-white pictures had on Hollywood. While *Vertigo* and *The Lineup* had to carefully choose locations, faster film stock allowed Edwards to more carefully control the tone of location footage, day or night, creating a low-key aesthetic on location that a few years earlier could only be achieved on the soundstage. San Francisco maintained an image of urban splendor for city planners and many Hollywood filmmakers, but Edwards demonstrated how readily the city's appearance could be manipulated. His improvisation on location, as well as his depiction of a dark, lurid city, set a precedent for San Francisco films of the early 1970s, but Hollywood's rapid shift to color in the mid-1960s abruptly ended the trend of downbeat black-and-white films. Once color film approached the speed of black-and-white, location filming in San Francisco followed a similar course, degrading the image of San Francisco to suit another wave of bleak urban cinematography.

DOWNBEAT PICTURES AND INDEPENDENT PRODUCERS

Jack Warner had reason to worry about *Days of Wine and Roses* based on several newspaper clippings filed with the film's production documents and specified for his attention. In January 1962, roughly two months before principal photography, the *Los Angeles Times* ran an article with the headline "Parade of Downbeat Pictures Continues." Adult content, it said, was threatening not only taste but also business, as "all too often shock or bitterness takes precedence over either entertainment or art. . . . Among the new outpouring on the decidedly downbeat and often flagrant side are such pictures as 'Tender Is the Night,' 'A Walk on the Wild Side,' 'A View from The Bridge,' 'Sweet Bird of Youth,' and 'Too Late Blues.'"[6] Another clipping worried about the effect of "low-key, downbeat subject matter" on the increasingly important youth audience. "Who wants to take his best girl to see people suffer to the bitter end?" was a representative question from a survey of college and high school students. Middle-aged screen characters appeared far more delinquent than teenagers.[7]

Edwards's gloomy depictions of San Francisco in *Experiment in Terror* and *Days of Wine and Roses* were part of an early 1960s wave of pictures with darker themes and more explicit content. Although less restrictive self-regulation fit a liberal shift in American culture and politics, the Production Code Authority (PCA) proved unable to rein in the independent production companies that now produced most Hollywood films. As studios competed for projects with proven stars and producers, creative workers increasingly dictated which films would reach the screen, including several theatrical properties with taboo subjects previously restricted by the PCA. As with runaway production, which benefited individual productions but in excess threatened industry stability, Hollywood leaders failed to stem the tide of downbeat and salacious features by independent producers. Edwards depicted San Francisco in a sinister light despite his success with dark but droll narratives for *Peter Gunn* and *Breakfast at Tiffany's*. The disturbing plot of *Experiment in Terror* and the cold realism of *Days of Wine and Roses* called for night-for-night shooting in seedy locations, offering hard shadows and sordid places largely absent from *Vertigo* and *The Lineup*.

The liberal Kennedy administration soon distinguished itself from the conservative culture of the Eisenhower era, which facilitated Hollywood's more lax censorship. For instance, in 1958, the Department of Justice refused to cooperate on *The Birdman of Alcatraz*, effectively scuttling the planned production; in 1962, a new production of the film premiered, mounting a harsh critique of the prison system without government interference.[8] The same year, *Lolita* represented the United States at the Venice Film Festival, marking a decisive break with the "niceness" of previous American entries. *Variety* observed, "It's quite in harmony with the New Frontier and the film's sophisticated tone would indeed seem to fit snugly under the White House culture umbrella."[9] Tellingly, every major studio but Fox bid on *Lolita*, a property that only a few years earlier would have been inconceivable to acquire.[10] Even the Legion of Decency shifted emphasis toward promoting moral films rather than threatening to boycott immoral ones, as the largest pressure group relinquished its strongest tactic for policing Hollywood content.[11]

A looser and more loosely enforced Production Code allowed previously unmentionable topics to reach the screen. Faced with the challenge of controversial high-profile releases such as *The Man with the Golden Arm* (1955) and *Baby Doll* (1956), the PCA made its first major revision to the 1930 code in December 1956.[12] While on paper the revision replaced bans on specific topics such as abortion and childbirth, Geoffrey Shurlock's looser interpretation of the code had a greater impact. He implied in 1959 that any subject but homosexuality could be presented, if properly handled.[13]

Regardless of intention, the PCA had already lost the authority to strictly enforce the code. *Variety* described "the new anarchy of the independents" as "a rampage of rival self-interests." Dozens of director-producers and actor-producers created the lion's share of films and stood to profit directly from exploitative hits.[14] In 1958, independent companies produced half of American films; by 1960, it was two-thirds.[15] With so many different entities involved, the Motion Picture Association of America (MPAA) struggled to enforce industry-wide measures. Calls for censorship, union pacts, and rules to curb runaway production all proved difficult to implement among a constellation of independent companies rather than among a cadre of studio heads.

By 1959, competition between major studios to sign a handful of top-flight independent producers had grown fierce. Studios like MGM and Paramount could offer large backlots and foreign facilities; lacking a physical plant, United Artists (UA) effectively wooed many of the top producers with creative freedom.[16] After *On the Beach*, a thoroughly downbeat picture, Stanley Kramer lauded UA for not being "afraid of the offbeat."[17] Along with conventional pictures, the company was credited with bringing "a new awareness" to the screen that "ranges from shock values to adult material." Pictures that followed, such as *The Apartment* (1960) and *Elmer Gantry* (1960), confirmed UA's boldness.[18] In 1960, *Variety* christened the company "the protagonist in the entire industry's modus operandi,"[19] but the practice of giving talent creative leeway led to more shocking pictures. Meanwhile, UA's success without a physical production plant highlighted the waning importance of the soundstage as location shooting became more efficient and prevalent.

European films made major gains in the American market in the early 1960s, buoyed by sexual themes and content beyond the limits of Hollywood productions.[20] They also helped sustain Hollywood distributors through product shortages. For instance, MGM stockpiled six foreign films as a hedge against a release gap caused by the 1960 Screen Actors Guild (SAG) strike.[21] In 1962, foreign films were "much more controversial," full of "inversions, abnormalities, and strange sex histories."[22] Hollywood responded with violence, as *The Birds* (1963) and *Whatever Happened to Baby Jane?* (1963) joined "films of mayhem from many lands" at Cannes.[23]

Sex and brutality in Hollywood films grew more audacious and more frequent. While films like *Anatomy of a Murder* (1959) tweaked the code, *Psycho* eviscerated it with graphic violence and psychosexual perversion.[24] Popular theatrical properties with taboo subjects also abounded. Although only four Tennessee Williams dramas reached the screen between 1950 and 1957, seven appeared between 1958 and 1962, including lavish star productions of *Cat on a Hot Tin Roof* (1958), *Suddenly Last Summer* (1959), and *Sweet Bird of Youth* (1962).[25] Old and new works by major literary and dramatic provocateurs hit theaters; the authors included William Faulkner (*The Sound and the Fury* and *The Long Hot Summer* [both 1959]), Norman Mailer (*The Naked and the Dead* [1958]), Vladimir Nabokov (*Lolita* [1962]), Lillian Hellman (*The Children's Hour* [1961], *Toys in the Attic* [1963]), William Inge (*Splendor in the Grass* [1961]; *All Fall Down* [1962]), and Eugene O'Neill (*Desire Under the Elms* [1958], *Long Day's Journey into Night* [1962]). These downbeat stories and wretched characters threatened to dampen audience enthusiasm for controversial subjects.

As one industry observer noted, "It's not the license but the flood which causes the trouble."[26] As in the 1930s, a glut of offensive pictures brought public calls for censorship, and in the early 1960s, the MPAA made an early attempt at establishing a ratings system as a new form of censorship, with at least two tiers separating child- and adult-appropriate films. MPAA head Eric Johnston floated the idea of a voluntary ratings system in 1961, but theater owners balked, again revealing the challenge of regulating a vertically disintegrated industry.[27] Independent producers like Blake Edwards continued to push the boundaries of explicit content without consequence. For instance, the PCA asked Edwards to remove sexual innuendo and images in *Days of Wine in Roses*, including racy milkmaid costumes for the servers at a wild company party.[28] Edwards ignored all of these suggestions and chose particularly revealing outfits. Greater license also extended to Edwards's choice of San Francisco locations: the Roaring Twenties, a nightclub where scantily clad women rode swings over the crowd, was featured in *Experiment in Terror*. In a sense this was cine-tourism for a more permissive era; the club was profiled in the *Washington Post* in early 1962, and in 1963 the *Chicago Tribune* included a photo of the swinging waitresses.[29]

Despite reservations over indecent content, the industry had a compelling reason to welcome a great many of these downbeat films: they were set and shot in the United States. As runaway production abroad threatened to permanently dislocate US filmmaking, a wave of medium-budget black-and-white films offered a potential alternative, saving both money and jobs for Hollywood. In 1963, Fox revealed a $20 million loss filming *Cleopatra* in Italy and temporarily shut down all film production; less than a year earlier, *What Ever Happened to Baby Jane?* had earned back its production cost in just eleven days.[30] Although unions praised pictures that stayed home, home was no longer limited to Los Angeles. Independent producers shooting realist dramas overwhelmingly favored authentic locations, shooting extensively throughout the country. Nonetheless, all but a handful films returned to Hollywood soundstages to complete principal photography.

RUNAWAY CRISIS

As discussed in chapter 2, runaway production had become common practice for many major studios by the mid-1950s, but it exploded into an industry crisis in the early 1960s. While the unions targeted foreign production as the critical threat to their workers, the struggle would have clear implications for domestic location shooting as well. The unions failed to limit the number of Hollywood productions shooting abroad, but union pressure helped close the tax loopholes that made foreign production so desirable for major stars and producers. The need for realistic locations remained the studios' best defense for shooting away from Los Angeles, solidifying location shooting as a key component of foreign productions and reinforcing an association between location shooting and cinematic realism. When filmmakers returned from foreign locations to shoot in the United States, they frequently continued to shoot extensively on location.

Lower-budget films and television productions remained the critical exception to foreign runaway production. Both took advantage of the abandoned facilities, workers, and even sets during Hollywood's surge in filming abroad. For the police procedural, location shooting still proved less expensive than set building, while for exploitation horror films, Hollywood's disused sets added production value. By 1960, television location shooting had developed domestically to reinvigorate a largely set-bound medium. Telefilm producers learned to shoot fast and imperfectly under small budgets and tight schedules, skills that proved critical for filmmakers like Blake Edwards working on location.

By 1957, the rise of telefilm production in Hollywood was providing enough jobs to temporarily dampen union protests against runaway production.[31] But studio facilities continued to shrink as the prevalence of foreign production made it easier for the majors to sell off property. With Los Angeles real estate prices still booming, selling land could not only offset losses but boost earnings reports to Wall Street, lifting stock prices and building liquid assets. Fox's 260 acre lot in Westwood sold for $56 million.[32] In fact, the studio sold so much studio space that in 1961 they had to consider renting stages on the Goldwyn lot to keep pace with production.[33] Tax laws favored this odd development: rent could be deducted as an operating expense if a company was willing to forgo potential profits as a landlord and real estate holder.[34]

Labor suffered another blow just prior to the SAG strike that began in March 1960. Anticipating the work stoppage, Fox, Columbia, MGM, and Warner Bros. all began downsizing staff and physical assets. At MGM, most of the layoffs were construction workers; set building, the backbone of the world's biggest backlot, had withered under the dual threats of runaway production and location shooting. Regardless of the outcome of SAG negotiations, Warner Bros. warned employees that the layoffs might be permanent.[35] The "industry-wide strike" appeared to be the first of its kind, a testament to the new power of noncontract talent.[36] Other workers proved less essential, as the studios discharged nearly 5,000 studio employees by the start of the strike.[37] Paramount began its first wave of firings in May 1960, the start of a "wholesale overhaul of personnel."[38] Despite the company's strong earnings and assets, studio head Barney Balaban challenged every employee to justify his or her position.[39]

Downsizing quickly paid off for the studios. By 1961, *Variety* saw signs that "the worst was over" for the industry. Stocks rallied, theater closings subsided, and companies found "a new kind of surer economy" through diversified holdings and less capital expenditure.[40] For the first time in over a decade, the crippling overhead was in check, balanced by fewer employees and more rentals to television productions.[41] These improved conditions removed a key obstacle to location production, particularly domestically. For Sidney Lumet's production manager, George Justin, it was "the old overhead that dictated production on the Coast."[42] As long as producers could shoot economically in New York, both in studio and on location, they need not head to Los Angeles to contribute to the cost of studio operations.

Conditions grew tenuous for union workers. As studios focused on a handful of lavish pictures like *Cleopatra* (1963) and *Lawrence of Arabia* (1962), the total number of pictures released approached a historic low. Meanwhile, the demand for a handful of top stars and directors to anchor major pictures further retarded production as studios waited for talent to finish the lengthy shoots required for spectaculars.[43] A trend toward hour-long television series left fewer productions for television crews. In April 1962, once the television season wrapped, 40 percent of Teamsters and 30 percent of cameramen sat unemployed.[44] While all of these factors affected American production workers, foreign production remained the unifying grievance for Hollywood labor in the early 1960s. IATSE was responsible for coining the term *runaway* in the 1950s, and the organization began to adamantly push the studios to finally take action.[45]

In June 1960, the AFL-CIO vowed to "reactivate" a five-year-old plan to urge Congress to address runaway production.[46] The pugnacious cameramen's union, led by Herb Aller, went further. They demanded dislocation benefits in the form of higher weekly unemployment pay due to pictures shooting abroad.[47] Aller also threatened to boycott the pictures of stars living abroad to avoid US income tax, which *Variety* deemed the first direct action against runaways. Targeting the star tax loophole proved a clever strategy; the exception seemed to benefit only a handful of wealthy actors and matched the popular industry argument that stars largely dictated foreign shooting.[48] In fact, Elizabeth Taylor only agreed to star in *Cleopatra* if the film would be shot abroad, which saved her from paying personal income taxes on her high salary.[49] The cameramen's opening salvo attacked William Holden for filming two pictures abroad, *The World of Suzie Wong* (1960) and *Counterfeit Traitor* (1962), as if Holden was a traitor to the country and industry that had made him a star.[50]

Realism remained a popular argument for shooting abroad. William Holden insisted that it was the rubble of Berlin, not tax benefits, that had dictated the decision to shoot overseas.[51] Yet *Spartacus* (1960), shot largely in the United States, looked just as realistic as *Ben Hur,* shot largely abroad. *Ben Hur* director William Wyler conceded that the decision to shoot entirely in

Rome had been solely financial.[52] Leading up to a 1962 congressional probe, Paramount's Y. Frank Freeman defended the use of runaway production when foreign locales were essential or the cost of shooting in Hollywood would be "prohibitive."[53]

By focusing on production expenses and realism, the industry sidestepped the other financial incentives available when shooting abroad. In 1960, *Variety* identified a third phase in overseas filmmaking. Phase 1 had relied on postwar fascination with Europe, exemplified by *The Third Man* (1949) and *Three Coins in the Fountain.* During phase 2, shooting in certain European cities actually became cheaper than Hollywood and offered spectacles to compete with television. Phase 3 revealed no clear economic benefits from shooting abroad or featuring foreign locales.[54] Studios could plausibly argue that for a given picture, cost savings were no longer a factor. The realism excuse helped placate the unions, but ensured that location shooting remained a significant part of foreign production and helped drive further development of location shooting practices. The question remained: if the costs were equal, why was Hollywood making so many pictures abroad?

Despite rising production costs in Europe and elsewhere, financial incentives more clearly impacted foreign production than realism. The president of the William Morris Agency, Abe Lastfogel, cited tax exemptions as the top reason for shooting abroad; his agency had sold talent packages for thirty-five recent films, seeking to maximize tax relief for their clients. He predicted that a proposed tax amendment would stem runaway production and mentioned *Days of Wine and Roses*, shot entirely in California, as a recent package deal.[55] However, stars could still benefit from having their living costs funded as a production expense during months shooting away from Los Angeles, a benefit gained in domestic cities like San Francisco as well. And hidden beneath the public outcry over tax subsidies was a fairly new development: cofinancing deals with foreign production companies, which according to one guild leader were "the most insidious form of runaway in Hollywood."[56] By cofinancing major British pictures like *Lawrence of Arabia* and *Dr. Strangelove* (1964), Hollywood studios qualified for financial assistance from the British government under the Eady Plan.[57]

In contrast to location shooting in Europe, shooting large-budget pictures on location in the United States could be prohibitively expensive. For instance, Otto Preminger claimed Hollywood was kidding itself about the cost of shooting domestically, which remained one-third more expensive than in Europe due to labor costs and union concessions. Preminger claimed that while shooting *The Cardinal* in Boston, union "blackmail" restricted him from hiring local workers and forced him to pay standbys in Hollywood; no such demands occurred in Italy.[58] These agreements help explain why the unions aggressively fought foreign runaway production without addressing domestic runaways; they also pushed location productions to return to the studio, with the key exception of New York productions, where union labor, including New York's industrial and commercial film workers, could be tapped.[59] These expenses helped limit location shooting in cities like San Francisco, particularly in color, which added additional expenses and difficulties. The four major color productions set in San Francisco in the first half of the 1960s—*The Pleasure of Her Company* (1961), *Flower Drum Song* (1961), *The Birds* (1963), and *Good Neighbor Sam* (1964)—all returned to the studio after capturing backgrounds and a few exterior scenes.

The maturation of Hollywood studios into diversified corporations backed by rising stock prices also pushed global productions. Producer Charles Schneer argued, "You can't confine the industry to Hollywood. It's a world industry now."[60] Investors pressured Hollywood to tighten budgets, and foreign savings could do so on paper, although the final cost rarely matched.[61] As one *Variety* writer wryly stated, "Foreign shooting skeds are estimated at a minimum with maximum up to gods," highlighting the continued uncertainty of foreign location shooting, where logistical problems such as weather, inexperienced crews, and local government restrictions could add months to production schedules.[62] Investors favored lower approved costs but failed to understand the murky production issues that caused frequent overages abroad. The expensive failures of *Mutiny on the Bounty* (1962) and *Cleopatra* called this strategy into question. Local IATSE members who owned stock in MGM spoke out at a 1963 shareholders meeting in New York and blamed the studio's dramatic decline in profits on a woeful neglect of its Hollywood lot. Years of runaway production had not only kept MGM's facilities underutilized but had degraded their value, spurring further location shooting at home and abroad.[63]

By 1961, Hollywood labor had the federal government's ear. In an April speech to Congress, President Kennedy asked for a repeal of the "total tax exemption" for citizens living abroad, a position publicly endorsed by SAG.[64] A House subcommittee scheduled a probe of runaway production for November.[65] The investigation, led by Democrat John Dent, failed to gain Kennedy's support and folded in April 1962.[66] Kennedy finally signed away the tax exemption in January 1963, but the government took no further action to curb runaway filmmaking.

The slow process of fighting runaway production weakened Hollywood unions, which struggled through years of underemployment only to achieve a partial victory through the federal repeal of tax exemptions for American citizens' foreign earnings. The threat of moving more productions abroad served as a weapon for the studios and top independent producers to wrest concessions from unions. For example, for the first time in its history, SAG asked for no upgrades in pay or working conditions for a 1962 pact, citing "realism in light of 'runaway.'"[67] Craft unions had to press IATSE for action, an indication of the umbrella group's alleged coziness with the studios.[68] Still, IATSE's public statements remained timid. It praised *Spartacus* for staying in Hollywood (with the exception of a major battle shot in Spain) and promoted it as a turning point against the runaway tide.[69] The declining power of the Hollywood unions became a crucial factor in the spread of domestic location shooting in the later 1960s. As with foreign location shooting, when union workers faced high unemployment and had to regulate practices among independent producers, they failed to slow location shooting in cities like San Francisco and New York.

Ironically, the unions' reduced bargaining power in the wake of rampant foreign production helped make shooting domestically more attractive. A turning point came in May 1962 following a series of secret negotiations between labor and management. Talks centered on George Stevens's mega-production *The Greatest Story Ever Told* (1965). At stake would be over 20,000 man-days of work for actors and craftsmen, but Stevens threatened to take those jobs abroad.[70] According to Stevens, costumes for 1,000 soldiers would cost $145,300 in California but only $7,500 to rent abroad. Similarly, 1,000 extras would cost $115,000 a day, compared to $5,000 (at a $5 per day rate) in Spain.[71] Despite Stevens's public accusations of featherbedding, the unions caved, beginning with the extras guild granting the production a special waiver. *Variety* crowed with the front-page headline "Action on 'Runaway' at Last."[72]

The celebration would be short-lived. By August 1962 the pace of runaway had only quickened, with twenty-five of thirty-six new pictures slated to film abroad, amounting to $75 million invested outside Hollywood.[73] By May 1963, only eight of twenty-five features were in Hollywood; ten would be shot entirely overseas, while seven would eventually return from Europe and New York.[74] Craft unions lobbied specific studios urging some runaway restraint.[75] *Variety* asked, "If [Runaway] Tide Turns, When Is It Due?"[76]

Location shooting often interfered with strict union guidelines, evidenced by two 1963 arbitrations. IATSE claimed that MGM owed its members a meal penalty for a flight to San Francisco to shoot for the *Sam Benedict* television series. While breakfast was served, the workers could only eat, clearly unable to leave the plane to attend to other business. In another case, union members asked for an extra day's pay after refusing to board a plane that appeared dangerously overcrowded, delaying their return home by a day. In his decision, the arbitrator cited "the reasonable changes and allowances" that kept the film in the United States, including location conditions, and sided with producer George Stevens.[77] The irregular schedule and unexpected changes in location production not only risked union penalties but also created regular conflicts for crew members forced to accept less favorable contracts. While production workers lamented jobs lost overseas, location shooting domestically remained a source of friction for beleaguered workers asked to make further accommodations for producers.

Despite declining union power, Hollywood crews cost as much as $5,000 a day in 1962, causing labor complaints to fall on deaf ears.[78] Certain studio heads showed no sympathy, including Fox's Spyros Skouras, who blamed runaway production on a 1959 pact for a five-day work week. Columbia's Mike Frankovich gave *Variety* the front-page headline "Don't Film to Please Unions."[79] Public fights over the causes of runaway production between studio representatives and union leaders created a tense production climate that encouraged some producers to stay away from Hollywood. As demonstrated by George Stevens and Elizabeth Taylor, star producers and actors largely dictated whether pictures would shoot domestically or internationally. Runaway production reflected the atomization of Hollywood filmmaking, no longer anchored to the physical studio or the dictates of central management. As unions and major studios failed to find adequate solutions to the phenomenon, a fragmented production system and inconsistent box office returns made it difficult to institute industry-wide regulations.

One devastating casualty of runaway production was Hollywood's self-image as a creative capital. Howard Koch, producer of *The Manchurian Candidate* (1962), declared Hollywood dead and wrote a stinging epitaph: "Today it is a dead place where people are being wedged ever more tightly into their own little corners too preoccupied with themselves even to want to know what anybody else is doing." By contrast, European film artists were "still unfettered by box office tentacles."[80] Columnist Sheilah Graham found far more energy among the American actors abroad, writing, "Hollywood has become stale for creative people."[81]

Such indictments inspired filmmakers working extensively on location, who relished "the breakdown of the old monarchies that ruled production."[82] The growing clout of independent producers and stars not only allowed them to pursue lucrative productions in Europe, but also to produce dozens of dark, challenging story properties, largely shot in black-and-white on American locations. A wave of early 1960s films shot in and around New York City, including *Butterfield 8* (1960), *The Hustler* (1960), and *Long Day's Journey Into Night (1962)*, paired real locations with realist dramas that sought to counter Hollywood make-believe in both aesthetics and theme.[83] Such films were rarely major hits, but they often brought critical acclaim to established talent. *Days of Wine and Roses* garnered Oscar nominations for Jack Lemmon, Lee Remick, and Blake Edwards; although Lemmon and Edwards had earned far more money making comedies, they had garnered less artistic recognition.

Producer Carl Foreman lamented, "No thought has been given to developing the people who will make the pictures 10 years from now." He added, "The only new people in the industry today come from television," a sad irony for a Hollywood veteran.[84] In an article titled "Make Way for Youth," producer-director Mervyn LeRoy wondered why Hollywood did not recruit bright young minds from colleges like other industries, such as Detroit automakers. He noted the increasingly gray-haired backlotters, but not the obvious cause: a decade of downsizing that left few new positions available.[85] A television executive, ABC's Lee Goldenson, saw a clear solution: television workers were talented, particularly with a limited budget, but were underused in feature film. *Whatever Happened to Baby Jane?* illustrated the profit potential for movies budgeted under $1 million. Like other industries, Hollywood needed streamlining and new thinkers; Goldenson named as examples Blake Edwards, Arthur Penn, George Roy Hill, and John Frankenheimer, who all thrived in feature filmmaking in the 1960s and 1970s.[86]

Lower-budget filmmaking offered an important exception to runaway production. Roger Corman noted that for his "medium-budget" pictures, the savings abroad would be minimal compared to a major studio epic.[87] In fact, Corman gained production value by scouring the neglected resources of the major studios. The impressive set for *The Pit and the Pendulum* would be a Frankenstein-like creation, patched together from architectural set pieces lying around various studio warehouses.[88] The same logic operated for studio producer-directors. William Wyler assured runaway critics that his next project would be shot in America, but the black-and-white drama, *The Children's Hour*, cost a fraction of *Ben-Hur*'s budget.[89] Similarly, Robert Aldrich followed up the epic *Sodom and Gomorrah* (1962), shot in color abroad, with the low-budget black-and-white sensation *Whatever Happened to Baby Jane?*. Domestic filmmaking increasingly relied on an economy of smaller scale and greater controversy.

Television faced similar budget constraints and far greater time constraints. Even by 1962, shooting television abroad remained largely unfeasible for American series, other than occasional location trips with a few principal actors.[90] But domestic location shooting became an integral part of telefilm, particularly in an era dominated by Westerns and a growing crop of police series. By 1959, "it became passé to have the cops and robbers shoot it out between narrow walls of a Hollywood set."[91] Cops and robbers still spent most of their time indoors, however, such as at the nightclub set and ubiquitous warehouses featured in *Peter Gunn*. Only rare series, such as *Sea Hunt* (1958–1961) and *Route 66* (1960–1964), went beyond the limited Southern California location work favored by 1940s features.

Television's demand for studio space gave birth to a different modus operandi than UA's, exemplified by MCA-Universal. Like UA, Universal used only independent producers; unlike UA, they had an entire lot entirely rented out.[92] As share prices soared, Universal embarked on a $10 million reconstruction of Universal City, phase 1 of which was modernizing the physical studio.[93] By 1963, their Revue television lot employed 5,300 workers on thirty-two stages and six backlot locations, and they still needed to rent additional space at Paramount's Sunset lot. This was "a bonanza to the industry's crafts and guilds," but the new production facilities lured feature filmmakers back to the lot as well.[94] Instead of shooting in Southeast Asia, *The Ugly American* (1962) built a 35 acre exterior set on Universal's lot; coupled with a massive interior set, construction cost $420,000.[95] Harold Hecht brought *Wild and Wonderful* (1964), set in France, to the Universal lot and bragged of saving $500,000. "Why runaway to Europe for authentic locations when for $350,000 one can be duplicated in Hollywood?"[96] Meanwhile, Universal reaped both the film distribution and the lot rental fees for these pictures.

San Francisco lacked the financial incentives of Europe or the production facilities of New York, and as the appeal of widescreen travelogues declined, location shooting in the city grew fairly infrequent. Several productions staged San Francisco almost entirely on the studio lot. Other than early establishing shots, *Flower Drum Song* built Chinatown at Universal City. The same was true at MGM for features such as *Go Naked Into the World* (1961) and *The Subterraneans* (1960), with a bobbysoxer rendition of Kerouac's North Beach staged on the Fifth Avenue standing set.[97] For other films, the cine-tourist style persisted. In *Pleasure of His Company* (1962), a color Fred Astaire and Debbie Reynolds comedy, the pair tour Fisherman's Wharf and other San Francisco sites through a rear-projected montage. Like *The Lineup*, *Man-Trap* (1961) augmented black-and-white standard fare with an extensive car chase down the Embarcadero past the Ferry Building and Fisherman's Wharf.

Blake Edwards's two 1962 films, *Experiment in Terror* and *Days of Wine and Roses*, were important exceptions, approaching San Francisco with the dark themes and crisp, low-key cinematography associated with New York filmmakers such as Lumet and Frankenheimer.[98] Befitting the realist black-and-white trend, Edwards shot extensively on location, even capturing key interiors in the city. Crews readily improvised to minimize the inevitable delays caused by unpredictable location conditions. San Francisco's noir shadows looked far blacker than *Dark Passage*, and for good reason: location technology had improved, and black-and-white film had reached a technological apex.

SHOOTING ANYWHERE BUT "THE DARK CAVE IN CANDLELIGHT"[99]

Much like *The Lineup*, *Experiment in Terror* shot numerous scenes in San Francisco, but there was a day-and-night difference in the depiction of city. *Experiment* opens with an image entirely absent from *The Lineup*: a night exterior. As Kelly (Lee Remick) drives home to face a terrifying encounter with a murderous extortionist, Red Lynch (Ross Martin), both the action and each point of light in the surrounding city appear crisp and clear, including helicopter footage relying only on the available light of city buildings, headlights, and the Bay Bridge (Figure 3.2). The establishing shot of Kelly's car pulling into her driveway in Twin Peaks appears lit by a single streetlight, while the San Francisco background looms as a constellation of lights. *American Cinematographer* described it as "one of the most striking exterior night shots ever seen."[100] Cinematographer Phil Lathrop benefited from major

3.2. A night exterior at the opening of *Experiment in Terror* demonstrates the greater photosensitivity of black-and-white film stock in the early 1960s.

improvements in film stock and lighting equipment that by the early 1960s allowed black-and-white location shooting in dark conditions and interior spaces that were previously too expensive or impossible to adequately light.

These technological developments facilitated more extensive location shooting with subtler lighting, evidenced by Edwards's two San Francisco films and myriad productions shot throughout the United States, especially in New York City. A realist black-and-white aesthetic complemented real locations, as well as the trend for bleak dramas in the early 1960s. Color film, particularly in widescreen and in large formats like 70 mm, required too much light to convey a similar aesthetic. *American Cinematographer* revealed a deepening aesthetic distinction between most color productions and low-key black-and-white films shot on location and praised for realistic cinematography.

By the early 1960s, improved film stock not only reduced the advantage of shooting at the studio but also of shooting in Southern California. According to director Jack Garfein, who shot *Something Wild* (1961) on location in New York, frequent sunlight, a fundamental reason why the American film industry relocated to Los Angeles, was no longer an asset. This was not a consequence of smog but a result of faster film stock. For black-and-white filmmakers, the Southern California sun sometimes shined too brightly for more light sensitive film stock.[101] Such technology clearly facilitated domestic location shooting, but this was merely a consequence of the production practices that drove this development: television and foreign location shooting.

In 1961, Eastman Kodak's film department director, Don Hyndman, reflected on the rapid improvement in black-and-white stock over the past decade. The introduction of Tri-X in 1954 greatly facilitated night-for-night shooting, "a tremendous boost toward ultimate realism."[102] Only six years later, Kodak's Double-X rendered it obsolete. Double-X was twice as fast as Plus-X, the industry standard, yet with almost identical sharpness and far less grain than Tri-X. Industry-wide evaluation suggested that Double-X could become the standard stock for indoor and low-light shooting. Pan-X permitted shooting in conditions previously deemed inadequate for proper exposure.[103] Tri-X would only be necessary in almost total darkness, such as "Tom Sawyer and Huck Finn sneaking up on Injun Joe in the dark cave by candlelight."[104]

The target market for Double-X was television, and not for aesthetic reasons. More sensitive film allowed for smaller and fewer lights, reducing power consumption as well as setup time. These seemingly modest budget reductions had a major impact since television films worked with "tight budgets and tight shooting schedules."[105] *The Jack Benny Show* (1950–1965) immediately switched to Double-X, which also facilitated camera pans to the audience. Less stage-bound shows, such as Warners' *Maverick* (1957–1962), became early adopters. Lower light levels also offered greater comfort to crews and actors working under hot lamps; television had far less tolerance for low-key lighting than theatrical projection.[106]

Historically, black-and-white film quality had steadily improved, requiring less light with less grain, and by the 1960s it still kept a relatively stable cost. *Anatomy of a Murder*, shot and edited entirely on location in Michigan, suggested that "light and speed problems were no longer a detriment in photographing a motion picture."[107] More sensitive stock also favored more portable equipment. Like its 1948 namesake, the television series *Naked City* (1958–1963) relied on photoflood lights and handheld cameras to capture roughly 60 percent of the series in New York exterior locations. Unlike Mark Hellinger's expensive noir, high-speed negatives and lightweight equipment allowed the show to film in "almost any location," with three- to four-day schedules for each half-hour episode.[108]

As shooting on location became less of a technological challenge for black-and-white films, filmmakers learned to better exploit unexpected situations arising on location. Gerry O'Hara, Preminger's assistant director on *The*

Cardinal, which shot extensively in Boston, praised the improvisation required to shoot on location; not merely capturing but adapting to real site conditions added distinct realism.[109] Shooting *Raisin in the Sun* (1961) in Chicago brought "happy little accidents," from the details of an African American liquor store to the unexpected sight of a man pushing a baby buggy.[110] Quicker setups and faster film stock gave filmmakers the opportunity to effectively observe and capture local eccentricities rather than smooth them away, as Jerry Wald had insisted upon during the difficult shooting of *Dark Passage*.

New lights opened further opportunities to shoot scenes on location that previously necessitated soundstage shooting. Hollywood quickly adopted a powerful new halogen light, the Sun Gun, debuting in 1962. The 3 pound, 1,000 watt light provided 5,000 watts of illumination, joining an array of photo lights as a staple of black-and-white location production. *The Lineup* series cinematographer Hal Mohr called it the greatest improvement in lighting equipment in thirty years. Once again, the immediate application was television, where the small size proved ideal for lighting location interiors for Screen Gems series; television alum John Frankenheimer used Sun Guns to light the Madison Square Garden catwalks for *The Manchurian Candidate* (1962). On the television series *Shannon* (1961–1962), director of photography Phil Tannura coupled two lights with a car-mounted 35 mm Arriflex and captured two characters driving without using a process shot.[111] The familiar through-the-windshield process shot still relied on a blue-screen process for color film in 1964; by 1962, black-and-white could accomplish the same on location.[112]

Color film stock failed to keep pace with black-and-white, although it improved dramatically in the late 1950s and early 1960s. In 1959, Eastman Color 5251 effectively eliminated three-strip Technicolor from the industry.[113] Following its debut in 1953, Eastman's single-strip process steadily gained on the cumbersome three-strip process, becoming the industry standard by 1958. Yet the single-strip process came at a cost, necessitating large, high-intensity tungsten lights; these behemoth units made sets uncomfortably hot and raised production costs. Eastman 5251 doubled in speed without quality loss and established Eastman Kodak as the dominant film stock provider in Hollywood.[114] As with black-and-white, color technologies responded to industry trends. Eastman 5251 was "expected to solve the numerous lighting problems encountered overseas in such underpowered areas as the Far East."[115] Faster stock also allowed longer shooting days at higher northern latitudes and could open new areas to color filmmaking that had only been feasible in black-and-white. The new color film primarily responded to and facilitated runaway location production, not aesthetic demands.

A host of new lenses and cameras developed by Panavision also made an impact on color cinematography. Panavision's anamorphic process streamlined widescreen production, where producers had gone so far as experimenting with curved sets to compensate for lens distortion. By 1960 they had also minimized the camera size, creating the first handheld 70 mm camera. Many of these improvements stemmed from new lenses developed to match existing cameras. One of these, the Ultra-Speed Panatar, promised to revolutionize 35 mm filmmaking in color. During camera tests, cinematographers captured night scenes with only a lighted store window as the key light. William Daniels, who innovated low-intensity lighting on *Naked City* (1948), raved about the new lens, capable of shooting long shots with light levels as low as 40 foot-candles.[116]

Despite faster film stock and lenses, color cinematography retained much of its familiar high-key aesthetic throughout the era. The Hollywood that fostered Panavision innovations also relegated their use. Rather than pushing low-key color filmmaking, Panavision compensated for the excessive lighting demands of shooting large-negative (70 mm) color film for ultra-widescreen exhibition, often in less sunny locations abroad or in New York. Particularly with the debut of Double-X in 1960, color film remained well behind black-and-white's light sensitivity. Meanwhile, Panavision lenses worked just as well in black-and-white, aiding the low-key cinematography of *Lonely Are the Brave*, shot on location in the mountains of New Mexico. As Eastman Kodak's Hyndman noted, "[A]t a time when color motion picture film seems to be growing into maturity, its black-and-white older brother is moving forward at a faster pace than ever."[117] *Experiment in Terror* and *Days of Wine and Roses* both depended on low-key scenes shot on location that not only remained beyond the reach of color cinematography but fit the continued association between black-and-white and dramatic realism.

The technical limitations of color compared to black-and-white reinforced formal associations between the two formats. *The Nun's Story* (1959) provided a telling conundrum for director Fred Zinnemann and cinematographer Franz Planer. The moody and repressive convent scenes favored black-and-white, but Zinnemann feared that the vibrant African locations for latter parts of the film would lose their appeal without color. The solution would be creating a severe monotone palette for the convent through costume and set design, essentially "shooting black-and-white in color."[118] Not only did color limit Planer's creative options, but largely worked against his dramatic goals. He noted that it was "more difficult in color to make something *un*beautiful than to make it beautiful. The object here was effectively to *destroy color*."[119] By the early 1970s, gritty films like *Dirty Harry* (1971) and *The French Connection* (1971) worked to systematically destroy color; a decade earlier, filmmakers more frequently decided to shoot tough stories in black-and-white rather than work against color's perceived strength.

The standards for realism in color also fell below black-and-white, due to both technical difficulties and generic associations. The color Western *They Came to Cordura* (1959) gained praise from *American Cinematographer* for never using an interior; although the film strived for "stark realism," it had to rely on the stylized process of day-for-night for one-third of the picture.[120] *The F.B.I. Story* (1959) shot in some actual interiors of FBI headquarters, but these were limited by "seemingly insurmountable lighting problems for color photography."[121] *West Side Story* (1961) adopted a "hybrid stylization" between the realist gang plot and fantasy musical numbers, yet the film's darkest moments remain brighter than almost a single image in John Frankenheimer's black-and-white gang drama, *The Young Savages* (1961). So-called sick tales would invariably favor black-and-white, except for a powerful gender determination. Murderous and salacious melodramas with female leads tended toward color. Despite its title, *Portrait in Black* (1961) starred Lana Turner in San Francisco in color; *Where Love Has Gone* (1964) flaunted sexual deviance, but with Susan Hayward as the lead, the lurid San Francisco story played out in producer Ross Hunter's lurid color scheme.

Meanwhile, black-and-white films reveled in low-key location shooting. *The Defiant Ones* (1958) won the Academy Award for best black-and-white cinematography. A frigid, rainy Southern California February was the background for 80 percent of the many location exteriors, contributing to a "stark, cold and unfriendly atmosphere."[122] For *The World, the Flesh and the Devil* (1959), black-and-white Cinemascope allowed "a mood of grim desolation that could never have been achieved in color."[123] Often straining to get exposure even on fast stock, the film captured New York City as a desolate, post-apocalyptic wasteland.[124] *Experiment in Terror* gained similar acclaim for its dark, frightening San Francisco atmosphere.[125]

American Cinematographer closely followed two filmmakers, Otto Preminger and John Frankenheimer, who pushed the boundaries of American location filmmaking in the late 1950s and early 1960s through improvisation;

Edwards would employ similar techniques in San Francisco. For *Anatomy of a Murder*, Preminger experimented with near-total location filmmaking at a remote site with a remarkably tight schedule. He planned to capture the best-selling book where it actually took place, in the home and courthouse of the author, Judge John Vockler, located in Michigan's Upper Peninsula.[126] He also hoped to rush the film for a July 4, 1959, release to quickly capitalize on the book's popularity; this required the unprecedented feat of editing the film and trailers on location in a three-room suite. The only production task performed in Hollywood was lab processing.[127]

According to director of photography Sam Leavitt, the location demands were daunting. Preminger's crew could not drive nails into the plaster walls of the judge's eighty-year-old house, in which the largest room was 10 by 12 feet. The jury box took over most of the courtroom, which required upward of six actors and 200 extras; naturally, Preminger, famous for long takes featuring camera movement, called for fifteen different camera moves despite the cramped quarters. A script change made on location called for the always challenging through-the-windshield shot, with dialogue and without process photography or a camera car. A "Rube-Goldberg" rig of lights and a camera on a low flatbed truck sufficed to film the scene.[128] Leavitt revealed only a handful of his techniques, but the film's seven Oscar nominations, including for best cinematography, demonstrated how far portable equipment and black-and-white film had advanced for location shooting. Both exteriors and interiors could be effectively captured on location, although Preminger wisely avoided the additional handicap of low-key lighting.

Although New York offered better production facilities away from Hollywood, less-photographed locations offered greater local support. The production bragged of spending $500,000 in a depressed region while hiring a thousand local extras; for its efforts, Michigan named *Anatomy of A Murder* its Product of the Year.[129] Cooperative locales also helped raise the production value of locations. Locals supplied a locomotive, loading crane, and seventeen cars to enliven the background for a brief scene of Jimmy Stewart and Arthur O'Connell lunching by the waterfront. An authentic absence of seagulls appeared inauthentic on camera, so the crew spread thirty pounds of fish around to attract birds and complete the mise-en-scène.[130] Edwards gained similar cooperation in San Francisco from hotels and nightclubs eager to associate themselves with Hollywood stars.

John Frankenheimer and writer J. P. Miller collaborated on the original television production of *Days of Wine and Roses*, which aired on *Playhouse*

90 in October 1958. They reteamed on *The Young Savages*, Frankenheimer's first feature film, as well as his first of four films with actor-producer Burt Lancaster (*Birdman of Alcatraz* [1962], *Seven Days in May* [1964], *The Train* [1964]). Another black-and-white "sick tale," *The Young Savages*, opens with a Hispanic youth gang stabbing a blind boy to death. Like *Sweet Smell of Success* (1957), Lancaster and producer Harold Hecht mounted an incisive critique of urban culture captured in low-key black-and-white.[131] Portable equipment and improvised multicamera shooting revealed a far different side of New York: Spanish Harlem. Frankenheimer demonstrated how improvisational techniques honed in television production could be applied to urban location shooting to reveal parts of the city rarely captured by filmmakers.

American Cinematographer lauded Frankenheimer's bravery working in a neighborhood where "even the police tread lightly," described as "a jungle loaded with ominously restless 'natives.'"[132] This hyperbolic description reflected cinema's popular association of violent ethnic youth gangs with New York City (as in *Asphalt Jungle* and *West Side Story*). Frankenheimer deeply infiltrated tenement neighborhoods with both off-screen and on-screen strategies. Local actors cast as gang members helped negotiate a payment to two youth gang leaders who controlled their turf to facilitate shooting. The dynamic opening sequence, in which several actors rush through the streets toward the scene of the stabbing, spanned several unbarricaded city blocks. Using battery-powered handheld cameras on luggage trucks, one cameraman trailed the actors; once a crowd of onlookers formed around the camera, a second cameraman wheeled after the actors while the first camera served as a decoy. Frankenheimer continued to steal shots with handheld cameras in difficult situations, particularly in *Seven Days in May*. He captured a staged protest and fight in front of the White House and grabbed a shot of Kirk Douglas entering the Pentagon without a shooting permit.[133]

This emergent semi-documentary style featured fluid camerawork and jarring compositions absent from the semi-documentaries of the 1940s and 1950s. Unlike the film newsreel, this style mimicked the run-and-gun technique of the television news exposé.[134] Shooting interiors on location also revealed urban destitution beyond Hollywood's darkest fantasies. After shooting inside an actual railroad-style tenement, "sets which had heretofore been considered sufficiently squalid were found to be vastly understated when compared to the real thing."[135] The experience of crossing the threshold of location façades not only produced realistic location footage, but augmented the realism of the soundstage sets. New York ghettos gained increasing visibility, but urban poverty and gang violence would remain largely ghettoed in New York settings. In 1960, a group of white youths attacked black patrons at a San Francisco first-run theater. The closing of every movie theater in the African American Fillmore District had forced black moviegoers to cross racial lines.[136] But on-screen, San Francisco's urban problems were virtually deracinated; white deviants rather than impoverished minorities roamed the dark alleys beyond the city lights.

Among the many early 1960s films combining dark themes with low-key black-and-white location shooting, the only movies set in San Francisco were produced by Blake Edwards. His provocative series, *Peter Gunn* (1958–1961), brought the style and violence of film noir to television, combined with the hip jazz culture of San Francisco. Moving from television production to feature filmmaking, Edwards gained enough time and funding to shoot extensively in San Francisco for *Experiment in Terror*. In this dark thriller, the city often appears as a shadowy criminal landscape reminiscent of *Peter Gunn,* but its themes and settings were too perverse for television. The production of *Days of Wine and Roses* demonstrated how effectively Edwards could use his television experience to efficiently exploit locations. The bleak story of an alcoholic couple found tragic undercurrents of San Francisco's celebrated nightlife. Although the city is more civilized than Frankenheimer's New York and features clearly articulated districts and regions, its cine-tourist beauty proves tragic and haunting with headlights and bar signs punctuating a deep black night.

BLAKE EDWARDS'S SAN FRANCISCO

Blake Edwards's two early 1960s films dramatically changed the depiction of San Francisco from the standards of 1950s cine-tourism. On television, *Peter Gunn* combined the style of San Francisco culture with the look of film noir, launching Edwards into the new wave of creative talent moving from television to feature filmmaking. For both *Experiment in Terror* and *Days of Wine and Roses*, Edwards's experience working fast and cheap helped him efficiently shoot on location and take advantage of local support in San Francisco. Both films present a jaded view of the city while still taking advantage of its unique scenic appeal. Between the San Francisco–inspired city of *Peter Gunn* and the latter two films, Edwards created a distinctive image of the city suiting larger trends in early 1960s location production.

Peter Gunn: Television Noir and San Francisco Style

Edwards's *Peter Gunn* was a breakout hit for NBC in its first season (1958–1959), drawing praise for its style but also occasional condemnation for its violent content. The detective series offered a more vibrant television image of San Francisco culture than CBS's *The Lineup* except for two details: the production never left Southern California and never mentioned the name of its city setting. However, the series fundamentally shaped Edwards's feature productions set in San Francisco and provided a clear precedent for the hip detective of *Bullitt* (1968). Edwards actually wrote San Francisco crime dramas for *The Lineup* when it was a radio series (1950–1953).[137] Henry Mancini's theme song and score for *Peter Gunn* was as popular as the show itself, which brought West Coast jazz to television, including on-screen performances by Shelly Manne.[138] The series so thoroughly revolved around Henry Mancini's jazz score that Peter Gunn (Craig Stevens) forewent an office, instead conducting business at Mother's nightclub, where most episodes featured musical performances.

Peter Gunn frequently relied on San Francisco imagery such as the waterfront location of Mother's (Figure 3.3), shadowy warehouse piers, and Chinatown, all largely constructed on Hollywood studio lots. Moreover, the title character embodied the Beat ethic of the urban traveler, knowingly frequenting the hippest African American jazz clubs and the best nightclubs in Chinatown. Peter Gunn was closer to Humphrey Bogart as Rick in *Casablanca* (1942) than as Sam Spade in *The Maltese Falcon*, equally at home in police, criminal, and nightlife settings. Steve McQueen's title character in *Bullitt* (1968) was a San Francisco detective who similarly bridged the eclectic urban culture and the tough world of police work.

Along with its jazz score and pseudo–San Francisco setting, *Peter Gunn* distinguished itself from other hip detective series like *77 Sunset Strip* (1958–1964) through a combination of violence and stylization. In September 1958, *Variety* saw little hope for the apparently formulaic show, with a script "reminiscent of TV seven to 10 years ago."[139] But the series became a top 20 hit in its first season, pushing *Variety* to reassess the show's slickness and brutality in a November review: "That the murder and mayhem was done with finesse was indisputable. But each climactic moment in the half-hour hinged on a shooting, a death house visit, slugging, a hypodermic needle and a novel, detailed electrocution scene of the non-prison variety."[140] In essence, *Peter Gunn* was a compendium of noir violence peppered with dry, witty banter.

3.3. A noir-styled waterfront added cinematic flourish to television in *Peter Gunn* (NBC, 1958).

The novelty of *Peter Gunn* and the crime shows that followed it, particularly *The Untouchables* (1959–1963), was not the detective plots but, as NBC described it, "the change in mood and accent."[141]

Peter Gunn's popularity was far more fleeting than its impact on television geography. While its style was forward, it relied on the fading model of advertising agency sponsorship. After changing time slots and networks (from NBC to ABC), Bristol Meyers dropped the show in 1961.[142] Despite its short network run, *Peter Gunn* sold quickly in syndication, billed as "the show that started it all," with its "sophisticated approach to danger—urbane story lines and some of the most fabulous jazz of our time."[143] In 1960, *Variety* observed, "The crime suspense program category is rapidly displacing the western as the staple of network programming."[144] Shows such as *Peter Gunn* and the highly popular *The Untouchables* (1959–1963) capitalized on the fading appeal of the television Western.[145] The urban present overtook the rural past as television's dominant violent setting. The growing alienation of suburbanites from the city, observed by contemporary scholars such as William Whyte and Lewis Mumford, had made an on-screen impact: for suburban

Americans, the city faded as a place of daily experience and blossomed as a fictional realm of danger and violent action.[146]

Variety credited Blake Edwards with "something of a revolution" in both television style and production organization. With the initial success of *Peter Gunn*, he became one of the earliest acclaimed television writer-producers. Such a hyphenate, commonplace among Hollywood filmmakers, became increasingly prominent in television by 1959, including writer-producers such as Rod Serling for *The Twilight Zone* (1959–1964) and Norman Retchin for *The Untouchables* (1959–1963).[147] Writer-producers helped fill a talent gap in Hollywood, where major studios had struggled to find competent production executives to run their growing television departments. For instance, Fox hired former television producer Martin Manulis to work on feature films, but lacking other producers with television experience, Spyros Skouras soon switched Manulis over to television pilots. Though Manulis's contract guaranteed his return to feature filmmaking, he left Fox in 1961 and took his feature project, *Days of Wine and Roses*, to Warner Bros.[148] Edwards's success getting *Peter Gunn* and a second series, *Mr. Lucky*, on the air earned him a six-series deal with MGM's television unit in 1961.[149]

Experiment in Terror and *Days of Wine and Roses*: The Logistics of Location Shooting in San Francisco

Edwards sought to use *Peter Gunn* as a springboard to expand his role as a producer of Hollywood features. In October 1959, he announced plans to write, produce, and direct a feature film version of the series.[150] Edwards continued to work as a director for hire, completing another famed collaboration with Henry Mancini on the hugely successful *Breakfast at Tiffany's* (1961). After finishing *Breakfast*, Edwards planned to write, direct, and produce *Experiment in Terror*, followed by producing and directing *Days of Wine and Roses*.[151] Although he did not receive screenplay credit for *Experiment* or producer's credit for *Days*, he oversaw both projects through to their completion. Edwards made his aspirations clear after partnering with Jack Lemmon on yet another company, a creative talent development firm. Prior to working with UA's Mirisch brothers on *The Pink Panther* (1963), Edwards praised their free hand with producer-directors such as William Wyler, Billy Wilder, Robert Wise, and Fred Zinnemann. He noted, "These men are left to their creative designs without anyone looking down their throats."[152]

Well before the young filmmakers of the Hollywood Renaissance, Edwards openly advocated for an auteur-director's cinema. Rather than citing European filmmakers, he lauded the most independent of the independents, UA's star producer-directors. Like Wilder, Edwards worked his way up through his writing; unlike the studio-trained Wilder, he gained his autonomy under the shoestring budgets and manic schedules of live and scripted television, from *Four-Star Playhouse* (1952–1956) to *Peter Gunn*. Edwards brought along his *Peter Gunn* cinematographer, Phil Lathrop, to shoot both of his early 1960s San Francisco features. The regular noir flourishes on the series could now be pushed beyond the dimmer, narrower frame of the television screen. Meanwhile, in shooting and planning, Edwards's pictures hinged on the ability to improvise and economize on location, skills honed through television production.

In *Experiment in Terror*, Red Lynch forces Kelly to steal money from the bank she works at, while FBI agent Ripley (Glenn Ford) tries to protect her and uncover Lynch, who effectively hides his identity through telephone threats and disguises. Lynch leads Kelly and investigators into seedier districts of San Francisco before Ripley learns his identity through his Chinese girlfriend (Anita Loo). Hoping to pick up the money from Kelly during a baseball game at Candlestick Park, FBI agents and police surround and kill Lynch on the pitcher's mound of the emptied stadium. Sensitive black-and-white film stock helped cinematographer Philip Lathrop create low-key lighting that fit the crime suspense film, including several night exteriors at San Francisco locations.

The night-for-night cinematography for the opening scene of *Experiment in Terror* required careful preplanning. Shooting almost entirely on Double-X, Lathrop captured Kelly driving through a pitch-black night on her way home, where Lynch surprises her in the garage (Figure 3.4).[153] Beginning in the afternoon, Lathrop employed three generators (strategically concealed) to power several Big Brute arc lights, establishing three planes of light to create depth of field and illuminate character actions. Smaller units hid throughout the location added effects lighting. Shooting at only 50 foot-candles, Lathrop captured staggering depth and sharpness in a vast wide shot that left few places to hang lights.[154] Ink black shadows effectively masked the requisite equipment. After hours of preparation, San Francisco fog rolled in after only a few takes. Yet the early establishing shot was worth the difficult setup. Paired with ominous Mancini riffs, these foreboding night images set the tone for the subsequent assault by Lynch, and the frightening world of the film. This shot also showcases the full capability of early 1960s black-and-white filmmaking, combining

3.4. Faster Double-X film not only allowed for darker scenes in *Experiment in Terror*, like this night exterior shot (*top*), but also opened up large interior locations that might have been too difficult to light, such as Crocker Bank in San Francisco (*bottom*).

the naturalness and subtlety of studio lighting with the striking real backgrounds provided on location.[155]

Double-X also opened the door to shooting location interiors, particularly Crocker Bank (see Figure 3.4). Lynch intimidates Kelly into stealing money from the bank, transforming her workplace into a tense trap. The high-key, evenly lit interior shows no trace of the difficult shooting conditions. The vast building with large windows forced Lathrop to balance and regularly rebalance the interior with the changing exterior light; meanwhile the bright white walls of the bank could exaggerate any increased grain or overexposure. The easiest solution, placing arc lights outside the windows, not only proved inadequate, but also drew large crowds that interfered with the shoot. Instead, Lathrop gradually increased the interior lighting with the waning daylight. Although Plus-X offered less grain, Double-X proved necessary, likely to allow a smaller aperture to handle the bright lights.[156]

Why not build a bank set on the Columbia lot instead? Edwards answers this question with his camera placements and movements. A high-angle crane shot pans across the large bank foyer, taking advantage of the high ceilings to capture a large sphere of activity. In another wide shot, the camera pans with Kelly walking toward the teller area, before tracking left as she turns the corner and walks past the teller windows. Thus the full height of the bank, along with all four walls, appear within a single shot. What would have required a massive set on the lot was captured on location over a weekend. Meanwhile, the camera angles and movements trace Kelly's every move, a visual reminder of Lynch's constant surveillance and threat. Aided by the latitude of black-and-white stock, an actual San Francisco bank simultaneously provided economic, aesthetic, and narrative advantages.

Smaller lights and cameras also compensated for the continued logistical problems that plagued urban location shooting. One scene called for Kelly to meet Lynch on a cable car, but not knowing his appearance, she allows a lascivious man whom she believes is Lynch to pick her up. As had been the case since the 1940s, cameras and lights attracted crowds like moths to a flame; Lathrop estimated nearly 5,000 people arrived and made shooting impossible. Unlike the 1940s, production could hardly be set back a day, and the filmmakers improved upon the "prosaic" cable car setting. The night before, Edwards had visited the Roaring Twenties, a wild San Francisco nightclub with showgirls on swings and an arcade shooting range (Figure 3.5). Determined to exploit the unique location, Edwards moved the cable car scene and the production team searched for small lights suited for a low-key night club; Lathrop further improvised, obstructing large arc lights with flags to create multiple, narrower rays of light. The club's evening hours left the crew ample time to shoot during the day.[157]

The improvised nightclub scene effectively replaced the colloquial image of San Francisco (the cable car) with a unique site of the city's famed risqué nightlife. Equipped with a handheld Arriflex, Lathrop grabbed effects shots,

3.5. Blake Edwards moved a scene to the Roaring Twenties nightclub to take advantage of the local erotic spectacle for *Experiment in Terror*.

including one from the seat of a swing, where the pendulum motion augments Kelly's disorientation within the club.[158] While Preminger and Frankenheimer improvised on location to capture specific features of real locales, Edwards instead used the features of actual places as a springboard for his imagination. Trained in television, where only ingenuity could squeeze production value out of tight budgets and schedules, Edwards wrung every potential visual flourish out of a location. In fact *Variety*'s major criticism of the finished film would be its "experiment in cinematography that emphasizes 'artistic' camera technique that is cute but does little to aid the story."[159]

Candlestick Park, the spectacular location for the finale, was no exception. As police scramble to locate Lynch during a Giants-Dodgers game, Edwards takes advantage of the massive scale of the stadium, from dark corridors to press boxes and aerial helicopter shots (with a mounted stabilized Arriflex) revealing the entire stadium (Figure 3.6). Once again, the sensitive film stock allows the shadow play to range across the height and depth of the stadium surroundings. Yet *American Cinematographer* was just as impressed with the minor, improvised visual effects. Lathrop creatively employed a zoom lens to capture Lynch eyeing Kelly's sister (Stephanie Powers) through his rear-view mirror.[160] What *Variety* found excessive, *American Cinematographer* deemed a "must-see" for students of cinematography.[161] Lathrop himself provided a narrative logic for the bravura cinematography; they wanted

3.6. Candlestick Park served as a climactic and recognizable location for a shadowy chase and a police helicopter confrontation in *Experiment in Terror.*

the audience to fear the killer could be lurking in any shadow, and indeed, the unrestrained extension of noir effects across real locations encouraged such anxiety.

The 1962 *American Cinematographer* cover story on *Experiment in Terror* not only positioned Phil Lathrop as a promising newcomer recently admitted to the American Society of Cinematographers, but also validated the impact of television production on feature filmmaking. Lathrop had a classical Hollywood pedigree, working for a decade as a camera operator for Russell Metty at Universal.[162] He then "followed the general trend of cinematographers to TV filming." Lathrop lauded his television experience, which gave him "unlimited opportunity to experiment with lighting effects and camera techniques."[163] Like John Alton, who famously developed noir lighting on B-films like *T-Men* (1947) and *Raw Deal* (1948), Lathrop honed his craft on 1960s television noirs like *Peter Gunn*, where creative lighting provided one of the only inexpensive methods to add production value.

Reviewers emphasized *Experiment in Terror*'s effective use of San Francisco settings. *The Motion Picture Herald* even argued that it used settings more imaginatively than any thriller since *North by Northwest* (1959).[164] *Variety* also praised the use of San Francisco landmarks, although with an important caveat: they noted the story could take place anywhere.[165] Despite the actual locations and street names, local baseball teams, and obligatory cable car shot, *Experiment in Terror* creatively photographed San Francisco locations but, other than the Roaring Twenties nightclub, showed few specific details of San Francisco city life.

Days of Wine and Roses transposed a story from another setting onto the city, adapting a teleplay set in Manhattan to a film set and shot in San Francisco. Joe (Jack Lemmon) and Kirsten (Lee Remick) fall in love and marry but descend deeply into alcoholism as Joe loses his career and Kirsten abandons their family. Joe recovers with the help of Alcoholics Anonymous while Kirsten cannot bear to stop drinking, leaving Joe to raise their daughter as she flees into the San Francisco night at the close of the film. The downbeat story of a couple's downfall motivated another black-and-white film with low-key lighting. While *Experiment in Terror* used this shadowy aesthetic to provide suspense, *Days of Wine and Roses*, also shot by Lathrop, used a similar look to explore the bleak despair of the urban drunk.

Although the San Francisco setting did not alter the plot of the film, it required careful location scouting and economic negotiation. As of May 1961, *Days of Wine and Roses* was set in New York. By January 1962, the doomed couple's first romantic moment had moved from the Hudson River bank of the Upper West Side to Fisherman's Wharf.[166] Unit manager Jack McEdwards laid the groundwork for shooting in San Francisco. Like Lathrop and Edwards, he moved fluidly between feature filmmaking and television. After serving as an assistant director in features throughout the 1950s, he became the production manager for *Peter Gunn* and rejoined Edwards for *Days*. The same year he also worked with Otto Preminger on *Advise and Consent* (1962), which shot extensively on location in Washington, DC. Just after New Year's 1962, Edwards, Manulis, writer J. P. Miller and art director Joe Wright joined McEdwards for a three-day location scout of San Francisco. His survey report reveals the constant negotiations between aesthetic and economic demands that shaped early 1960s location shooting.[167]

San Francisco businesses and residents remained eager to participate in Hollywood filmmaking, and McEdwards exploited this interest to stretch the budget. For the four-day location trip, the premier hotel, the Fairmont, offered their minimum rate. Yacht owners and club members were excited to provide their vessels for the film's wild boat party scene. Each night, the production team dined at a potential location. For a nightclub setting, they chose the Owl and the Turtle, whose manager was extremely interested in the publicity, over the Roaring Twenties. Yet all the production promised was to use the restaurant as a cover set, available for a three-and-a-half-page scene in case of bad weather.[168] The club Place Pigalle charged only a dollar a day if the production mentioned it by name, whereas Ernie's, the restaurant famously featured in *Vertigo*, required $150 a day plus three employee salaries. The production paid no exorbitant rental fees, which peaked at $250 a day to shoot at San Francisco's most famous location, the Golden Gate Bridge.[169]

Lower hotel rates promised even greater savings, and McEdwards effectively leveraged the Jack Tar Hotel's need for publicity. McEdwards had already negotiated steep discounts for rooms, with $85 a night suites rented at $50 a night. He thought he could do even better and shaved another $5 off the suite rate and $2–$4 off each room. Considering the production would pay for over 900 nights at the hotel between February 8 and February 24, each dollar off saved nearly $1,000. Bob Holden, the manager of the Jack Tar, soon conceded in a letter reiterating his hopes and fears. Having Lee Remick and Jack Lemmon stay at his hotel would be fantastic publicity, while having them stay with a competitor could damage the hotel's image. For the sake of two star guests, the entire cast and crew stayed cheaply, and the strategy ultimately backfired for Holden. Likely unimpressed with their suites, "Jack and Lee, Blake Edwards and most of the more important people had moved to the Fairmont."[170]

The police point-person, Bob Kane, who had worked with Blake Edwards on *Experiment* the previous summer, remained vital to securing locations. He now had an official title within the San Francisco Police Department as a public relations officer. Kane not only accompanied the production team to locations such as the Yacht Club, but also contacted the Recreation and Parks Department to find out whether the pier could support the large camera boom. He personally introduced the filmmakers to the owner of the Telegraph Hill apartment chosen for exteriors of Kirsten's apartment. Kane's cousin lived next door and vouched for the owner's cooperation. Kane knew to avoid shooting the popular Maiden Lane shopping district except for Sundays to avoid the delivery trucks that often clogged the street. He even helped secure a church for an AA meeting scene, because as a fellow Catholic, he knew the priest. Edwards could not proceed regardless of local conditions, like *Dark Passage* did, or rely on reshoots and process shots to overcome local conditions, like *Vertigo* did. Instead, he followed the advice of local experts like Kane, who charted the path of least resistance for location shooting in a city still bound together by networks of personal relationships.[171]

If potential locations fell short of narrative or pictorial demands, Edwards shot them in Southern California. Despite the willing club members, the San

Francisco yachts were not "pretentious" enough for the debauched corporate party where Joe first meets Kirsten. Meanwhile, nearby Sausalito proved inadequate for the cinematography due to logistical and aesthetic problems, and potential bad weather. Aside from establishing shots at the San Francisco marina, the party scenes were filmed in Balboa, an Orange County seaside town.[172] Another key sequence—in which Joe leaves a cheap motel, stumbles through the woods, and robs a liquor store in a desperate alcoholic search—was filmed entirely (exteriors and interiors) on Warners' Jungle stage.[173] With enough location footage to concretely establish San Francisco, Edwards could afford to shoot a few scenes closer to home, especially when actual San Francisco locations proved disadvantageous.

Securing locations proved less complicated than securing personnel on location. Production manager Charles Greenlaw had to negotiate the involvement of local San Francisco IATSE workers and their union jurisdiction over a racetrack outside the city. Using a still photographer on location required paying a standby salary to a union photographer in Los Angeles. The Coast Guard oversaw the boat scenes, but a rear admiral wrote to reject any gratuities, which were against regulations. (Whether the $1,200 "donation" to the Coast Guard on the final budget solved or created this impropriety remains unclear.) Lee Remick's hairstylist negotiated every possible additional compensation in her contract before traveling to San Francisco. The apparent freedom of independent production in 1960s filmmaking came with at a price: independent negotiations with dozens of involved parties and individuals.[174]

Successful location shooting, particularly on a midbudget film like *Days of Wine and Roses*, depended on anticipating the unexpected. Bad weather always threatened to disrupt exterior shooting, and rather than add shooting days, budget-strapped producers might be forced to scrap entire scenes. Warner Bros. had the National Weather Institute provide forecasts specific to movie shooting schedules, including the number of expected good shooting days and likely cloud cover for February through April 1962. April looked sunnier, but location shoots had to be completed prior to studio work, so Edwards took his chances. Securing location interiors ensured that poor weather rarely ground production to a halt. The Golden Gate Park scene was scheduled for a Monday, but if it rained, they would move to the milkmaid party scene. The long night scene of the couple at Fisherman's Wharf relied on clear weather; yet as the beginning of the romance, it was also the most important exterior location in the film, worthy of postponement if necessary. Despite a major weather delay shooting exteriors at the Yacht Club, the production returned to the studio on schedule after ten days. The majority of the film was shot in the studio over forty-five days, and Edwards finished five days ahead of schedule. A seasoned television producer used to ironclad time and money constraints, Edwards never came close to going over budget or schedule.[175]

Days of Wine and Roses gained immediate critical and commercial success. Henry Mancini won an Oscar for the title song, Jack Lemmon and Lee Remick earned nominations for best actor and actress, and two more nominations came for black-and-white art direction and costume design. A *Variety* reviewer worried that "an almost intolerably depressing 117 minutes" might limit its box office potential.[176] Nonetheless, *Days* earned nearly $4 million on a $1.7 million budget. Jack Warner wired Lemmon, "[Kalmenson and I] feel we have hit every jackpot in Las Vegas without even pulling a handle."[177]

Both of Edwards's San Francisco films demonstrated how the speed and resourcefulness required for television production translated into more efficient production strategies on location. Aided by faster black-and-white stock, Edwards and Lathrop succeeded in capturing location footage without sacrificing aesthetic quality, lighting real locations with studio polish but without major expense. Improved location shooting practices opened new San Francisco locations to filmmaking while casting familiar sites in a darker light. In both films, the city's sleazier districts and characters appeared to suit an explicit thriller and a bleak alcoholic drama. But the characters, not the city itself, descended into desperate conditions; San Francisco had its vices, but they remained part of a coherent image of the city.

San Francisco in *Experiment in Terror* and *Days of Wine and Roses*: Dark Lives in the Imageable City

> When a city begins to grow and spread outward from the edges, the center which was once its glory . . . goes into a period of desolation inhabited at night by the vague ruins of men, the lotus eaters who struggle daily toward unconsciousness by way of raw alcohol. . . . And then one day perhaps the city returns and rips out the sore and builds a monument to the past.[178]

In *The Heart of Our Cities*, Victor Gruen begins his proposed counterattack against urban decay with this quote from John Steinbeck's *Travels with Charley* (1962). The alcoholics who roam downtowns at night were seen as symptoms of urban sickness, a cancer that would have to be removed before the city could be rebuilt. Edwards's bleak San Francisco films suggest the opposite. Early 1960s San Francisco, on- and off-screen, lacked the formlessness of other cities. Instead, urban American misfits descended a clear path into the city's lower depths. Edwards elaborates the illicit side of the city not as a sign of urban decline, but as a designated part of an imageable city.

Kevin Lynch's 1960 book *Image of the City* presented a new method of evaluation for urban studies. Rather than focusing on urban structure, he examined the urban perception of the city dweller. He selected pedestrians to draw maps of their urban environment and found urban enjoyment was greatest in cities where residents could visually orient themselves: "A highly imageable (apparent, legible, or visible) city in this peculiar sense would seem well formed, distinct, remarkable. . . . The sensuous grasp upon such surroundings would not merely be simplified but also extended and deepened."[179] Parts of San Francisco, as well as New York, Boston, and the Chicago lakefront, typified a highly imageable environment.[180] Lynch's studies matched popular sentiment for San Francisco, particularly in comparison to the overwhelming landscape of Los Angeles. A 1959 *New York Times* piece contrasted San Francisco's "cosiness," walkability, and cohesion to Los Angeles's "far-flung aggregation of variegated communities and interests."[181]

Lynch identifies five structural components—paths, edges, districts, nodes, and landmarks—that distinguish the visual experience of a pedestrian moving through the city. Edward Dimendberg adapted Lynch's concepts to the movements of film noir protagonists through urban neighborhoods, suggesting that characters fight the growing formlessness of a declining modern city through these "walking cures."[182] The tools of Hollywood continuity editing provided a more effective cure, particularly establishing shots, which offer a ready formal solution to urban formlessness. Through establishing shots of San Francisco's landmarks and distinctive districts, Edward reinforces a transparent orientation through the city in both *Experiment in Terror* and *Days of Wine and Roses*.

In *Experiment in Terror*, Red Lynch operates within the private cracks of an enforceable, legible public space. In the opening sequence of *Experiment in Terror*, Kelly drives into San Francisco across the Bay Bridge. The bright bridge stands in high contrast to the deep blackness of the bay at night. As she drives through her neighborhood, a sign clearly designates it as "Twin Peaks." Landmarks like the bridge and sign, combined with details such as the affluent suburban architecture, demarcate districts while eliding indefinite in-between spaces. When Lynch ambushes Kelly in her garage, he invades an organized and safe world. He overpowers her in a private domestic space rather than a public area. Lynch continually intrudes upon private spaces both directly, such as dressing in drag and confronting Kelly in the ladies' room, and indirectly, such as calling her at her home on the telephone.

The police and FBI, led by Agent Ripley, display a remarkable visual mastery of the public space.[183] During several shots of vistas, including a hilltop view of the city against the bay and a wide shot of Fisherman's Wharf, the camera pulls back to reveal surveillance agents watching from their vehicle. The vast public realm falls within the omniscient "see" of authorities. Aside from the home invasion, criminal incidents in the film occur in specific districts. Lynch's Asian mistress, Lisa, lives in Chinatown, and a stool pigeon inhabits a seedy movie theater and eventually dies in a dark back alley, a staple setting for noir violence. During the finale, the killer attempts to hide within the public chaos of a baseball crowd at Candlestick Park. Ripley eventually spots him and pursues him toward the brightly lit, empty field; the criminal inevitably protrudes from the crowd of spectators, exposed and corralled at the spectacular center of the stadium.[184]

The finale begins at Fisherman's Wharf, showing a helicopter overhead as Kelly speaks to Lynch at a phone booth. Here new law enforcement technology adds another layer of visual control over the city. Rear projection within the frame of the helicopter allowed for a controlled, panoramic view as the helicopter follows Kelly's car to Candlestick Park. In the final moments of the film, Agent Ripley shoots Lynch as the helicopter, FBI agents, and police swarm onto the empty baseball diamond of Candlestick Park. Lynch breathes a last asthmatic breath on the pitcher's mound under the bright stadium lights. The film's final two shots swoop backward, dissolving into an extreme wide shot showing the entire stadium, an island of light and activity within the night sky. Institutional authority has eliminated the insidious criminal and restored its command of this vast visual landscape. The fly in the affluent ointment of San Francisco has been lethally excised.

As William Luhr and Peter Lehman note in their analysis of *Experiment*, Ripley and his fellow FBI agents are inhumanly cold, robotically responding to Kelly's terror with unsympathetic instructions and procedures.[185] Meanwhile, the killer reveals greater character depth as the film progresses. Well into the film, Lisa tells Ripley that Lynch has paid for her son's hospital bills; Ripley merely sees this as an investigative opportunity and badgers the son for information on Lynch's whereabouts. Lynch's face is revealed halfway through the film as he wakes up to an asthma attack and clutches for his inhaler. His gasping breath now appears less lascivious and more painful. He similarly defies expectations when, after kidnapping Kelly's sister and forcing her to undress, he makes no sexual advances toward her. By the time Lynch heaves his dying breaths, he is more sympathetic than Ripley. Like Dancer in *The Lineup*, Lynch is a criminal outsider who despite incredible effort cannot disguise himself from police surveillance. Although the San Francisco of *Experiment* looks far darker than this earlier noir, the overbearing civil order of the city remains.

Edwards's sympathetic portrayal of derelicts like Red Lynch extends to Joe and Kirsten in *Days of Wine and Roses*. Drinking offers an escape from the corrupt corporate culture of public relations, where the urban businessmen indulge in outrageous public events that drive Joe's alcoholism outside of work. Meanwhile, the bar districts of San Francisco call Kirsten away from an unfulfilling life as a housewife. John Frankenheimer was the obvious choice to direct the feature film version of *Days of Wine and Roses*, which he did so effectively for *Playhouse 90*. However, Jack Lemmon wanted a director who could do comedy.[186] While *Days* marked a dramatic departure from Lemmon's broader comedies, his recent hit, *The Apartment* (1960), was a dark comedy that dealt seriously with corporate lechery and suicide, and like *Days* earned him an Oscar nomination for best actor. Whereas the television version of *Days* is downbeat throughout, Edwards amplifies the tragedy and character identification by capturing Lemmon as a laugh out loud, funny drunk. As it is for the doomed couple, carousing is fun for the viewer until the consequences become emotionally wrenching.

In one of the most effective scenes, Lemmon does a classic comedy routine, drunkenly picking flowers for Kirsten, walking into a glass door, and then closing the flowers in the elevator door. Yet moments later, he rages at Kirsten for not drinking with him while breastfeeding rather than using formula, and wakes their sleeping child. As Joe mouths in disbelief, "How can I do this to a child?," he draws the viewer's shattered sympathy back. At the moment he nearly takes responsibility, Edwards cuts to Kirsten sipping a drink, a dagger in the couple's progress. Lemmon's early comic behavior as a drunk at first lightens the depressing film, but disarms the viewer to subsequent harrowing scenes of addiction.

San Francisco offers an outrageous, entertaining nightlife that only later in the film reveals despair. The corporate yacht party brims with soused models and executives. A later business event is even more audacious, featuring skimpy outfits and a shot featuring a businessman leering at a woman's backside (Figure 3.7). These excesses tie Joe's alcoholism to a seedy world of public relations and corporate hedonism, the subject of sharp black-and-white critiques such as *Sweet Smell of Success* (1957) and *The Apartment* (1960). Similarly, Kirsten's return to alcoholism follows her dissatisfaction as a housewife and mother. In a haunting scene, she watches cartoons on the

3.7. *Days of Wine and Roses* (Warner Bros., 1962): *top*, a yacht party depicts a hedonistic downtown corporate culture; *bottom*, Kirsten's alcoholism is tied to her dissatisfaction as a housewife and mother. In this scene she is watching cartoons while pleading for the baby, who is in another room, to stop crying.

couch, pleading for the baby in the other room to stop crying (see Figure 3.7). Jim (Jack Klugman), Joe's AA sponsor, teaches him that alcoholism is a disease. But Edwards suggests it may be a social as well as a physical disease, a refuge for men disenchanted with a sleazy business culture and women isolated in the domestic sphere.

As Joe and Kirsten drift further into alcoholism, their accommodations grow bleaker. They begin their marriage in a luxurious apartment. The next apartment set is far shabbier, taken after they fail to sober up at Kirsten's father's house away from the city. Later a sober Joe finds Kirsten in a dark, cheap motel where another binge leads him to detox in a hospital. In her book *The Apartment Plot*, Pamela Wojcik suggests that 1960s films centered on apartments offer narratives of young urbanites reinventing themselves in a buzzing city; unlike the nostalgia for modernity that Dimendberg describes in noir, characters look toward the future in a new sphere of action in the city.[187] Holly Golightly (Audrey Hepburn) in Edwards's *Breakfast at Tiffany's* is an icon of this era's bohemian culture. *Days* ties the freedom of apartment life, as opposed to the suburban house, to the potential transience of addiction. Joe's fight with Kirsten over not drinking while breastfeeding pits the contrasting demands of drunken nightlife and family life against each other within the limited space of the apartment. The ease of moving between apartments ties moral downfall to a progression of worsening living spaces.

As alcohol use turns from pleasure to despair, the nightlife that defines a vibrant San Francisco sees its shadow. In *The Exploding Metropolis*, Jane Jacobs describes San Francisco's Maiden Lane as the exemplary street, where a group of stores crowd around a narrow alley off of Union Square.[188] Yet Maiden Lane is also lined with bars, whose neon lights often define San Francisco's night life on film. In *Days*, gray daylight location footage of Maiden Lane suggests a shabby haven for drunks to drink away the day (Figure 3.8). A haunting image at the close of the film casts the sad refuge of the bar against the beauty of San Francisco. In the film's final scene, a briefly sober Kirsten visits Joe in his new apartment, a spartanly furnished but roomy place where he cares for their child. She cannot bring herself to see her daughter or stop drinking; without a drink, she says, "I can't get over how dirty everything looks." She leaves, and Edwards closes the film with the same effective shot that Frankenheimer used years earlier: the camera slowly zooms on Joe staring out his window as the flashing bar sign reflects against the glass. Freed from the limitations of live television,

3.8. *Days of Wine and Roses*: *top*, the Maiden Lane District; *bottom*, the closing shot of the film. A popular tourist destination and shopping district, Maiden Lane also has many bars.

Edwards inserts a penultimate wide shot with inky black location cinematography akin to *Experiment*. Kirsten walks downhill into the distance on a deserted San Francisco street, past the bar flashing in Joe's window. Distant streetlights and headlights establish the depth below under a black sky. The downhill panorama, the stock beauty shot of San Francisco, yawns as the dark, empty path of the barfly (see Figure 3.8).

Edwards's San Francisco films resonate with other critical black-and-white films of their era, including their exploitation of adult content. The heavy-breathing killer in *Experiment* finds one victim undressing before forcing Kelly's sister to slowly undress for him and the audience. Edwards clearly suggests profanity in the killer's telephone calls, cutting to shots of Kelly listening but eliminating the last word of lines like, "You're a lying little. . . ." *Days* exploited not only revealing costumes, but also the shocking depths of alcoholism. Lobby cards ignored the advice of *Variety*'s reviewer, who cautioned against selling the picture on "superficial sordidness."[189] One ad featured a shirtless Lemmon strapped to a table during detox, with the tagline: "They will let him up soon and he will look for his wife and he may pray that he doesn't find her." Another featured no image, just white text on a black background with the quote: "It's your wife, Joe. In another motel. Come pick her up."[190] Kirsten's infidelity was clearly implied in the film when Jim warns Joe that she will find another playmate.

In both films, San Francisco appears dark and ominous but still beautiful, particularly in the night-for-night location exteriors. Edwards includes familiar landmarks like Fisherman's Wharf, allowing for a familiar cine-tourist publicity strategy. The *Days* press book promoted the use of "some of the better-known San Francisco area sites." Similarly, notes for the trailer for *Experiment* listed five strategies to sell the picture. These included "the locations involved," as well as exploitation elements such as "a beautiful girl in jeopardy" and "the shock scenes."[191]

In the last sentence of *The Death and Life of American Cities*, Jane Jacobs notes that "lively, diverse, intense cities contain the seeds of their own regeneration."[192] Edwards's 1962 films, particularly *Days*, suggests that seeds of self-destruction also lie at the heart of vibrant cities. Like other so-called sick urban films—such as *The Young Savages*, *The Hustler*, and *Butterfield 8*—*Days* explores troubled individuals disaffected by American culture and its institutions. Early 1960s urbanists such as Jacobs and Gruen suggested that the contemporary American city was fading, and these films offer personal stories of cultural decline in America's urban centers. The bleak *Days of Wine and Roses* does not suggest that San Francisco was declining as much as it reveals the city through the downcast eyes of outcasts struggling within American society.

Through 1968, San Francisco maintained its reputation as exceptionally immune to urban decay, but in just a few years the city would undergo its greatest image transformation. As the new American capital of the counterculture, San Francisco ceased to be an on-screen alternative to cities like Los Angeles, New York, and Los Angeles. No longer an urban or tourist backdrop, San Francisco became the primary destination for films exploiting the youth revolution. Meanwhile, the critical, dramatic, and aesthetic power of black-and-white filming met an abrupt end in Hollywood. After 1963, Hollywood exclusively shot San Francisco in color. As a wave of filmmakers descended on the city in the second half of the 1960s, filmmakers and city alike worked to extend and accommodate location filmmaking.

4

COUNTERCULTURAL CAPITAL

Hollywood Chases the Summer of Love

BY 1967, SAN FRANCISCO HAD EMERGED as an international mecca for a young counterculture, and Hollywood followed a wave of media attention focused on the city. Industry discourse grew hyperbolic, suggesting not only that the city was a profitable setting for youth exploitation films, but even that its mere inclusion in any film promised box office success. San Francisco's appearance in several of the biggest hits of the late 1960s led *Variety* to attribute a near mystical appeal to films set there. The exceptional hit of 1967, *The Graduate*, shot a handful of scenes in San Francisco and Berkeley, as did the fourth highest box office earner, *Valley of the Dolls* (1968). *Guess Who's Coming to Dinner*, which had the second highest earnings, benefited from a San Francisco setting despite a minimum of location shooting. Two of the top three hits of 1969, *The Love Bug* and *Bullitt* (both released in 1968) were also set there.[1] In just a few years, San Francisco went from being an occasional location for Hollywood films to a potential threat to Los Angeles production as the city continued to pull filmmakers northward. A crucial transition for San Francisco began in 1968 as the new mayor, Joseph Alioto, began an ambitious attempt to transform the city from a desirable location into a full-fledged production center for feature and television filmmaking.

In 1964, Art Seidenbaum of the *Los Angeles Times* had welcomed news of the launch of a film production company in San Francisco. He surmised it was the most ambitious local production plan since 1908, when Bronco Billy Anderson began producing hundreds of Westerns in the Bay Area. But despite its appeal for artists, technicians, and East Coast executives on business trips, it was far from a viable competitor with Hollywood. Seidenbaum concluded, "Better to have a few people visiting in San Francisco than watch them dodging taxes around the world."[2]

Less than three years later, Robert Joseph, writing for the *Los Angeles Times*, noted that Hollywood personnel had become worried; while European production had sagged, "several film creators were unobtrusively slipping out the back door of Hollywood on their way north to that other increasingly active rival foreign film capital—San Francisco."[3] In April 1967, at least eight major pictures were shooting there, making it "the latest answer to Cinecitta."[4] Adding insult to injury was the extent of the location work in San Francisco. For instance, *Point Blank* (1967) ignored Hollywood's long-established precedent of recreating Alcatraz on the studio lot. Filmmakers shot San Francisco's slums rather than Los Angeles's oft-photographed downtrodden districts.[5] By late 1968, the city was mobbed with cameras shooting features, underground films, television episodes, concert films, and news specials. Producer Aaron Beckwith, filming an ABC news special on the Generation Gap, gave a simple explanation: "It's where everything is happening."[6]

Variety ran a major article on the city's media boom in late 1968 titled "California's Camelot."[7] Their San Francisco correspondent, Rick Setlowe, streamed through famed Bay Area products, listing Hollywood films such as *Guess Who's Coming to Dinner*, *The Graduate* (1967), and *Petulia* (1968) alongside musicians such as Jefferson Airplane and the Grateful Dead, television figures like the Smothers Brothers, political movements such as Berkeley Free Speech and the Black Panthers, and even troop deployments to Vietnam. Hollywood's commercial incentive to join the youth movement was transparent: "In their wake trekked the camp followers—television and filmmakers—to drop in, turn on and cash in on the Frisco Mystique. A street sign at the corner of Haight and Ashbury Streets became the most photographed inanimate object in the world."[8] As early as April 1967, San Francisco had gained the nickname "Psychedelphia" for its combination of rock shows, underground films, light shows, and often nude dancing. Advertisers adopted psychedelic styles, and stories on San Francisco hippies multiplied in major magazines and television news stories, causing police and city leaders to brace for the inevitable onslaught of young émigrés and tourists.[9] The consequent Summer of Love was as much a media phenomenon as a cultural one, and Hollywood tried to catch the hippie wave on film.

As San Francisco became the filmic focal point for the social revolution of the youthful counterculture, Berkeley, across the bay, had come to symbolize the political revolution being led by campus activists around the country. Meanwhile, a handful of Hollywood films set in San Francisco in 1967–1968 highlighted a generational conflict in terms of production methods. Both Otto Preminger's *Skidoo* (1968) and Richard Lester's *Petulia* featured the hippie scene and stylistic experimentation. The clearest difference was in shooting approach, keenly observed by *Variety*'s Setlowe:

> The older tradesmen from Sam Katzman to Otto Preminger, traveling in long trains of moving vans like a gypsy exodus and loaded down with heavyweight brutes and Mitchells, shot and cut back to the Hollywood studio setups. A New Breed of filmmakers, including such disparate talents as Richard Lester and Woody Allen, utilized television techniques and its lightweight, mobile technology, shot entire features on location while still using the Hollywood labs, and money, less than an hour's shuttle away by jet.[10]

Preminger was a pioneer in adapting studio techniques to actual locations in films such as *Anatomy of a Murder* and *Advise and Consent*. In the 1960s, British filmmakers pioneered a different solution, adopting a quick, less continuous style of shooting and editing to meet the temporal and spatial demands of location shooting. Instead of carefully preplanning each shot to streamline shooting and editing, these filmmakers often improvised on location, grabbing a variety of footage with multiple cameras before sorting out a rough continuity during post-production. John Boorman (*Point Blank*), Richard Lester (*Petulia*), and Peter Yates (*Bullitt*) all left London to shoot Hollywood-produced films in San Francisco. Financially and stylistically, *Petulia* blurred the lines between European and Hollywood production. *Bullitt* successfully harnessed similar production techniques to Hollywood genre filmmaking and fundamentally changed Hollywood's location aesthetics, not only in San Francisco but in cities across the country.

The continued decline of feature filmmaking in Los Angeles and major improvements in location shooting technology promoted extensive location shooting in other urban areas. Shooting within months of each other, *Petulia* and *Bullitt* were the first two films shot entirely on location in San Francisco. Myriad film and television productions tapped into San Francisco's cultural cachet in the late 1960s, but most made only cursory use of the city as a location and a dramatic setting. *Petulia* and *Bullitt* presented two different location production practices that allowed filmmakers to shoot exclusively in San Francisco, only returning to the studio lot for post-production. Despite a shared goal of capturing San Francisco's unique late 1960s culture, the films reveal two remarkably different cities, demonstrating how location filmmaking transformed rather than reflected San Francisco. Despite offering urban critiques, these energetic films matched the national excitement over the city. *Bullitt*'s successful deployment of a new style of semi-documentary police film had a profound impact not only on San Francisco's location shooting boom, but also on its declining screen image in the early 1970s.

REBUILD THE LOT OR RUN AWAY?

Hollywood's dilemma over whether studio lots would become albatrosses or rental profit centers continued throughout the 1960s with no prevailing consensus. The mid-1960s marked the first major building campaign in decades as Universal Studios expanded just north of Hollywood in the San Fernando Valley. By 1968, cries against runaway production had grown as loud as in the early 1960s. In any given year, a backlot might be brimming with television and feature production or practically shuttered. Caught between the unpredictable economies of real estate, television, and global filmmaking, workers and moguls alike struggled to adapt.

Cities like New York, Miami, and, by 1968, San Francisco capitalized on Hollywood's uncertainty, pitching lower shooting costs to lure productions away from Los Angeles. Domestic competition for production, largely ignored by labor leaders fighting foreign runaways in the early 1960s, had emerged as a legitimate threat by the end of the 1960s. The prevalence of location shooting further depressed Hollywood's labor market, employing far fewer crew members than a picture requiring major set construction.

As workers eagerly campaigned for expensive, labor-intensive features like *Camelot* (1967) to return to Hollywood, breakout hits shot in domestic locations, such as *Bonnie and Clyde* (1967) and *Bullitt*, provided greater returns on investment.

MGM exemplified Hollywood's struggle to monetize the studio lot. In 1968, a new management team dithered on whether to sell, cut, or rent. Selling the entire studio to a real estate developer in booming Los Angeles would fetch a hefty profit (valued at $27 million in 1965).[11] MGM could also rid itself of a backlot whose aging, poorly maintained streets had visible signs of urban decay.[12] On the other hand, a massive backlot full of television series rentals would bring in regular income, not just a one-time profit. The previous management had optioned a site for an all-new studio in the Conejo Valley, on the periphery of Los Angeles, hoping to profit from the real estate value of Culver City while building modern facilities on cheaper land.[13] Selling some of the lot and renting the rest was a third option. Before any substantial action could be taken, however, Edgar Bronfman Sr., who had owned the studio for only two years, sold it in 1969 to Kirk Kerkorian, a successful Las Vegas property developer.[14] MGM's real estate value proved easier to assess than its production value or strategy.

Earlier in the decade, MCA-Revue-Universal, the studio with the tightest integration of film and television production, had "paved the way for the potential of new and improved facilities."[15] The studio launched a multimillion dollar makeover in 1963, beginning with the construction of the MCA office tower and several service buildings. After leveling acres of hills, the next phase added stages, parking, and Visitors Village, which was the starting point for a major innovation, the modern studio tour, a source of significant ancillary profits to this day.[16] Set-building at the revamped studio was just as ambitious, including an $80,000 set for the Rock Hudson–Doris Day film *Send Me No Flowers* (1964). As director Norman Jewison suggested, building the set would be cheaper than location shooting during winter weather.[17] Meanwhile, Revue could regularly fill the expanding state-of-the-art stages with either in-house or rental television productions.

Buoyed by Universal's success, Darryl Zanuck pushed the idea of a superstudio—an updated version of his 1950s plan for Fox and Warner Bros. to share a single lot.[18] In 1963, Fox, MGM, and Columbia copurchased a 75 acre site in Malibu for $800,000 hoping to build a studio panacea. They would leave behind wasted real estate values in Hollywood, high taxes, empty stages, and obsolete facilities. Malibu also offered dramatic terrain for backlot shooting, less traffic, and less smog, which had already begun to degrade outdoor photography in Los Angeles. Building anew, the majors could add the soundproofing and lighting features of more recently built studios in Europe. With ample, inexpensive land, sets could remain standing for future exploitation. All the expensive sets built abroad for *Cleopatra* (1962) had to be destroyed after production, and Hollywood studios could not afford to save idle sets for future use on valuable Los Angeles land.[19]

A super-studio also held the potential to regularize employment for craftsmen. With major studio production concentrated on a single lot, workers might once again report daily to work on any given production, as they had in the pre–World War II studio system. Unmentioned were the duplicated studio jobs that would be lost under such an efficient consolidation.[20] The studios ambitiously promised that the facility would "dramatize anew the revitalization of Hollywood as a production centre," albeit by moving the "centre" north of Los Angeles.[21] Rather than relying on the inconsistent cost savings of runaway production, modern facilities might restore the cost-efficiency of the classical studio system.

Instead, by the end of 1965, the super-studio plan was dead. The steady demand for stages by television production had halted a major studio land sell-off. By August 1965, several studios were operating at near capacity with television production.[22] Even though studios hiked their rental rates, television work grew so abundant that by 1966 several unions were anticipating a labor shortage.[23] Fluctuations in the television market had defeated long-term plans to revamp studio production, allowing runaway feature filmmaking to continue unchecked.

Runaway feature production peaked in 1961 and again in 1965, a decade after shooting abroad had ceased to offer below-the-line savings.[24] Even between these years, more than 40 percent of major productions were shot abroad.[25] Rising production costs in Europe and fewer tax advantages stoked the eternal hope for pictures to return to Hollywood.[26] The challenge of meeting release deadlines for massive productions shooting abroad, such as *Doctor Zhivago* (1965) and *The Dirty Dozen* (1967), did push some pictures back to Hollywood, particularly for post-production and sound looping.[27] After six weeks shooting in Spain, *Camelot* returned to the Warner Bros. lot, where forty-five sets sprawled across twenty-three soundstages, a record for a single production; four cargo planes hauled 22,000 pounds of equipment back to Burbank.[28] This left little room for *Bonnie and Clyde*, which Jack Warner reluctantly allowed to shoot on location in Dallas; the latter strategy, domestic location shooting, soon reached its heyday as expensive set-bound features like *Camelot* buckled under their own weight.[29]

Despite the incipient problem of domestic runaway production, the unions remained intently focused on foreign production. Unions gained congressional attention again in 1966 when Democratic representative John Dent tried to revive his failed legislative effort of the early 1960s.[30] In late 1967, the runaway battle reached an unprecedented fever pitch when a group that included every Hollywood guild and union, representing some 30,000 workers, rallied California's two Republican senators to action.[31] The winter of 1967–1968 proved particularly harsh for Hollywood craftsmen; as production began an annual slowdown to mitigate Los Angeles taxes on film inventories, 31 percent of Hollywood craft workers sat idle. Unemployment for grips and electricians, dependent on active production, was 75 percent.[32] In May, two months after the inventory tax, unemployment remained high, but "no one in management, labor or government had come up with a solution to the problem or even a proposal."[33]

Hollywood workers had struggled in vain against runaway production for well over a decade, suggesting that this trend was more than an economic loophole to be closed. The system of studio filmmaking had fundamentally shifted away from mass production, empowering the individual producer to choose the most opportune economic situation for shooting anywhere around the globe. *Variety* asked the question labor leaders could not acknowledge: "Is the Hollywood job market overpopulated?"[34] Not only were fewer films being produced there, but extensive location shooting required fewer production workers. Typical Hollywood crews now had twenty-five to thirty members, but films like *Bullitt*, shooting semi-documentary style on location with available light, provided far fewer jobs than set-bound productions like *Guess Who's Coming to Dinner*.[35] Producer Jerry Fairbanks, who relocated a production from Spain to Hollywood with union cooperation on crew size, argued, "We are paying more to fewer people but turning out more and better work in a shorter time."[36]

That same summer, of forty-five movies in production, twenty-seven were shot in Europe, twelve in Hollywood, and six in other parts of the United States.[37] The latter six seemed like a minor threat, but domestic runaways soon proved nearly as troublesome as overseas production. The glut of television production, including commercials, opened opportunities for cities other than Los Angeles to build production economies. And as location production techniques and technologies continued to improve, Los Angeles increasingly had to compete with other American cities, not only as a production center, but also as a desirable location.

Miami was one of the first cities outside of New York and Los Angeles to build professional production facilities for film and television. Studio City, a $5 million full-service studio complex, opened in 1966. The 65 acre site became home to three New York production companies, a New York equipment rental house, and a color film lab. By early 1966, Miami boasted twenty-seven producers working on various productions, including the television series *Flipper* (1964–1967); two Bond films, *Goldfinger* (1964) and *Thunderball* (1965); television commercials; and Spanish-language production and dubbing.[38] Over a year later, Studio City remained largely unused except for television commercials. Yet the revived sales pitch, offering 20–25 percent production savings over New York and Hollywood, resonated with the global economics of runaway production. For producers who preferred to stay in the United States, the cost of shooting in Miami fell somewhere between cheap international locations like Mexico and major American production centers such as New York and Los Angeles.[39]

New York—with its established production facilities, union workforce, and aesthetic appeal as a film location—proved a greater threat to Hollywood than Miami, particularly after recently elected Mayor John Lindsay formed the Office of Film, Theater, and Broadcasting in 1966. By streamlining the bureaucracy and cost gauging that had plagued location filmmakers in the 1950s, Lindsay hoped to lure Hollywood filmmaking back to the city.[40] The Hollywood AFL bristled when Lindsay sent representatives to meet with producers in Los Angeles, demanding action from Los Angeles mayor Sam Yorty and accusing Lindsay of starting a war between cities.[41] They claimed Lindsay underbid producers with local union contracts; Lindsay said he only approached producers who were already planning to shoot in New York. Deftly deflecting the issue to the union's primary target, foreign production, Lindsay argued that there were enough films shooting abroad to keep production workers busy in every American city. Lindsay wanted production companies to stay beyond the location trip and complete principal photography in New York. This idea of turning a desirable urban location setting into a full-phase production center through incentives for Hollywood companies soon arose in other cities, particularly San Francisco.[42]

In 1968, which saw an explosion of filmmaking in the city, San Francisco joined the competition. Like New York, it had specific production assets to build upon. San Francisco's beautiful urban settings and varied landscapes had established the city as a favored location for television commercials, including the Rice-A-Roni ads featuring ringing cable cars. Meanwhile, the greater Bay Area could approximate locations much farther from Hollywood than San Francisco. In *The Russians Are Coming* (1966), Mendocino stood in for Cape Cod, and in *Cool Hand Luke* (1967), Stockton became the Deep South. But San Francisco's cultural revolution truly drove the production boom, with thirteen features shooting partially in the city between 1967 and 1968. *Variety* suggested that being "both physically and philosophically set in large part in the culturally churning Bay Area" explained the incredible box office numbers for *Guess Who's Coming to Dinner* and *The Graduate*, even though neither film shot extensively on location.[43] Elected in 1968, Mayor Alioto, a former attorney for Sam Goldwyn in a suit against Fox, was eager to maintain Hollywood's appetite for the San Francisco zeitgeist. He moved quickly to sustain the film boom, contacting *Bullitt* producer Phil D'Antoni even before he took office. Soon Woody Allen was in town shooting *Take the Money and Run* (1969), and his producer, Charles Joffe, dubbed Alioto the "West Coast Lindsay."[44]

Although Alioto made every effort to lure filmmakers to San Francisco, the wave of production in San Francisco had actually preceded his election. The pace of production had accelerated due not only to the city's cultural cachet, but also the increasing efficiency of location shooting. Earlier in the 1960s, location technology was primarily soundstage equipment adapted to location demands. By 1968, technologies specifically designed for shooting on location and favored by documentaries, television commercials, and European art films had gained wider acceptance in feature filmmaking. Tools and techniques adopted from these lower-budget productions proved crucial for major studio features like *Petulia* and *Bullitt*.

TECHNOLOGY DESIGNED FOR LOCATION SHOOTING

In April 1965, Hank Stockert of *American Cinematographer* asked, "Is Filming Technology Losing Ground?"[45] While industries like aerospace and electronics were surging ahead with new technology, motion picture and television production still relied on cameras designed and, in some cases, manufactured in the 1930s. Professional cameras lacked the tools such as automatic exposure and motorized zooms that were common to consumer 8 mm cameras, leading Stockert to lament the industry's lack of attention to research and development. Indeed, after over a decade of shedding labor overhead, innovations increasingly came from outside manufacturers, not studio camera departments.[46] Almost all of these innovations made location shooting more fiscally and stylistically competitive with soundstage production.

Ideas for the future of motion picture technology mirrored speculation over modern super-studios versus location shooting. Some proposals sought to reestablish an efficient, controlled studio environment through electronics. These ideas included a camera that could generate superimposed backgrounds on live television and a system of remote-control cameras monitored from a central console on the stage or backlot.[47] Others saw the future of production in further advances in portability and mobility. Don Norwood envisioned a "camera of the future" that would be small and quiet enough to operate surreptitiously for "natural street scenes, mob scenes, riot scenes, actual battle scenes."[48] Large camera rigs were dinosaurs, incapable of entering the real drama playing out on the streets and in the war zones of the late 1960s. By 1967, the future camera had become present reality. In a discussion with several cinematographers about the present and future state of Hollywood moviemaking, George Folsey acknowledged that the quartz-iodine light, the handheld camera, and the zoom lens were the most important production innovations of the past decade.[49] All of these technologies emerged to improve location production for documentary, industrial, and television filmmakers. By the late 1960s, Hollywood had adapted these tools to a new style of feature filmmaking, evident not only in off-kilter youth-oriented hits like *The Graduate* and *Bonnie and Clyde*, but in mainstream Hollywood features such as *In the Heat of the Night* (1967) and *Bullitt*.

The quartz-iodine light, popularized by the Sun Gun in the early 1960s, became a staple item for Hollywood cinematographers shooting on location, particularly in actual interiors. Even at lower intensities, these small, portable lights offered a far different lighting scheme than conventional three-point lighting. Rather than relying on powerful key and fill lights, cinematographers used several to dozens of small quartz-iodine units to precisely light a scene. Cinematographer Arthur Miller compared it to having a fine brush as a painter.[50] These lights not only offered artistic advantages but logistical and economic ones: "mobility with less manpower."[51] Quartz-iodine lights lasted three times longer than conventional bulbs without fading (which disrupted color temperature), and even higher wattages, from 2,000 to 10,000 watts, appeared possible in the near future.[52]

Quartz-iodine lights solved several location problems. On a low-budget color picture like *A Swingin' Summer* (1965), they allowed faster setups to meet the ten-day shooting schedule.[53] On *The Night They Raided Minsky's* (1968), cinematographer Andrew Laszlo needed fill light for a block-long shot of New York City. He attached seven Lowell lights, quartz-iodine lamps with flexible mounts, directly to the camera.[54] On location, lighting setups that were speedy, mobile, and unobtrusive opened up new spaces to the camera, particularly where property owners could afford to rebuff filmmakers.

Introduced in 1963, the Angénieux 10:1 zoom lens became a fundamental component of the handheld cameras favored by European New Wave filmmakers in Britain and France, as well as cinema verité documentarians in America.[55] They later gained ground among Hollywood filmmakers confronting similar location difficulties. Haskell Wexler put a zoom lens on one of several hidden cameras deployed for the Boston bank robbery exteriors in *The Thomas Crown Affair* (1968). With the cameraman standing in a doorway across the street, zooming in on the robbers exiting the building provided a sense of being on the street without alerting the crowd to the crew or the actors.[56]

The handheld camera was nothing new to Hollywood, nor had portable camera technology undergone significant changes since the early 1960s. What had clearly changed was the association between handheld camerawork and the exciting stylistic changes in New Wave and cinema verité. For many observers and advertisers, these two styles often collapsed into one. In 1965, an equipment rental firm asked, "Shooting Documentary Style? Behrend's has all the New Wave Equipment you need!"[57] By 1968, Arriflex was trumpeting its role in this style as it increasingly appeared in American feature filmmaking. The ad proclaimed: "'New wave'; 'cinema verité'; call it what you will. Today's young film craftsmen are pursuing new patterns in cinematography with a vigor that amounts to a crusade."[58] This description suggests an art film, but the subject was the use of an Arriflex on a studio feature, *The Incident* (1967). While camera manufacturers like Arri and Éclair benefited from a broad definition of the newest trends in filmmaking, cinematographers were struggling to define the new style of films like *The Graduate*: "Surtees calls it 'ultra-modern'—but it is something more than that. It has touches of 'Mod' and a faint aura of avant-garde, overtones of the 'Underground' and flashes of Cinema Verité.'"[59]

The growing acceptance of handheld camerawork had a practical tradeoff, with filmmakers tolerating less polished photography in exchange for greater access to real places. Direct cinema exemplified the benefits of this approach. For instance, David Wolper wanted to shoot at the New York

Stock Exchange, but after a large Hollywood crew disrupted trading, the governing board had banned cameras from the floor. Wolper gained access by showing off his small equipment package, consisting of only an Éclair and a Nagra portable sound recorder; he shot with available light, without tripod or power cables, and Éclair promoted his success in a print ad.[60] Meanwhile, Wexler began using Éclair cameras on location for Hollywood films, winning an Oscar for Cinematography for *Who's Afraid of Virginia Woolf?* (1967) and shooting Best Picture winner *In the Heat of the Night*.[61]

Every technological change of the late 1960s seemed to favor location shooting. The Nagra—a 13 pound, synchronized sound-recording device that debuted in 1958—would earn a 1965 Academy Award, signaling its growing acceptance for Hollywood location work.[62] Also, a new crab-dolly debuted that was small enough to carry cameras through doorways and narrow hallways.[63]

The television networks' shift to all-color programming in 1965 precipitated a daunting challenge to location filmmaking. As the market for color film sales to television networks boomed, Hollywood would all but phase out black-and-white production by 1968.[64] Eastman Color quickly responded to the challenge. In June 1967, Eastman 5251 required four times the light of the "almost obsolete" black-and-white Double-X; however, a new, extended development process offered to double the effective speed of color film with little quality loss.[65] In June 1968, Eastman introduced 5254, twice the speed of 5251 with absolutely no loss of quality.[66] The immediate application was location shooting, enabling color filming "earlier in the morning, later at night and in bad weather." Faster film required less light and promised "more realistic location coverage."[67]

American Cinematographer noted how the late 1960s boom in location filmmaking coincided with various technological innovations, but could not determine which was the cause and which was the effect.[68] Certainly trends in film style and film technology were mutually reinforcing, but the confluence in the late 1960s was also a confluence of film industries and new international styles. Equipment manufacturers no longer responded to Hollywood trends alone, but to a larger market working faster, cheaper, and often without soundstages. Smaller cameras and lights benefited filmmakers in various fields, including European art cinema, documentary, industrial, commercial, television, and war coverage. Runaway production and overhead reduction further displaced Hollywood as the center for technological development in filmmaking.

Cinematographer Andrew Laszlo observed the historical irony. As better lights and film stock created ideal conditions for studio filmmaking, most filmmakers were fleeing the studio for the unpredictable locations of pre-studio filmmakers.[69] Such a trend was particularly puzzling for the old guard of directors and cinematographers whose professional pride rested on their ability to control the film image.[70] The new style favored capturing the moment in actual conditions over shaping the setting and precise movement. Better technology made it easier to capture an image with available light and less expertise, challenging the importance of the professional cinematographer.

With the rapid abandonment of black-and-white, cinematographers also had to find new ways to build dramatic realism and maintain a downbeat tone in color. Since color films could not match the low light levels of black-and-white, they had to grow duller and bleaker. Established cinematographers learned not only how to make the image look better, but how to make it look worse. Ironically, as San Francisco became increasingly desirable as a location, filmmakers labored to make the city appear less spectacular.

SEMI-DOCUMENTARY COLOR

In the second half of the 1960s, filmmakers not only adapted the tools of cinema verité to narrative features but also brought a similar ethos of unadulterated realism. They faced a new challenge when Hollywood all but abandoned black-and-white film in the late 1960s. Realist dramas like *Days of Wine and Roses* featured crisp, shadowy black-and-white location cinematography; now stark realism had to be achieved on color film, a format still strongly associated with happier stories and highly saturated hues. Filmmakers largely achieved a new semi-documentary aesthetic in two ways. First, they insistently muted the color scheme through lighting and choice of settings. Second, while shooting extensively on location, they employed the imprecise framings, camera movements, and lighting associated with late 1960s documentary and avant-garde filmmakers. This lack of polish became a badge of realism compared to the traditional aesthetics that persisted in many Hollywood features.

Shooting *You're a Big Boy Now* (1966) for Francis Ford Coppola, Laszlo noted a "sharp turn" in Hollywood cinematography. Viewing the early camera tests, Coppola complained that they looked "too good." The film largely featured everyday New York locations, such as "a drug store or a meat market," rather than landmarks, and Coppola wanted his footage to "come as close to the actual look of these places as possible."[71] Laszlo credited these instincts to Coppola's background in student filmmaking, but Alfred Hitchcock expressed similar goals shooting *Torn Curtain* (1966). Relying on reflected light, he wanted rooms to appear on film as they did in actual life.[72] Although old guard filmmakers cautioned against certain techniques popularized by younger directors, they all faced the same paradigm shift. Technological improvements allowed for subtler lighting that made earlier studio realism appear increasingly artificial. The industry's full conversion to color forced filmmakers to adapt color aesthetics to fit stories that would have previously been shot in black-and-white. Finally, the growing scope and prominence of location shooting favored a new semi-documentary style, with cinema verité techniques suggesting greater realism and a stronger sense of place.

Cinematographer Arthur Miller was a master of classical Hollywood realism whose work included *How Green Was My Valley* (1941), *The Ox-Bow Incident* (1943), and *Gentleman's Agreement* (1947). Yet decades after his final film, *The Prowler* (1951), Miller showed little nostalgia. He noted that despite cinematographers' boasts about "natural" lighting, "for the most part we were only fooling ourselves."[73] Faster film stocks and smaller lamps revealed how much technical limitations had restrained filmmakers; both in staging and lighting, cinematographers had compromised ideals of naturalism with the bright, bulky lights needed to gain exposure. Miller shared lighting diagrams from scenes he shot with smaller lights, such as a candlelight scene in *The Mark of Zorro* (1940), hoping that current cinematographers could better achieve subtle interior lighting with more advanced tools.[74]

The same technological improvements that made interior lighting appear less stage-bound also made interiors less stage-based. *Bonnie and Clyde* shot almost entirely on location in Texas, spending ten weeks in small towns outside of Dallas. With the ability to film in actual building interiors, the crew could take advantage of a number of towns that had hardly changed their appearance since the 1930s. A string of holdups spanning Indiana to East Texas were all covered by moving from town to town in North-Central Texas without the time and cost of building or redressing studio sets. In fact, 1960s urban decline suited Depression-era period pieces. A "somewhat crumbling neighborhood in Dallas" resembled Joplin, Mississippi, during the 1930s. Woody Allen found a similar boon in San Francisco for his Depression-era crime comedy, *Take the Money and Run*. The decaying, depopulated buildings slated for redevelopment in the Yerba Buena project served on-screen as the 1930s slums of Camden and Union City, New Jersey.[75]

Despite clear improvements in color film stock, the demand for color films checked a seamless expansion of location filmmaking. When Eastman introduced its faster 5254 stock in 1968, it hoped the speed increase would inspire not only cinematographers but also screenwriters, who might write settings for color films that previously could only be captured on black-and-white.[76] Technological improvements opened up new territories for color filmmaking, but Hollywood needed to overcome previous assumptions governing color in the age of black-and-white.

The use of color film had strong generic associations, but these needed to rapidly change due to the virtual elimination of black-and-white by 1967.[77] For instance, after gaining an Oscar nomination for the black-and-white war film *King Rat* (1965), Burnett Guffey chastised Hollywood's use of "color for color's sake." He believed black-and-white was the best medium for mystery, action-adventure, or "stark" drama.[78] By 1967, however, black-and-white was no longer a real choice. For *In Cold Blood* (1967), writer-producer-director Richard Brooks had to fend off multiple studio attempts to shoot the film in color; the next successful studio film shot in black-and-white would be *The Last Picture Show* (1971).[79] As color film became universal, cinematographers had no choice but to develop a realist aesthetic in color. In 1967, Guffey meticulously desaturated the color palette for *Bonnie and Clyde* to provide a more realistic look for a shockingly violent film. He won the Oscar for Best Cinematography and helped set off a trend of using muted colors for increasingly bleak narratives.[80]

Older directors such as Alfred Hitchcock and Otto Preminger began experimenting with new color aesthetics just as black-and-white filmmaking was declining. Hitchcock believed color could convey the same mood as black-and-white, but he distinguished between "vulgar and delicate" color, where "the colors are not shouting at us."[81] For *Torn Curtain*, cinematographer John Warren bounced nearly every interior light off of a reflector and even crafted new canvas reflectors to create soft, shadowless light.[82] John Huston mounted a more ambitious experiment with delicate color. After half a year experimenting with lab processing, Houston selectively desaturated *Reflections in a Golden Eye* (1967), resulting in a sepia palette with the exception of red, which could brightly explode from a flower or other intensely red objects. While Huston hoped his restricted palette would shield the story's psychological drama from garish color, he ironically drew greater attention to the use of color than to the story.[83] As they struggled to define a new color aesthetic, filmmakers largely agreed that current Hollywood color aesthetics needed to be drastically dimmed for realistic stories; shooting *Bullitt*, director Peter Yates and cinematographer Bill Fraker assiduously toned down the color reproduction of San Francisco locations.

Aside from a few elder craftsmen like Hitchcock and Huston, a distinction between vulgar and delicate color largely followed generational lines, with younger directors such as Coppola, Mike Nichols, and Arthur Penn favoring chromatic restraint. Robert Surtees highlighted the gap between the old and new aesthetics by shooting two strikingly different Best Picture nominees, the high-key musical *Doctor Dolittle* and the softly lit youth hit *The Graduate*. Dubbed a cinematographer with a "split-personality" by *American Cinematographer*, Surtees suggested how the new school of color fit with broader changes: "On *The Graduate* I had to forget all the years of trying for perfect photography. On that film it was not how beautiful the photography was that counted, but how emotional and exciting it was."[84] *The Graduate* struck a significant balance between the unreality of its innovative camera techniques and the natural appearance of its lighting, color, and settings. Guffey echoed these sentiments describing *Bonnie and Clyde*, which also combined droll fantasy and stylistic flourishes (the slow-motion finale) with realist cinematography: "Color in itself sometimes detracts from realism because it comes out pretty whether you want it or not. We tried very hard to subdue the color in this picture. . . . I think he [Penn] succeeded because this is one film that can never be called 'pretty.'"[85]

Two stylistic influences helped resolve this seeming opposition between realism and overt stylistic techniques: cinema verité and European New Wave cinema. *American Cinematographer* rarely ran articles about foreign filmmakers, but the impact of *The Battle of Algiers* (1966) occasioned a piece written by its director, Gillo Pontecorvo. Pontecorvo emphasized his preference for available light, bouncing sunlight to fill out natural settings. He shot the entire film with an Arriflex (William Fraker would do the same for *Bullitt*), giving the small crew better access to locations in the crowded urban setting of Algiers. While creating a palpable sense of realism, Pontecorvo aggressively violated a hallmark of classical Hollywood realism: unobtrusive style. He remarked, "I believe that the motion picture camera has been used too passively for the most part. It should be the most creative thing about the entire business of filmmaking. It should truly move."[86] A new realist aesthetic was being forged, one that prized fidelity of place but championed the active presence of the camera, moving through the action rather than seamlessly framing it.

The growth of direct cinema in American documentaries further reinforced the association between imperfect mobile camerawork and realism. These films had a larger impact on young filmmakers, circulating through college campuses and focusing on the music counterculture in *Don't Look Back* (1965) and *Monterrey Pop* (1968).[87] Veteran filmmakers who had built their careers on polished realism were largely dismissive. In October 1968, an industrial-documentary filmmaker, Mike Waddell, addressed the budding verité trend: "If a technique calls attention to itself, it is bad because it will divert the audience's attention from what you are attempting to say . . . some of the most common being out of focus scenes, awkward zooms, and the most common—camera D.T.'s or the hand-held jiggle approach."[88] Hollywood veterans were no kinder. For Edward Dmytryk, the handheld camera was nothing new; it had been successfully used by James Wong Howe for boxing scenes in *Body and Soul* (1947). According to *American Cinematographer*, handheld cameras and long zoom lenses were merely a current European gimmick.[89] The magazine's editor, Herb Lightman, directed a similar jab at a colloquium on lighting: "Except for a few, very new directors who feel that all there is to cinematography is grabbing a hand held camera and available light in order to create an automatic masterpiece, the vast majority of my fellow directors have a tremendous respect for the Director of Photography."[90] Many industry professionals regarded the newfound ability to quickly point, shoot, and film in 35 mm as a threat to professional standards and the standing of established cinematographers.

Wexler, the only respected cinematographer who regularly used documentary techniques, became the interlocutor for the new style of filmmaking. Despite shooting Academy Award–winning features, he still considered himself a documentary cameraman.[91] His stylistic influences for *The Thomas Crown Affair* were *Battle of Algiers* and *The War Game* (1965), a semi-documentary portrait of a nuclear war. Rather than criticizing established techniques, Wexler advocated for greater experimentation.[92] With less cumbersome and less costly equipment, documentary filmmaking allowed for trial and error: "I learn more when I go out with a Bolex or a 16mm Éclair and, as you might say, just 'play around' with film."[93] Other cinematographers wondered how to translate freewheeling location photography to the studio set; Wexler's response was to treat the set like a real location.[94] Thus by the late 1960s, location shooting had become a viable alternative to the studio, and location aesthetics had begun to shape soundstage production.

While films such as *Bonnie and Clyde* and *The Graduate* signaled the rise of an American New Wave, Hollywood studios and producers also recruited upcoming foreign filmmakers. Robert Chartoff and Irwin Winkler capitalized on the growing popularity of British films and actors, releasing *Darling* (1965) in the United States and securing its budding star, Julie Christie, for the MGM blockbuster *Doctor Zhivago*. They described themselves as "an American outgrowth of the English revolution in movie-making."[95] Their first film, *Point Blank*, considered an "offbeat film," featured Hollywood stars and California locations (San Francisco and Los Angeles) but also included "a sleek contemporary look" and "an elliptical style in the European manner."[96] Warners' *Petulia* and *Bullitt* both paired British directors, key crew members, and actors with Hollywood stars, San Francisco locations, and studio financing. In fact, when *Petulia* arrived at Cannes as an official US entry, observers debated whether it was actually a British film with a "Yank label."[97] The new look of American films emerged not only from the influence of European filmmakers, but through their active participation.

Prolonged runaway production had helped stifle Hollywood creativity. At the 1966 IATSE conference, MPAA head Jack Valenti acknowledged a void of new talent in Hollywood, and IATSE had a share of the blame.[98] Many key union chapters were closed to new membership by 1966.[99] The cameramen's local union—whose leader, Herb Aller, had been a vocal opponent of runaway production—was deemed a monopoly in 1967 by the National Labor Relations Board following its third unfair labor complaint in three months.[100] As Hollywood unions closed ranks to protect their remaining job opportunities, a new generation of young talent trained in Hollywood filmmaking abroad. Europe offered more opportunities for young production workers, who gained technical expertise and increasingly competed with American workers.[101] Reflecting on the studio lots that in the summer of 1966 were filled with television series but devoid of feature filmmaking, Peter Bart wrote, "Nearly all of the potentially important movies—big budget pictures as well as the small 'art' films—are being shot in Europe, not Hollywood." He concluded, "Hollywood's once limitless creative resources seem to be running thin."[102] Fittingly, English filmmakers John Boorman, Richard Lester, and Peter Yates indelibly captured California's new creative capital, San Francisco.

Changes in both popular taste and production practices promoted this British invasion of San Francisco. American foreign film preferences shifted from French to British in the second half of the 1960s, with films like John Schlesinger's *Darling* and Richard Lester's *The Knack* (1965) reveling in the fashionable London scene.[103] The British style of rapid location shooting and unconventional editing allowed filmmakers to capture the popular moment in San Francisco with less concern for classical continuity. Moreover, the city drew British directors seeking the same revolutionary cultural force as American teenagers, advertisers, and media producers. San Francisco journalist David Talbot described the 1960s counterculture as "essentially a cultural dialogue between San Francisco and London."[104] By 1967, San Francisco had the louder voice. After shooting *Georgy Girl* (1966) in London, British producer-director Silvio Narizzano planned to shoot his next project in San Francisco, which he dubbed "the most exciting city in the world today."[105]

SAN FRANCISCO: SETTING, LOCATION, AND URBAN FORM

Between 1967 and 1968, San Francisco became a highly popular setting for feature films and television series. Sharply different approaches to depicting the city revealed a widening gulf in production practices. *Petulia* and *Bullitt* relied on the newest technologies and location shooting styles, whereas the backlot looks of *Guess Who's Coming to Dinner* and *The Love Bug* could largely have been achieved by the mid-1950s. Over seven seasons, *Ironside* (1967–1975), a television detective drama starring Raymond Burr as a wheelchair-bound San Francisco police chief, likely spent less time shooting on location than either *Petulia* or *Bullitt*. Case studies of these two films reveal how new techniques and urban aesthetics began to quickly transform San Francisco's role as a location and setting through the mid-1970s. Both productions sought a more authentic image of San Francisco than the bulk of late 1960s productions that had exploited its popular image without carefully exploring the city.

Staging the City

Before *Bullitt* ushered in a wave of extensive location shooting in San Francisco and other cities in the 1970s, studio reproductions of the city still met professional standards.[106] The cheapest way to cash in on the San Francisco scene remained a quick location trip, supplemented by psychedelic set dressing in Los Angeles. This strategy appealed to the tight budgets of exploitation and television filmmakers, as well as the tight production constraints imposed on Stanley Kramer for *Guess Who's Coming to Dinner*. Although *The Graduate* shot few scenes in San Francisco, *Variety*'s inclusion of the film on its list of San Francisco hits is not incidental. The film highlighted opposing styles of filmmaking as well as the opposing symbolism of Southern and Northern California. Both San Francisco and *The Graduate* became metonyms for new stylistic and cultural practices.

The rural outskirts of Northern California provided fertile ground for shooting a number of exploitation biker films such as *Devil's Angels* (1967) and *Angels from Hell* (1968). Capturing downtown San Francisco proved less cost-effective. Sam Katzman, "the Speedy Gonzales of exploitation films," cashed in early on the exploitation value of rock music and free love with *The Love-Ins* (1967), "the first film set in San Francisco in the jet age that was shot entirely on a Hollywood lot."[107] American International Pictures' *Psych-Out* (1968) would go to further lengths to harness the San Francisco scene. Produced by Dick Clark, the film featured a soundtrack from current psychedelic bands such as Strawberry Alarm Clock and the Seeds. The film opens with a montage of handheld, documentary-style footage of the Haight-Ashbury district, including the sign at the intersection and the de rigueur shot of a San Francisco cable car. Yet like most films set in San Francisco in previous decades, the early action moves away from actual locations to interior sets of hippie clubs and crash pads. Haight-Ashbury thus serves as a stylistic marker rather than a location, with cinematographer Laszlo Kovacs (who shot *Easy Rider* the next year) deploying an array of camera movements, colored lighting, and focus pulls to complement the trippy set dressing and costumes.

Ironside debuted in 1967, perfectly timed to capitalize on the rising popularity of San Francisco, but it was a typical Universal television production, "confined to the backlot, except for a couple of postcard shots of the SF police HQ and the Golden Gate Bridge." When it premiered, a *Variety* reviewer advised producers to take better advantage of San Francisco location shooting, beyond "a lot of stock cut-ins and rear screen loops."[108] Half a year later, *Ironside* remained a fixture of the NBC schedule, and *Variety* faintly praised the show for going against the trend toward television location shooting by "playing down the Frisco locations" and "making it without the scenic crutch."[109]

Ironside gestured to San Francisco's youth culture through casting. Raymond Burr, a veteran television star in *Perry Mason* (1957–1966), was paired with a younger white male detective (Don Galloway), a stylish young, white female investigator (Barbara Anderson), and a young black assistant with a criminal past (Donald Mitchell). They were a tamer version of *The Mod Squad* (1968–1973) with adult supervision. On rare occasions, *Ironside* dealt with crimes specific to San Francisco. In *Groove Tube*, Aniko Bodroghkozy places a 1968 episode of *Ironside*, "A Trip to Hashbury," within the context of other series, such as *Dragnet '67*, that devoted episodes to condescending depictions of young runaways swept up by villainous hippies taking advantage of a drug-fueled, promiscuous cultural scene.[110] The settings were equally cartoonish, with "Hashbury" staged as an isolated mansion (nonexistent in the densely urban, rundown Haight), with psychedelic decorations, a flower-painted car, and flower children extras. Likely shot on the Universal lot, this Haight was an episodic flight of fancy, and San Francisco remained a trivial detail throughout *Ironside*'s series run.

While economics dictated the style of *Ironside*, *Guess Who's Coming to Dinner* faced different limitations. The first was Stanley Kramer, who largely favored the controlled environment of the studio lot, where he could focus on performances rather than logistics. (Despite an ocean setting, Kramer shot *Ship of Fools* [1965] entirely on the Columbia lot.)[111] The bigger limitation was Spencer Tracy's health as he struggled to finish the picture while dying of cancer. Production revolved around efficiently recording Tracy's performance, relying on simple staging for his scenes while shooting the rest between his short, painful visits to the set.[112] With most of the story set inside the parents' house, *Guess Who's Coming to Dinner* required little location work, but all of Tracy's scenes had to be captured on the lot. Never a master technician, Kramer's attempts to meet these challenges degraded the film's aesthetics. Although rear-projection driving shots were still common in 1967, the painted San Francisco backgrounds of the mansion terrace and rear projection of Tracy walking into an ice cream parlor look cheap and dated.

The mixed critical response to the very style of *Guess Who's Coming to Dinner* suggested that the aesthetic preference for location shooting followed generational lines. Newer critics like Andrew Sarris attacked Kramer's "lumbering machinery" of filmmaking, and Joe Morgenstern pilloried the decades-old aesthetic of Kramer's film.[113] Coupled with the celebrated performances of its older stars, Tracy and Katharine Hepburn, the film served as a swan song for Hollywood's studio era. But despite minimal location shooting, the narrative invocation of San Francisco powerfully shaped the film's appeal. According to Setlowe, "It was set entirely in San Francisco, because the revolutionary movie storyline of an ideal, live-happily-ever-after inter-racial romance was somehow more acceptable there, even to the moviegoers in Lester Maddoxland who broke box office records in Atlanta."[114] The fantasy of San Francisco bounded social change within a West Coast peninsula, comfortably distant from a South still roiling over civil rights. The city's revolutionary image reinforced a rather timid crossing of cinematic boundaries.

The Graduate relied on a similar symbolic geography. As Benjamin breaks away from the plastic, materialistic Southern California world of Mrs. Robinson and his parents, he travels north through San Francisco and into Berkeley. Nichols famously shot Benjamin driving the wrong way across the Bay Bridge (toward San Francisco), which allowed for camera cars and helicopters to capture the open sky rising above him (Figure 4.1).[115] As he chooses Elaine and a young, rebellious generation, epitomized by Berkeley campus activists, he almost inevitably drives away from Los Angeles toward the Bay Area.

Aside from the film's narrative, the unique stylistic flourishes in *The Graduate* further associated it with San Francisco, booming with experimental film and music artists. Like *Petulia* and *Bullitt*, *The Graduate* employed mobile equipment and improvised staging. Most of the film was confined to the studio lot, but as Surtees suggested, Nichols built and shot sets to function like real locations. He had Mrs. Robinson's house built in its entirety on the Paramount lot rather than as a series of sets. Thus if he decided to film actors moving between rooms, he could do so on the fly. The house even

4.1. Benjamin crossing the Bay Bridge in *The Graduate* (Embassy, 1967). On film, the Bay Area's youthful freedom frequently contrasts with Los Angeles's bourgeois culture.

included a bathroom, despite no scene in the script taking place there. Such a realistic space offered the constraints that spurred creativity on location, while the technical resources of the studio provided a safety net. At one point, Nichols decided he needed a wall removed to facilitate his camera placement. Although a wild wall would have saved time, the crew could still accomplish the task, whereas such destruction of a real location would be inconceivable.[116]

When *The Graduate* did shoot on location, the crew found creative and effective ways to use new equipment to open otherwise impossible to capture locations. *The Graduate* features one of cinema's most famous zoom shots, where the extreme telephoto lens captures Benjamin seemingly running in place toward the church in the film's climax. Yet the zoom proved just as important for catching subjects unaware on location. When Benjamin and Elaine walk through a crowd of hippies outside a Sunset Strip venue, a 500 mm lens hidden at a gas station across the street recorded the action. Wearing wireless microphones, little-known actors Dustin Hoffman and Katharine Ross blended in with the unsuspecting concertgoers.[117]

The Graduate employed low-power quartz-iodine lights to circumvent noise restrictions. Filming Benjamin meeting Mrs. Robinson at the bar of the Ambassador Hotel with conventional studio lights would have required a generator, a loud disturbance for the hotel guests. Instead, cinematographer Robert Surtees hung a hundred or so quartz-iodine lights throughout the lobby. Later, shooting in Beverly Hills, a municipality with a generator ban, he ran the same lights on household power from helpful residents.[118] In sharp contrast, *Petulia* caused a major disturbance shooting for days at San Francisco's marquee hotel, the Fairmont. Unlike the wealthy residents of Los Angeles, where regular production spurred restrictions on filmmaking, San Franciscans in the late 1960s were still enjoying the novelty of film production.

Hits like *The Graduate* and *Guess Who's Coming to Dinner* gained cultural currency through a limited engagement with San Francisco. Director Richard Lester and producer Steve McQueen shared a different, more ambitious approach, seeking to authentically depict the city by shooting entirely on location. Rather than copying a psychedelic aesthetic, as so many filmmakers and advertisers had done, they attempted to capture the inimitable energy of San Francisco through location shooting. Effectively filming a city now defined by its young residents rather than its architecture required new techniques and equipment. With small crews, mobile cameras, and a willingness to improvise, British directors Lester and Yates scoured the area and shot dozens of locations in San Francisco. They found two different cities.

Petulia: Collage City

Petulia was the first feature financed by a major studio that was shot entirely in San Francisco (excluding a two-day shoot in Tijuana). Even a handful of scenes set in Acapulco were shot in nearby Sausalito.[119] This decision was remarkable (and galling to Los Angeles observers) because the source novel, *Me and the Arch Kook Petulia*, was set in Los Angeles, including Hollywood (Figure 4.2).[120] *Petulia* not only ran away from Los Angeles, but also London, where the key production personnel were based.

By 1967, *Petulia* director Richard Lester had established himself as one of the most creative filmmakers in the industry and one whose films returned major box office profits. Lester's multiformat experience prepared him for the frenetic pace of shooting a modish, moderate-budget feature entirely on location. Before establishing himself as a British filmmaker, Lester had worked in Canadian television.[121] After moving to London, he directed an improvisational comedy series, *The Goon Show*, as well as 500 television commercials. His first feature was a low-budget rock-and-roll film, *It's Trad, Dad* (1962), for Columbia. Lester's next film, *A Hard Day's Night* (1964), starred the Beatles and revolutionized the rock film to enormous commercial success.[122] Unlike French and Italian films of the 1960s, which grew more opaque and cerebral, British films drew criticism for commercial and sexual exploitation, and Lester's style toed the line of advertising pizzazz and avant-garde experimentation.[123] The result was a string of stylistically innovative and commercially successful films, including a second Beatles film, *Help!* (1965), and two successful comedies, *The Knack . . . And How to Get It* (1965) and *A Funny Thing Happened on the Way to the Forum* (1966).

For *Petulia*, Lester joined first-time film producer Raymond Wagner, who worked for years in American television as a new projects executive for MCA-TV.[124] Wagner packaged Richard Lester and Julie Christie for *Petulia* in March 1966 and then sought a distributor. The original plan was to shoot in February in both London and San Francisco.[125] The London locations were likely included to qualify the film as a British production and thus eligible for Eady Fund money. Despite being financed by Warner Bros., Lester insisted the film was still British, even after scrapping the London shoot;

4.2. Richard Lester's nonlinear style allowed him to capture dozens of disparate scenes on location for *Petulia* (Warner Bros.–Seven Arts, 1967)—including this fashion pose shot of Petulia (Julie Christie) and Archie (George C. Scott) beneath the Golden Gate Bridge. These were later incorporated during editing.

since a largely British crew had shot the film, he argued that San Francisco was merely a location, not a place of origin. Throughout production, *Petulia* was classified as British, but upon release it failed to meet quota restrictions. The film played at Cannes as a US entry, and even Lester enjoyed the irony.[126] Born in Philadelphia before becoming a filmmaker in Canada and London, he was just as transatlantic as *Petulia*.[127]

Lester and San Francisco were a natural pairing. Like *The Knack*, *Petulia* was a quirky urban romance whose characters whimsically roam the city. Like *A Hard Day's Night*, the film had a rock-and-roll angle, shooting during the height of the San Francisco rock scene. *Petulia* premiered in June 1968, the same month that Jefferson Airplane graced the cover of *Life* magazine. A special section on "new rock" began with a photo spread of Janis Joplin with Big Brother and the Holding Company—the same band that plays in *Petulia*'s opening scene.[128] Originally, Jefferson Airplane had been slated for *Petulia*, but manager and Fillmore concert promoter Bill Graham pulled them, rightly predicting that by the film's release, the band would be too famous to be merely a background act.[129]

Lester's rapid and playfully discontinuous editing was a key influence on the "new look" of Hollywood films of the late 1960s, setting a precedent for the celebrated use of slow motion in *Bonnie and Clyde*, as well as the dreamy montage of *The Graduate*.[130] This style was particularly suited to San Francisco, where nontraditional editing was a staple of the underground cinema that often played behind local rock performances. *Variety* even placed *Petulia* under the subheadline "Underground Films" in a piece on the San Francisco music scene, placing this studio-financed feature alongside avant-garde films by Bruce Conner and Kenneth Anger. While Lester was shooting, Michelangelo Antonioni was screening underground films at the Fillmore; like Lester, Antonioni followed the zeitgeist from London to San Francisco after *Blow Up* (1966).[131] The convergence of innovative European filmmakers in San Francisco suggested a confluence between European New Wave and the American avant-garde.

For *Petulia*, Lester hired British cinematographer Nicolas Roeg, who had shot Lester's last picture, *A Funny Thing Happened on the Way to the Forum*, and Julie Christie's previous picture, *Far from the Madding Crowd* (1967). A seasoned location cinematographer, Roeg invented a color filter spray as a replacement for the costly window gels used to control color temperature, saving both time and space.[132] Expedient solutions such as this proved critical to *Petulia*, whose narrow interiors and use of a freewheeling handheld camera left little off-screen space for production personnel.

Lester's and Wagner's resumes suggested they could deliver a hit while staying under budget, having both worked within the tight budget and time constraints of television production. But *Petulia* began principal photography without an approved budget, and in a memo to Warner Bros., executive Walter McEwen doubted that the independent producers, Lester's Petersham Films Ltd., had made enough effort to minimize costs. He added, "The only trouble with economies effected after a picture starts shooting, is that they usually end up being minor—because the fixed costs involved for cast etc. cannot be reduced."[133] Less than a month later, production continued after Lester agreed to cut the shooting schedule by nearly 25 percent, from seventy-two to fifty-six days.

Lester's shooting method defied Hollywood's established methods for ensuring that pictures remained under budget: daily production reports tracking how many feet of film rolled and the number of script pages completed. This allowed studio executives to assess whether productions were moving too slowly or overshooting, and then quickly intervene. Warners' executives faced a dilemma about Lester's overshooting. In May, McEwen wrote Jack Warner:

> I am afraid it is too much to hope that Lester will depart from his established technique of multiple cameras, including hand held cameras. That appears to be the only way he knows how to make a film—making use in the cutting room, of bits and pieces of almost everything he shoots. In my opinion, any attempt to clamp down on Lester in this regard could be disastrous—also deprive us of the full value of the unique talent of the man we bought as director.[134]

Production reports failed to clarify that Lester was actually two days ahead of the new, shorter shooting schedule.[135]

Departing from classical Hollywood continuity was not only a stylistic challenge but a challenge to the entire production apparatus. Pictures were scheduled and budgeted based on scripted scenes and settings. Lester instead shot as much as he could capture in the given schedule, regardless of the screen duration of a given scene. Thus Warner Bros. had no idea what picture they had paid for until well after shooting had wrapped. For instance, toward the end of shooting, Lester spent five days on the opening scene at the Fairmont Hotel ballroom, where Archie and Petulia first meet as Big Brother and the Holding Company entertain a room full of formally dressed socialites. Yet aside from principal settings like Archie's apartment and the hospital, Lester covered most locations in a single day.[136] The film featured nondiegetic inserts, including fashion poses by the principal actors under the Golden Gate Bridge, and rapidly cut flashbacks and flash-forwards breaking into various scenes. Such montage elements were a signature of Lester's style and the European New Wave, but a greater number of cuts threatened to extend post-production and further confused the executives trying to track the film's progress.

Warner Bros. hesitated to rein in Lester not only because they realized his unconventional methods paid off on-screen, but also because of competition with other studios for talent. During shooting, Lester's attorney informed Warner Bros. that he had signed a multipicture deal with United Artists, including no budget restrictions and a 50 percent profit share. United Artists' confidence kept McEwen hopeful that as Lester's "track record" suggested, *Petulia* would be a major hit; it was not, although it easily outperformed *The Bed Sitting Room* (1969), the one picture Lester completed as part of his UA deal.[137]

In its early stages, the growing power of the auteur director that peaked in 1970s Hollywood was not only an issue of talent competition but of executive expertise. New shooting methods made the time-tested data of budgets and daily production reports a less precise indicator of progress toward completion. Instead, to manage budgets, executives had to rely on contract language and track records. On a medium budget, it led to false expectations for *Petulia*; on a large budget, it led to *Heaven's Gate* (1980), with which Michael Cimino, a seemingly reliable talent after the success of *The Deer Hunter* (1978), essentially bankrupted United Artists by shooting an expensive box office failure.[138]

Lester quickly proved the value of his flexible approach when, as was so often the case, rain fell on San Francisco. Undeterred, Lester lost no time and played up the rain to set the mood of his characters' bittersweet romance.[139] Shooting in a small Telegraph Hill apartment, crew members hid in closets and stairwells to stay out of frame.[140] Roeg's ability to capture the urban landscape of San Francisco, coupled with Lester's discontinuous editing style, allowed abstract scenic images to punctuate the film (Figure 4.3).[141] San Francisco location shooting never affected the film's bottom line; instead, the downbeat tone and disorienting style limited the film's box office appeal.

Petulia begins with the newly married title character (Julie Christie) seducing Archie (George C. Scott) at a charity ball also attended by her husband (Richard Chamberlain). Petulia and Archie begin a sporadic love affair as she brings youthful irreverence to his staid routine as a doctor. The story

4.3. Abstract scenic shots punctuate the narrative in *Petulia*, creating a patchwork image of San Francisco.

takes a dark turn when Archie finds Petulia beaten nearly to death by her husband. Her powerful father-in-law (Joseph Cotton) helps convince Petulia to return to his son, and they leave San Francisco on his yacht. Upon her return, Archie sees Petulia, ready to give birth, at his hospital. In this final scene, he asks her to run away with him, but neither one has the courage to abandon their established lives.

Although Petulia plays an eccentric flower child for Archie, she refuses to leave an abusive and manipulative high society family. This resembles the story of *The Graduate*'s Mrs. Robinson, not Benjamin—one possible reason for the film's limited commercial success. Yet Lester offers a striking picture of late 1960s San Francisco, where members of Nob Hill high society, fixtures of 1940s and 1950s films, were struggling with a youth movement in direct opposition to their bourgeois culture. From the opening scene, Lester introduces this contrast with abrupt dialectical edits between wheelchaired dowagers in an elevator and Janis Joplin playing at their charity ball (Figure 4.4).

Petulia's bravura opening scene also exemplifies Lester's improvisational shooting style. The production reserved a ballroom at the Fairmont, but upon seeing the voluminous lobby, Lester could not resist staging the ball there. This large space required "about half the lighting needed to flood Candlestick Park," a reminder of the still daunting demands of shooting location interiors in color; somehow enough power remained for the Holding Company's sound equipment. The lobby contained a car placed on a platform for a convention; Lester wrote this into the script as the grand prize at the ball. Hotel management let the company shoot in the lobby, but only between two and six in the morning so as not to inconvenience hotel guests. Not surprisingly, a late night rock concert with 150 extras generated several complaints from guests trying to sleep. For the next four nights, the band played the opening riffs to establish the dance beat, and then the party proceeded in silence. In the final film, the scene ran for only a minute and a half.[142]

This production anecdote reveals as much about shooting in San Francisco in the late 1960s as it does about Richard Lester. Even prior to Mayor Alioto taking office in January 1968, the city had proved remarkably amenable to an influx of filmmakers, even when they rankled guests at the ritziest hotel in town for nearly a week. The society page of the *San Francisco Chronicle* provides a key clue to the lack of resistance: Hollywood courted the very blue bloods satirized in *Petulia*. One "Junior Leaguer" who took

4.4. Dialectical editing in *Petulia* contrasts San Francisco's high society with the youth culture, here typified by wheelchaired dowagers in an elevator (*left*), and Janis Joplin performing at their charity ball with Big Brother and the Holding Company (*right*).

drama classes at Stanford landed bit roles in both *Petulia* and *Bullitt*. About *Petulia* she quipped, "I think all of San Francisco society worked in that one." The same article, titled "Elite in the Act," featured an image of socialite James Wyatt II dancing as an extra in the opening party scene.[143] While the San Francisco filmmaking boom remained novel, city residents, particularly the influential citizens who often found their way onto sets, tolerated the requisite disturbance caused by urban location shooting—an attitude that quickly changed in the early 1970s, when Hollywood productions were commonplace.

In *Petulia*, Lester exploded the paradigm of San Francisco cine-tourism. First, he expanded the travelogue montage to encompass the entire film. Sightseeing is not isolated in *Petulia*, nor is the rapid editing between different places. Instead, Lester staged the principal actors moving through various tourist sites, ranging from the Fairmont Hotel, the Japanese Tea Garden, Chinatown, Alcatraz, and Fisherman's Wharf. He even captured a dialogue scene with Petulia aboard a trolley car, the same shot that fell apart during *Experiment in Terror* when it drew too large a crowd. The television pace and willingness to patch scenes together without strict continuity editing allowed Lester to quickly capture dozens of locations with lead actors.

Unlike previous Hollywood filmmakers, Lester explicitly acknowledged the commercial tourism industry flourishing in San Francisco's beautiful scenery. When Archie tours Muir Woods with his children, the mystical setting from *Vertigo* hosts a commercial camera crew using the ancient forest as the background for a cigarette ad. When he picnics with a date at the Japanese Tea Garden, a loudspeaker intrudes upon the natural setting, directing visitors to the gift shop. When he tries to entertain his kids with a boat ride to Alcatraz, they reveal that his ex-wife's new boyfriend has already taken them there. Hoping to outdo the boyfriend, Archie sneaks them past the fences, and they frolic through Alcatraz in an escape from the structured tour ironically staged in a prison.

Even San Francisco's adult spectacles prove underwhelming in the film. Archie regularly has lunch with a friend at the Roaring Twenties, the same club featuring nearly nude girls on swings in *Experiment in Terror*. Off-screen, the North Beach club was now famous not only for its swinging girls, but the first bottomless striptease in the city.[144] As girls in pasties parade past the camera, the men seem, for the most part, detached from the erotic display. The girl on the swing has her back to them as they strain to read the menu in the dimly lit club. Archie briefly glances at her, triggering a flash cut to Petulia, before returning to the menu. Lester then cuts away to a nude dancer, draped in a towel, eating a sandwich beyond the shadow of the band (Figure 4.5). Behind the scenes, the dancers are having a working lunch as well, and the club, charged with sex and seediness in *Experiment in Terror*, appears almost as mundane as Archie's hospital.

4.5. In *Petulia*, Richard Lester undercut the erotic appeal of the Roaring Twenties nightclub by cutting from a shot of Archie (George C. Scott) having lunch (*top*) to a nude dancer, draped in a towel, on her lunch break (*bottom*).

Like the dancer on the swing, San Francisco's counterculture largely appears as mise-en-scène rather than part of the plot. After their first tryst, Archie walks Petulia to her cab. As she leaves, a flower-painted VW Bug rolls backward past him. Hippies appear pantomiming rock songs on a stage in Golden Gate Park, drawing chalk patterns on hillside steps, and leaving psychedelic posters throughout the city (Figure 4.6). For a film set during the peak of the San Francisco hippie scene, Lester decidedly framed the youth movement within the scenery rather than as an active participant in the story, suggesting an alternative lifestyle beyond the view of his wealthy protagonists. By 1967, it was hard to distinguish so-called happenings from tourist events because the city's youth culture had become the focal point of San Francisco's tourist economy.[145] By using the hippies as a leitmotif,

4.6. Hippies appear as a leitmotif throughout *Petulia* rather than as central characters, shown doing things such as leaving psychedelic posters throughout the city (*top*) and drawing chalk patterns on public walkways (*bottom*).

Lester suggests something subtler. Although staged as a spectacle for the upper class (exemplified by the charity ball), the hippie lifestyle remains beyond their comprehension, a direct challenge to their sterile culture.

If Archie fits squarely, albeit joylessly, within San Francisco high society, Petulia toes the line between the hippies and the urban elite. Her floral name, style of dress, and reputation as a "kook" clearly place her within the counterculture. As a prime example, she irreverently breaks a pawnshop window to steal a tuba. Yet once her husband reveals himself as not just a rich stiff, but also an abuser, her independence appears far more ambivalent. Late in the film, Archie confronts her in her bedroom, where trendy floral fabrics drape a four-poster bed and a posh room in a modernist mansion (Figure 4.7). The character of Petulia echoes Christie's role as the hip but feckless Diana in *Darling*, and similarly suggests that the sexy free spirits of the era were beholden to a wealthy establishment. Yet unlike Diana, who effortlessly moves between men, Petulia suggests a more cynical reality, in which her hippie fashion overhangs a golden cage. In a damning shot, Petulia's radiant sun dress stands out against a trolley car filled with uniformed soldiers, the second reference to Vietnam after an earlier transitional shot of a television news report (see Figure 4.7): the same class funding Petulia's wardrobe is also complicit in the Vietnam War.

As socialites Petulia and Archie fail to embrace the social freedom represented by the hippies, Lester embellishes the opposition between the professional class and the youth movement by intercutting shots of psychedelic rock shows with scenes featuring the mechanical aspects of Archie's world. The opening scene introduces this crosscutting as the camera sways horizontally with Janis Joplin's wailing rock show, producing a sonic and visual contrast to the party guests, doubly trapped in wheelchairs and an elevator cage, rising vertically to a creaky mechanical sound. Later in the film, Lester overlays sound and image to create a similar disjunction. As Archie gives dry medical descriptions at the hospital, Lester cuts in footage from another rock show (which Archie attends much later in the film), and his technical language becomes the soundtrack for the silent performance footage. The same technique brutally reappears when Petulia is taken from her apartment on a stretcher after the savage beating by her husband; a sound montage of neighbors' gossiping and the ambulance wailing again bleeds over inserted images from the rock show. These flash-forwards, which initially seem to be nondiegetic images intercut with emotionless medical procedures, provide the rare moments when youth culture

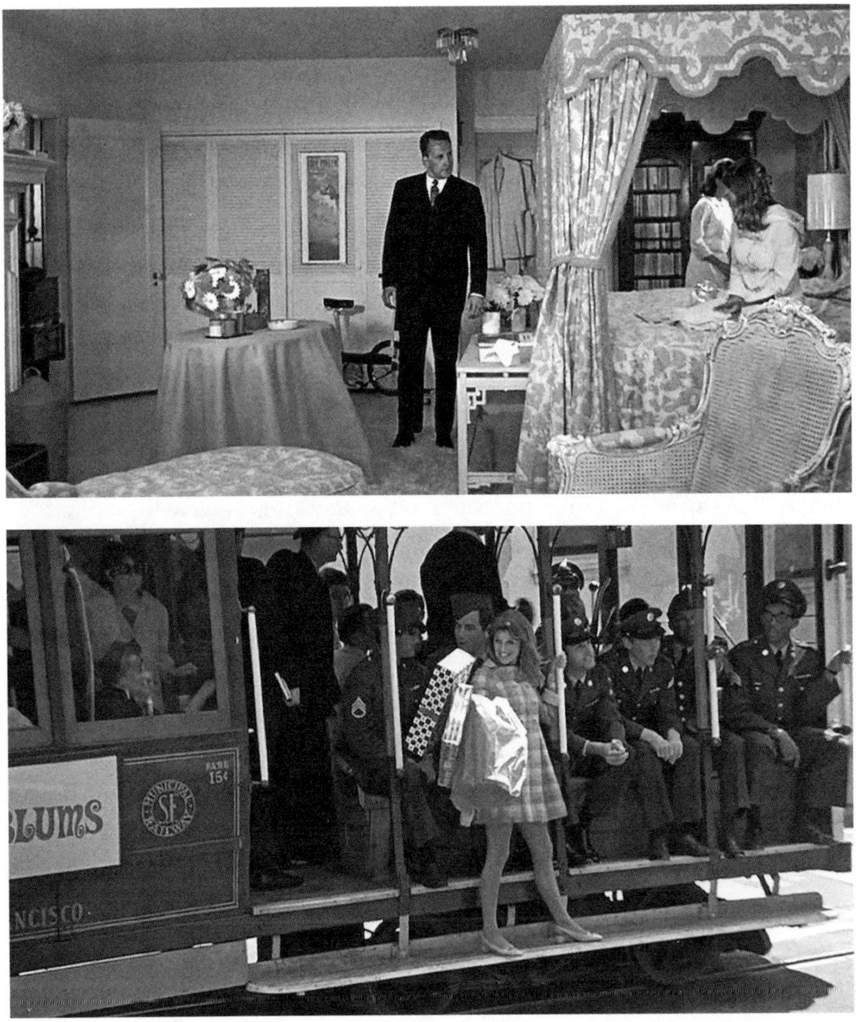

4.7. Color décor and fashion create visual conflicts between Petulia and her surroundings: *top*, her posh bedroom; *bottom*, Petulia in a radiant sun dress on a trolley car filled with soldiers headed for Vietnam.

abruptly jumps to the forefront of the film. They heighten the sense of soullessness and dread hidden beneath Archie's and Petulia's upper-class lives. Rather than emphasizing the growing commercialism of the Summer of Love, Lester emboldens the counterculture through disruptive interjections of music and image with the force to cut through images of a failing mainstream culture.

Petulia stages cultural conflict on the scale of the city through a creative use of San Francisco's diverse architecture. Jet-set mansions and hotels contrast sharply with infinite expanses of tract homes. In Archie and Petulia's first tryst at the ultramodern San Francisco Hilton, the couple walk up the elegantly slanted concrete parking structure, use strange key cards, and fiddle with electronic devices throughout their room. These comical space-age trappings strike a chord similar to that of the high-tech machinery Archie employs at the hospital. The modern domestic architecture of the husband's family home features an audacious cobweb window, an elegantly engineered dream home that entraps rather than comforts. Here the father conducts the family like a business from his desk.

These sterile spaces clearly contrast with the swirling colors, organic lines, and dark interiors of the rock show sequences. Yet Lester introduces a remarkable third space of San Francisco by including a rarely filmed part of the peninsula: Daly City. In a subplot, Archie investigates Petulia's adoption of a Mexican child and finds himself lost in rows of identical houses climbing the hills into the horizon. A pair of hippies fail to orient him, looking equally out of place in this vast, seemingly uninhabited housing development. Wide shots reveal an endless supply of domestic mass production, with working-class homes spread autonomously across the landscape (Figure 4.8). Downtown San Francisco offers the illusion of a dense playground full of culture and landmarks, an antidote to the sprawl of Los Angeles. Unlike Hitchcock, who visited outlying areas to extend the dreamscape of the city, Lester highlights the incompatible forces at play in the American city. If Lester found crass commercialism in the social realm of downtown San Francisco, he also found the physical expansion of this ethos in suburban landscapes, and his film forcefully defines San Francisco as the sum of irreconcilable parts.

Beyond Lester's specific social, aesthetic, and architectural critiques in *Petulia*, his urban montage provides a city symphony. Unlike earlier films of this type—such as *Berlin: Symphony of a Great City* (1927) and *A Man with a Movie Camera* (1929)—*Petulia* is a narrative feature focused on two urban characters, not the city itself. However, Lester's montage exceeds the travelogue interludes featured in films such as *The Pleasure of His Company* or the opening sequences of countless San Francisco films. Instead, jarring cuts draw comparisons between disparate spaces, such as the rock show and the hospital; different times, through flashbacks and flash-forwards; and

4.8. Daly City, a rarely filmed location just south of San Francisco, provides a visual disjunction between working-class suburban sprawl and downtown high society in *Petulia.*

inherent contradictions within spaces, such as the commercial shoot in the natural preserve of Muir Woods. Lester staged scenes, not just establishing shots, at dozens of San Francisco interiors and exteriors. These background settings are imbued with signification, populated by hippies, commercial intrusions, and new technologies. One reviewer who noted the stunning locations of the hotel and the modern mansion described the film as "a gaily-colored patchwork quilt," although she found it lacking in meaning.[146] Indeed, Lester built a patchwork San Francisco composed of distinct, meaningful spaces that clash with each other.

During the 1960s and 1970s, urban designer Colin Rowe developed the concept of the "collage city," which like *Petulia* approaches urban form through montage and juxtaposition. He noted: "Collage is a method deriving its virtue from its irony, because it seems to be a technique for using things and simultaneously disbelieving in them, it is also a strategy which can allow utopia to be dealt with as image, to be dealt with in *fragments* without our having to accept it *in toto*."[147] In *Petulia*, Lester created a similar playful tension between San Francisco's dual identities as a mainstream tourist center and countercultural youth haven, impishly bringing these elements into conversation and into question. His provocative montage and mélange of striking locations offers no final verdict on the city, youth culture, or even Archie and Petulia; although they fail to escape their social mores, they are no less charming or sympathetic in their failure. There is no climactic confrontation between generations, as in the wedding scene in *The Graduate* or the violent shootout in *Bonnie and Clyde*. Rather, San Francisco's charms and failings are its eclecticism, its conglomeration of urban lifestyles, and its mix of generations that can neither coalesce nor escape each other.

In Lester's film, and public perception, urban collage also explains why San Francisco won out as a location over Los Angeles. Lester commented, "Los Angeles is too powerful a city. The images would overwhelm the story. San Francisco is more subtle: therefore more suitable for our picture which is a sad love story. I'm not sure you can tell that kind of a story in Los Angeles." Producer Wagner added, "I consider San Francisco the only city in the world with an honest contemporary flavor."[148] But with such dramatic scenery, how could San Francisco be a more intimate, realistic urban setting than Los Angeles? First, it offered a pedestrian scale, a vibrant core to be traversed by the characters. Second, because the cutting edge of the youth movement remained in San Francisco and Berkeley, the increasingly commercialized hippie aesthetic appeared more authentic there. As one cameraman quipped, "Sure, there's a peace march in L.A. today. But we don't build them like they do up here."[149] By contrast, Los Angeles appeared to be a ruthless corporate town of detached houses. Films set in both San Francisco and Los Angeles, like *The Graduate* and *Point Blank*, dramatically staged this popular distinction.

Bullitt somehow combined these conflicting urban experiences within San Francisco itself. The title cop, played by Steve McQueen, straddles a vicious criminal world and a countercultural paradise. And in the most influential car chase in film history, *Bullitt* transforms San Francisco from a pedestrian oasis into an automotive dreamscape. Although *Petulia* relied on semi-documentary production techniques to efficiently capture dozens of San Francisco locations, *Bullitt* fully embraced the late 1960s aesthetic for semi-documentary realism. Unlike *Petulia*'s kaleidoscopic color portrait of the city, *Bullitt* aggressively deploys dim lighting and dismal locations. And as *Petulia* faded from theaters, *Bullitt* became a runaway hit, not only accelerating the growth of location filmmaking in San Francisco, but also strongly shaping the police genre and gritty cinematography that typified depictions of the city for the first half of the 1970s.

Bullitt: Automotive City

Wagner and Lester described San Francisco as "the most exciting and dynamic community in the Western world today."[150] *Bullitt* directed this energy not toward the people of the city, but toward San Francisco itself, converting cultural energy into vehicular momentum and turning the city's topography into an automotive arena. *Petulia* attempted a realist portrait of San Francisco's cultural landscape; *Bullitt* instead offered the realism of the semi-documentary, heightening the authenticity of the action through an emphasis on physical locations and nontheatrical lighting. *Petulia* explored the internal struggles of its characters within a beautiful city; *Bullitt* captured a sordid city that only a hero could navigate. *Petulia* earned only $1.5 million on a $3.5 million budget;[151] at a cost of $5.5 million, *Bullitt* earned at least $16.4 million during its domestic release, becoming one of the top three films of 1968.[152] Due to its box office success, *Bullitt* became a prototype for Hollywood's urban police films of the 1970s staged in San Francisco and other cities.

Premiering a year before *Bullitt*, *Point Blank* set a clear precedent in both production practice and style. Producers Robert Chartoff and Irwin Winkler hired John Boorman to direct with only one picture to his name, *Having a Wild Weekend* (1965), a rock music comedy in the vein of Richard Lester starring the Dave Clark Five. This was a curious decision, considering *Point Blank*'s gangster plot, in which Walker (Lee Marvin) seeks vengeance on the partner and criminal organization that stole his money and left him for dead. The producers believed that the young audience wanted to see the latest artistic trends, and that a young filmmaker from the hip London scene would prove more valuable (and cheaper) than a Hollywood veteran. On a modest budget of $2.5 million, they hoped for $9 million.[153] The quirky action film grossed only $3.5 million, but *Variety* lauded Boorman's "superior exercise in cinematic virtuosity."[154]

Bullitt producers Phil D'Antoni and Robert Relyea, working for Steve McQueen's company, Solar Productions, made a more calculated risk. They also hired a sophomore director from England, Peter Yates, whose first film, *Robbery* (1967), was a suspenseful restaging of *The Great Train Robbery* shot in cinema verité style.[155] Yates had proven how effectively this style could be applied to an action film. Cinema verité revitalized the semi-documentary with the newest trends and equipment from documentary filmmaking. By contrast, Boorman infused the formulaic gangster genre with an artistic flashback structure associated with European art films. The results elevated *Point Blank* beyond its generic peers, but placed it squarely between two disparate audiences: the younger art cinema crowd and the older action movie audience.

With its ambitious use of locations, *Point Blank* expanded feature filmmaking in San Francisco. Alcatraz had been abandoned as a prison after 1963, but in 1967 it had not yet been fully converted to tourism. Yearly maintenance of the federal facility cost $24,000; MGM offered $2,000 a day for a week or more of location shooting for *Point Blank*, and the agency in charge of the site was more than happy to oblige to save taxpayers the expense.[156] Although a Los Angeles journalist chided the production for not simply using a set, the difference was unmistakable. With free rein over the large, rundown prison, Boorman exploited the location's full value in an opening scene where Reese (John Vernon) shoots Walker after they rob a helicopter making a cash delivery. The massive scale of the desolate ruin of Alcatraz at night allowed for deep-space compositions throughout the eerie interiors and exteriors. The island also has perhaps the best view of downtown San Francisco, against which Boorman staged Walker in the foreground. Alcatraz is the defining location of the film—not only as the site of the betrayal that drives Walker's relentless revenge, but also as a symbolic prison of the past that sets a classical gangster against the dispassionate ruthlessness of a corporatized criminal syndicate.

The conflict between the old-school Walker and the new-school syndicate—nearly indistinguishable from a Fortune 500 company—did not suit San Francisco, the original setting for the entire film. As Boorman later explained, "[San Francisco] was all soft, romantic, pastel shades—a very beautiful place—but the complete opposite of what I wanted for the film. I wanted my setting to be hard, cold and, in a sense, futuristic. I wanted an empty, sterile world, for which Los Angeles was absolutely right."[157] He convinced the producers to move the primary location to Los Angeles, which also lowered location costs. There he staged the principal action at used-car lots, under highways, in guarded penthouse apartments, and at suburban mansions with swimming pools. As Allan Siegel observes, *Point Blank* suggests the postindustrial city's incompatibility with the noir criminal.[158] Walker is a determined man with a code of honor and vengeance facing an abstract landscape concerned only with finance and corporate hierarchy. This value distinction parallels the film's invocations of Los Angeles and San

Francisco, the former portrayed as shallow and materialistic, the latter as passionate and authentic.

For *Bullitt*, Steve McQueen also pushed the association between San Francisco and realism—specifically, the realism inherent to location shooting. In one interview he claimed: "We want to capture the feeling of the city . . . the movement, the productivity, the people along the streets—the whole upbeat feeling of San Francisco. Most films miss that. The Europeans are able to get it—Antonioni, Godard, DeSica."[159] Here McQueen points to the tensions in realism that define *Bullitt*'s aesthetic. Like other productions, the film's goal was to capture the popular energy of late 1960s San Francisco. Yet it also leaned toward neorealism, a location shooting style that depicted the city at its cruelest and most quotidian. The extravagant chase sequence, the cornerstone of the film, pairs a realist style with the highest form of spectacle. All the while, a detective plot and a series of dangerous, dimly lit interior locations make it appear worlds away from Haight-Ashbury. *Bullitt* is remarkably ambivalent, alternatively realistic and fantastical, critical and escapist. While Lester's creative editing in *Petulia* played up the cultural conflicts inherent in San Francisco, Frank Keller's celebrated editing helped smooth out *Bullitt*'s tonal oscillation.

Bullitt also had to balance its police story line with an antiauthoritarian San Francisco counterculture. The source novel, *Mute Witness*, is set in New York, but like *Petulia*, producers adapted the story to the popular San Francisco setting.[160] In mid-1967, *Variety's* Setlowe compared the relationship between police and hippies to an Arab-Israeli truce, making it difficult to imagine a hip San Francisco police detective like McQueen's Frank Bullitt.[161] He could not simply be a tough cop, like the title detectives in *Madigan* (1968) and *Coogan's Bluff* (1968). Rather, as McQueen put it, "This guy Bullitt is an oblique person. . . . He's a man who's earnestly interested in society. . . . Not all police nowadays represent the long arm of the Establishment."[162] The archetype for the antiestablishment detective in San Francisco was the title character in *Peter Gunn*, and Bullitt showed many of the same traits. After escorting a witness to a dingy hotel, he meets his girlfriend, Cathy (Jacqueline Bissett), at her design studio in a modern loft. They go to dinner at a hip restaurant featuring a folk band, with hippies and African Americans among its patrons. Like Peter Gunn, Bullitt is equally adept at navigating San Francisco's youth culture and policing the city's most dangerous corners. While not a private eye, he behaves like one, bucking police and political authority to pursue suspects.

Bullitt benefited from Mayor Alioto's earliest efforts to lure filmmakers to San Francisco. In January 1968, he announced a new plan for the annual San Francisco Film Festival. Claude Jarman Jr., a former child actor who played the boy in *The Yearling* (1946), not only drew high-profile films to the festival, but used it as an opportunity to convince visiting filmmakers to shoot in San Francisco. Indeed, filmmakers were practically given a key to the city that year. *Bullitt* occupied up to eight city blocks at a time for the epic chase sequence, which despite this generous allotment still took several weeks to shoot. San Francisco's architecture added further danger since many doors and garages open directly onto the sidewalk, meaning an uninformed resident could accidentally pull out in front of a careening stunt car. To prevent such accidents, cooperative police officers walked the entire route of each driving shot with the crew, securing whole blocks for filmmaking.[163]

Like *Petulia*, *Bullitt* benefited from San Francisco socialites' desire for cameos. Producers secured a ritzy home in Russian Hill as the setting for a political benefit for Senator Chalmers (Robert Vaughn), who interferes with Bullitt's case. The owner, Kate Morrissey, appears briefly in a non-speaking role (Figure 4.9).[164] Alioto recognized this enthusiasm as well, turning the San Francisco premier of *Bullitt* into a benefit for construction

4.9. Producers helped secure a mansion on Russian Hill by giving the owner, Kate Morrissey, a cameo in *Bullitt* (Warner Bros.–Seven Arts, 1968).

of a swimming pool in Hunter's Point. Warner Bros.–Seven Arts donated $25,000 to the project and in turn received publicity for a gala premiere. The first 150 people who purchased $100 tickets were invited to a champagne pre-reception at the Palace of the Legion of Honor and, after the movie, dinner at the Imperial Palace restaurant.[165] Hollywood, the mayor, and the starstruck socialites all got their money's worth.

Despite San Francisco's hospitality, the complicated and expansive car chase put *Bullitt* three weeks behind schedule, and Warner Bros. tried to clamp down the way studios always had: wrapping the location shoot and finishing the car chase on the backlot. The filmmakers found this preposterous, and McQueen had to flex his industry muscle to preserve *Bullitt*'s location aesthetic.[166] After a weekend meeting in Hollywood, he returned with a promise to finish the film in San Francisco. The cost was forfeiting a six-picture deal between Warner Bros. and McQueen's Solar Productions after just the first picture. *Bullitt*'s immediate success was likely a bitter pill for the short-lived Seven Arts studio heads, who might have prevailed over a lesser star. Yates, who had insisted on shooting entirely on location, scrapping the originally scheduled studio days, credited McQueen for having both the power and conviction as an actor-producer to defend the look of the picture.[167]

Seven Arts' predicament reveals how much uncertainty extensive location shooting introduced to production. McQueen estimated that television-trained directors like Yates and Lester averaged sixty to seventy setups per day, compared to the studio average of eight to twelve. At that pace, the major savings on set construction and studio rentals balanced higher transportation and living costs. But Yates suggested, "Studios don't like shooting of this kind. They don't have a close control. It's the beginning of total independence. This is the first major film of this kind ever shot entirely on location with an all-American crew."[168] How could a studio predict whether this freedom was warranted? Lester had a far better track record on location than Yates, but the San Francisco locations provided far more box office value for *Bullitt* than *Petulia*. The daily value of shooting on location also varied tremendously. The car chase in *Bullitt* and the party scene in *Petulia* required far more days for fewer pages of script than any other sequences.

Both films' reliance on editing heightened the uncertainty of location production. While Lester could shoot more setups per day, he also needed to overshoot the script, building the film in post-production from a variety of fragmented clips. Editor Frank Keller, who would win an Oscar for *Bullitt*, faced a similar task. Other editors credited Keller with figuring out an ingenious way to cover up a mistake during the car chase, when a stunt car filled with dummies triggered the climactic car explosion too early. A short montage hides the mistake and preserves the excitement.[169] Nonetheless, the car chase stretches the limits of continuity editing, tracing an impossible path through the city that knocks five hubcaps off the villain's car.[170] Upon completion, the chase looked so remarkable that the producers arranged to show the whole scene on *The Ed Sullivan Show* to promote the film's release,[171] even though as unedited footage, it looked messy enough for the studio to kill a six-picture deal.

One of *Bullitt*'s editing innovations came even before shooting began. In San Francisco, the production rented a large vacant room so Keller could edit throughout principal photography.[172] He screened dailies and cut sequences at a projection space around the block from his cutting room. Keller took immediate note of the intended style and construction from the producers on site, who could also confer on added scenes without delay. Through the cooperation of Warners' editing department and San Francisco's proximity to Los Angeles, dailies arrived in sync just a day after shooting.[173] On-site editing helped balance the uncertainty of location footage that required a consistent look despite being shot in multiple locations over several days. When they left San Francisco, the producers could be reasonably certain that they had the picture they wanted in the can.

Working entirely on location, Yates and cinematographer Bill Fraker chose to shoot exclusively with Arriflex cameras. Although this small, often handheld camera had been regularly used by Hollywood filmmakers throughout the 1960s, it had been limited to specific tasks, such as action scenes on location; typical setups relied on the industry-standard Mitchells. The most celebrated use of the camera came when it was mounted inside and outside of speeding cars, which was as much an achievement of the rigging as of the camera itself. With so much time devoted to shooting the chase, the crew experimented with aluminum railings and flatbed mounts that gave previously impossible but remarkably stable images from the point of view of the car and driver. Meanwhile, by using up to five cameras at a time, Fraker could cover the high-speed stunts from various angles. Cameramen could test out new techniques while traditional methods, such as panning with the cars' movement, clearly covered the action.[174] Keller's final cut involves a clever mix of traditional shots to orient the viewer and car-mounted shots to accentuate the speed and danger.

The signature car chase relied on both improvisation and collaboration on the streets. The stunts had to be carefully choreographed, and Yates welcomed suggestions from cameramen and stuntmen. For instance, if a stuntman recommended a better hill a few blocks away, they would readjust the setup. Fraker remembers that Yates began the picture with storyboards but abandoned them as the film seemed to take on a momentum of its own for the entire crew.[175] With large tracts of the city open for shooting, the filmmakers let the locations dictate what should happen on film, and the results took full advantage of nearly every twist, turn, and elevation that San Francisco had to offer. This was a far cry from Hitchcock's minute instructions to the second unit for the driving sequences in *Vertigo* (1958).[176]

While the choice of Arriflexes for action scenes was conventional, its use for the remainder of the film was intrepid. Crews worked in daunting interior locations, particularly two poorly lit, seedy hotels with very small rooms.[177] Here the smaller size of the camera proved even more essential, particularly when it required a larger rig for recording sound (Figure 4.10). Tire screeches could be added during post-production, but attempting to capture dialogue on location necessitated a large camera blimp. The Arriflex opened up cinema verité techniques to the entire picture. Fraker had left studio work as a cinematographer to shoot television commercials and documentaries, hoping to learn less formal techniques.[178] He applied this experience to *Bullitt*, revitalizing the semi-documentary by combining established Hollywood visual storytelling with documentary techniques that depended on the maneuverable Arriflex.

Real locations such as hotels and an actual hospital set a dark, understated tone that helped make the otherwise outlandish car chase believable. They also revealed an underworld of San Francisco never before pictured on-screen. In one scene, as Bullitt scopes out a hotel room for stashing a witness, he peers through a filthy, cracked window overlooking the stained concrete overpasses of the Embarcadero Freeway, the climactic set piece in *The Lineup* (Figure 4.11). This ugly view also holds potential danger, leading Bullitt to caution the witness to avoid the window in case of a sniper. As the cars stream by, we see the automotive landscape that Bullitt will soon need to traverse. But unlike the later spectacle of hills and surrounding mountains at full speed, we see the interstitial eyesores of a slum hotel.

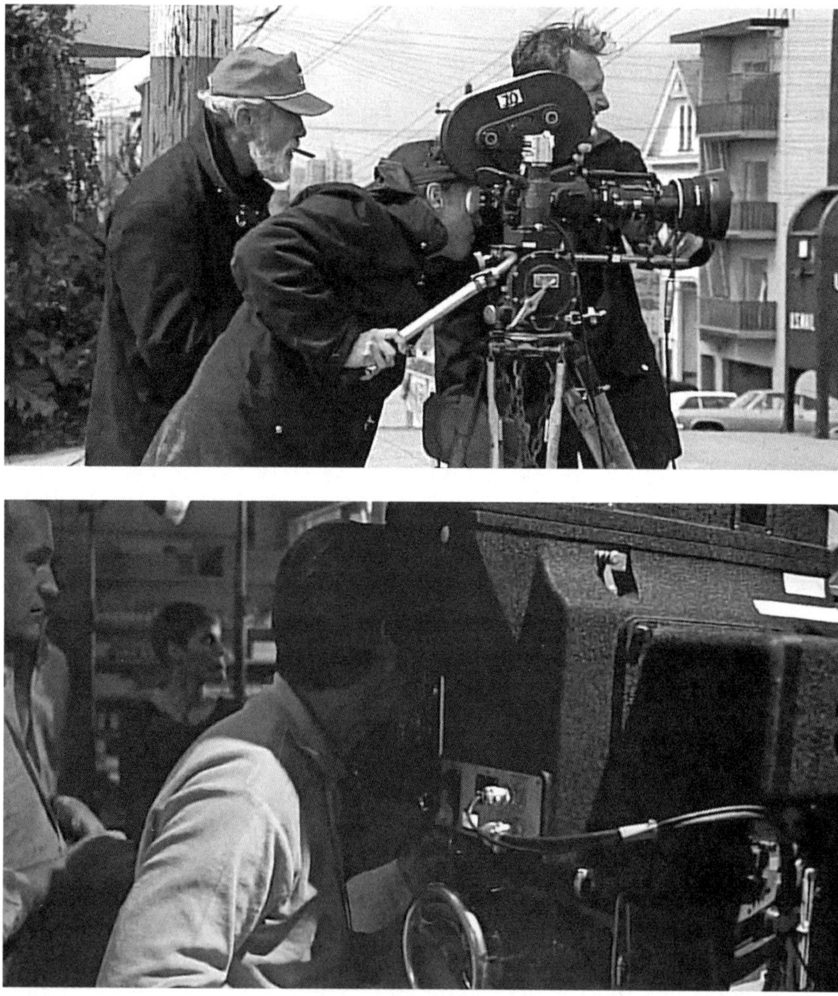

4.10. The unblimped Arriflex camera (*top*) offered flexibility for shooting in the streets, while the bulkier blimped camera (*bottom*) still proved more maneuverable than the standard studio Mitchell for shooting location interiors for *Bullitt* (*Steve McQueen: A Commitment to Realism* [Warners Bros.–Seven Arts, 1968]).

The bleakest setting in the film is the interior of an actual hospital, the setting for several scenes in the first half, including the foot chase of a would-be assassin through the corridors. Working on closed floors of the hospital, the crew could set up scaffolds of lights; otherwise, they changed out fluorescent ceiling lights or filtered them to prevent creating a greenish hue on film. A few times they left the lights unfiltered, casting

4.11. A dreary hotel room overlooking the Embarcadero Freeway reveals the ugly side of San Francisco in *Bullitt.*

an alien green glow over the dark institutional setting.[179] Ironically, by testing the limits of low lighting on color stock, the low-key look associated with black-and-white realism at times appeared unrealistic. For instance, a shaft of daylight through the windows reveals a hospital inexplicably bathed in shadow (Figure 4.12). As Bullitt walks through the hallways, he nearly drops out of sight between the staggered ceiling lights. Seeking semi-documentary realism, Fraker relied on dim source lights, but the lighting bears as little resemblance to a daytime hospital as any theatrically lit film noir.

The film's finale at the San Francisco airport further tested the limits of exposure and realism. The script called for Bullitt to chase his suspect through an airfield at night, but the actual runway left few lighting options; there was nowhere to place a generator, and no way to run cables across an active runway. Relying on battery-powered lights, Fraker pushed the exposure a stop; Yates insisted on two stops. The result is one of the lowest-key color sequences of the 1960s, but the brightly lit planes and the sounds of gunfire help orient the viewer. McQueen added realism by performing a dangerous stunt, running under a moving plane.[180] Thus by eking out an image and risking the actor-producer's safety, *Bullitt* gained authenticity and production value that would have been unattainable and prohibitively expensive on the studio lot.

4.12. A dim color film aesthetic connotes realism in *Bullitt* despite the fact that this hospital location is implausibly dark for a daytime scene.

The film also offers more delicate touches of realism, such as a short sequence in an actual corner grocery store. Bullitt enters the store, moves to the freezer, and grabs a stack of frozen TV dinners. The art director cleared an aisle and rearranged the food to facilitate a dolly shot.[181] This moment encapsulates one of the mundane aspects of Bullitt's life, the bland meals of a policeman too wrapped up in a case to bother cooking. It also provides a glimpse of San Francisco where apartments over storefronts underpin walkable, personable districts. Other moments, like when Bullitt's partner wakes him at his apartment, show not the indomitable driver of the car chase but the unglamorous policeman in his daily grind. These types of scenes are absent from *Dirty Harry* (1971), where Detective Harry Callahan's life away from the case—if he has one—exists only off-screen.

Most of *Bullitt*'s settings reveal none of the San Francisco culture that producers had hoped to capture. Fraker raved about the energy of the city, as well as its various social districts, but aside from the date scene at the restaurant, these places rarely appear in the final film. Instead, San Francisco's postcard views and landmarks stand in for the city's people and culture. Fraker composed shots around famous sites, such as the Bay Bridge or Alcatraz, sometimes panning past the action to end shots on popular landmarks.[182] The speed and danger of the car chase precluded showing many San Francisco residents. Instead, the physical traits of San Francisco invigorate the pursuit. As cars bounce over the famous hills, the city's topography becomes part of the drama. The creative geography of the chase circles around the city streets before exceeding them, pushing into the surrounding hills, meadows, and bay vistas beyond the Golden Gate Bridge.

Bullitt includes weak attempts to reconcile scenic images of the city with the film's bleak semi-documentary interiors. Late in the film, Cathy (Jacqueline Bissett) sees a corpse after intruding on a murder scene in yet another dim hotel. She says, "You're living in a sewer, Frank," and questions whether she really knows him. In the background, industrial structures contaminate the bucolic setting outside the city. The closing scene of the film returns to this idea of Bullitt's duality as a hard-boiled policeman and conscientious member of the city's counterculture. A panning shot shows Cathy's yellow car by the street. Next, Bullitt stares obliquely into the mirror before Yates cuts to a shot of bullets lying on the dresser. This narrative closure suggests a far deeper and more complex figure than the one developed over the course of the film. Cathy's dissatisfaction abruptly appears late in the story, soon after the car chase. Rather than reconcile the competing pleasures of the cosmopolitan and reckless cop, the film feigns resolution by framing Bullitt as one of the ambiguous protagonists common to late 1960s youth-oriented films.

The depiction of San Francisco in *Bullitt* is far less personal than it is in *Petulia,* but equally indebted to authentic locations. Rather than seeking places that captured San Francisco's cultural contradictions, *Bullitt* chose dynamic locations that activated a latent image of the city in automotive motion. Following an opening sequence in Chicago and the film credits, the first image of San Francisco is a bird's-eye view of its streets, with the camera perched above the tall buildings on Nob Hill. A slow zoom draws closer to the street, resting on a taxicab turning. The San Francisco plot begins in this taxi, with a passenger introduced as a witness against the Chicago mob. Yet the zoom also announces the visual logic of the city: the focal point of the urban action will be the movement of cars. Yates often begins scenes with establishing shots where Bullitt parks his Ford Mustang at the next location. Even away from his famed car, Bullitt remains in automotive motion, interviewing a gunshot victim in the back of a moving ambulance or driving through the countryside in his girlfriend's yellow convertible. Highway ramps regularly appear in the background, alluding to the pivotal car chase.

For over a decade, these structures had appeared antithetical to San Francisco's image; *Bullitt*'s ten-minute chase scene recoded these concrete barricades as the most exciting avenue to experiencing San Francisco.

As cars careen through the city, there is a far greater articulation of motion than place. Match cutting created the perception of a continuous ride, with the speed of the chase activating a dormant pleasure in San Francisco's hills. They become rhythmic undulations rather than viewing points, although with each cut Yates offers yet another one of the city's picturesque urban backdrops. There is no clear articulation of direction, and also no time to perceive buildings and districts as more than a backdrop for the action in the streets. The only real delimiter of the distance traveled is the change in scenery from downtown to the surrounding hillsides. Shifts in landscape primarily introduce new obstacles, such as oncoming traffic on one-lane roads and sharp curves etched by rocky hills. Traffic never arrests movement, but merely adds another obstacle to provoke another screaming turn of the wheels. Small details, such as background continuity or a fifth hubcap coming off, are nearly imperceptible within the sheer momentum of the chase. In a single sequence, *Bullitt* exhausts nearly the entire landscape of *Vertigo*.

San Francisco's Summer of Love is what drew *Bullitt* to town, but the film's urban action aesthetic would soon be transplanted to other cities. Neither the scale of highways and airports nor the grim corridors of hospitals and hotels left room for more than cursory gestures toward the specific city of the moment. *Bullitt* instead offers a hybrid of Los Angeles and San Francisco, energizing the former's grit and automania with the latter's spectacular sights and cultural cache. *Bullitt* and *Petulia* both heralded the expansion of studio-backed urban location shooting in the late 1960s. *Bullitt* proved the value of exploring a location not only as a place, but as a set piece.

Despite the film's reliance on some dismal locations and an unvarnished semi-documentary style, the San Francisco of *Bullitt* appears halcyon compared to the San Francisco of *Dirty Harry*, shot only three years later. By the time of its release, *Petulia*'s image of the American city had already fallen out of step with the growing sense of an urban crisis. Warner Bros. asked that *Petulia* be completed by early November for an Easter release, providing six months for the distribution department.[183] Those six months brought the Tet offensive and the assassination of Martin Luther King, followed by riots in many American cities. Returning from Cannes, *Petulia* had its US premiere just days after Robert Kennedy was assassinated in

Los Angeles. San Francisco ceded its spotlight to Chicago in August 1968, when protestors and policemen battled outside of the Democratic National Convention. America was on the verge of chaos, and the primary flashpoints were its cities. Hollywood responded with ruinous urban depictions, and for the first time, San Francisco no longer appeared as the exception to urban blight. By the early 1970s, this filmic city had come to resemble the towering decay of Manhattan.

5

THE MANHATTANIZATION OF SAN FRANCISCO

Dirty Harry and *The Streets of San Francisco*

BULLITT'S SAN FRANCISCO PREMIERE in October 1968 also served as a fundraiser with a goal of $50,000 to defray construction costs for a new swimming pool in the Hunter's Point neighborhood. Following a $25,000 donation from Warner Bros.–Seven Arts, the city built the pool before public funds were allocated, and by the time of the *Bullitt* premiere, it was already in heavy use. There was a pressing reason for the city's rush to build before the project was fully funded.[1] In September 1966, the largely African American community of Hunter's Point was the site of a six-day riot.[2] The new recreation facility was a literal attempt to cool the tension. Alioto had also pushed *Bullitt* producers to hire Hunter's Point residents as extras. In a *Playboy* interview, Eldridge Cleaver, the fugitive spokesman for the Black Panthers, derided Alioto's attempt to buy off pockets of Black revolution with "little handouts" that included paid film and television appearances.[3]

By the end of the 1960s, the violence, property destruction, and racial animosity of a wave of riots had sharply redefined the public image of the American city. The 1965 Watts Rebellion heralded summer uprisings in urban areas throughout the rest of the decade. An August issue of *Life* magazine featured a cover photograph of a Watts resident fleeing his flaming house under the headline "Arson and Street War—Most Destructive Riot in U.S. History: 11 Pages in Color."[4] What many hoped was an isolated tragedy became an ongoing national phenomenon. By the end of the summer of 1967, at least thirty-one cities had experienced riots, including a conflagration in Detroit that required President Johnson to send in the National Guard. This number rose to 125 cities in the week following Martin Luther King's assassination in April 1968. The imagery of the riots became emblematic of an urban crisis. Richard Nixon emphasized urban disorder in his acceptance speech for the Republican presidential nomination: "As we look at America, we see cities enveloped in smoke and flame. We hear sirens in the night."[5]

In a study of American urban decline, Robert Beauregard argues that race riots created a "sharp break" with the previous fifteen years of postwar discourse. By 1968, urban decline had become "urban crisis" as violence and crime in the central cities became the second biggest political issue after Vietnam.[6] In fact, these two crises quickly grew visually and linguistically intertwined. Beauregard notes that the common descriptors of the riots, including "anarchy, guerilla war, snipers . . . race war," were terms that could also easily describe the conflict abroad.[7] By the early 1970s, they could also describe Hollywood's image of the city in police dramas like *Dirty Harry* (1971) and *The Streets of San Francisco* (1972–1977). Such depictions fit the bleak reality of New York, a nearly bankrupt city that faced numerous social and financial crises from the late 1960s through the early 1970s.[8] Yet San Francisco had carefully preserved its image as the American urban exception, making the city's aesthetic degradation far more jarring.

The Hunter's Point riot failed to mar San Francisco's distinct national image. Kenneth Clark, whose *Dark Ghetto: Dilemmas of Social Power* (1967) harshly criticized America's racist urban policies, listed the Bay Area as the possible exception to "creeping blight."[9] Neighboring cities overshadowed San Francisco's own struggles with race and campus violence, with Oakland gaining attention for the Black Panther movement and protests at Berkeley drawing attention away from a prolonged student strike at San Francisco State.[10] On the national stage, San Francisco's Summer of Love seemed a direct contrast to the summer of riots in other American cities.[11] Mayor

Alioto helped quell a near riot following the King assassination, and San Francisco largely preserved an internal and external perception as an oasis from racial conflicts.[12] While other cities fought for downtown investment, San Francisco continued its so-called vertical earthquake, with skyscrapers rising throughout the 1960s and 1970s. Neighborhood activists decried what other critics called "Manhattanization," which drove up rents and blocked cherished scenery.[13] But in national news coverage, San Francisco still merited its slogan, "Everybody's Favorite City"; as the *Chicago Tribune* put it in 1971, "despite all the change, the city is still one of the most beguiling in the world."[14]

On-screen, Hollywood performed a different type of Manhattanization—a reflection of new production strategies and aesthetic paradigms for location shooting. As San Francisco grew as a filmmaking center, the city drew production not only for its aesthetic and cultural appeal, but also for its financial and logistical advantages. Ironically, San Francisco leeched films from a struggling New York City only to appear just as grimy and crime-ridden. This bleak urban aesthetic reflected not only cultural pessimism about American cities, but major advancements in location shooting technology. Filmmakers now had an unprecedented ability to capture nearly any part of the city, day or night, at a time when the most desired locations were the dark corners that defined a revived semi-documentary form of urban realism. The setting of *Dirty Harry*—a city marked by pervasive crime, red-light districts, and macabre violence—made the San Francisco of *Bullitt* look like an urban paradise. *The Streets of San Francisco* reinforced and serialized this image of the decaying, crime-ridden city.

Although the urban crisis had altered the image of the city, a devastating recession between 1969 and 1972 fundamentally altered Hollywood production. Mounting debt on expensive films with middling box office prospects had left Hollywood studios with little money to invest in new productions. As a result, the focus switched to relatively inexpensive films shot largely on location, taking advantage of both new location equipment and union exceptions. By the early 1970s, location shooting had become the dominant method of Hollywood filmmaking, particularly for young filmmakers shooting low-budget features. San Francisco mayor Joseph Alioto took advantage of this trend and lured filmmakers from Hollywood with extensive cooperation and production support. *Dirty Harry* epitomized this confluence of location shooting and an aesthetic of urban decay. Taking full advantage of San Francisco locations and local government support, it depicted the city as a chaotic wasteland. The film's surprise box office success helped popularize the image of a dangerous, blighted San Francisco, seen also on *The Streets of San Francisco*, whose depictions of a city overrun by violent crime appeared weekly in prime time.

A MATTER OF SURVIVAL

In 1972, the University of Southern California titled its annual film conference "A Matter of Survival." The conference logo was a film canister stamped with the epitaph "Here lies the Hollywood film industry, 1910–1970" (Figure 5.1).[15] Major directors such as Blake Edwards, Peter Bogdanovich, Rouben Mamoulian, and Sydney Pollack participated in panels along with industry leaders such as Fox president Gordon Stulburg and other figures, including screenwriter John Milius and cinematographer John Alonzo. Although encouraged by recent hits like *The Godfather* (1972) and *The French Connection* (1971), Professor Arthur Knight estimated an 80 percent industry unemployment rate, an overstatement reflecting the public and private fears of Hollywood's total collapse. Two weeks later, MPAA president Jack Valenti and *French Connection* director William Friedkin addressed another event at Babson University, a seminar titled "Who'll Save Hollywood?."[16] What scholars now term "the Hollywood Recession" was at the time commonly referred to as "the Hollywood Depression," indicative of the industry's veritable collapse between 1969 and 1971.[17]

Hollywood acutely suffered from the social upheaval of 1968. In "perhaps the most civil violent year of the 20th century," urban fear had an immediate impact at the box office.[18] Fearing racial violence, both commuters and inner-city residents avoided downtown theaters. The youth audience, shaped by a cultural revolution, remained a key but increasingly unpredictable demographic. New York, the most important urban movie market, was particularly hard hit by everything from a flu outbreak, to a Broadway strike, to the "intangible box-office loss" in and around Harlem due to "black militancy and white backlash."[19] New York's slogan, "Fun City," became a punchline, referred to as "a sad joke" in a 1969 travel article lauding San Francisco's tourist appeal.[20] *Variety* labeled it "not-so-Fun City."[21]

These external factors proved far less damaging to Hollywood than an internal industry crisis. By July 1968, the slate of Christmas and winter releases included major hits such as *The Graduate* ($40 million), *Guess Who's Coming to Dinner*, and the second run of *Bonnie and Clyde* ($16.5 million).

5.1. A tombstone for Hollywood served as the logo for a USC film conference in 1972, symbolizing the depths of Hollywood's early 1970s recession (*American Cinematographer*, June 1972).

A year later, *Bullitt* was the sole film approaching a $15 million gross. The only promising summer hits in wide release were *Midnight Cowboy* (1969) and a Cinerama picture, *Krakatoa, East of Java* (1969). Expensive roadshow releases, particularly dependent on struggling downtown theaters, played poorly, with rare exceptions including *Funny Girl* (1968) and *Oliver!* (1968). Hollywood's hopes were riding on a record $200 million inventory of just twenty to twenty-five expensive films.[22]

Even before the failure of films like *Paint Your Wagon* (1969) and *Darling Lili* (1970), Hollywood's record inventory had come at the worst possible time. The 1969 national recession had spiked interest rates for film production effectively above 10 percent. With some $1.2 billion in total inventory in Hollywood between 1969 and early 1970, the $120 million in interest was roughly equal to the entire yearly box office gross for a major studio.[23] Coupled with poor box office returns for most of this inventory, studios were able to survive only through various financial maneuvers facilitated by the Nixon administration.[24]

As in previous decades, spiraling debt immediately led to backlot divestment. In January 1969, Paramount sold its Cahuenga lot for $9 million, ostensibly to honor a consent decree for purchasing the Desilu lot in 1967.[25] In September 1969, Paramount laid off 150 workers, putting the Cahuenga sale in the context of a major restructuring to reduce overhead. Paramount not only needed to save money, but also to become more competitive as a rental lot. Independent producers increasingly chafed at hiring studio personnel such as crews and set designers as part of a production deal, making many backlot employees not worth the overhead cost. Meanwhile, Paramount had a surplus of about forty finished pictures, so in-house production employees were largely superfluous. Paramount's downsizing was the most visible, but every studio gradually shed weekly employees over the first half of 1969.[26] Even Universal, which as late as January 1969 had planned to add two new stages, cut 100 to 150 workers in November, shaving roughly $2 million off the payroll.[27]

By 1970, the cuts had grown drastic, resembling the production downturn and overhead slashing of the late 1940s. A reeling Fox decided to reduce production from eighteen to twenty features a year to twelve to sixteen. This echoed recent announcements by MGM, Paramount, and other companies. The goal was an $11 million spending decrease, $6 million of which had already been achieved by gutting operating costs. A restructured Fox looked to better exploit its realty assets, but it still took years for the studio to emerge from debt. Despite a string of hits, including *Butch Cassidy and the Sundance Kid* (1969), *Hello, Dolly!* (1969), *M*A*S*H* (1970), and *Patton* (1970), Fox took a $17 million second quarter loss in 1970, with substantial box office profits merely chipping away at the massive debt interest. In September 1970, Fox still had $159 million tied up in film inventory, just 25 percent less than at the start of the year. Despite slashing employment and production budgets, the studio still lacked funds to mount any major new productions.[28]

Another solution involved increasing cash assets by selling physical ones, evidenced by MGM, which sold off the vast majority of its studio real estate. New owner Kirk Kerkorian and his studio head, James Aubrey, planned to sell all but 20 of MGM's 140 acres of Culver City lots. They not only off-loaded the studio's real estate, but also sold its camera department to Panavision and held a public auction of studio memorabilia, including Judy Garland's ruby slippers from *The Wizard of Oz* (1939). The biggest parcel of land went to a real estate developer, not a production company, revealing how little contemporary filmmakers valued MGM's famous standing sets. A 1970 internal study found that only demolition costs lowered the estimated real estate value; on paper, the value of existing structures was negligible.[29] Part of this devaluation stemmed from decades of neglect; MGM's New York Street served as the post-apocalyptic setting for *Soylent Green* (1973), and the decaying sets needed little alteration.[30] Surrounding these blighted urban sets were acres of fallow lots enclosed by chainlink fences, creating a dismal gray zone in Culver City. As the wrecking balls began swinging in 1972, a television documentary and a *60 Minutes* special on MGM publicized the death of the Hollywood dream factory.[31]

Despite such dire images and a common refrain from filmmakers that studio sets were unrealistic, *Variety* suggested in a December 1970 lead story that "the demise of the backlot is somewhat exaggerated." Neither Universal, Columbia, nor even Fox had sold off major backlot properties, including Fox's Malibu ranch, which usefully doubled as Korea for *M*A*S*H*.[32] By 1971, with no end in sight for Hollywood's financial crisis, plans for studio facility mergers began reappearing, as in the 1950s and 1960s. Columbia discussed becoming a co-tenant on the Warner Bros. lot so it could sell off its main lot and ranch. Other mergers, such as a "tri-studio complex" for Fox, MGM, and Columbia (or another three-studio lot with separate entrances housed on the Paramount lot) gained less traction. As in previous decades, corporate competition stymied such mergers, and *Variety* expressed the hope that the current desperation would overcome these obstacles to efficiency.[33]

An aside in a *Variety* article on plans for new studios provided a compelling argument for the economic value of the backlot: "Some corporate owners of the studios have been waging a war of attrition, hoping to outlast other lots and therefore sharing in the windfall of increased usage when factors induced other studios to close."[34] With MGM shutting down production, and other studios contemplating selling land to pay down debt, studios that had weathered the depression could see a major payoff. MCA-Universal, with the best monetized and most modern facilities, including their profitable studio tour, stood to become the biggest winner.[35] The steady rise of independent production and the steady demand for television production space meant that the surviving lots could earn far more from rentals than they could save by shooting their own films on the lot rather than on location.

Employment conditions off the lot had grown desperate too, as high inventories, runaway films, and dwindling financing left few active productions employing crews. In late 1969, several craft unions reported upward of 50 percent unemployment. Production workers suffered the most. In fall 1968, the cameramen's local had virtually full unemployment, with 159 members out of work.[36] A spokesman for the propmen's union called it the bleakest employment situation since 1933. Despite IATSE's successful lobbying of Los Angeles to repeal its film inventory tax, which regularly caused end-of-year slowdowns, Hollywood production work remained sparse.[37]

Unemployment persisted even as the pace of runaway production abated. Hollywood began to pull out of Britain, which had been a major destination, due to a combination of factors, including the anti-runaway campaign, the popularity of American stories such as *The Graduate* and *Rosemary's Baby* (1968), and a reduction in Eady Fund subsidies.[38] And like *Petulia* and *Bullitt*, other European-helmed films, including *Midnight Cowboy* and *Zabriskie Point* (1970), avoided Los Angeles entirely. British director Michael Winner shot United Artists' *Lawman* (1971) in Mexico and estimated saving $1 million on a $3.5 million below-the-line budget by avoiding studio overhead and union labor costs.[39] With the support of Mayor Yorty of Los Angeles, production workers continued to hope for an American version of the Eady plan that never materialized.[40]

The biggest impediment to production continued to be high inventory and interest expenses, which ate up funds for new production. Not only did approved budgets tighten, but the so-called front money needed to start production was as scarce as it had been in years. Several pictures already in motion on "step deals" were dropped well before shooting when studios refused to pay for the next stage of development.[41] When Yorty asked for federal assistance to address the "catastrophic" employment situation, *Variety* took issue with the implication that the studios were nearly bankrupt.[42] Indeed, the financial maneuvers and tax shelters built by the Nixon administration may have saved the studios, but they left production workers to fend for themselves.

These dire straits left unions with little leverage to negotiate. In early 1969, IATSE secured a 22 percent raise by the fourth year of its new contract, but the union's demands for television residuals and a percentage on runaway films, intended to curb foreign production, were flatly refused.[43] Labor-saving production devices such as the Cinemobile soon gained industry-wide acceptance, despite early resistance from the Hollywood Teamsters.[44] There was also a rise in non-union companies, often crewed by union members too desperate for work to report the violation. As one labor executive suggested, "The unions have lost control."[45]

The overwhelming beneficiaries of the Hollywood Recession were the up-and-coming young filmmakers. On the heels of the success of *The Monkees* television series, young production executives Bert Schneider and Steve Blauner joined producer-director Bob Rafelson to form BBS, a small production company focused on low-budget films for the youth market. After *Easy Rider* (1969) became a major hit for BBS on a miniscule budget, Hollywood increasingly hired young filmmakers to target a countercultural youth film market that older producers were struggling to understand.[46] The success of *Easy Rider* was particularly attractive in a depressed market; with so little capital to invest in production, the low-risk, high-reward strategy of low-budget filmmaking offered an alternative to the more conventional blockbusters that cash-strapped studios could barely afford to finance. Following *Easy Rider*, Columbia struck a six-picture deal with BBS, with each picture guaranteed to cost no more than $1 million.[47] The success of *Five Easy Pieces* (1970) and *The Last Picture Show* (1971) more than offset losses on unpopular films like *Drive, He Said* (1971).

The $1 million number was far from arbitrary. IATSE had agreed to special exemptions for pictures budgeted under $1 million provided they shot in Los Angeles or used Hollywood crews on location. The immediate beneficiaries were American International Pictures and BBS.[48] On the one hand, this was a reasonable compromise; union regulations were crafted around large studio productions, where hard-won concessions amounted to a much smaller fraction of the below-the-line cost than on low-budget films. On the other hand, this move spoke to how desperate union members had become, particularly when these skeleton-crewed productions offered few jobs in return for the exemptions. By the end of 1972, BBS was still clashing with the unions, arguing that their regulations put an undue burden on low-budget filmmakers. The historically protective cameramen's union refused to allow Néstor Almendros, a French citizen, to shoot *Gone Beaver* for BBS without hiring a union standby cameraman; Almendros's Hollywood career was delayed for years until *Days of Heaven* (1978), a landmark achievement in cinematography.[49]

Francis Ford Coppola also benefited from union concessions, making *The Rain People* on a $750,000 budget. He assembled a crew of ten—hired from New York, Los Angeles, and Chicago—and hired additional technicians at each location in eighteen different states. This small picture helped launch his new San Francisco production house, American Zoetrope. Despite various problems with the sound mix for *Rain People*, an indication of Zoetrope's limited professional experience, Warner Bros. allowed Coppola and his young partners, including George Lucas, to continue learning on a low budget. A five-picture deal, each budgeted under $1 million, constituted a minor investment with the potential for major returns if Coppola produced even a modest hit. Although Coppola emphasized the virtues of intimate films, a *Variety* headline underscored the benefit to the studio: "Hollywood's New Breed of 'Personal' Films Has Corporate Angle: Modest Budgets."[50]

Tighter budgets paid off for more expensive, more conventional films as well. Ted Ashley, Warners' new production head, gave his first green light to *Woodstock* (1970), an inexpensive documentary that grossed $13.5 million domestically. He pushed "lean negative costs" not only for youth films, but for the full 1971 slate of thirteen features, averaging a mere $1.7 million budget. With a reasonable budget, Warner Bros. could take risks, such as the seedy plot of *Klute* (1971); the film paid off handsomely at $6 million in rentals, without needing a broader audience to justify its budget. While many companies budgeted films to break even in the United States and begin earning abroad, Warner Bros. doubled production costs on several domestically targeted films, including *Dirty Harry*, *McCabe and Mrs. Miller* (1971), and *A Clockwork Orange* (1971). By focusing on the US market, Warner Bros. also focused on specifically American settings, including in three of the above-mentioned films, as well as *Deliverance* (1972), *Steelyard Blues* (1972), *Cotton Comes to Harlem* (1972), and *What's Up, Doc?* (1972).[51] This was a far cry from the expensive European epics of the 1960s, although each production marked a return to America, not Hollywood.

Despite the Hollywood Recession, enthusiasm for tightly budgeted films, cheaply produced films rarely paid off. Coppola and Lucas had incredible success on big-budget features but struggled to make a profitable "personal" film, from Coppola's *Rain People* to Lucas's debut, *THX 1138* (1971). Warner Bros. looked brilliant for backing *Woodstock*, but similar attempts at cashing in on the youth counterculture, such as *Dusty and Sweets Mcgee* (1971) and *Medicine Ball Caravan* (1971), went nowhere. Meanwhile, *Billy Jack* (1971), an inexpensive Warners' acquisition, was a surprise hit with the middle-American youth market.[52] Other than their low costs, no formula explained the success of disparate films like *Easy Rider*, *Woodstock*, and *Billy Jack*—nor the failure to replicate it.

With dozens of low-budget features by young filmmakers failing to produce another hit like *The Graduate* or *Easy Rider*, veteran producers such as Walter Mirisch questioned Hollywood's cheap, "Don't trust anybody over thirty" production strategy. Producers seemed to ignore the enormous returns on ambitious mainstream projects such as *Airport* (1970) and *Love Story* (1970), as well as overseas audiences with far different tastes than those in the US. While not advocating for outrageous budgets, Mirisch saw less opportunity for cheap, youth-targeted films to expand beyond that audience. Following the success of *The Godfather*, Kerkorian questioned his company's approach to rapid filmmaking. MGM got its inexpensive films to market in an average of five months instead of the average ten-month lag between the start of production and a film's release. This allowed them to quickly capitalize on relevant topics and market trends. But as Kerkorian lamented, "It remains difficult to get a 'Godfather,' 'Fiddler on the Roof' or 'Cabaret' to market five months after putting it into production."[53] As Hollywood's financial crisis subsided and tight-fisted production strategies yielded little profit, studios renewed their emphasis on more expensive productions with wider box office appeal.

The French Connection (1971), which won the Academy Award for Best Picture, exemplified Hollywood's new economics. Producer Phil D'Antoni managed to finish the film for $2.2 million, which was half the cost of *Bullitt* but saw similar box office success. Crucial savings came by hiring less-established talent, as with Dustin Hoffman in *The Graduate*. With Gene Hackman starring rather than Steve McQueen, above-the-line costs dropped from $1.7 million to $500,000. D'Antoni also reduced below-the-line costs by $1 million, despite the same shooting schedule of seventy days. This was not a matter of belt-tightening but, primarily, the result of key technological improvements in the three years since *Bullitt* had premiered. These developments made location shooting far more efficient, reducing budgets and production schedules while allowing cinematographers to shoot effectively in almost total darkness. With below-the-line costs rising from 60 percent for *Bullitt* to 77 percent for *The French Connection*, location shooting had come to rival star power.[54] *Dirty Harry* followed this trend in San Francisco. As in other cities, the most desirable places to shoot were oddly enough the dark corners and dim, cramped interiors of blighted districts.

SHOOTING IN THE DARK

Much of *Dirty Harry* was shot on location in San Francisco at night, including sequences where actors are barely visible in the darkness. These shadowy settings not only provided an atmosphere of urban dread for the gritty police films of the early 1970s, but also offered a sense of adventure for filmmakers. Faster film stock allowed cinematographers to shoot with so little light that they could barely see their equipment. Representative of the urban crisis, low-key interiors and dark streets also prompted urban exploration, with filmmakers seeking out locations that were only feasible with new technologies.

When Eastman's 5254 stock appeared on the market in 1968, filmmakers had limited access to the fast new film. Not surprisingly, Haskell Wexler, who preferred shooting documentary-style on location with available light, found a way to acquire some for *Medium Cool* (1969). Directing his first feature film for a major studio, Wexler staged actors within real scenes of American upheaval, culminating in the melee between policemen and protestors at the August 1968 Democratic National Convention in Chicago. The innovative film blended documentary and narrative filmmaking to capture actual revolutionary events, but Wexler was also excited about a handful of dim interiors shot on Eastman 5254, which made him realize the implications of the faster negative. For natural interior lighting, he simply put a brighter bulb in a household lamp, supplemented slightly with professional lights. The result saved five hours of preparation time and, in his opinion, looked better.[55]

Wexler gained further light sensitivity from a fast new pair of still photography lenses adapted to fit his small custom Éclair camera. He soon learned that he could "push" the 5254 one f-stop in development without noticeably more grain, gaining even more effective speed and allowing him to capture a sharp image of the lead actress (Verna Bloom) crossing a Chicago bridge at night without additional lighting. Taken together, the faster stock, faster lenses, and pushed development reached a photographic milestone. Wexler marveled, "Everything you can see with your naked eye you can photograph in color."[56] Cinematographers had long prided themselves on their ability to create natural lighting using high-powered lights to simulate the world as seen through the human eye. Now color filmmaking technology could do almost the same with available light, and for the first time, virtually any location could be filmed, often without additional lighting.

Wexler's unconventional shooting style and embrace of non-studio equipment tempered the impact of his breakthroughs with low light. But a few months later, the venerable James Wong Howe performed his own experiment. In what *American Cinematographer* described as "a radical departure from traditional technique," Howe shot the big-budget feature *The*

Molly Maguires (1970) using quartz lights instead of brute arcs. He originally wanted to shoot the feature in black-and-white due to the difficult lighting conditions and gritty tone of a coal mining drama, but Paramount refused, knowing this would hurt its resale value for television. Despite challengingly low-lit settings, arc lights were "hellishly expensive," and 70 percent of the film was shot on location in rural Pennsylvania and Ohio. Arc lights required massive generators, operators for the generators, and trained operators for each individual light. They also frequently smoked and flickered, halting filming while operators changed carbons and waited minutes for them to fully ignite. After years of downsizing and protectionist union practices, most skilled arc light operators had retired, and few young technicians knew how to properly handle them.[57]

The Molly Maguires was an expensive box office failure, but Howe's cinematography helped lower the cost of future Hollywood productions by proving the efficacy of smaller lights.[58] Once shooting wrapped, Paramount had Howe perform a direct comparison test between conventional lights and quartz lights. The detailed findings ran alongside an article on making the film in *American Cinematographer*. Both exterior and interior shots looked nearly identical.[59] In the midst of an economic crisis, Hollywood grew more willing to challenge basic production practices and came to realize that newer technologies could not only complement but supplant standard equipment. Approval from an old master of naturalistic lighting signaled a period of greater flexibility for cinematographers, much like the late 1940s, when another industry crisis had forced them to adapt to stricter schedules.

An early 1970s boom in new production equipment greatly reduced production costs and increased mobility on location. Since the 1940s, outside technology such as the photoflood lights used by William Daniels on *The Naked City* had occasionally trickled upward, moving from industrial and commercial producers to television and finally Hollywood feature production. Yet the ongoing use of arc lights in the 1970s, nearly a decade after quartz lights had gained professional attention, speaks to the reluctance of Hollywood cinematographers to abandon familiar tools. Studios also had little incentive to pay for new equipment if the old equipment was still effective. For the most part, new technologies like the Arriflex and quartz lights had specific rather than general applications, particularly on location, when studio equipment more often proved clumsy.

The speed of Eastman 5254 reduced lighting requirements to the point that arc lights became largely obsolete. The new stock accelerated the boom in location filming during the 1970s, opening the door to a host of other new technologies. While established Hollywood companies like Mitchell and Technicolor struggled to evolve, newer innovators such as Panavision, Nagra, Arri, and Cinemobile flooded Hollywood production. After years of overhead reduction, studio camera departments were no longer hubs of research and development. Instead, companies reliant on non-feature filmmakers built technologies best suited for economical location shooting. This practice became the norm rather than the exception during the Hollywood Recession, and thus feature filmmaking underwent rapid technological change.

In 1969, Wexler still had to retrofit faster still-photo lenses onto movie cameras, but by the early 1970s, new professional cinema lenses appeared in response to the growing demand. Working in concert with the Motion Picture and Television Research Center, Canon built three models of the modern zoom lens, debuting in mid-1971. Unlike earlier zoom lenses, these were lightweight, added little distortion, and were just as fast as conventional lenses, even at close range. Adaptors fit both Arri and Mitchell cameras. Filmmakers could now carry far fewer lenses on location and easily maneuver the ring focus on the zoom, even while shooting handheld. An effective zoom lens provided a cheaper alternative, if not exact equivalent, to dolly shots, notoriously difficult to perform on location due to uneven surfaces and other local conditions.[60]

Panavision developed faster prime lenses that when coupled with pushing in development allowed for incredibly low light levels. For instance, using several Panavision lenses, Jack Priestley shot most of the interiors for *Across 110th Street* (1972) between 5 and 25 foot-candles, using available light whenever possible.[61] Panavision claimed its cameras added roughly a half stop of exposure, while ultrawide lenses could capture night exteriors with a quarter of the normal light requirements. The biggest detriment to further adoption of Panavision was its profitable business model. The company did not sell their products, which were more expensive than other equipment to rent, leading some producers to choose cheaper rentals or accept studio equipment included in production deals.[62] Clint Eastwood's Malpaso Productions embraced Panavision despite the expense, and the superior technology proved essential to the low-key lighting on location for *Dirty Harry*.[63]

New sound- and video-assist technology added further efficiencies to location filmmaking. The 1970 model of the Nagra sound recorder was palm-sized, designed to easily carry and operate on location.[64] Crystal sync, a technology for wirelessly recording synchronous sound developed in the 1960s, became a regular rather than occasional tool as Hollywood expanded location shooting. This wireless technology made a new video replay system, developed by Video West, more practical to use on location.[65] Locations could never promise the quiet of the soundstage, but wireless microphones made location dialogue far more attainable and surreptitious. Video replay helped safeguard getting adequate footage before abandoning the location. Better sound recording saved filmmakers extensive automated dialogue replacement (ADR) work in post-production, particularly when shooting in noisy urban locations, while video replay helped them avoid expensive reshoots.

A number of less successful inventions highlight the overwhelming shift from soundstage to location. An "air bubble" location stage, an inflatable soundstage for distant locations, served as a convenient ad hoc studio space and a backup set for inclement weather.[66] Even special-effects technology became portable. Bill Hansard, a background-projection specialist for television series such as *Green Acres* and *Petticoat Junction*, developed a front-projection system "packed down into the minimum amount of space . . . with everything redesigned for mobility."[67] These products suited an era when many filmmakers saw Hollywood as a place to finish films, not make them. Michael Ritchie, who shot *The Candidate* (1972) entirely on location, largely in the Bay Area, praised Hollywood's technical facilities, including those for special effects, sound and music, and titles; he avoided Los Angeles production facilities.[68]

The Cinemobile was the culmination of these various technologies and inspired several imitators. Fouad Said developed the prototype for an all-purpose production van working on *I Spy* (1965–1968), the first television series to shoot on location throughout the world, despite a typically restrictive budget. As early as 1967, Said built new vehicles intended for television series and movies. In 1969, Said debuted larger models of the Cinemobile to accommodate feature production. The elegant design of the Cinemobile allowed quick access to any piece of equipment, eliminating the need to fully unpack and repack trucks on location. Aside from a few tools designed by Said, such as a smaller generator, the van compactly assembled the smallest and lightest of existing technologies. These included Nagra recorders, zoom lenses, Colortran lights, and Arriflex cameras, advertised as "one-eighth the weight and one-tenth the cost of conventional U.S. made-Mitchells."[69] *American Cinematographer* reprinted a promotional story for Cinemobile, originally published in *Business Week*, paid for by Colortran and Arri, the equipment manufacturers that directly benefited from Cinemobile's further adoption.[70]

The Cinemobile held the greatest appeal for low-budget films and television work, where below-the-line costs constituted a greater portion of the negative cost. In dense cities, which typically had limited and expensive parking, the compact production vehicle became essential. Thus in 1971, three features (*The Strawberry Statement*, *Harold and Maude*, and *Fools*), two series (*McMillan and Wife* and *Ironside*), and two television movies (*Cross Current* and *Incident in San Francisco*) all used Cinemobiles to shoot in and around San Francisco; the following year, Quinn Martin, who produced *Incident*, returned to the city for *The Streets of San Francisco*. While Cinemobile gained higher-budget clients on two major Westerns, *Little Big Man* (1970) and *Jeremiah Johnson* (1972), *The Godfather*, a blockbuster shot in crowded urban neighborhoods, gave it the best publicity.[71]

Location shooting technology progressed to a point in the early 1970s where cost was no longer an obstacle to shooting in San Francisco and other cities. This facilitated a surge in urban location shooting that coincided with the redefinition of American cities as centers of crime and chaos. A trend toward bleak, semi-documentary realism reinforced the popular image of the blighted city as filmmakers actively worked to drain beauty from color film. San Francisco may have suffered less off-screen blight than other American cities, but this emergent aesthetic effectively blighted its on-screen image.

FILM STYLE AND URBAN CRISIS

Jan Dawson opened her 1969 *Sight and Sound* review of *Midnight Cowboy* with a comparison to two recent films set in Los Angeles and San Francisco:

> Unlike John Boorman's *Point Blank* and Peter Yates's *Bullitt*, both of which managed to uncover some cinematically virgin aspect of America's urban landscape and to flesh out their criticisms of the society they found there with an obvious pioneer enthusiasm . . . British director John Schlesinger's first American feature confines itself to the now familiar terrain of the American Dream turned nightmare.[72]

Dawson's allusions to the western frontier suggest a paradigm shift in America's image-myth of city and frontier, which I discuss in detail later in this chapter. She also indicates more immediate shifts in Hollywood's urban production style between 1968 and 1969. Although offering gritty cinematography and social criticism, *Bullitt* and *Point Blank* both reveled in the thrill of expanded access to urban locations; while abandoning the overt tourism of previous decades, they approached America's new cultural capital as a cache of visual treasures. *Midnight Cowboy*'s bleak depiction of "New York's neon wasteland" heralded an era where urban location shooting favored the vice districts and rundown neighborhoods of American cities.[73] On film, urban realism became synonymous with urban decay.

The advent of the ratings system in 1968 brought a wave of films for "mature" audiences that treated adult subjects with brutal realism. Partly due to the success of *Bullitt*, shooting entirely in an urban location went from exceptional to commonplace the following year. Filmmakers continued to aggressively chase low light levels, approaching absolute darkness with faster stock and faster lenses. Later in her review, Dawson criticizes Schlesinger for failing to distinguish the transcendent dreams of the characters from "the ugly environment" they intimately inhabit. Such a critique could extend to Hollywood cinematography, where fidelity to often depressing locations took priority over characterization.

Midnight Cowboy famously won the Academy Award for Best Picture with an X rating, and a host of other controversial films, ranging from the acclaimed *A Clockwork Orange* (1971) to the sensational *Deep Throat* (1972), became top-ten hits in the early 1970s. More typical genre films with M and R ratings also favored the stark realist aesthetic, pushing cinematographers to spend more time degrading the image than beautifying it. The cops and criminals featured in *The French Connection* and *Dirty Harry* were far more disturbing than those in *Bullitt*. An action film could feature rape, as in *Deliverance*, while hit crime films like *The Getaway* and *The Godfather* contained explicit violence previously reserved for exploitation films. Even successful musicals like *Cabaret* addressed taboo sexuality and Nazi violence. In response to uglier narratives, cinematographers creatively stripped the beauty away from color cinematography.

On *The Godfather*, Gordon Willis labored to decrease rather than increase image quality. He wanted the film to "look like a newspaper photograph in bad color—a black and white print out of the New York Times, with a little color introduced."[74] Along with desaturating the palette, he produced a prominently grainy look. This image degradation was not limited to period pieces, where historical distance might justify a weathered aesthetic. The futuristic *THX 1138* frequently shot under uncorrected fluorescent light in San Francisco locations, which "destroyed the features of people and their humanity." Filmmakers did "everything that would 'uglify' the color."[75] On

The French Connection, William Friedkin and cinematographer Owen Roizman even avoided "fancy compositions" that might aestheticize the semi-documentary approach. Friedkin described the story as "dirty, stark and ruthless," adjectives that defined the cinematography as well.[76] In the early 1970s, gritty realism approached cinematic brutalism, where not only embellishment but even photographic polish was meticulously avoided.

After shooting *The New Centurions* (1972), yet another bleak police film, cinematographer Ralph Woolsey noted the continued impact of the virtual elimination of black-and-white filmmaking. Coupled with faster stocks, smaller lighting units, and extensive location shooting, the studio practice of beautifying the image had fallen out of favor. The goal now was almost exclusively to "make things and people look the way they really are," and as a result, locations like San Francisco often looked worse than in reality.[77] America's ongoing crises at home and abroad suggested that the visual truth of any city must be an ugly truth. Meanwhile, as lighting on location for color film ceased to be a significant challenge, filmmakers tested their ability to shoot in near total darkness. Roizman shot a nightclub scene for *The French Connection* with table lights providing only 4 to 6 foot-candles for the actors.[78] On *THX 1138*, the young filmmakers shot in locations where they needed a flashlight to view the light meter, which sometimes failed to register a reading. Their motto became "just put on your fastest lens, open it up all the way and shoot."[79]

For veterans like James Wong Howe and experienced cinematographers such as Roizman and Willis, the subtlety of approximating natural lighting, particularly in dim locations, became hallmarks of their craftsmanship. Less than a decade earlier, the lighting demands of color cinematography had placed far more emphasis on proper exposure and color temperature, eliminating the smaller lights that facilitated fine detail. By shooting at low light levels and pushing the negative, cinematographers like Willis left little room for laboratories to alter the final image, preventing the studio from brightening the print for release.[80] Cinematographers like Roizman prided themselves on creating the look of available light with carefully placed small lighting units.[81] Less experienced, low-budget filmmakers like George Lucas approximated this style by shooting with available light. This method was far less precise, but it facilitated speedy location shooting, and new technology provided a safety net against wasteful underexposure.[82]

As Paul Ramaeker has demonstrated, the Hollywood police film most completely embraced the location techniques of French New Wave and direct cinema, with *Bullitt* serving as the exemplar. By the 1960s, the police genre was almost exclusively set in "seedy metropolitan locations."[83] *Bullitt* featured a mix of blighted locations, such as shady hotel rooms, and scenic attractions, such as Grace Cathedral. By 1971, scenic districts had all but disappeared from the genre, replaced by slums, gray zones, and red-light districts. For the *French Connection*, an "important goal was to not make New York look pretty. So the approach in scouting locations was to pick places that would make the city look the way it really looks."[84] Roizman sought a "dismal" and "dreary" atmosphere, although tellingly, if this was the only true image of New York, careful location scouting would be unnecessary. Gene Polito, cinematographer for *Prime Cut*, made a similar association between realism and squalor: "This rat infested flop house transcends our world of make believe. It stands out in my mind as a grim reminder of the spectre of human misery that exists today."[85] Ralph Woolsey listed the range of Los Angeles locations for *The New Centurions*, emphasizing adult theaters and bookshops, "nudie cafes," and Skid Row.[86] Poor urban neighborhoods and sleazy night districts had long been hallmarks of film realism. The era's new urban aesthetic suggested these sites had taken over the city; in *Coogan's Bluff* (1968), a crowd of derelicts even overtakes the halls of a New York police station.

Certain filmmakers described themselves as urban frontiersmen, daring to penetrate dangerous neighborhoods. The "Blaxploitation" film *Across 110th Street* provoked a particularly breathless account of production risks in *American Cinematographer*. While author Charles Loring described shooting entirely on location as standard practice for "rawgut realism," he emphasized "the special problems of shooting in the teeming ghetto of Harlem." Studio executives wanted director Gary Shear to abandon "probably the worst ghetto in the country," but "he refused to be intimidated."[87] The crew hired local residents for security and were shocked that observers enjoyed watching the location shoot rather than mounting a resistance. Director of photography Jack Priestley bragged about shooting in actual brothels, as well as apartments filled with rats and junkies that smelled "worse than a Himalayan yak."[88] With the same bravado that 1950s and 1960s Hollywood filmmakers had celebrated the challenge of shooting in distant locations, he crowed over the danger and exoticism of shooting in previously unphotographed pockets of poverty in urban African American neighborhoods.

Medium Cool served as a limit case for the integration of documentary and narrative filmmaking in Hollywood, as capturing actors against the unfolding of real events in cinema verité style became a common flourish. *The Candidate* took particular advantage of this technique throughout the Bay Area. The story of a California senate campaign allowed the camera operators, shooting handheld with available light, to appear on-screen as television news cameramen. Shooting wide open with pushed Eastman 5254, Victor Kemperer, who had just shot *Husbands* (1970) for John Cassavettes, took advantage of both available light and available events. Instead of the numerous extras and expensive locations required to stage political rallies, they used existing crowds. Director Michael Ritchie filmed candidate Bill McCay (Robert Redford) among a crowd of 20,000 at a high school football homecoming rally in rural Tracy, California. And knowing that every December 31, financial firm employees in San Francisco showered Montgomery Street with shredded calendars, Ritchie played it as a ticker-tape parade for McCay, and the jubilant crowd's response to movie star Robert Redford doubled for a political celebration. The production team asked for permission to embellish nearby spectacles, such as the army's burning of old barracks on Angel Island. They even convinced them to light a bigger fire, then added a scene where McCay and his opponent race to the site of a wildfire.[89]

The verité style perfectly suited the economic, technological, and stylistic developments of the Hollywood Recession. Young directors like Michael Ritchie and older directors trained on tight budgets, like Don Siegel, flexibly adapted scripts and staging to the uncertainties of actual locations. Obstacles to consistent or polished cinematography became production assets in the form of gritty, realist aesthetics. *The Candidate* cost only $1.5 million but covered a large number of locations, some of which allowed for only a single take. Yet with the use of multiple handheld cameras and a faster editing style, improvised scenes could be efficiently shot and stitched into the narrative.[90] Rough continuity and compromised photography supported rather than hindered the new mode of semi-documentary realism.

Hollywood films now regularly covered dozens of locations and incorporated local people and events into the drama. This required municipal cooperation, particularly in dense urban areas where location shooting could inconvenience or even endanger large groups of residents. Yet Hollywood's economic crisis was less prolonged than that of most American cities, where deindustrialization and white flight had decimated the tax base. As Stanley Corkin observes, filmmaking offered a clean industry that employed blue-collar workers, and New York took the lead in wooing producers to town.[91] While San Francisco weathered the economic slump of the 1970s, film production boosted revenue for local services like hotels and restaurants. Ritchie estimated that *The Candidate* pumped $750,000 into the San Francisco area, half of the film's budget. Mayor Lindsay set the precedent for luring filmmakers to the city, but quick on his heels, Mayor Alioto capitalized on New York's struggles, launching his own campaign to lure filmmakers to Northern California.

BECOMING NEW YORK

Among Mayor Alioto's personal papers on San Francisco filmmaking is a newspaper clipping titled "Lindsay Signs New Film Pact" containing two relevant points of interest. The first is the $40 million that Mayor Lindsay claimed filmmakers contributed annually to New York's economy. The second is the four-month suspension of filmmaking due to a union fight with producers over starting times, which were resolved in a new 1971 agreement.[92] New York's economic returns inspired other cities to court Hollywood location filmmaking, but its specific challenges allowed San Francisco to lure productions away from the East Coast.

By 1970, New York's Times Square district was a public embarrassment. In March, a lead article in *Variety* described the latest crime, in which a transit cop shot a subway drifter in front of the Taft Hotel. The subheadline read: "Porno Sinema Tone Hurts N.Y." The rise of midtown office buildings left behind tracts of poorly lit construction sites adjacent to a growing vice district populated by "muggers, hustlers and assorted Times Sq. flotsam." A ten-month survey identified "fear" as the most common word used to describe the area, now pithily referred to as "The Great Dark Way."[93] The decaying core of a once thriving entertainment district gained further notoriety as the milieu of the popular and acclaimed *Midnight Cowboy*.[94] In contrast, on the same front page of *Variety*, a story profiled a group in San Francisco making family-friendly films under the headline "Frisco's Good Clean Fun."[95]

Hollywood documented and embellished New York's precipitous decline, from *Coogan's Bluff*, to *The French Connection*, to *The Taking of Pelham One Two Three* (1974), but for Lindsay, luring production jobs and money to the city was worth the price of negative screen portrayals. In 1965, the year before he took office, only two features had been shot entirely in New York. By the end of his second term in 1974, 366 films had shot in the city. In his first year in office, Lindsay set up the New York Film Office to both coordinate and promote filmmaking.[96] In 1968, California senator George Moscone described Lindsay as "a one-man task force to seduce the motion picture industry to New York." He cited urban location incentives as an alternative to a California-wide film subsidy.[97] Mayor Alioto began following suit in Moscone's hometown of San Francisco.

A key innovation at Lindsay's film office was a streamlined permit process. Rather than dealing with dozens of local agencies, filmmakers had a centralized system to efficiently and economically reach agreements.[98] In December 1971, Los Angeles approved its own one-stop permit office at City Hall in another effort to slow runaway production. As the threat of domestic runaway production grew, Los Angeles now had to compete with other cities as a potential location rather than as an alternative to location shooting.[99] San Francisco struggled to adopt such a model, relying on a mayor's committee with no authority over production permitting. The primary focus of location filmmaking in Los Angeles and New York was jobs, but San Francisco instead focused on tourism, tracking location crews' downtown spending on hotels and restaurants while courting the international promotion and publicity gained from the film industry. In mid-1972, the San Francisco Film Committee joined the San Francisco Convention and Visitors Bureau, indicative of the city's emphasis on filmmaking as a catalyst for the existing tourist economy.[100]

Unfortunately for Lindsay, strong local unions in New York clashed with Hollywood producers, just as they had during the city's 1950s boom in location shooting.[101] In 1971, an agreement with New York studio mechanics took more than eleven months to settle. This led to further negotiations with the Teamsters, the camermen's union, and scenic artists over flexible start times and shared lunch hours. Teamsters bristled at Cinemobile's non-union drivers, while art directors fought producers who considered them unnecessary on location.[102] Paramount president Frank Yablans publicly blamed the New York unions for driving below-the-line costs of *The Godfather* from an expected \$600,000–\$700,000 to as high as \$1.7 million. A representative for the New York cameramen's union instead blamed *The Godfather* producers' indecision and bad planning for escalating costs. The film's unprecedented box office success made these below-the-line costs negligible, but it had immediate consequences. Paramount pulled two pictures out of New York, including *Play It Again, Sam* (1972), which moved to San Francisco. Columbia followed suit and moved *Butterflies Are Free* there as well.[103] Defenders of New York filmmaking acknowledged the problem but adopted a condescending tone, suggesting that Hollywood producers did not know how to handle New York.[104]

Unlike the unions in New York, San Francisco's local unions implored the mayor to emulate Lindsay. This strong support stemmed from San Francisco's place on the precipice of becoming a steady film production center. Although Hollywood remained active in San Francisco in the early 1970s, the film committee urged the mayor to keep pushing to sustain regular employment for local film workers.[105] Mayor Alioto and union representatives allied against San Francisco's powerful Board of Supervisors, who were more worried about the impact of filmmaking on the local environment. Alioto emphasized economic growth, actively promoting the downtown office construction that became an ancillary benefit for filmmakers, who used San Francisco's skyline as an alternative to New York's.[106] The influential citizens who opposed new construction as a disruption of San Francisco's historic urban form and culture would later challenge the urban disruption caused by Hollywood filmmaking.[107]

Bullitt not only showcased San Francisco as a dynamic location but also initiated the direct involvement of Alioto and city government to promote the city as an attractive Hollywood destination. This production push brought over fifty-six film and television productions to San Francisco between 1968 and 1973.[108] Alioto's initial 1968 filmmaking campaign gained extensive publicity but few results. *Take the Money and Run* followed *Bullitt* and *Petulia* as just the third film shot fully in San Francisco in 1968, leading to the front-page *Daily Variety* headline "Mayor's Campaign to Make Frisco Hollywood's 'Backlot' Succeeding."[109] The low-budget feature, a parody of 1930s crime stories, is set in the urban East Coast and rural Midwest, but the greater San Francisco area provided enough geographical variety to play both of these regions.[110] The city had some production facilities, such as a Mission District warehouse converted to a television office and production space.[111] San Francisco even managed to turn its local blight into a desirable location: the Yerba Buena project, then a decaying area in South of Market slated for redevelopment, stood in for the 1930s slums of Camden, New Jersey.[112]

Attracting films without a San Francisco setting, such as *Take the Money and Run* and *The Boston Strangler*, proved more practical than promoting San Francisco screenplays. But despite Alioto's efforts, the number of projects shot in San Francisco declined from seven or so in 1968 to five in 1969. The immediate cause was the overall production decline brought by the Hollywood Recession. San Francisco's national profile had also waned from the peak attention it received during the Summer of Love; the countercultural music and experimental film scene had declined, while strip clubs and pornographic films had gained national attention.[113]

The most prominent San Francisco films reflected the current urban pessimism. After scouting Oakland and Los Angeles, Michelangelo Antonioni chose San Francisco as the site of a "Negro riot" for *Zabriskie Point*, later changed to a violent student protest.[114] *The Strawberry Statement* (1971) more centrally focused on campus violence, including a prolonged student strike, building takeover, and militaristic police raid on the protesters. *Point Blank* producers Irwin Winkler and Robert Chartoff returned to the city but shot most scenes in nearby Stockton, with some urban footage to suggest San Francisco State. Hoping to quickly capitalize on the protests at Columbia and UC-Berkeley, filmmakers saw the city as a fitting stage for youth liberation turning to pitched rage and violence.[115] Although the box office failure of both films spared most Americans from these negative portraits of the city, the films also dispelled San Francisco's reputation for box office magic.

In early 1969, San Francisco's Recreation and Parks Commission eliminated permit fees, making popular locations like Golden Gate Park more affordable to smaller film companies. Lindsay had done the same thing in New York. The mayor's office also suggested an annual license for companies rather than a long series of permit requests.[116] Yet over a year later, San Francisco's IATSE office complained that companies who had balked at the $250 fees were now being charged again, for $200, still a hefty price for smaller operators.[117] The local chapter of the Screen Actors Guild complained to the mayor that the film committee was not receiving adequate funding. Faced with a short-term fiscal crisis, the mayor proposed a model of direct assistance from the business community that would benefit from an uptick in local production.[118]

Despite San Francisco's disorganized production apparatus, location production boomed in the city in the early 1970s, including eleven productions in 1970, eighteen in 1971, and seven in the first half of 1972. Even prior to the start of *The Streets of San Francisco* series in 1972, the city estimated $40–$45 million in revenue from feature film, commercial, industrial, and documentary production combined in the previous five years (1968–1972). This number did not include the potential revenue from increased tourism promoted by San Francisco's screen appearances.[119] While big-budget films like *Dirty Harry* and *What's Up, Doc?* would gain the most attention, less expensive films were the key to San Francisco's production boom, particularly television movies.

Debuting in 1966 on NBC, television movies had become a fixture of network programming by the early 1970s and served as a brilliant way to mitigate the risk of launching new network series.[120] Movies such as *Incident in San Francisco* (1971), which appeared as a two-hour *ABC Sunday Night Movie,* also functioned as pilots, promoting new series while providing a test run with audiences before the network ordered additional episodes. *The Streets of San Francisco* followed this launch pattern, whereas failed pilots like *Incident* and Warners' *Cross Current* (1971) ran only as television movies (which also had lower budgets and fewer union restrictions than feature films).[121] San Francisco clearly benefited from the IATSE exemptions and other union concessions for pictures with budgets of less than $1 million, which allowed producers to hire more local cast and crew without compensating Los Angeles unions. *Crosscurrent* (1970), *Fools* (1970), and *Play It Again, Sam* all had a $1 million budget, and several other inexpensive films shot in San Francisco likely fell below this threshold.[122]

The variety of San Francisco productions expanded in the early 1970s. The city still elicited some bright, picturesque portrayals of the city. For instance, the series *McMillan and Wife* and *What's Up, Doc?,* in knowing reference to classical Hollywood, depicted the city in cine-tourist splendor, the former with a colorful bicycle chase through the city and the latter with a posh hotel setting and a slapstick car chase through Chinatown. Now increasingly mobile, television series used San Francisco as an exciting change of scenery, including *The F.B.I.*, *Mission Impossible*, and *Lassie*.[123] Other films tapped into the hippie and drug culture, such as the 1972 films *Thumb Tripping*, *Dealing*, and *Butterflies Are Free*. San Francisco's liberal reputation also made it a plausible setting for African American–led dramas. Sidney Poitier reprised his *In the Heat of the Night* role as Virgil Tibbs in *They Call Me Mister Tibbs!* (1970) and *The Organization* (1971), relocated to San Francisco, Tibbs's happy home, where a lack of prejudice seemed more believable than in the Deep South or even Tibbs's hometown of Philadelphia. *Cross Current*, a police show pilot, was expected to become the first hour-long drama starring an African American (Robert Hooks). Airing in a two-hour version on ABC in 1971 and a ninety-minute version on CBS in 1972 (retitled *The Cable Car Murder*), *Variety* praised the San Francisco locations, which the reviewer said gave "the immeasurable sense of the city's vaunted charm"; nonetheless, the program never became a series.[124] Even the unconventional romance of *Harold and Maude* appeared more plausible set in San Francisco and Northern California.

A final piece of the San Francisco production boom was the establishment of Francis Ford Coppola's American Zoetrope studio. In 1969 Coppola used seed money from his multipicture deal with Warner Bros. to build a filmmaking plant that he planned as a new form of cooperative feature film studio. But displeased with the Coppola-produced *THX 1138*, Warners' head Ted Ashley terminated the deal at the end of 1970 and called in the loan, essentially bankrupting the fledgling film complex. Zoetrope survived, in large part by tapping into San Francisco's thriving television commercial market as well as educational and industrial films.[125] By investing heavily in new camera equipment and flatbed editing machines, Coppola positioned Zoetrope to become a small production house akin to New York rental and production facilities. Filmmakers like Michael Ritchie, who moved to San Francisco and became a regular at Zoetrope, took advantage of its state-of-the-art equipment. In fact, Ritchie was able to begin post-production work on *The Candidate* there before returning to Los Angeles.[126]

Indicative of the rise of location shooting, Coppola decided to build American Zoetrope without a soundstage. This decision proved overly optimistic for Coppola's first production, *THX 1138*, which required science-fiction set pieces that forced him to rent a Hollywood soundstage.[127] Yet the ability to shoot at very low light levels helped George Lucas exploit San Francisco locations that doubled as futuristic sets. Gaining access to the newly constructed BART stations and tunnels, Lucas found empty space-age facilities that added immeasurable production value to the film. Bay Area architecture—such as the Oakland Coliseum, the Pacific Gas and Electric Building (built in 1971 and also featured in *Dirty Harry*), and the Marin County Civic Center (Frank Lloyd Wright's final commission)—provided voluminous, modernist settings for the future dystopia. On location, Lucas pushed almost every shot for available light except, tellingly, shots needed for optical effects.[128] Years later, Lucas's pioneering use of optical effects made him a fortune and also drew him and the Hollywood industry back from the extensive location shooting employed for *THX 1138* and *American Graffiti* (1973).

Mayor Alioto needed the support of both Hollywood producers and San Francisco residents to increase location shooting in the city. In 1968 he rebranded the San Francisco Film Festival, which had started in 1957, as a celebration of American film. He introduced the Samuel Goldwyn Award, named after his former client, for "the best American-made picture." Like Mayor Lindsay in New York, he framed his efforts to promote production in his city—and the United States—as part of the larger cause of promoting

American over foreign production. He said that he named the award after Goldwyn for his role as "a long-time critic of 'runaway' motion picture production." *Variety* wondered whether this would finally convince the major studios to participate in the film festival, but reporter Thomas Pryor gave credence to Alioto's jingoism, hoping it might "bring the controlling forces of the European festivals to their senses and rekindle a respect for the U.S. industry, which has been treated with contempt of recent years."[129]

Alioto built local support for film production by ensuring that producers contributed something to local interests, starting with the charity premiere of *Bullitt*. The *Dirty Harry* premiere raised $10,000 for the Police Activities League, which even Herb Caen, a vocal critic of the film, had to acknowledge; a smaller film, *The Organization,* gave $2,500 as an unspecified cultural donation.[130] In 1972 Alioto began asking production companies shooting in San Francisco to donate to the film festival; he even suggested requiring producers to meet with the mayor before the final granting of a shooting permit, which would give him an opportunity to make a personal "pitch" for donations.[131] Location production helped build up the festival, and the festival helped build interest in further location production.

Both *Dirty Harry* and *What's Up, Doc?* shot on location in San Francisco in 1971. *Dirty Harry*, with its violent portrayal of the city and its ambivalent stance on police vigilantism seemed like a film that would begin to sour residents on the boom in local filmmaking. Surprisingly, the instigator was *What's Up, Doc?*, touted by director Peter Bogdanovich as "A G-rated comedy with no redeeming social values."[132] Decrying the scarcity of the escapist fare that had defined classical Hollywood, Bogdanovich captured San Francisco in near-Technicolor glory in a screwball comedy starring Barbra Streisand as a cross between Bugs Bunny and a Howard Hawks female lead. Unlike Hawks, Bogdanovich shot almost entirely on location, including a wacky car chase through Chinatown. Producers secured a permit to drive a single Volkswagen down the steps at Alta Plaza, a park in the wealthy Pacific Heights neighborhood, provided it was equipped with a rubber piece to protect the stairs. Instead, an unmodified Volkswagen and four full-sized sedans "plummeted down the stairway," chipping the old concrete. This innocuous incident might not have made the news in another city, but in San Francisco the headline read, "Outrage at Alta Plaza."[133]

At the time of this October 1971 incident, four films were busy shooting in San Francisco's compact and densely populated urban core. Warners' insurance easily covered the damage to Alta Plaza, but the tony residents were angered that the Hollywood filmmakers had cavalierly ignored an agreement with the Parks and Recreation Department. Complaints drew the attention of Supervisor Robert Mendelsohn, who moved to hold board hearings on location filmmaking. While not seeking to discourage filmmakers, he suggested that "the enormous growth in filming on our streets and parks has raised a number of questions which deserve study." He sought to ensure that producers adequately paid for services such as police officers and street closures, and sufficiently protected property, what he saw as "reasonable guidelines."[134] Caen, the legendary columnist for the *Chronicle*, not only approved of Mendelsohn's suggestion but took the concern a few steps further.

Caen was quite amenable to the major cultural shifts of 1960s San Francisco, but the impact of filmmakers associated with Los Angeles seemed antithetical to San Francisco's unique urban culture.[135] He wrote, "The chutzpah of these Hollywood invaders is wondrous to behold" and listed the traffic problems, costs for police protection, and property damage that the city had endured in exchange for publicity. Yet here he pivoted to the specific content of these productions: *Bullitt*'s high-speed chase, which showed no squad cars responding on the scene, and the ineffectual police commissioner of *McMillan and Wife*, both suggesting, at best, an inept San Francisco police force. Even worse was the "brute of a cop" in *Dirty Harry* and the city's depiction in *The Organization*, where "S.F. crime runs rampant."[136] Although local papers had previously described residents as starstruck, San Franciscans now appeared to bristle at the intrusion of location filmmaking. More fundamentally, the city's deteriorating screen image was seen as inaccurate and destructive to its reputation.

In December 1971 public criticism of location filmmaking made the front page of *Variety* under the headline "Frisco Has Some Second Thoughts On Wooing Film Productions." Although writer Jim Harwood attributed some of the uproar to San Francisco's "anti-auto sentiment," citing the still unfinished Embarcadero Freeway featured in *The Lineup*, he also blamed the city for never making a clear effort to coordinate production. Although successful in luring filmmakers to town, San Francisco still lacked a dedicated production office like New York's, and the resulting disorder threatened to bring about filming restrictions. Although he acknowledged Caen's overstatement, Harwood agreed with his second point: "As today's films strive for realism, one seldom sees any flattering side of urban life unspooled on screen once the crews are gone from town." While New York continued to fight for production jobs, "the consistent movie view of Gotham these days is hardly glamorous."[137] The confluence of ugly realism and expanded urban location shooting created a dilemma for cities vying for film production. San Francisco may have wanted the production economy of New York, but it did not want to inherit its blighted image.

Alioto responded quickly to assuage Hollywood's doubts about the city's desire for production, even taking the stage at *Dirty Harry*'s premiere in San Francisco to say, "We'll continue to make pictures in San Francisco, and we're not going to worry about a couple of chipped steps in Alta Plaza."[138] Although location production irked residents, local production companies and unions lobbied city government to do more to attract Hollywood filmmaking. San Francisco's union cameramen pushed for greater city assistance. Representative Gerald Smith wrote Mendelsohn that he was "perplexed by your obvious prejudice" against San Francisco filmmaking and copied Alioto on the letter. He cited greater incentives offered by other states and Canada, where helicopter scouting and police assistance were free, and services like cars and cheap hotel rates were included.[139] Local filmmakers and officials begged the mayor to do even more. San Francisco commercial filmmaker Greg Snazelle shared a letter he received from Los Angeles mayor Sam Yorty that established a one-stop permit office.[140] Another letter advocated for building a soundstage, which might convince filmmakers to shoot both exteriors and interiors in the city.[141]

With Alioto's cooperation, a group of local film companies and union representatives formed the San Francisco Film Committee, initially housed in the mayor's office. Chairing the committee was Ann Brebner, who along with her husband ran a casting agency that provided extras for nearly every Hollywood location production in the city. A month after the Alta Plaza incident, committee member George Burrafato outlined an ambitious proposal to streamline San Francisco's production policy for the immediate future. He argued that a city production coordinator should be hired and furnished with an office, and that the committee should prepare a directory of local production services to become "the San Francisco bible for anything a filmmaker may need in the Bay Area." He also suggested selling ads in the directory to offset the cost, and including a promotional cover letter from the mayor's office. Yearly ads could be placed in industry publications like *Variety* and *American Cinematographer*, which in 1971 ran a cover story and a special section on San Francisco filmmaking. A regional Kodak representative extolled the virtues of shooting in San Francisco alongside articles on

American Zoetrope, *THX 1138*, and a new, filmed tourist attraction called "The San Francisco Experience."[142]

The committee planned a major meeting in late June 1972 at the Fairmont Hotel, assembling local union representatives and government officials from various agencies such as BART, the Golden Gate Bridge Authority, and the city's Recreation and Parks Department. They put forth an ambitious agenda, planning to send a delegation to Los Angeles and give a press conference announcing their new role as a clearinghouse for location production matters, coordinated with a mass mailing to producers in Hollywood and New York. They also proposed an annual award, which would first go to Francis Ford Coppola, the city's most celebrated filmmaker.[143] In the press, Brebner promoted San Francisco filmmaking beyond credulity, citing a "hospitable climate" and frequent clear days, where available light largely sufficed, as if Los Angeles filmmakers had brought the weather north with them.[144]

Despite their high aspirations, the film committee never gained the authority to centrally oversee film production. For undisclosed reasons, in June 1972 it moved out of the mayor's office into the Convention and Visitors Bureau.[145] A production directory appeared by 1974, but producers still worked directly with the mayor. Alioto's ongoing interest in networking with filmmakers, such as his proposal to tie permits to a personal meeting, suggests he never wanted to relinquish his role to a more efficient committee. Without a centrally organized film office, location production challenges and local resistance persisted, particularly following the success of *Dirty Harry*. Not only did the film depict the city awash with crime and vice, but its box office success prompted sequels and imitators that made violent police dramas a staple of location production in San Francisco throughout the 1970s. A salient example of this trend appeared on television, where *The Streets of San Francisco*, although less disturbing than *Dirty Harry*, broadcast a picture of a brutal, crime-ridden city every week to a national audience.

DIRTY HARRY AND URBAN DECAY

Upon its release in 1971, the politics of *Dirty Harry* largely shaped discussions of the film. The initial backlash came from movie critics such as Pauline Kael, Andrew Sarris, and Roger Ebert, who described the film as a fascist and paranoid portrayal of the country's police and legal system. Warner Bros. expected controversy upon the release of *Dirty Harry* and found it—not only in the critical backlash, but also an Oscar protest where demonstrators held signs reading "Dirty Harry Is a Rotten Pig."[146] Film scholars have mounted similar critiques as well. In *American Films of the 1970s: Conflicting Views*, Peter Lev nuances these arguments, but suggests that Harry Callahan personifies a simplistic version of law-and-order, right wing conservatism, and the film follows this credo.[147] Although Lev and others attribute the film's success to the rise of the so-called silent majority, *Dirty Harry*'s motifs and references are multivalent, a product of the complicated interweaving of production technique, location, and cultural context.

Writers and scholars who have focused more closely on *Dirty Harry*'s visual style than its narrative tend to see the film as more complex and morally ambivalent, including those writing at the time of the film's release. As Gordon Gow cautioned in 1972, despite the film's undercurrent of social criticism, "the danger is that many will keep on seeing things from Harry's viewpoint."[148] Four sequels made by Eastwood's production company, Malpaso, further distorted the film's immediate context as the Dirty Harry character grew into a simpler franchise hero. The issue of political identification with *Dirty Harry* was reignited when Clint Eastwood delivered his trademark line, "Make my day!," to a cheering crowd at the 2012 Republican National Convention. Ronald Reagan famously repeated this line from the fourth Dirty Harry film, *Sudden Impact* (1983), and the later identification of conservative politicians with Harry further distorts his more ambiguous characterization in the original film.

Regardless of its politics, looking at *Dirty Harry* as a San Francisco film shot largely on location places it more squarely in the specific production context of its era. The successful transformation of America's most scenic city into a shadowy cesspool shows how determinant the new semi-documentary urban aesthetic had become by the early 1970s. The city government's active participation in its own image destruction also followed a larger trend. But *Dirty Harry* proved remarkable in collapsing so many elements of location shooting, urban form, and national crises into violent set pieces. Scenography such as snipers' rifles (paired with zoom shots) and police helicopters are loaded symbols associated with race riots and Vietnam. As the urban crisis created central loci for cultural anxieties, *Dirty Harry* offered a thrilling city of action where the urban nightmare comprised the totality of San Francisco.

Dirty Harry follows Detective Harry Callahan as he tracks Scorpio, a sniper who kills random victims and then taunts the police with cryptic notes, similar to the actual Zodiac killer, who killed several people in and around San Francisco in 1968 and 1969. Between a series of encounters with Scorpio, Harry fights other crimes that appear to be daily chores for San Francisco police, including a bank robbery and an attempted suicide. Harry finally captures Scorpio in a deserted Kezar Stadium, shooting him and pressing his foot into the wound to torture him into revealing the whereabouts of his kidnapping victim. Harry is too late to save the girl, and charges of police brutality improbably free Scorpio on all charges. He eventually hijacks a bus full of schoolchildren. Harry confronts Scorpio at an industrial plant on the outskirts of the city, kills him, and throws his badge into a wastewater pool where Scorpio floats dead. In this troubling portrait of San Francisco, the forces of law and order fail to protect the city or restrain Harry's and Scorpio's violence.

Dirty Harry made a profound impact on Eastwood's career and San Francisco filmmaking, but the script originated with a different star and a different setting. It began as a Frank Sinatra vehicle set in New York, an appropriate follow-up to his 1968 film, *The Detective*. After four drafts, Sinatra withdrew from the film, leading Clint Eastwood and Don Siegel to develop the project at Warner Bros. They decided a location change to San Francisco would help distinguish the film from *Coogan's Bluff* and allow Eastwood to shoot close to his Carmel home, both a convenience and a promotional angle for the local press.[149] The location shift also gave Siegel and writer Dean Reisner, who rewrote the script for *Coogan's Bluff*, a chance to incorporate actual San Francisco locations into the finished screenplay, including Kezar Stadium and Mount Davidson Park, striking sites for Harry's violent physical encounters with Scorpio.[150]

The new setting also matched a rare subject of negative national press for the city. In 1969 and 1970, *Life* magazine ran two profiles of tough cops working dangerous beats in San Francisco. The first piece was a book excerpt set in Haight-Ashbury, which under the strain of so many new residents had descended from a communal haven into a slum. Descriptions of African American criminals and misguided revolutionaries assailing the "pigs" foreshadowed the city of *Dirty Harry*, as well as San Francisco's reaction; several residents wrote letters to the editor to decry what they considered an inaccurate portrayal of their police and their city.[151] The second article, about a family of policemen, also emphasized hippies and African Americans, openly disparaged by the older officer. *Life* also ran photos of the eighteen police officers killed in the United States in 1970 in "unprovoked attacks," promoting a universal sense of the urban lawlessness dramatized in *Dirty Harry*.[152] Despite stories like these and the Zodiac killings, travel writers continued to rave about San Francisco and its familiar tourist locations, including the Golden Gate and Bay Bridges, Maiden Lane, and Fisherman's Wharf.[153] In *Life*, San Francisco crime appeared isolated to a few parts of the city, such as the Fillmore; in *Dirty Harry*, it appeared pervasive.

Extensive location shooting contributed to the expansive urban landscape of *Dirty Harry*. With the exception of an early scene where Harry confronts a bank robber (with the famous line "Do you feel lucky?"), the entire film was shot on location. This was typical for Malpaso, which by 1973 had shot over 200 days in four years and spent only six in a studio.[154] Despite the logistical complications, Malpaso producer Robert Daley felt crews worked more efficiently on location due to an "esprit de corps." Using the same key technicians on several productions maximized this team-building. For instance, Bruce Surtees worked as a camera operator on *Coogan's Bluff* before becoming a director of photography for *The Beguiled* (1971) and *Dirty Harry*. *Dirty Harry* was Siegel's fourth Malpaso picture, while editor Carl Pingitore edited all three of Malpaso's 1971 productions.[155] Despite the higher rental costs, adopting Panavision lenses and later the flexible Panaflex camera was critical for Malpaso, which distinctively shot in low-light conditions. Surtees acquired the nickname the "Prince of Darkness" for his dark cinematography with minimal fill light, an aesthetic that became a signature style for Malpaso productions.[156]

Dirty Harry relied heavily on city-owned locations, including subway and streetcar stations, two city hospitals, Mount Davidson Park, and Kezar Stadium. The biggest show of city support came while shooting at three city hall locations, including three days in the mayor's reception room. Location manager Harry Zubrinsky not only secured these requests directly with the mayor's executive deputy, John DeLuca, but also requested additional services. He asked the city to clear both the emergency room at San Francisco General and the City Hall rotunda. For hospital scenes, they requested ambulances and hospital police, and motormen for the subway and streetcar chase. Even though the 49ers had finished their season at Kezar Stadium, the *Dirty Harry* producers requested that yard line markers be drawn and goal posts erected. The city cleared a wide area around the stadium for the ascending helicopter shot and gave filmmakers full control of the stadium lights.[157] The police department ostensibly had to approve scripts shot on location, but they cooperated fully on *Dirty Harry* as the

San Francisco government helped prepare locations for one of the city's most controversial films.[158]

Certain sites, however, proved impossible to secure, such as the Hall of Justice. Rather than return to the studio, the production rented a floor in the Pacific Gas and Electric Building. Ironically, *The Organization* had recreated the exact setting on another floor of the building.[159] Freed from the power consumption and size of larger lighting units, productions often used empty floors in local buildings and warehouses as soundstages. Existing structures required only set dressing, saving the cost of constructing or assembling a standing set. But one particularly challenging scene, a shootout with bank robbers on a crowded street, proved much easier to film on the backlot. The controlled mayhem and property destruction caused by a car crashing into a fire hydrant was much too unwieldy for location shooting (Figure 5.2).

Despite similar complications, Siegel managed to capture a rooftop shootout between Harry and Scorpio on location. The neon "Jesus Saves" sign, constructed atop the Blue Shield office high-rise in North Beach, could be seen for blocks by perplexed local residents. Until midnight, gunfire rang out from the rooftops while floodlights lit several buildings around Washington Square Park.[160] Siegel recalled using seven cameras for a particularly difficult shot, with lighting cables running for blocks below. He worried about the lights temporarily blinding some drivers (they may very well have caused some minor accidents), and also the danger of shattered glass and wires falling from the neon sign (Figure 5.3). His attention to safety pushed

5.2. The only scene in *Dirty Harry* (Warner Bros., 1971) shot on the Universal lot was the bank robbery, which involved the complicated logistics of a car crashing into a fire hydrant. The image of law enforcer Harry (Clint Eastwood) striding across a backlot street also connects the film to the Western genre.

5.3. A neon "Jesus Saves" sign was constructed atop the Blue Shield office high-rise in North Beach for a rooftop shootout between Harry and Scorpio. This dangerous shoot highlights the growing scale and ambition of location production in San Francisco.

the shooting well past midnight as police handled a barrage of neighbors' complaints.[161] That this commotion was only a local interest story, whereas damage to the Alta Plaza steps had prompted government hearings, suggests an ancillary benefit of Hollywood's infatuation with seedy urban locations such as North Beach: wealthy residents had the political voice to threaten local shoots, while downtrodden neighborhoods could be invaded by filmmakers in the name of economic development with little or no consideration for residents.

With the mayor's office facilitating filmmaking, the police force provided direct assistance, not only in securing locations but also, as they did in North Beach, addressing residents' complaints. During the production of *Dirty Harry*, police chief Alfred Nelder expressed disapproval of parts of a script for a promotional featurette. The San Francisco police force likely objected to the film's depiction of crime, bureaucracy, and rogue police work, particularly while they were assisting the roughly two-month shoot. But Claude Jarman, Alioto's appointed film festival head, wrote to chastise the police chief for his remarks. He concluded that in the future, Warner Bros. should instead coordinate production with "the men in your department who are more familiar with the details." In other words, not even the chief of police should interfere with filmmakers, and the head of the film festival could bluntly say so, copying Alioto on the letter.[162] Nonetheless, the stress that location production placed on San Francisco police helps explain the tribute to fallen policemen at the opening of *Dirty Harry* (which was pilloried by liberal critics), as well as Warners' contributions to the Police Athletic League.[163] But location filmmakers depend on police cooperation and enthusiasm, and these gestures proved particularly important when *Dirty Harry* spawned several sequels, all shot in San Francisco. Don Siegel had thanked the San Francisco Police Department years earlier on *The Lineup*, as did the producers of *The Organization* in 1971. Although criticism from San Francisco police officers over their screen depiction was effectively quelled, trade papers like *Variety* and local newspapers continued to fret over the violent portrayal of the city.

Variety saw limited box office potential for *Dirty Harry*, less for its politics than its graphic attention to brutality by both police and criminals. Its review of the film suggested that it spoke to extremists across the political spectrum, including "sadists, revolutionaries and law-and-order freaks." The reviewer acknowledged the film's striking technique, including Siegel's "flair for hard-hitting urban cinematics," Surtees's cinematography and Lalo Schifrin's eerie score. Yet the plot seemed like television pulp rather than a feature-worthy story, like "an updated, freaked-out Peter Gunn episode." *Variety* predicted the film would be a serviceable programmer.[164] Instead the film was "a major surprise," a hit that helped lift Warners' fortunes.[165] Part of the film's appeal lay in its successful transplantation of the Western genre, in which Eastwood rose to fame, onto the image of the American city as a violent frontier in the early 1970s.

Eastwood clearly understood this analogy. When, during shooting, a San Francisco journalist asked Eastwood about the lack of a female lead, Eastwood explained, "It's kind of a western."[166] While this genre reference neatly ties the film into Eastwood's early career, it also connects *Dirty Harry* to Siegel, Eastwood, and screenwriter Dean Reisner's first collaboration on *Coogan's Bluff*, which *Rawhide* writers Herman Miller and Jack Laird had first developed for television. (After the film's release, Miller and Laird brought the same concept to television for the long-running series *McCloud* [1970–1977].)[167] As Coogan, Eastwood plays a cowboy-hatted Arizona deputy chasing Ringerman (Don Stroud), a fugitive in New York City. Here his independent, violent approach to justice clashes with the city's police bureaucracy, where criminals lounge about the precinct and harass Eastwood's love interest, a forgiving social worker (Susan Clark). Ringerman is a violent hippie, drawing Coogan further out of his element into the psychedelic scene. In many ways, *Dirty Harry* is also the story of a cowboy cop operating in a city that resents his violent but effective crime fighting. Harry wears no cowboy hat, but Scorpio wears a peace sign belt, combining a symbol of youth liberation with the violence of assassinations and Vietnam, forces that all contributed to urban conflicts.

Coogan's Bluff creates striking visual contrasts between rural landscapes and urban areas, reasserting the critical geography of the Hollywood Western. The opening sequence is a modern Western showdown in the style of the Old West. Coogan arrests a half-naked Native American who nearly kills him with a sniper rifle from his position in the high rocks above the Arizona desert. The open landscape is juxtaposed with the cramped interiors and crowded streets of New York, where Coogan's cowboy stands out just as sorely as Joe Buck in *Midnight Cowboy*. Later in the film, a scene staged at one of the city's protected natural spaces, the Cloisters, further links the Western to the urban crisis. The scene opens on a low-angle shot of an American flag before the camera moves to cover Coogan and the social worker entering the plaza. The camera continues to pan as they stroll past the Hudson River, lined with trees in the foreground and the deep background of the far bank. They pause in a postcard composition, the space between them revealing the Cloisters in the background, an apparent medieval abbey along a sylvan river. Coogan stalks away from this vista toward a view of the city, where the dense urban texture appears nearly monochromatic in beige and brick. Massive housing projects and smoke stacks dominate the frame. Coogan tells Julie, "I'm trying to picture it the way it was, just the trees and the river, before people came along and fouled it all up." Just as it had for the gunfighters of a Peckinpah Western, the frontier has closed on Coogan. The mythical civilization that cowboys helped forge has overtaken all but a few remnants of a virgin territory. An ugly urban expanse has achieved the totality of the western landscape; like the film's establishing shots of Manhattan, urban space appears to blanket the realm as an endless megalopolis.

Dirty Harry deepened this pessimistic vision of the Western hero in an urban landscape, consonant with the American crises of its era. In *Gunfighter Nation* (1993), Richard Slotkin details the persistent American frontier myth of the savage war fought away from the established city as a form of American expansion and masculine, cultural regeneration. In literature and film, this Western mythos reached a crisis point during the Vietnam era, when fighting in what soldiers dubbed "Indian Country" proved both futile and morally corrupt.[168] Slotkin notes how the Vietnam and urban crises bled into one another, quoting a Chicago resident who believed thousands of My

Lai massacres were happening in America every day, and brutal racism in the inner city was making the killing of civilians or a Black Panther leader an everyday reality.[169] Slotkin identifies two related critical inversions in the frontier myth that occurred in late 1968. The first, suggested by the riots, frames racial conflict not as the foundational triumph over savagery, but the fundamental flaw of American culture. The second, based on the urban locus of violence, shifts the center of conflict from the frontier to the metropolis.[170]

There is yet a third inversion inherent in *Dirty Harry*, one that inscribes a mythical inversion in physical space. The central city is not only the new center of violence, but the new frontier. After decades of postwar suburbanization, business decentralization, and white flight, downtown was no longer the central hub of most Americans' lives. Hollywood was acutely aware of this trend, particularly in the early 1970s, when fear of muggings and racial unrest further eroded downtown movie attendance.[171] The rural frontier had long served as a distant fantasy realm of action and violence. Now, a central city populated by social outcasts and African Americans, who were frequently depicted as savages, took the frontier's cultural role, evident in the decline of the Hollywood Western and the rise of the police genre in the early 1970s. *Dirty Harry* depicted the city as a frontier without redemption, an arena for violence and sadism that ultimately resists civilization. In the fallen city, a cowboy cop fights under his own code of vengeance in a lawless wilderness, futilely policing a frontier that no one will endeavor to recivilize.

In the bank robbery scene shot on the Universal lot, San Francisco briefly resembles a western town with a central street. Harry cockily strides across the road to playfully threaten the African American robber into submission. The scene plays out on a backlot street set where likely dozens of Westerns had been staged, and where the law is enforceable on foot. The robbery also occurs across the street from Harry's favorite hot dog joint, suggesting that the few safe spaces in his world are just a step away from violent crime. Scorpio suggests the same omnipresent threat, killing a beautiful woman blithely swimming in a rooftop pool on a sunny day. Senseless violence can strike anywhere, whether atop a tony high-rise or in the neon squalor of North Beach. Unlike *Bullitt*, *Dirty Harry*'s home is never shown; he sleeps off his injuries on a police office couch. He has no home or family to protect; a fleeting reference to his wife reveals that she was also a victim of a random crime, killed by a drunk driver.

Invoking the Western genre provides a critical context for the image that bookends *Dirty Harry:* a police badge appears at the center of the backdrop for the written police tribute that opens the film, and at its close, Harry throws his badge into the murky water of the industrial site where he has just killed Scorpio. Writing on the Western, André Bazin argues that "the sheriff's star must be seen as constituting a sacrament of justice, whose worth does not depend on the worthiness of the man who administers it."[172] This observation underscores the bleakness of Harry's urban frontier, where not only the authority but the city itself seem unworthy of justice. His gesture references the ending of *High Noon* (1952), where Marshall Kane (Gary Cooper) throws his badge in the dirt in front of the townfolk who failed to support him. For all their failings, at least some of them support Kane's work without joining his posse, and Kane saves the city before abandoning his job. In *Dirty Harry*, citizens and even fellow officers abhor his methods, and he earns his nickname doing "dirty" jobs such as pulling a suicidal jumper off a rooftop ledge. Nearly every urban site appears dangerous and perverse. Eastwood and Siegel argued over the ending; Eastwood worried that Harry was quitting, while Siegel suggested he was merely rejecting the city's bureaucracy.[173] The corrupt city on-screen suggests an even worse possibility: there is nothing left to save.

The location of the final confrontation between Harry and Scorpio reinforces the sense of a lost urban society. Rather than fighting in the heart of the city, Harry battles Scorpio in an abandoned rock quarry whose conveyor belts continue to run without human supervision (Figure 5.4). In late 1960s Westerns such as *The Wild Bunch* (1968), the presence of industrial products like cars suggest the end of the western frontier. The conclusion of *Dirty Harry* suggests the opposite, as the remnants of a productive society rot away, and civilization returns to seed. Many 1970s films feature the ruined factories of a deindustrialized urban core, but *Dirty Harry* ends in the wasteland at the edge of a declining city. Rather than a final image of San Francisco, a wide, ascending helicopter shot reveals a dull plain crisscrossed by concrete overpasses and industrial water channels. This murky industrial site that dwarfs Harry is the forgotten detritus of the city and a reminder of the absence of an urban society worth fighting for (see Figure 5.4).

Harry not only lacks a place to defend but also struggles to retain visual mastery over the city. The film opens with Scorpio's omniscient view from a sniper's nest, and he repeatedly asserts visual dominance over Harry. Sensitive color film stock helped reinforce the police officers' marked lack of

5.4. The finale of *Dirty Harry* takes place not in the heart of San Francisco, but in a decaying frontier on the fringe of the city: *top*, a rock quarry; *bottom*, a postindustrial wasteland.

vision. As Harry pursues a suspect through dark streets, the suspect appears as a barely perceptible flash of motion in the night. Windows offer a seductive visual agency that consistently undermines Harry. For example, he steals a peek at an unconventional domestic scene including an Asian man and a large, topless woman in a skid row apartment. After stumbling from his perch, Harry is assaulted by a gang of street dwellers for peeping at "Hot Mary." Later, on a stakeout, Harry peers through binoculars, and his gaze lingers on a naked hippie woman. This voyeuristic indulgence nearly prevents him from spotting Scorpio on the rooftop.[174] Scorpio then shoots out the neon "Jesus Saves" sign above Harry and his partner, reclaiming the cover of darkness. The shattered glass rains down on the police as the killer's machine gun annihilates the source of light.

North Beach, with its strip clubs and neon signs, provided not only derelict urban settings but also an ideal streetscape for Surtees's cinematography. Harry drives at night past blocks of the red-light district and follows Scorpio into one of the clubs. Neon lights provide just enough exposure to glimpse figures but leave swathes of dark shadows. Uncorrected fluorescents, used for realist expediency in *Bullitt*, point up the seedy landscape of the city by bathing Harry in sickly colored light, particularly when he stands beneath the "Jesus Saves" sign. Even the choice of props, such as a yellow bag holding Scorpio's ransom money, provides just enough color to remain barely visible as Harry runs through a darkened tunnel. During this exceptionally dark foot chase, phone booths serve a similar role, again creating small pools of colored light in a shadowy urban landscape.

Other elements of Harry's footrace from phone booth to phone booth highlight the unique urban geography employed in the film. Harry moves from car to train to streetcar to finally running on foot. Analogous to Scorpio's manipulation of Harry and the rest of the city, Harry's mode of transportation gradually weakens. On foot, the full decline of the city becomes readily apparent. The obstacles that deter Harry from reaching his destination are all indications of urban blight. A gang of young, leather-clad thugs tries to mug Harry for his bag of ransom money. A vagrant answers the phone despite Harry's protests. Finally, in the forest of Mount Davidson Park, a stereotypical gay hustler tries to pick up Harry, a scene Herb Caen wryly described as "a bit of local color."[175]

As Scorpio directs Harry from place to place, Harry crisscrosses the city, and the darkness of the images helps smooth the creative geography. Surtees's ability to create a disturbing environment largely through lighting was particularly useful in San Francisco, where fewer locations resembled the dilapidated buildings, stained walls, and trash-strewn streets of Manhattan as depicted in *Midnight Cowboy* and *The French Connection*. Harry descends from downtown streets into tunnels, back alleys, and finally, an urban forest, where Scorpio assaults him under a giant concrete cross. As he delves deeper into the city under Scorpio's command, he moves from civilization to wilderness, where an older sign of cultural order, the cross, provides no more protection than its neon counterpart. Whereas *Vertigo*'s tourist itinerary covers San Francisco's scenic public sites and cultural institutions, Harry's nightmare tour reveals the backside of the city, full of interstitial pathways and threatening people and subcultures. Just as *Vertigo* preserved its cinetourist aesthetic by avoiding eyesores like the Embarcadero Freeway, *Dirty*

Harry painstakingly avoided shooting in the picturesque districts that still flourished in San Francisco in the early 1970s. A grim story, shadowy lighting, and a careful choice of locations created a facsimile of New York's urban decay in San Francisco.

Surveillance is a major motif of *Dirty Harry*, beginning with the opening scene, where Scorpio kills a swimmer with a sighted rifle, displaying visual authority over the police and presenting one of the era's dominant criminal archetypes: the sniper. Snipers appear in several urban and ex-urban thrillers of the era, including *Targets* (1968), *The Organization*, *The French Connection*, *Across 110th Street*, and *Get Carter* (1971). These surreptitious killers were not only threatening soldiers in Vietnam, but also police, as seen in the sensationalized coverage of urban riots. The initial shock of the sniper assassination of John F. Kennedy in 1963 would become a recurring trauma with the Charles Whitman Tower shootings at the University of Texas in 1966 and Martin Luther King's assassination in 1968. Not coincidently, the recently improved zoom lens became a frequent analogue for the sniper's scope. In *Dirty Harry*, we first see a telephoto image of the female swimmer before Siegel slowly zooms out to reveal Scorpio taking aim from another rooftop. This scene perversely takes advantage of San Francisco's growing skyline. Several other scenes filmed on high-rise rooftops reveal broad scenic vistas that would be the envy of 1950s cine-tourist films; yet this broader view reveals a broader kill zone, and the beautiful sunlit scenery provides a false sense of security from the imminent threat.

The pairing of the zoom lens and sniper scope is both an optical equivalency of distant vision and a continuation of the link between visual technology and military force explored by Paul Virilio in *War and Cinema*.[176] The presence of a sniper militarizes both point-of-view and telephoto shots of the city, equating the ability to see with the ability to kill. By point of contrast, Scorpio remains difficult for Harry to see for much of the film, disappearing into the shadowy streets or hiding behind a mask in the Mount Davidson confrontation. Additionally, the practice of dominating the landscape with a rifle from the high ground or rooftop is another Western trope, notably appearing in *Winchester '73* (1950), *The Wild Bunch*, and the Western-style opening of *Coogan's Bluff*. The ability of the zoom lens to capture both the distant detail and the wider scope of the urban landscape fluidly extends the scope of danger from the street to the city at large.

Scorpio's visual technology proves far more effective than a police technology equally loaded with symbolism: the helicopter. The first news helicopter, a former Korean War unit adapted as a "telecopter" for KTLA News in Los Angeles, covered its first major story in 1965: the Watts riots. During four days of national coverage, the helicopter overlooked blocks of bungalows covered in smoke and flames.[177] As in Vietnam, helicopter pilots soared above the destruction but failed to understand the complex reality below. Having emerged as a technologically advanced tool for military surveillance, helicopters soon came to represent the failure of technological might and vision to control the confusing violence on the ground. The Air Cavalry would emerge from the same division that had "won the West" from Native Americans.[178] The failures, horrors, and historical parallels of Vietnam played out not only in Hollywood Westerns like *Soldier Blue* (1970) and *Ulzana's Raid* (1972), but also in the contemporary urban frontier of *Dirty Harry*.

Helicopter shots provide stunning overhead views, and they were growing more common in the mid-1960s with the Oscar-winning development of a helicopter camera mount that minimized vibration.[179] Aerial shots became a staple of the *Dirty Harry* films and provide some of the brief touristic views of San Francisco. Views from the cockpits and footage of the helicopters swirling past the city's skyscrapers, with the bay in the background, show that the urban crisis had hardly damaged the city's beautiful vistas. Yet as Harry scours a rooftop for sniper shells, the helicopters circle above a dense urban landscape they can survey but not penetrate. Even when a police helicopter swoops down on Scorpio, foiling his attempt at another rooftop murder, and the police order him to desist over a loudspeaker, he disappears through a door as the helicopter fails to bridge the distance between the sky and the ground. Siegel cuts to the cost of this failure: a policeman lying prone in the dim street, shot to death by Scorpio. Unlike the sniper's rifle, the police helicopters lack lethal force. By contrast, at the conclusion of *Experiment in Terror*, a state-of-the-art police helicopter tracks Lynch's car to Candlestick Park. Police surround him on the pitcher's mound as the helicopter descends, trapping him from above, as officers on foot surround him from below. The sequence ends with two smooth ascending helicopter shots separated by a dissolve, creating a seamless transition to an extreme wide shot high above the stadium, an island of light and activity within the night sky. Institutional authority has eliminated the insidious criminal and restored its command over a vast urban landscape.

In *Dirty Harry*, Siegel chose an identical camera movement to punctuate a similar event: Harry's apprehension of Scorpio on the field of the deserted

Kezar Stadium.[180] After shooting him, Harry grinds his foot into the gunshot wound in a desperate attempt to discover where Scorpio has hidden a kidnapped girl. Scorpio bleats and protests the excessive use of force as authorities move toward the field, preventing Harry from administering vigilante justice. With Lalo Schifrin's discordant score heightening the palpable sense of uneasiness, the camera rapidly jags away from the empty stadium. Unlike the majestic swoop upward in *Experiment in Terror*, the speed and agitation of the camera movement show a city spinning out of Harry's violent grasp. The final shot of *Dirty Harry*, another ascending helicopter shot, reveals the desolate landscape of San Francisco's exurbia. In an inversion of *Experiment in Terror*, Harry becomes the tarnished symbol of authority, sinking like his badge into a filthy, disordered urban landscape.

One scene in particular summarizes how *Dirty Harry* mobilized new cinematic technology to directly attack San Francisco's historical cinematic beauty. Because it was shot in extremely low light, the Golden Gate Bridge's shining red beams turned black, and the gorgeous view of San Francisco beyond the bay turned dull blue and hazy. Despite the muted colors, Harry standing in the foreground, overlooking the bridge, forms a postcard composition (Figure 5.5). Yet such careful framing merely sets up a contrast with the following shot, where a handheld camera with a telephoto lens roughly follows the motion of workers pulling the nude corpse of Scorpio's fourteen-year-old victim out of a drainage ditch. As San Francisco's

5.5. Harry and the Golden Gate Bridge at dawn. Because of the extremely low light, the red beams appear black, and the view of San Francisco beyond the bay looks dull blue and hazy. The fast Eastman color stock facilitated the low-light shooting.

touristic beauty turns monochromatic, the semi-documentary camerawork exposes the interstitial space below the urban splendor, a police scene of macabre, senseless violence.

TV COPS FOR THE URBAN CRISIS: *THE STREETS OF SAN FRANCISCO*

Dirty Harry cost $3 million. By point of comparison, in the early 1970s, a typical half-hour television show cost just over $100,000, and two-hour television pilots came in under $1 million.[181] Thus *Streets of San Francisco* could not emulate the action spectacles of *Dirty Harry*. Nor could it air the film's graphic violence and teeming sex districts on network television. Nonetheless, it distinguished itself from older network series with extensive location shooting. The series included scenic shots of the city, but it also gravitated toward seedy areas and decrepit districts, a badge of gritty television realism. Crime series demand a weekly crime, and as in *Dirty Harry*, murders in *The Streets of San Francisco* often implicated the city itself.

Quinn Martin, the successful producer of long-running television crime series such as *The Fugitive* (1962–1967) and *The F.B.I.* (1965–1974), shot a handful of productions in San Francisco in the early 1970s, including the television movie *Incident in San Francisco* (1970), followed by a one-week shoot in 1971 for *The F.B.I.* Seizing upon the promise of a regular series shooting largely in the city, Mayor Alioto drew close to Martin. In the summer of 1973, as *Streets* began its second season, Alioto wrote to thank "Quinn" for a personal favor: having Karl Malden speak on Alioto's behalf at the Robert Kennedy Club. Alioto added, "Please do not hesitate to call on my office if we can be of any assistance to you."[182] Martin soon became a regular participant and contributor to the annual film festival.[183] More importantly, after its first season, *Streets* began shooting entirely on location in San Francisco.[184]

Location shooting in various cities was a notable trend in urban police shows debuting in 1972, including *Streets*, *The Rookies* (Los Angeles), *Banacek* (Boston), and *Jigsaw* (Sacramento). San Francisco hosted several television cops, and *Variety* joked about Karl Malden, Raymond Burr (*Ironside*), and Rock Hudson (*McMillan and Wife*) all working out of the same office.[185] *Ironside*, which over two years (1970–1971) spent only a week shooting in San Francisco, looked increasingly dated as location shooting became a staple of police series.[186] And as television shows grew more action-oriented, Ironside's wheelchair became a ratings handicap. A staple of NBC's Thursday night lineup, *Ironside* struggled to attract new viewers.[187] A top-ten rated show in 1972, it fell out of the top twenty-five the following year, when *Streets* first cracked the top twenty-five.[188]

For the first season, the *Streets* crew shot exteriors in San Francisco and interiors in Los Angeles. For greater efficiency, they would shoot two episodes of interiors followed by two episodes of exteriors. This saved money, but star Karl Malden recalled that it hurt performances as actors alternated scenes for different episodes.[189] A Cinemobile reduced below-the-line costs for location shooting, and the series helped sell the production vehicle in a full-page *Variety* ad, claiming that the Cinemobile had proved as dependable as the trolley, having logged over 1,800 hours for the show by the end of 1973.[190] *McMillan and Wife*, shooting regularly in San Francisco during the early 1970s, was another Cinemobile customer.

Variety appreciated *Streets of San Francisco*'s two-hour pilot but questioned the sustainability of location shooting: "It's hard to judge this cop meller off a splashy two-hour premiere with all that location detail when it all may wind up between interiors on the Warners' lot and a Nob Hill phone booth come midseason." The reviewer listed San Francisco locations and Karl Malden as its two biggest production assets.[191] Rather than retreat after the pilot, the series spent close to three weeks per month shooting in San Francisco during its first season.[192] For the second season, producers rented a warehouse in the city where they built the interior sets. The show favored San Francisco exteriors over interiors, though this interfered with high-quality sound recording. Undeterred, technicians installed a looping facility in the warehouse to efficiently record and postdub dialogue compromised by noisy locations.[193]

By 1973, *The Streets of San Francisco* had filmed twenty-six episodes a season over the course of eight months in San Francisco. This rapid pace necessitated thirteen-day schedules for each one-hour episode, split between six days of preparation and seven days of shooting. While crews shot one episode, other personnel planned the next one. Location scouting, led by series location manager Tom Piskura, formed a large part of the preparation. The day the script arrived, Piskura would list potential locations for every scene. He spent the remaining days evaluating locations and building a shooting schedule. He had three criteria for locations: photographic concerns, local cooperation, and logistical concerns. Ideal locations not only fit the story but facilitated quick lighting setups and camera dollies. Piskura favored locations with helpful owners or administrators, as well as ones with parking for production vehicles and within close proximity of other locations. One episode involved exterior shots of six churches and interior shots of two; Piskura spent nearly a full day visiting San Francisco churches with a member of the Archdiocesan Communications Office to find those that best fit his criteria.[194]

Piskura carefully informed location owners and residents about the realities of location production. He compared the arrival of the production company to "a band of gypsies bringing a side show," which could be a shock to location owners expecting less equipment, fewer crew members, and often, a chance to participate.[195] Despite the efficiency of the Cinemobile, production still required as many as eight trucks, half a dozen cars, a handful of buses, and twenty to fifty people. A reporter documenting the process referred to the "familiar white signs announcing, 'No Parking.'"[196] In a dense city of narrow streets, frequently tying up parking spaces and traffic affected many local residents and was a source of irritation that contributed to the backlash against location production.

In its initial review, *Variety* aptly described *Streets* as a modernized version of *The Lineup*, a 1950s San Francisco cop series featuring far more location work than *Peter Gunn* or *Ironside*. The opening credits of *The Lineup* show a police car turning atop a hill to reveal a scenic view of the city. *Streets of San Francisco*'s credits also favor scenic spots, updated as a modern montage of snap zooms toward various tourist sites, like the famous opening credits of *Hawaii Five-O* (1968–1980). Occasionally the production's sustained engagement with the city spurred greater authenticity. Piskura saw a difference in the depiction of the minor characters, often questioned on location by the detectives. Rather than appearing in generic settings, they worked on cable cars or sold flowers, adding local flavor. Other scenes lacked such specificity. Major dialogue sequences were written in Hollywood and dispatched north to San Francisco. While full-day shoots in the warehouse studio offered a welcome respite from the logistical demands of location shooting, interior sets were indistinguishable from their Hollywood counterparts.[197]

As with *Dirty Harry*, the producers of *Streets of San Francisco* never let an appreciation for the city soften their gritty depiction of the violent and illicit urban realm common among 1970s police dramas. The two-hour pilot reveled in ugly settings and macabre images, opening on a stretch of dirt and asphalt by the bay, where a dead woman floats. Other locations included a seedy motel in a North Beach–like vice district, the underside of the Embarcadero, and various dockside warehouses. In a clever zoom shot juxtaposing images of urban blight and cine-tourism, the camera opens on a dumpster before zooming out to reveal a macabre crime scene (Figure 5.6) and then

5.6. A macabre scene in *The Streets of San Francisco* (ABC, 1972), which serialized the tarnished, crime-ridden city of *Dirty Harry* for television.

a beautiful San Francisco vista. More frequently, scenic images appeared uncritically as establishing shots or transitional images for when the show returned from commercial; the Golden Gate Bridge and Chinatown were common sights. As in *Bullitt* and *Dirty Harry*, *Streets* featured extensive driving sequences and high-speed pursuits, revealing larger stretches of the city. Smaller cameras facilitated rear-mounted camera shots, as well as shots from the backseat of the squad car; *Bullitt*'s innovations could now be achieved on a television budget. Like Malpaso, Quinn Martin employed Panavision equipment to maximize shooting efficiency on location.[198]

While locations oscillated between gritty urban districts and scenic views, the crime stories were particularly grim. The first case leads Detectives Stone (Malden) and Keller (Michael Douglas) into the local drug scene, where San Francisco aristocrats are taking advantage of young runaways. A final confrontation pits the cops against a Satanist (loosely modeled on San Francisco's notorious Church of Satan founder, Anton Lavey), whose mansion brims with black magic décor. This villain not only killed the teen siblings at the center of the investigation, but murdered and molested a number of children in another unsolved case. Instead of emphasizing the resolution of the crime, the show lingers on photographs of the victims, including a haunting image of the teenagers holding a "California or Bust" sign. Runaway youth meeting bad consequences was a staple of crime series, as were fear-mongering exposés on destinations like Haight-Ashbury and Greenwich Village, but for broadcast television, *Streets* offered an incredibly bleak reflection on the California dream.[199]

The pilot was no exception to other downbeat urban stories, with crimes that challenged the partners' professional restraint as if threatening to push them to become like Harry Callahan. In the first regular episode, Stone seeks revenge for the shooting of his best friend, while the second episode draws Keller into a romance with a prostitute. Other first-season episodes feature crazed Vietnam veterans, cop killers, rapists, and assassins. In a direct nod to *Dirty Harry*, one show centers on a burglar who killed a child but is released on a technicality. Television budgets precluded the extensive night exteriors and elaborately degraded cinematography that set the tone for the urban crisis in feature films. Yet *Streets* brought a similar definition of urban realism through depictions of horrific crimes and stark settings, supplemented by a less pronounced "documentary look."[200] A half-blighted, crime-ridden San Francisco became a weekly television setting.

Other series shot in San Francisco briefly or sporadically, such as *San Francisco International Airport* (1970–1971) and *McMillan and Wife*, but *The Streets of San Francisco* was the city's only resident television production. Months of frequent location shooting further desensitized San Francisco residents to the presence of professional film crews. Location mishaps—such as when actual police responded to a crime near the University of San Francisco location set, or when the series constructed a one-day mock cemetery for an episode—were frequently the subject of local columns.[201] As the influx of film production continued into the mid-1970s, local enthusiasm for film and television production waned. Some residents grew inured to moviemaking and, like New Yorkers and Angelenos, barely paused to notice the film crews. Others raised tough questions about the benefits of the Hollywood occupation of the city. Was San Francisco developing a local production industry or merely selling its sites to Los Angeles workers? And how would an imaginary on-screen crime wave affect its carefully cultivated image? This was no minor concern for a city whose film committee was part of its tourist bureau.

While San Francisco grappled with its production boom, Hollywood started to reassess its production strategies as blockbuster pictures and new technologies began to pull production back to the lot. In 1974, *The Conversation* became the first studio release to be set, shot, and edited entirely within San Francisco. The same year, *The Towering Inferno*, also set in San Francisco, staged a disaster too large and too dependent on special effects to mount on location and spent far more time and money shooting on Hollywood backlots than in the city. Despite its local origin, *The Conversation* said more about Americans' deep disillusionment with US cities in general than it did about San Francisco itself, which largely served as a local backlot for Coppola's personal vision. As a high-concept blockbuster, *The Towering Inferno* reasserted the advantages of the soundstage and made only cursory use of San Francisco. The film's tremendous success indicated that fantastical effects held more box office appeal than real locations, signaling the end of a thirty-year expansion of Hollywood location shooting.

6

HOLLYWOOD NORTH / HOLLYWOOD RESURGENCE

The Conversation and *The Towering Inferno*

THE GODFATHER DOMINATED THE 1972 BOX OFFICE and won the Academy Award for Best Picture, establishing Francis Ford Coppola as San Francisco's first filmmaking superstar. Irwin Allen's disaster film *The Poseidon Adventure* came in second and earned the third most Oscar nominations.[1] For the 1974 Oscars, Allen and Coppola squared off again with two films set in San Francisco, *The Towering Inferno* and *The Conversation*, nominated for Best Picture along with Coppola's *Godfather Part II*. Coppola won the Oscar for *Godfather II*, but even the combined gross of his two Best Picture nominees paled in comparison to *The Towering Inferno*, the top earner of 1975. By early 1977, it had become one of the ten highest-grossing films of all time and, with $55 million in domestic rentals, had outearned *Godfather II* by $16 million.[2] *The Conversation* was a much smaller film, an intense character study of a reserved surveillance expert that earned critical acclaim but, on a $1.6 million budget, merely broke even. *The Towering Inferno* was *The Poseidon Adventure* with bigger stars, bigger explosions, and more complex special effects.

Both films were shot in San Francisco, but in an entirely different fashion that pointed to another sea change in location shooting. With *The Conversation*, Coppola proved that a major studio release, from pre- through post-production, could be entirely crafted in San Francisco. *The Towering Inferno* proved that a new scale of spectacle could only be accomplished on the back-lot. No filmmaker could build a set for the tallest building in the world and burn it to the ground in the middle of downtown San Francisco. Awash in film and television production, San Francisco courted a film that not only staged the city's destruction, but heralded its decline in location production. Meanwhile, citizen support for Hollywood filmmaking continued to erode as residents tangled with location filmmakers, and the city's on-screen image continued to suffer.

The films employed vastly different production strategies and location shooting practices, but in each, San Francisco was largely incidental. Despite being a resident, Coppola treated the city like an urban backlot for his interiorized story. *The Conversation* reflected American disillusionment with the central city, concerns not unique to San Francisco.[3] *The Towering Inferno* minimized location shooting to focus on spectacular pyrotechnical effects and physical sets built on Fox's soundstages and backlot. This minimized the role of San Francisco, which served as a generic urban background for scenic establishing shots and the climactic rescue. *The Towering Inferno* revealed nothing about the city beyond Mayor Alioto's continued ability to woo producers amid growing local dissatisfaction with film production.

Allen's disaster pictures—along with *Airport* (1970), *Earthquake* (1974), and the semi-disaster picture, *Jaws* (1975)—pointed toward the crowd-thrilling, mass audience blockbusters that came to define post-1975 Hollywood. As Charles Champlin observed in early 1975, "It has been a time of blockbusters and small, hard gems, with not much in the middle."[4] *The Conversation* was one of the latter, an inexpensive, incisive picture with limited box office appeal. As the American film industry recovered from the Hollywood Recession, a handful of phenomenal mass audience hits proved to be more profitable than the early 1970s production slate of low-budget, downbeat, and young adult–oriented features. The stark realism of early 1970s hits like *The French Connection* and *The Godfather* gave way to the adventure fantasies of *The Towering Inferno*, *Jaws*, and *Close Encounters of the Third Kind*

(1977). Location shooting remained a requisite component of feature filmmaking, but the specificity of place receded into the background. Unlike *Vertigo* and *Bullitt*, the success of *The Towering Inferno* owed as little to San Francisco as *Jaws* did to Martha's Vineyard.

The second half of the 1970s brought far greater advances in special effects than in location shooting. Introduced in 1975, the Steadicam facilitated smooth camera movement on the uneven surfaces of various locations, but this technology had a minimal effect on location shooting compared to Eastman 5254 film stock, Panavision cameras, and the Cinemobile. By contrast, the optical effects employed on *Star Wars* (1977) and *Close Encounters* changed the paradigm for special effects, displacing the most cumbersome physical effects of *The Towering Inferno* and expanding the role of visual effects throughout Hollywood cinema. Nonetheless, the location aesthetic of the early 1970s persisted, as filmmakers combined location footage and certain semi-documentary techniques with optical effects, using a realist style to lend credence to fantastical events. A growing emphasis on special effects pulled production work back to the controlled environment of both the backlot and the high-tech post-production studio. Even spectacular locations such as Devils Tower in *Close Encounters* needed to be recomposited in post-production with the overwhelming illusion of an alien spaceship.

In the early 1970s, as Hollywood appeared on the brink of collapse, San Francisco dreamt of luring the entire industry northward. Hollywood's blockbuster success ensured that San Francisco remained primarily what it had always been, a location for Los Angeles filmmakers. Television series, movies, and commercials kept San Francisco's nascent production industry alive, and the city continued to draw feature filmmakers for prolonged location shoots, but with less regularity. By 1975, San Francisco's boom in location shooting had subsided, and while the city remained a popular site for film and television producers, Hollywood paid far less attention to its specific culture and its less familiar sites. At the same time, the city faced growing competition from other cities, states, and countries aggressively seeking location production dollars.

With two Best Picture nominees shot in San Francisco, 1974 was a marquee year for Alioto's campaign to draw Hollywood filmmakers to the city; nonetheless, the production of *The Conversation* and *The Towering Inferno* showed that San Francisco was still a location, not a self-contained film industry. Meanwhile, residents and commentators were growing more frustrated with the negative impact of both Hollywood crews and Hollywood depictions of the city. *The Conversation* was a landmark for San Francisco film production, and perhaps the closest Coppola came to his goal of personal filmmaking, but it offered a desolate view of his home city, consonant with how other Hollywood filmmakers were representing San Francisco and other American cities. *The Towering Inferno* offered a more tourist-friendly image of the city, but daunting production demands relegated San Francisco to a scenic backdrop, largely recreated on the Fox lot. The qualities that made the *Towering Inferno* an enormous hit helped check the steady expansion of domestic location shooting that had benefited San Francisco since the late 1960s.

"LET THEM MAKE THEIR MOVIES SOMEWHERE ELSE"

In 1973, Alioto's production campaign paid off with seven features shooting in the city. This success came at a price, with a boom in gritty police films portraying the city as rife with violent crime. In 1968, San Francisco high society had gladly welcomed filmmakers and the chance to appear as extras in *Bullitt* and *Petulia*. But by the mid-1970s, a growing number of residents and downtown businesses were questioning the value of location shooting. San Franciscans felt betrayed by Hollywood companies that took advantage of local cooperation and caused traffic and other disruptions, only to negatively depict the city on-screen. Popular columnist Herb Caen supported and publicized the Downtown Business Association's rebuke of Hollywood filmmakers, proclaiming: "Let them make their movies somewhere else."[5]

Alioto and local film industry leaders responded to complaints by trumpeting the annual $10 million or more that Hollywood production brought in jobs and services. In 1973, Jesse Unruh, running for mayor of Los Angeles, suggested, "San Francisco probably has more production right now than we have down south."[6] Such rhetoric imagined San Francisco as an emerging film industry center to rival Los Angeles, but the reality was that it was still by and large a location, reliant on projects originating from Hollywood studios and, after principal photography, edited and processed in Los Angeles. Unlike pre- and post-production, phases that provided regular work and few logistical challenges, San Francisco rarely had enough feature production to provide full-time employment for local workers. And unlike sprawling Los Angeles, San Francisco's tightly packed downtown struggled to accommodate multiple productions without inconveniencing numerous residents. American Zoetrope was the key exception, but Coppola's facility could only handle small, location-shot films like *The Conversation*, the type of films that Hollywood increasingly ignored in favor of blockbusters like *The Towering Inferno*.

Through the mid-1970s, Hollywood location shooting in San Francisco was frequent enough for local columnist Jack Rosenblum to run a recurring column titled "Hollywood North" about major movie companies shooting in town. At least two columnists, Jack Rosenblum and Judy Warrenfeltz, spent a day as a local extra, providing additional publicity for Hollywood production, now an everyday event in the city.[7] That same year, when CBS premiered a show about a Chinese detective, each major network had a series shooting in San Francisco (*The Streets of San Francisco* for ABC, and *Amy Prentiss* for NBC).[8] A 1975 clipping about a Hitchcock movie scheduled to shoot in San Francisco epitomizes the city's now blasé response to Hollywood production: "Ho, hum, another big-budget movie will be filmed here."[9] As San Francisco residents grew more accustomed to Hollywood location shooting, they also grew less tolerant of it.

A wave of police films set in San Francisco, inspired by *Bullitt* and *Dirty Harry*, created both representational and logistical problems for the city. A *Los Angeles Times* article on San Francisco's film popularity identified John DeLuca, the deputy mayor, and police sergeant Bill McCarthy as the key people to call in order to stage a difficult scene. The two examples were "a school bus full of children crashing into a city playground" (for *The Laughing Policeman* [1973]) and "a sniper spraying bullets around campus" (for an episode of *Streets of San Francisco*). Of the six theatrical films shot in San Francisco through July 1973, three were police films, one was an Italian-produced gangster film, and the other, *The Conversation*, centered on a murder investigation. Disney's sequel *Herbie Rides Again* (1973) was the rare nonviolent depiction of the city, although it still featured the de rigueur car chase.[10] Car chases closed off local streets and, occasionally, highway sections and tunnels, causing traffic and parking problems for hundreds of residents in the densely populated downtown core.

In the opening scene of *The Laughing Policeman*, a masked gunman kills eight bus passengers with a machine gun. As a reporter observed, "[I]f Hollywood film companies are keeping score, the statistics of 'crime victims' in San Francisco should be impressive."[11] Based on a novel set in Stockholm, Sweden, the film capitalized on the success of *Dirty Harry* by adopting a San Francisco setting and providing gruesome violence. *The Laughing Policeman* even outdid *Dirty Harry*'s depiction of vice and urban decay. The list of locations for approval included three topless bars, a porno theater, boardinghouses, and a massage parlor.[12] The plot involved pornographic snapshots, a cop cruising a gay bar in pursuit of the killer, and scenes staged in both Hispanic and African American ghettos. In one strip club, a patron obscures an image of a bottomless dancer lifting her legs in front of the crowd. From explicit sex districts to downtrodden ethnic neighborhoods, San Francisco appears as an amalgamation of sites symbolizing the fears, fantasies, and moral outrage of the urban crisis.

Television series like *Ironside* and *Streets* also grew more violent, as did the *Dirty Harry* sequel *Magnum Force*. Herb Caen griped about a *Streets* episode that featured a sniper randomly shooting across the University of San Francisco campus, and the fact that the university and local police had given production support to this frightful portrayal of the city.[13] Frequent depictions of San Francisco as crime-ridden weakened the argument that location production was a great form of publicity. Caen, a longtime critic of Hollywood filmmaking in the city, amplified the growing opposition of concerned civic groups. In 1974, the San Francisco Planning and Urban Research Association (SPUR) confronted MPAA head Jack Valenti about the number of violent movies being shot in the city. A few months later, the Downtown Association echoed these concerns, saying that the glut of crime films had given San Francisco "an undeserved Chicago-like reputation."[14] In 1968, the Chicago convention riots were the antithesis of San Francisco's Summer of Love; by 1974, the reputations of both cities had suffered from Hollywood's gritty crime aesthetic.

San Francisco's on-screen crime boom had begun with *Bullitt* in 1968, but the city now faced an actual wave of salacious crimes. Between late 1973 and early 1974, the city would see the reappearance of the Zodiac killer, the kidnapping of Patty Hearst by the Symbionese Liberation Army, and the Zebra murders, committed by a radical offshoot of the Nation of Islam that targeted white residents. In January 1974, San Francisco's streets were empty at night as racial tensions seethed.[15] National stories on crime in San Francisco, along with labor and redevelopment issues, showed the persistence of the city's exceptional reputation. Two *New York Times* headlines from 1974 and 1975—"Big City Problems Peril San Francisco's Charming Image" and "Magical 'Happy' San Francisco Also Has Problems, and Tears"—suggest that the mere existence of typical urban challenges in the city was news to most Americans. In turn, San Francisco's halcyon image was particularly vulnerable to any appearance of urban decline or unrest.

Some critics went so far as to blame violent movies for inciting crime or, at the very least, causing just as much damage to San Francisco's image.[16] *Variety* reporter Jim Harwood asked whether several incidents of police violence in San Francisco might be in response to "San Francisco's new popularity as a beautiful bloody backdrop for two-fisted police films"; he noted the popularity of several such films with local police officers, as well as two premieres that had benefited police causes.[17] While advocating against outright censorship, the Downtown Association pressed city government to more closely vet scripts that discredited San Francisco. Businesses earned far more from tourists than film crews and showed little tolerance for Hollywood exacerbating the city's newfound reputation for shocking crimes.

Complaints about screen content were intimately tied to off-screen problems caused by location shooting. The Downtown Association asked, "Why should traffic on Broadway, for instance, be detoured for an hour, requiring the presence of dozens of police, so that a movie can be made showing a daredevil, law-defying motor chase?"[18] *Freebie and the Bean*, a police comedy featuring three wild car chases, ran into major production problems not only for its location demands but also its unflattering script. Like another comedy, *What's Up, Doc?*, *Freebie* caused more public and private outrage than violent police films like *The Laughing Policeman*.

Producer-director Richard Rush acknowledged that *Dirty Harry* and *The French Connection* had inspired dozens of cop films, often set in San Francisco. Rush shifted *Freebie* from Cleveland to San Francisco for what he called "obvious reasons," implying the city's strong association with police films and car chases. Although some officers might enjoy a tough cop bending the rules, Sergeant McCarthy took exception to scripts depicting police as "hopelessly inept or corrupt."[19] Freebie (James Caan), the lead character, gained his nickname by abusing his detective position to pocket items like clothes and alcohol during investigations. His partner, the Bean (Alan Arkin), is equally corrupt and inept. The film suggests police involvement in graft and prostitution and features embarrassing conduct, such as when the partners brawl with a woman on the street. They are not only profane but—not surprisingly for a film with a Mexican American racial slur in its title—spew racial epithets throughout the film.

DeLuca and McCarthy met privately with Rush and his production manager to discuss police concerns about the script. McCarthy publicly stated that the police department had offered suggestions and technical advice, not censorship, but he voiced strong and specific objections to various parts of the script during the closed-door meeting.[20] Rush argued that nearly all of these scenes were comedic embellishments, but McCarthy flatly rebutted that no police officer would behave that way. In the end, *Freebie* faced a type of censorship not unlike the Warner Bros. policy for *Dark Passage*. No mention of the city was made, and references to local newspapers and utility companies were omitted. The police department withheld the official decals usually issued to productions, so the detectives drove unmarked cars and used non–San Francisco badges. Producers even agreed to avoid key landmarks such as the city's famous bridges, while acknowledging the impossibility of completely hiding its identity.[21] As McCarthy later announced, clearly in reference to *Freebie*, films casting police officers in a bad light could shoot in the city, but the on-screen setting would be "Anywhere, U.S.A."[22]

The film's production demands reinforced McCarthy's insistence on script changes. He openly worried about the major chase sequence, featuring a car crashing over the lower deck of the Embarcadero Freeway. This sequence was Warners' primary reason for shooting *Freebie* in San Francisco, so working on a tight schedule, Rush quickly devised a feasible route.[23] Rain delays further tightened the schedule. Either due to time pressure or a poor decision by one of the dozens of agencies overseeing production—in this case, the Department of Public Works—the production closed traffic through the Stockton Tunnel during morning rush hour.[24] The inevitable traffic jam inspired another Herb Caen broadside and a potential investigation by the Board of Supervisors.

The column began by describing the "honest taxpayers" delayed from reaching work. Caen noted another day when *Freebie* parked ten wrecked cars on location, preventing residents from pulling out of their parking spaces: "Fumed one irate woman, 'who needs these people, anyway?' Cop: 'Alioto.'" At the end of his column, Caen posed the woman's question to his readers in light of both the ugly film depictions of San Francisco police and the commuter problems caused by location shooting.[25] This challenged Alioto's production policies on both the publicity front and the economic front, highlighting incidents where location shooting directly harmed local businesses and employees. New York, verging on bankruptcy, would gladly accept traffic problems in exchange for production jobs and revenue; San Francisco, with a thriving tourist economy and financial stability, could reasonably question whether hosting Hollywood was worth the trouble.

Soon after the *Freebie* incident, city supervisor (and future San Francisco mayor) Dianne Feinstein contemplated new legislation governing location production. Members of the city's film committee and local labor leaders helped dissuade her from pursuing new laws. They later persuaded Supervisor Dorothy von Beroldingen to not hold public hearings on location filmmaking in the city. The film committee remained at arm's length from the mayor's office, but they collaborated closely whenever the Board of Supervisors moved to wrest control over film production.[26] The board's occasional regulatory threats exposed the fragility of San Francisco's production economy, predicated on local cooperation by residents and several government offices instead of direct financial incentives for Hollywood filmmakers.

Alioto weathered the public outcry over location shooting, and his active recruitment of Hollywood filmmakers remained effective through the end of his term in 1976. In a 1973 publicity piece for *The Towering Inferno*, producer Irwin Allen twice cited a "marvelous mayor" as the main reason he chose to film in San Francisco, and why he would consider the city for future projects.[27] Alioto also received private shows of support for his strong cooperation with filmmakers. Malpaso producer Robert Daley sent along location audits for *Magnum Force* that documented the over $1 million spent in the city, providing evidence against his critics. The production team for *The Killer Elite* (1975) met with both Alioto and DeLuca, who not only offered to help clear locations but also suggested alternatives to ward off potential problems.[28]

The San Francisco Film Festival remained the centerpiece of Alioto's production campaign. In June 1973, festival head Claude Jarman hosted a Los Angeles luncheon to honor Alioto and, ostensibly, to promote the event. The guest list clearly emphasized location production over film appreciation, including studio executives such as Peter Bart and Peter Guber, television executives like Screen Gems' John Mitchell, Freddie Fields (Steve McQueen's power agent), *Streets of San Francisco* producer Quinn Martin, Irwin Allen, and *The Towering Inferno* screenwriter Stirling Silliphant. Jarman planned to follow up with Allen, and a few months after the luncheon, Allen announced he would shoot in San Francisco.[29]

The actual festival, financed by donations from major productions shot in San Francisco, provided ample publicity for these features and series. An aptly titled *Variety* item, "Frisco Fest Name-Drop," listed stars in attendance, including Gene Hackman, Michael Douglas, Stacy Keach, and Jack Lemmon, all of whom were working on San Francisco–based productions. Francis Ford Coppola received a newly created award, a marketing idea suggested by the film committee; the trophy was a magnet shaped like Saint Francis of Assisi, the city's and also the director's patron saint, and a symbol of Coppola's ability to draw filmmaking to the city.[30] While local festival attendees focused on the visiting celebrities, Alioto focused on Hollywood producers, celebrating and extending their partnerships with the city.

Urban renewal continued to provide useful locations for filmmakers, creating city-controlled, depopulated structures that required little heed for property damage. In scenes featuring gunfights and explosions in *The Killer Elite*, an area slated for demolition could provide "a place that doesn't have to be reconstructed after we have had a shoot up in it."[31] With help from city hall, producers substituted dynamite for a wrecking ball and blew up a firehouse slated for redevelopment.[32] *The Laughing Policeman* inquired about an abandoned police station for a principal set.[33] The ease and limited liability of shooting in urban development zones provided further incentive for filmmakers to shoot in the most blighted districts. Similarly, the double-decker highway structure that made the Embarcadero an eyesore also held a production advantage: the city could easily close off the lower deck for filmmaking, providing a sheltered route for car chases.[34] In contrast to *Bullitt*'s scenic automotive tour, *The Laughing Policeman* and *Freebie and the Bean* both featured car chases through this dingy underpass.

By the mid-1970s, San Francisco boasted far more production service firms than in the late 1960s, as detailed in the film committee's twenty-four page booklet "Location: San Francisco," which appeared in July 1974.[35] The city now had four equipment rental companies, seven film labs, six recording facilities, and two small soundstages. Nonetheless, locations were still the key selling point, with a third of the booklet devoted to lists of potential filming sites along with contact information for the maze of municipal offices and private businesses that managed landmarks, districts, transportation, and surrounding Bay Area counties and cities. The booklet concludes with a summary of San Francisco's history and geography, including an optimistic description of nearly year-round "springtime," despite a cool average temperature range of 50–63° F. These general facts were widely known in Los Angeles, but the last page of the booklet addressed international producers, mentioning Rome and Tokyo alongside New York and Hollywood.[36]

This comprehensive booklet lent the appearance of industrial efficiency to what remained a patchwork set of practices and facilities for Hollywood productions. In New York, Mayor Lindsay had established a one-stop film permit office in the late 1960s; San Francisco could only claim the same in 1976, and months later, *The Hollywood Reporter* exposed this as merely a new way to describe the film committee's office. The city charter divided permit authority between agencies such as police, airport, and parks.[37] Additionally, all major studio productions still directly reported to the mayor's office.[38] Consequently, San Francisco maintained a reputation as "a great place to shoot but a lousy place to get any film work done."[39] In other words, casts and crews enjoyed their stay and the beautiful scenery, but despite its recent efforts, San Francisco remained a relatively inefficient site for filmmaking.

The city's growing number of production facilities were best suited for nontheatrical work such as commercials. Coppola bragged that American Zoetrope had better editing equipment than Hollywood, but it lacked other essential post-production tools.[40] Sam Peckinpah visited Zoetrope on a scouting trip for *The Killer Elite*, noting the impressive sound facilities and adequate editing rooms. But the small studio lacked an ADR system, a key tool for fixing dialogue recorded on location. Peckinpah instead viewed Zoetrope as a high-end production office with a screening room for dailies and some editorial work during shooting. While Coppola cut his low-budget personal features at Zoetrope, Peckinpah found the facility inadequate for a studio feature and completed *The Killer Elite* in Los Angeles.[41]

Lacking state-of-the-art facilities, San Francisco was not a feature production center except for a handful of films by Coppola and George Lucas. The city also faced growing competition from rival cities and states. The Texas Film Commission ran a quarter-page ad in *Variety* promoting location shooting there, which ran below a tiny column announcing the San Francisco location booklet.[42] Both highlight the wide range of settings available in their respective regions. In June 1973, filmmaking in Florida was the focus of a multi-article section in *American Cinematographer*, similar to San Francisco's spread in October 1971.[43] Although the Bay Area's picturesque settings and proximity to Los Angeles remained advantageous, other scenic corners of the country soon joined the fray.

Even at its peak, film and television production in San Francisco rarely offered full-time work for residents. Ann Brebner, leader of the city's film committee and head of the largest local casting agency, supplied local actors with roles as extras, but these jobs were short-term, paid modestly, and required actors to respond at a moment's notice. The only steady source of work was *The Streets of San Francisco*, by far the biggest employer of extras.[44] Nonetheless, Jim Bloom, the show's assistant director, conceded that "there's nothing more degrading than working as an extra." He added, "It's inane for extras to think they can get a break working in San Francisco."[45]

For crew members, the situation was even more desperate. Despite Malpaso's local ties to San Francisco, *Magnum Force* rented a hundred rooms at the Quality Inn for three months, a sign of how many production jobs were filled by out-of-towners.[46] In 1971, a peak year for location production, local film workers protested "foreign white hunters who use San Francisco as a game preserve, bag some scenery and hire a few native bearers."[47] Little had changed by 1975, and aside from local Teamster and IATSE members, the major beneficiaries of location revenue were restaurants, hotels, and local production service companies.

As an early center for location filmmaking, San Francisco learned what other North American cities like Toronto, Vancouver, and New Orleans would experience in the future. Cooperation and financial assistance might lure producers to town, but converting revenue and work experience from Hollywood location shoots into a stable local film industry remained an elusive goal. In San Francisco, local objections to filmmaking were already threatening to send Hollywood filmmakers elsewhere. By the second half of the 1970s, lower bids from other cities helped deflate San Francisco's production economy. Without the professional production resources of New York or Los Angeles, few filmmakers saw fit to stay in San Francisco beyond production, the shortest phase of filmmaking.

Despite its limitations, American Zoetrope offered the best hope for a local feature film industry. If Coppola could complete a successful studio film entirely in San Francisco, he would demonstrate that location filmmaking supported by a small post-production facility could fully untether filmmakers from Los Angeles. *The Conversation* was conceived, shot, and edited in the city and, unlike Lucas's film *THX 1138*, took place in present-day San Francisco. But rather than reviving the vibrant culture of the city, Coppola's film portrays a sinister urban landscape defined by surveillance, deception, and alienation. This introspective, understated film gained more critical accolades than box office returns, unlike the enormously successful *Godfather* films that bookended it. Despite the director's avowed love of his home city, the film's defeated tone matched that of Hollywood and American urbanism. Moreover, it revealed the fading box office prospects for modestly budgeted, auteurist films that relied heavily on locations like San Francisco.

ZOOM AND GLOOM

The Conversation was the ultimate San Francisco film—and ultimately not about San Francisco. Location technology allowed Coppola to shoot practically anywhere in the city, yet aside from an ambitious opening sequence in

Union Square, Coppola largely favored interiors for his guarded protagonist, Harry Caul (Gene Hackman). San Francisco locations met all of the production needs for a film expressing a larger American urban anomie rather than a story line specific to that city. Coppola's choice of locations, including his omissions, suggests the mutability of San Francisco, which provided a cold, paranoid setting to match the story. The city's most famous filmmaker depicted it as a bleak landscape of corporate sangfroid and urban decay.

The Conversation opens with Harry Caul leading a complicated audio surveillance operation to record a couple in Union Square. As he scours multiple recordings working to improve the audio quality, he grows convinced that the corporate director (Robert Duval) who hired him plans to kill the couple. As he continues to work on the tapes, his elaborate personal security erodes. Following a convention at a San Francisco hotel, Harry hosts an impromptu party for fellow security experts and conventioneers. After sleeping with one of the women, he awakens to find the recordings stolen. In an ambiguous scene, Harry either overhears a murder at the Jack Tar Hotel or suffers a paranoid delusion. At the end of the film, he realizes that he had misinterpreted the conversation; the couple had been plotting together to murder the corporate director. In a final scene, Harry rips apart his apartment when he realizes he has been bugged.

The film's downbeat and ambiguous narrative was born out of the Hollywood Recession, but *The Conversation* was released in the early blockbuster era. In January 1969, before purchasing facilities for American Zoetrope, Coppola (then insignificant enough for his name to be spelled "Cuppola" in *Variety*) planned for *The Conversation* to be the first film produced there.[48] By late 1969, when Zoetrope became operational, only *THX 1138* was ready for production. The box office failure of Lucas's debut caused Warner Bros. to divest from Zoetrope and pushed the fledgling studio toward financial ruin.[49]

The enormous success of Coppola's *The Godfather* and films by two other young directors, Peter Bogdanovich and William Friedkin, led Paramount chairman Charles Bludhorn to form the Director's Company, where these three promising filmmakers would have wide creative freedom provided they kept their pictures under $3 million. Plans for a future stock issue served to keep these highly sought after directors' fees in check.[50] Soon the choice of personal films such as *The Conversation* and Bogdanovich's *Daisy Miller* rankled not only Friedkin but also Paramount executives, who doubted their box office appeal. Gene Phillips suggests that disaster films such as *The Poseidon Adventure* dimmed studio interests in personal films, which had been desirable, low-cost risks during the Hollywood Recession. However, the success of *The Godfather* and the promise of its sequel gave Paramount sufficient reason to finance *The Conversation* at a reasonable budget of $1.6 million.[51]

Zoetrope's early investment in editing equipment had a profound effect on *The Conversation*, which relied on complex cuts between sound and image to convey Harry Caul's mental reconstruction of a murder plot from a distorted set of audio tracks. In 1969, Coppola's first major purchase for Zoetrope was the newest flatbed editing system, which was featured at the annual German trade fair for photography, Photokina.[52] Independent equipment companies were booming in the 1970s, and Photokina approached 100,000 attendees by 1974.[53] The surveillance trade show attended by Harry Caul in *The Conversation* provides a corollary for Photokina, where technical experts pursued the latest high-tech equipment. Coppola hired Walter Murch, a sound engineer on *The Rain People*, as both a sound and picture editor. Murch had the audio expertise for a film centered on audio surveillance, utilizing the full potential of Zoetrope's editing facilities, including an eight-track KEM and a six-track Steenbeck. These new tools also helped Zoetrope's bottom line, renting out for $1,200 and $600 per month, respectively—much higher than the $120 per month rate for the industry-standard Moviola.[54] Thus while *The Conversation* was a small, personal film, its reliance on technically advanced post-production was a notable similarity with *The Towering Inferno*. Both films' most distinctive effects came well after principal photography wrapped, in the form of a complex soundscape for *The Conversation* and a skyscraper-scale illusion for *The Towering Inferno*. This growing emphasis on post-production technology pointed toward an industry-wide expansion of post-production work, largely brought about by American Zoetrope veteran George Lucas following the success of *Star Wars*.

Another key collaborator was Haskell Wexler, who shot the opening scene in Union Square, providing image and sound that reappears throughout the film. At the University of Southern California, George Lucas befriended Wexler, who helped the young student filmmaker and later did some consultation and shooting for *THX 1138*.[55] Wexler went on to shoot Lucas's low-budget hit *American Graffiti* (1973) in Northern California. In late 1969, Wexler even considered making a film about a prison farm, "Santa Rita," at Zoetrope.[56] However, early in the filming of *The Conversation*, Coppola fired Wexler and shut down production for ten days. Wexler later justified the firing as Coppola's way of buying time for a film quickly running over schedule, giving him time to work on the script. Yet the two argued throughout their brief working relationship, primarily over locations.[57]

The opening scene, which begins with a three-minute zoom over San Francisco's Union Square, represented the height of the film's logistical, technical, and artistic challenges. Wexler, who effectively used hidden cameras in Boston for *The Thomas Crown Affair*, was the perfect cinematographer for the shoot, which featured perhaps hundreds of pedestrians unaware that their lunch break in the park was being filmed. The ambitious sequence relied on six cameras and various long-range shotgun microphones, with sound recordists appearing on-screen as surveillance operators, and cameramen occasionally walking through each other's shots. While Coppola had police permission, officers still arrested some of the sound recordists who looked like snipers (Figure 6.1).[58] The shooting strategy resembled *Medium Cool*, where actors walked through crowds of event participants, albeit in safer circumstances. Once Wexler had five cameras strategically concealed, he told Coppola to "have the actors do just what they would do in the park, and to let the park go."[59] The semi-documentary sequence deployed several independent cameramen shooting the couple as if they were unwitting subjects, a corollary to Harry's audio surveillance work in the film.

6.1. A sniper-style microphone was used to record actual production sound in the ambitious Union Square location shoot for *The Conversation* (Paramount, 1974); it also appears on-screen.

The zoom lens offered a visual counterpart to the long-distance microphone. In the opening shot, an inexorable zoom bridges the distance between an overview of the entire square to a detailed shot of individual figures (Figure 6.2). The source of the audio, a sound recordist on a rooftop, appears in the following shot. Wexler had a 20:1 zoom lens custom built for the scene, far longer than the 10:1 zoom that was standard equipment in the

6.2. Start and end frames of the opening zoom in *The Conversation*. Haskell Wexler used a custom lens to move from the wide urban scale (*top*) to that of human figures (*bottom*), all from a distance that hid the camera from the local crowd.

early 1970s. With zooms becoming so prevalent, Wexler felt that audiences could anticipate the end of it; by zooming far past this perceived limit, he created an unnerving effect of surveillance covering a seemingly impossible distance. The electronically distorted distant sound of the crowd and the couple's dialogue accentuate the camera distance. The effect is a frightening scale of clandestine observation and a powerful invasion of privacy, themes that define the rest of the film.[60]

A tight budget exacerbated the conflict between Wexler and Coppola. Wexler later claimed that his careful preparation allowed him to shoot the opening sequence in a day and a half instead of the scheduled ten or more days.[61] But Coppola faulted him for spending too much time on preparation; working on a low budget for personal projects like *You're a Big Boy Now*, *The Rain People*, and *THX 1138*, Coppola often shot first and gambled with the results. Wexler replied by criticizing Coppola's choice of locations.[62] Despite San Francisco's welcoming overtures to filmmakers, there was little room in the budget or schedule for locations with difficult lighting and logistical challenges. After suspending production, Coppola looked to make up time by hiring a younger, easier to manage cinematographer, Bill Butler, who had shot *The Rain People*. Coppola still lost every day that he had waited to resume production after firing Wexler. Murch later estimated that ten shooting days, covering about fifteen script pages, were never shot.[63]

For nearly a year, Murch oversaw post-production, meeting with Coppola as little as once a month once pre-production began for *Godfather II*. Murch built new plotlines and tweaked existing narrative threads. As a rule, Coppola preferred few costume changes, not only as a mark of realism and characterization (Harry's drab raincoat), but for greater flexibility, allowing Murch to intercut footage intended for different scenes.[64] Near the close of *Classical Hollywood Cinema*, David Bordwell analyzes how *The Conversation* incorporates art cinema strategies into a classical detective story, particularly through ambiguous montage sequences and subjective images cued by Harry listening to the recordings.[65] Production dynamics largely necessitated this strategy. A script still under revision during production, multiple cameras shooting, missing scenes, an absent director, and high-end editing equipment all encouraged art cinema solutions to restructure a film out of disparate and incomplete footage. Like *Petulia*, *The Conversation* stylistically resolved the vagaries of location shooting with frequent nonlinear cutting.

One of Coppola's location choices proved particularly damaging: Alta Plaza, the site of the public outcry over the chipped steps from *What's*

Up, Doc?. Smoke machines used to create a foggy atmosphere for a dream sequence drew neighborhood complaints as the oily smoke wafted around. When a local reporter arrived at the scene, Coppola warned him, "Stop taking pictures—you're making me look bad." He then assaulted the reporter in an effort to disable his news camera, leading to a $300,000 suit against the director and Paramount. The *San Francisco Examiner* noted two ironies: a filmmaker who refused to be filmed, and *The Godfather* director acting like a Mafia thug.[66] The third irony, in light of his violent treatment of a local reporter, was Coppola's Saint Francis Award at the annual film festival. Despite being a San Francisco resident, Coppola had acted just as heedless of local citizens as any other Hollywood location crew.

Coppola avoided further incidents with his remarkable choice for a San Francisco film: shooting almost entirely interiors. With the exception of San Francisco films based on stage plays, such as *Butterflies Are Free* (1972) and *Play It Again, Sam* (1972), filmmakers came to the city for the scenery. By contrast, *The Conversation* takes place almost entirely in a sparsely lit warehouse, cramped apartment buildings, and a windowless convention hall. The only clear view of the bay, a feat for a film shot in a peninsular city, is through the windows at the top of the office tower run by Harry's sinister employer (Figure 6.3). Here the vertical risers of the tower and a shadowy balcony bisecting the screen place Harry in limbo rather than a position of scenic mastery. The cramped interiority of the settings provides a fitting mise-en-scène for Harry's guarded personality. They also suggest an urban disillusionment that extends across San Francisco's rising downtown.

Like other filmmakers shooting in San Francisco, Coppola found economic and aesthetic value in urban renewal sites, taking advantage of low-priced real estate in declining districts. Harry's office was an empty warehouse blocks away from the former Zoetrope warehouse in the Mission District, and his apartment was in a district designated for redevelopment.[67] While offering clear advantages for location shooting, these abandoned urban sites also reinforce Harry's alienated existence. Twice urban decay becomes a visual symbol of his psychological decline. Discovering the site of the murder, a room in the Jack Tar Hotel, Harry sees (or imagines) blood pouring out of the toilet. A hard cut reveals a nearly demolished building as Harry hurries away from the disturbing scene, as if the collapse of the neighborhood mirrors the collapse of his grounding in reality (Figure 6.4). The final denouement has Harry frantically pulling apart his apartment in a failed search for a surveillance bug. Here he tears down his private sanctuary

6.3. Francis Ford Coppola assiduously avoided San Francisco's scenic beauty in *The Conversation*. This scene provides the only view of the San Francisco Bay in the film.

6.4. As Harry Caul (Gene Hackman) hurries away from a possible murder scene, a hard cut reveals a nearly demolished building, tying the physical decline of the city to his personal decline in *The Conversation*.

in a tear-down neighborhood, as physical space betrays his every precaution, leaving him vulnerable and unsheltered.

The corporate executive skyscraper has the opposite effect, as shiny pillars and glass walls create a hygienic geometrical space. The choice of odd angles and underexposure presents the office space not as a brighter alternative but as a different force of alienation; as the skeletons of new skyscrapers rise in the distance, the audience glimpses the orderly business structures overtaking the older, fading architecture of Harry's world (Figure 6.5). The midcentury modern style of the Jack Tar Hotel provides a similarly rational and sanitary space, down to the paper seal over the toilet. In both spaces, violence punctures the architectural order, from the menace of a Doberman at the CEO's side to the clumsy, bloody murder at the Jack Tar.

San Francisco's resident auteur stages the old city and new city as incompatible traps. Harry's personal sphere lies hidden among older buildings divorced of human community, while a rising business hub looms, coldly devoid of human compassion. Camera and audio surveillance encompass and truncate the only important public space in the film: Union Square. For both the corporate executives and Harry, the crowd provides no camaraderie; instead, its unpredictable sounds and movements conceal a private conversation. At the party after the trade fair, Harry lets his guard down to socialize and immediately jeopardizes his inner sanctum; a competitor bugs him with a hidden microphone, and a woman seduces him, stealing the recordings.

While offering a bleak image of San Francisco, *The Conversation* brought critical acclaim to filmmaking in the city, winning the Palme d'Or at Cannes and several other awards. Released during the Watergate scandal, its plot involving secretive tape recording proved more topical than it would have in 1969, when Coppola first planned to start production; *Variety* suggested that the film could have played as science fiction five years earlier. But neither the connection to Watergate nor Coppola's growing celebrity overcame the understated, cerebral tone of the film. While calling *The Conversation* "Coppola's most complete, most assured and most rewarding film to date," a *Variety* reviewer suggested a platform release relying on "intimate, sophisticated situations" to drive interest prior to a general release.[68] Though it garnered near unanimous critical acclaim, the quiet film found a quiet box office and barely broke even with production costs.[69]

6.5. Modernist buildings (*top*) in *The Conversation* are associated with ruthless corporate executives and create a visual counterpoint to the rundown building occupied by Harry Caul (*bottom*).

Perhaps *The Conversation* would have been a sleeper hit during the Hollywood Recession, but it paled in comparison to the record-breaking *Towering Inferno*, the paradigmatic blockbuster of 1974. This disaster film was San Francisco's biggest hit, but its parade of stars and pyrotechnics completely overshadowed the setting. And while the enormous budget offered an attractive source of location revenue, the complexity of the production signaled Hollywood's retreat from its location heyday of the early 1970s. A movie that size could afford to shoot anywhere, but, just as importantly, required teams of professional technicians and studio facilities that could only be found in Los Angeles.

DOUBLE FANTASY

The *Towering Inferno* required two studios, two source novels, two leading men, two directors, and two cinematographers (three counting effects specialist L. B. Abbott). Both the film and its production conjured the lavish spectacles of classical Hollywood cinema, with one reviewer comparing producer Irwin Allen to Cecil B. DeMille.[70] It also suggested the long dreamt of return to the backlot, providing jobs for craft workers and less uncertainty for producers. But rather than a return to the golden age of the studio, the production of *The Towering Inferno* pointed to a readjustment of the location versus soundstage calculus. The realist aesthetic of location shooting still shaped the look of studio-shot films, but improvements in special-effects technology offered more realistic depictions of spectacles impossible to capture in actual places, such as the overturned ocean liner for Allen's earlier hit, *The Poseidon Adventure* (1972), and the burning skyscraper for *Inferno.*

The Towering Inferno took little from its San Francisco setting other than requisite shots of the Golden Gate Bridge. The story concerns a massive fire in a just opened record-high skyscraper that menaces a cross-section of characters that could be drawn from any city or town. New York and San Francisco were the two most likely settings for a film centered on a large new structure, and since the obvious point of reference was the recently completed World Trade Center, the choice of San Francisco diffused real estate industry complaints about portraying high-rise buildings as unsafe.[71] Alioto's hospitality, the city's proximity to Los Angeles, and gorgeous locations for aerial footage also favored San Francisco. The city is merely a pretext for the disastrous tower, a vertical rendition of the doomed ship in *The Poseidon Adventure*. The *Towering Inferno* said little about San Francisco or American urbanism, but revealed a great deal about the tide of blockbusters that would threaten the city's importance as a location.

Thus although *The Towering Inferno* was another success for Mayor Alioto's ambitious production campaign, it signaled the beginning of the end for San Francisco's feature film prominence. The prevalence of special effects, first in the 1970s disaster cycle and later in *Jaws* and *Star Wars,* leeched into location budgets and, as in *Towering Inferno*, rendered extensive location shooting impossible. The disaster film's reliance on thin characterization and high-concept narrative left little room for the nuances of San Francisco's urban culture. Although the spectacular action of *Bullitt* and *Dirty Harry* had played out entirely in the streets, disaster films like *Poseidon* and *Inferno* relied on voluminous sets rigged with mechanical tools to simulate destruction and instability; even disasters staged in the streets, such as *Earthquake*, relied heavily on sets to mount a scale of destruction beyond what could be achieved on actual city blocks.

In late 1968, Mark Robson shot part of *Daddy's Gone A-Hunting* in San Francisco, including the climax at the panoramic Top of the Mark. Nonetheless, he predicted in *Variety* that "the days of extensive shooting on location are numbered." His observation had little to do with current complications, but rather the groundbreaking use of front projection in *2001: A Space Odyssey* (1968).[72] Exceptional locations still offered production value, but more-realistic studio recreations offered filmmakers greater control. Rather than shooting at the top of an actual hotel, *Inferno* constructed a panoramic promenade deck on an 11,000 square foot soundstage surrounded by a 340 degree cyclorama reproducing the San Francisco skyline (Figure 6.6).[73]

By 1973, Robson's prediction was coming true, not only regarding technological improvements but also economic changes affecting location production. A declining dollar hampered foreign runaways, and directors trained on location shooting came to realize the ease of studio shooting while learning methods to avoid a backlot look. The most successful rental studios, such as Universal and the new Burbank Studios, now offered modernized facilities that streamlined operations better than facilities built decades ago for classical mass production.[74] Studio operators exaggerated the decline of location shooting, but the process was subtler, with many pictures returning to the hybrid studio-location practices of the 1950s and early 1960s. As in *Vertigo*, location shooting for *The Towering Inferno* focused entirely on images that could not be as effectively captured in Los Angeles, such as helicopter footage of San Francisco and exterior shots of characters and emergency vehicles in the plaza outside the Bank of America Building, a realistic urban setting depicted as the ground floor of the tower.[75]

Declining box office returns abroad for the American-centric, location-based features associated with the Hollywood Renaissance further encouraged a return to the lot. In a 1974 *Variety* article titled "U.S. Antihero Films Flop Overseas," a foreign sales veteran rapped Hollywood for abandoning

6.6. The promenade set with cyclorama for *The Towering Inferno* (Fox–Universal, 1974) was the film's most expensive set piece and would have been impossible to build and destroy on location in San Francisco.

escapist pictures. He blamed *The Graduate* and *Easy Rider* for sparking a wave of alienating pictures, and saw the success of *The Poseidon Adventure* and the sunny projections for *The Towering Inferno* as a reaffirmation of Hollywood's strengths. At FilmEx, audience reactions suggested that even young viewers, the target audience for antihero pictures, preferred generic entertainment to "innovative (if boring) pix."[76] While films like *The Conversation* won awards at Cannes, viewers were flocking to action pictures starring Clint Eastwood and Steve McQueen.

The rise of large-budget, technically ambitious productions suggested that amid the cheap youth-picture movement of the Hollywood Recession, American studios had forgotten their historical advantage over foreign competitors: the ability to mount grander spectacles than any other national film industry. *American Cinematographer* praised the "genius of Hollywood set builders" on *The Poseidon Adventure* who constructed an enormous ocean liner set capable of being inverted 180 degrees and restaged as the capsized ship.[77] *Variety*'s review of *Inferno* crowed, "Nowhere else in the world does a pool of talent like this exist, and nowhere else in the world can a physical production achievement like this be made."[78] Producers working on location for lower-budget films like *The Conversation* preferred small crews to minimize expense and public attention. But this approach had failed to distinguish Hollywood methods from those of filmmakers working abroad. Throughout the 1960s, foreign filmmakers could match Hollywood's small artistic efforts, but they could never produce a film on the scale of *The Towering Inferno*, with a $12 million budget that went about $3 million over.[79]

The film starred Steve McQueen and Paul Newman, and featured William Holden, Faye Dunaway, Fred Astaire, Jennifer Jones, and O. J. Simpson, among other household names, drawing comparisons to MGM's all-star cast for *Grand Hotel* (1932).[80] Ironically, as MGM lay in ruins, Hollywood revived its old strategy of outstaging and outstarring its worldwide competitors. Screenwriter Stirling Silliphant openly admitted that the disaster formula left little room for "meaningful characters and complex emotional relationships." With fourteen major characters, even five minutes of screen time each would chew through half of the 140-page script.[81] Like television guest stars, the characters had quickly recognizable types with obvious points of conflict. Nothing could be further from the opaque antiheroes of films like *The Last Picture Show* (1971), *Five Easy Pieces* (1971), and *The Conversation*. As reviewer John Dorr observed in the *Hollywood Reporter*, with thrilling action scenes, "it hardly matters that the characterization is scanty and contrived."[82]

Irwin Allen's mega-productions provided welcome opportunities for a beleaguered Hollywood labor force struggling through the early 1970s. A IATSE Bulletin triumphantly described the scale of work for *The Towering Inferno*. Set builders constructed fifty-seven sets, including five floors of the skyscraper, on Fox's old Malibu ranch, as well as the enormous promenade deck set, 150 percent larger than the ship built for *The Poseidon Adventure*. Under a tight deadline for a Christmas release, Allen employed four complete camera crews working simultaneously, and hired double the usual number of crew members. Over 200 stunts and a "huge staff" of special-effects workers added further manpower to the complex production.[83] Unlike the producers who demanded union concessions during earlier runaway production crises, Allen invested heavily in Hollywood craftsmen who offered the best chance of realistically staging scenes with daunting technical challenges. Other disaster films, such as *Earthquake*, which required ninety-six sets, also provided opportunities for legions of workers.[84]

The expensive sets and disaster effects proved every bit as valuable as the marquee cast. In his review for the *Hollywood Reporter*, John Dorr noted, "Movie technology is the star of this awesome Irwin Allen production, a formula disaster picture made into an event by the sheer size of its inflating production values."[85] Realistically photographed urban locations were commonplace by the mid-1970s, losing the distinctive appeal they held in police films like *Bullitt* and *The French Connection*. But realistic depictions of spectacular events like a massive high-rise fire held tremendous box office appeal. After recovering from the Hollywood Recession, studios reinvested production capital into elaborate sets and special effects in a technological shock and awe that generated substantial profits for disaster films. While still an attractive location, San Francisco could never compete with or accommodate the pyrotechnical destruction that *The Towering Inferno* achieved on soundstages and backlots.

The film's daunting $15 million cost reflected new production strategies and financing arrangements that promoted more expensive features. Successful films like *Airport* and *The Poseidon Adventure* had driven studios to bid highly on disaster story properties. As the height of the World Trade Center stoked popular fear of unsafe skyscrapers, two novels capitalized on it: *The Tower* and *The Glass Inferno* both featured a catastrophic high-rise fire. Warner Bros. snapped up *The Tower* for $400,000, but weeks later, Irwin Allen convinced Fox to buy *The Glass Inferno*, yet to be published, for $410,000. Allen set up a meeting between the two studios and brought along artists' illustrations of a combined story.[86] Convincing executives that it would be "suicidal" to make competing pictures with identical story lines, the studios agreed to equally cofinance the film.[87] Widely recognized as the first major studio coproduction deal, similar financial arrangements for mitigating risk would later become commonplace.[88] The cofinancing decision allowed for a larger production budget than either studio could have justified on its own; *Variety* praised the collaboration, where "for the price of about two average pix each, they have what looms as an international blockbuster."[89] The deal also revealed that major studios had emerged from the recession largely as financiers, not active producers, giving the successful Allen near-complete autonomy over production.

Despite the expensive production demands in the script, the $12 million budget left enough leeway to hire two leading men. In early talks between Steve McQueen and agent Freddie Fields, McQueen agreed to play the architect, with Ernest Borgnine playing the fire chief in a supporting role, much like his role in *The Poseidon Adventure*. McQueen gravitated toward the firefighter character, and after another Fields client, Paul Newman, accepted the architect role for $1 million plus 7.5 percent of the gross, McQueen agreed to an identical contract to play the firefighter. The remaining issue was who would receive top billing. As he had for *Butch Cassidy and the Sundance Kid*, Fields got his clients to agree that their names would appear at the same time, with the order reversed for American and European prints. McQueen further insisted that Silliphant, already tasked with integrating two novels and over a dozen name actors into one film, must ensure that the fire chief had the same number of lines as Newman's architect.[90]

Silliphant, a veteran writer of television and film, including *The Poseidon Adventure* (and the feature version of *The Lineup*), peppered the script with escapist adventure segments and, as Dorr criticized, "weak liberal posturing." Like *The Poseidon Adventure*, a greedy businessman ignores safety for profits in the form of construction kickbacks, similar to the lone rogue banker prevalent in Production Code–era films. Thus *The Towering Inferno* conceded to a mass market by acknowledging but isolating the social critiques that had helped define America's countercultural cinema. Peter Biskind describes the audience for the film as "Nixon's *Towering Inferno* middle-Americans," but like *Jaws*, the film does offer soft critiques of profit motives; the corrupt builder serves a similar narrative function to the mayor preoccupied with tourist profits in *Jaws*.[91] But by soft-pedaling corporate corruption for a mass audience, Silliphant effectively neutralized San Francisco's contribution as a liberal cultural setting.

The Towering Inferno had enough money but barely enough time. With a seventy-day production schedule, principal photography stretched into early August, leaving less than five months to edit and distribute the film for Christmas of 1974. With costumes and sets progressively deteriorating under fire and water, Allen had to shoot in sequence, as he had on *The Poseidon Adventure*, further prolonging the schedule.[92] He saved time by deploying four separate crews, all shooting at once, including two major units led by different directors and cinematographers. The first unit, directed by John Guillermin and shot by Fred Koenkamp, covered most of the dialogue scenes, including three weeks of location shooting in San Francisco, largely devoted to scenes outside the Bank of America Building. An accomplished cinematographer (*Patton* [1970]), Koenkamp had experience shooting special effects dating back to his work on *Dark Passage*. The second unit, or action unit, directed by Allen and shot by Joseph Biroc, spent only a few days in San Francisco. The third unit shot special-effects sequences at Fox supervised by L. B. Abbott, a key collaborator on *Poseidon*. The fourth unit shot aerial footage by helicopter in San Francisco and Los Angeles.[93]

Like the screenplay, the tower itself was a composite of different locations, miniatures, and mattes. The only complete version of the tower was a 100 foot high "miniature." For establishing shots, Abbott used a matte to combine the model tower with helicopter footage shot in San Francisco (Figure 6.7). While the exterior of the Bank of America Building served as

6.7. A "miniature" tower (actually 100 feet high) was matted into helicopter location footage for *The Towering Inferno* to integrate the illusion of studio sets with the realistic setting of San Francisco.

the hotel entrance, producers chose the architecturally stunning lobby of the Hyatt Regency for the interior. Along with five complete floors built on the Fox ranch, nineteen other floors and the promenade were built on studio soundstages. The basement of a Century City office in Los Angeles doubled for the tower's computer control center.[94] Like *The House on Telegraph Hill*, San Francisco buildings provided only the bottom floors of an imaginary edifice that was optically completed in post-production.

Like Eastwood and his Malpaso studio, Allen relied on regular collaborators to delegate responsibilities across the demanding production. Malpaso reemployed directors and cinematographers on location, but Allen's core team focused on previsualization, production supervision, and spectacle. Over fifty crew members for *Inferno* had worked on *Poseidon*, including associate producers, production managers, art department heads, stunt and mechanical-effects supervisors, and production designer William Creber. He supplied hundreds of storyboards well before shooting to ensure proper construction of the multistory illusion.

Perhaps the hardest facet to coordinate was a consistent look for the cinematography shot by four crews in two different cities. Most often, Koenkamp's drama unit shot first—before Biroc's action unit damaged the set. Biroc typically consulted with Koenkamp as he finished shooting and watched most of his dailies to match his style.[95] Although Koenkamp focused primarily on figure lighting for the stars, Biroc concerned himself with lighting large areas of the set that featured numerous performers in action.[96] *Variety* praised the film's pictorial consistency across multiple units, and Biroc and Koenkamp shared the Academy Award for Best Cinematography.[97] Creber and the art department also earned Oscar nominations. These honors spoke to how convincingly *The Towering Inferno* integrated San Francisco locations, standing sets, practical effects, and optically printed composites. For decades, studios and filmmakers had cited an audience demand for realism as the driver of runaway production and location shooting; *The Towering Inferno* reasserted the value of studio-manufactured realism and found a large audience eager to suspend disbelief.

San Francisco received more attention from the helicopter unit, including a cine-tourist opening to establish the setting. Notes from a meeting with Irwin Allen suggested an aerial shot of a helicopter breaking through the fog to reveal the Golden Gate Bridge, followed by the bridge span itself, a version of which appears in the final film.[98] Allen cleverly tied an existing landmark to the manufactured image of the tower, buttressing an optical illusion with a dreamy infrastructural monument. Other aerial point-of-view shots instead relied on an optical printer used by effects specialist Linwood Dunn to mimic the motion of a smooth, twisting helicopter descent.[99] As in the 1950s and 1960s, location footage established and reestablished photographic realism through wide shots, creating a sense of real place that carried over into studio sets and matte composites.

The film's emphasis on complex sets and pyrotechnics rendered extensive location shooting superfluous. The action unit shot only one day in San Francisco, capturing fire engines racing down the streets in documentary style. Entire soundstages had to be fireproofed and ceilinged for dozens of fire sequences, making it impossible to capture much of the disaster on location.[100] During its three weeks in the city, the drama unit primarily focused on an urban spectacle: large crowds surrounding dozens of emergency vehicles descending upon the Bank of America Plaza (Figure 6.8).[101] For the largest crowd scene, 350 of the "Brebner Commandos" (a nickname for the extras hired by casting agent and city film committee member Ann Brebner) worked from 7 p.m. to well after midnight. Curious onlookers joined the extras but complained when they realized Robert Vaughn, rather than Paul Newman, was the star of the scene.[102] Despite the scale of the picture, its time in San Francisco was short and contained compared to the recent spate of police films. With a 120-person cast and crew required for the large crowd scenes, even such a well-funded production could not afford to stay in the city for long.[103]

6.8. Actors and crew preparing for one of the film's large crowd scenes. Exteriors for *The Towering Inferno* were shot at San Francisco's Bank of America Building, offering a real ground floor for a skyscraper that existed only in a number of disconnected sets and optical effects.

Regardless of *Inferno*'s escapist story and reliance on mechanical and optical effects, filmmakers still paid careful attention to the wave of location shooting that preceded them. According to *American Cinematographer*, Biroc had to contend with "audiences which have been fed a steady diet of realism during recent years and know how to recognize fakery."[104] Similarly, Koenkamp emphasized naturalistic lighting due to audience familiarity with location shooting. Wide night shots at the Bank of America Building required almost an entire city block to be lit. Low-key lighting, typically associated with location realism, was inadequate and inappropriate for the scene; instead, Koenkamp shot with multiple cameras and zoom lenses while pushing the film in development, giving a semi-documentary feel to the arrival of emergency crews and vehicles. Back at the studio, Koenkamp shot with both Panavision cameras on dollies and handheld Arriflexes, alternating polished pans and tilts with rough semi-documentary camera movements befitting the panicked immediacy of the action sequences.[105]

Biroc also relied upon tools and techniques associated with location shooting as he navigated massive sets built largely for visual emphasis rather than camera and lighting concerns. The need for fire-safe ceilings left Biroc without room to hang lights, so he often used smaller quartz lights. Fast film and fast Panavision lenses allowed him to shoot certain sequences with only the fire illuminating the actors and set. In order to capture the reactions of a large cast amid the controlled chaos of the fire, Biroc adopted multicamera

6.9 A location shooting style featuring rougher camerawork added a sense of realism and was also a good method for camera operators having to navigate the chaotic sets of *The Towering Inferno*.

setups; he used eight cameras to capture the flooding of the enormous promenade set, an event too destructive to stage more than once. With camera movement often obstructed by debris, zoom lenses added dynamic motion under difficult conditions (Figure 6.9).[106] A disaster that necessitated shooting at the studio also interfered with studio efficiencies, from hanging lights to executing camera movements. Yet shooting practices developed on location helped cinematographers work around difficult setups, allowing producers to focus on the appearance and mechanical effects of a set rather than its suitability for photography.

While minimizing location production in San Francisco, *The Towering Inferno* made typical concessions to the city, particularly the local firefighters who gave assistance and technical advice. Allen agreed to donate $20,000 to the annual film festival.[107] Initially galled by the "horror story" for the city's fire prevention work, the firefighters later promoted the film once producers had decided that the premiere screenings would benefit the Fire League Athletic and Musical Events (FLAME).[108] Allen also made a gesture equivalent to the one for police officers in *Dirty Harry*, offering a visual dedication to fallen firefighters at the opening of the film and also thanking the Los Angeles and San Francisco fire crews in the closing credits.

As anticipated, *The Towering Inferno* was a phenomenal box office success. After debuting on Christmas, it earned $16.5 million, more than its extraordinary budget, in only seventeen days.[109] Bringing in $55 million domestically and at least as much abroad, the film was the biggest hit of the year and quickly climbed the all-time box office list. Meanwhile, widespread critical acclaim suggested that Hollywood could once again make well-crafted mass-market pictures for a global audience. Coppola's personal film, *The Conversation*, was overshadowed at both the box office and the Academy Awards by *The Towering Inferno* and his own mega-production with extravagant sets, *The Godfather II.*

BACKLOT REVISITED

American Cinematographer saw *The Towering Inferno* as a change of tack in Hollywood. "[The film] is in a large sense a throwback. During recent years most of the big money-making pictures have strived for the economies and reality of location filming."[110] By the end of the 1970s, *Towering Inferno* proved to be not only a return to the studio-bound spectacles of the classical Hollywood system, but also a glimpse of the future. With unprecedented box office returns from the wide release of high-concept films, the money spent on elaborate but thrilling productions seemed more than worth the cost. In San Francisco, George Lucas reaped enormous profits by investing in studio fantasy over location realism in *Star Wars*. With rising budgets and greater industry stability, extensive shooting in popular cities like San Francisco was no longer an important source of production value or economic savings. The ability to shoot anywhere had to contend with the ability to shoot anything, from a skyscraper holocaust to an intergalactic war, on the backlot.

Just a year later, *Jaws*' record-breaking profits dwarfed those of *The Towering Inferno*. A major difference between the two productions was Steven Spielberg's extensive location work, although like *Inferno*'s San Francisco setting, Martha's Vineyard had little to do with the film's success. A quarter of *Jaws*' $12 million production cost went to special effects.[111] Unlike *The Towering Inferno*, technology proved inadequate, in part due to the difficulty of working on location. The mechanical shark malfunctioned and looked unrealistic on film, while cinematographer Bill Butler (*The Conversation*) struggled to match backgrounds due to unpredictable New England weather. Inconsistent lighting and cloud cover presented editing difficulties and also precluded one solution to the special-effects problems: using documentary footage of sharks.[112] Like *The Towering Inferno*, *Jaws* rushed into production to target a holiday release and capitalize on the publication of its source novel, further exacerbating production problems.[113] The experienced Allen went 20 percent over budget; Spielberg, on his first major-budget film, went 300 percent over budget and 104 days over schedule, pushing the film's cost close to that of *The*

Towering Inferno without the benefit of an all-star cast.[114] Ultimately, the studio delayed the premiere until the summer, which following the film's success became Hollywood's prime window for blockbuster releases.

As with *Bullitt* and *The Conversation*, the effectiveness of *Jaws* only emerged in post-production. Following a Dallas sneak preview after a showing of *The Towering Inferno*, *Jaws* emerged as an epochal blockbuster, and its problematic production history just became part of its lore.[115] Yet the lesson in location production was not lost on Spielberg. He shot much of his next blockbuster, *Close Encounters of the Third Kind*, on the backlot and in the Los Angeles suburbs, and relied on optical effects and set pieces over mechanical monsters. The film's most famous image, a monumental spaceship hovering over Devils Tower, artfully combines a spectacular location with a physically impossible special effect. Like Hitchcock's meticulously planned matte shots for *Vertigo*, Spielberg's composite images required careful previsualization, limiting improvisation on location, a defining aspect of *Bullitt*'s influential style, which established San Francisco as a favored site for cinematic exploration and experimentation through the mid-1970s.

The Conversation and *The Towering Inferno* arrived in 1974 like two ships passing in the night. Coppola rode toward the horizon of location shooting, perhaps reached by his monomaniacal location production *Apocalypse Now* (1979) and Michael Cimino's disastrous *Heaven's Gate* (1980); ironically, both pictures required major sets to be built on real locations. *The Towering Inferno* beat a path back toward the controlled environment and mechanical prowess of the physical studio. The decline of Hollywood's popular art cinema and the rise of escapist blockbusters was clear-cut, but the changes in location production were subtle. As innovations in location shooting technology plateaued, special-effects technologies rapidly improved. As blockbusters inflated production budgets, filmmakers could take advantage of both spectacular locations and high-end studio technology. Although *Star Wars* used locations in Death Valley and Tunisia to simulate the terrain of distant planets, Lucas created his most memorable scenes with studio sets, miniatures, and optical effects.[116]

San Francisco began struggling to attract a declining number of feature films being released by the major studios. In 1974, Hollywood put out roughly 240 films, but for the rest of the decade, fewer than 200 features were produced each year.[117] As high-budget blockbusters devoted more days to studio production and their choice of world locations, San Francisco's advantageous position of the early 1970s declined, and its feature production schedule returned to the norm of the 1950s and 1960s. In the second half of the 1970s, a handful of pictures shot in town each year, with a few midbudget pictures like *Foul Play* (1976), *High Anxiety* (1977), and *Invasion of the Body Snatchers* (1978) shooting extensively there. San Francisco remained a desirable location for television commercials, particularly car ads, and occasional television series, although the end of *The Streets of San Francisco* in 1977 dealt another blow to the city's production economy.[118]

A gritty aesthetic for urban pictures such as *The Conversation* persisted through the 1970s: in Philadelphia for *Rocky* (1976), New York for *Saturday Night Fever* (1977), and San Francisco for *The Enforcer* (1976), the third *Dirty Harry* film. But as the disaster genre mutated into *Jaws*, and *Star Wars* precipitated a boom in adventure and science-fiction pictures, the city ceased to be Hollywood's new frontier, although it remained a popular site for police stories.[119] Nonetheless, location techniques honed in the tight, dim urban quarters and streets of cities like San Francisco proved readily adaptable to the complicated setups of the new blockbusters. On *The Towering Inferno*, multiple cameras, zoom lenses, fast film stock, portable equipment, and ad hoc compositions allowed cinematographers to navigate crowded sets rife with obstacles to lighting and camera movement. With a shift in place and emphasis, the same production methods that crafted the introverted nightmare of *The Conversation* on location enhanced the extravagant nightmare of *The Towering Inferno* on the backlot. A key consequence of this production strategy was San Francisco's highly diminished role in both the production and the narrative.

While the urban location aesthetic of the late 1960s and 1970s had a tangible impact on the look and practice of studio shooting, the economic advantages of location shooting were short-lived, except of course for the lower-budget pictures that historically could not afford the cost of prolonged studio rentals and expensive soundstage technologies. Under Mayor Alioto, San Francisco had effectively parlayed the media attention of the Summer of Love into a filmmaking boom that perfectly coincided with the high-water mark of Hollywood location shooting. It had become one of the most filmed cities in the world, first as an embellishment of its own urban image and then as a prime setting for the urban crisis that likely left a greater mark on the city on-screen than off. San Francisco soon regained its cine-tourist image as America's picturesque urban gem. But to the disappointment of local boosters and industry workers, the city receded to the background of Hollywood film production.

CONCLUSION

Hollywood's San Francisco

A "SAN FRANCISCO" STYLE?

This study of Hollywood films shot over a thirty-year period in San Francisco (1945–1975) follows the development of location shooting from a minority to a majority practice for American filmmaking in the postwar era. Between the 1940s and mid-1960s, every attempt to shoot outside of the studio had to be justified against the efficient standard practices of soundstage and backlot production. By the late 1960s, shooting a film entirely on the lot was the rare exception, with major set-building reserved for those scenes impossible to capture on location. Across the American film industry, and specifically in San Francisco, location shooting peaked in the first half of the 1970s, near the end of Hollywood's rocky transition from a relatively stable mass production economy to a relatively stable blockbuster economy.

Following *The Towering Inferno*, San Francisco locations resumed a supporting role for both Hollywood narratives and special-effects spectacles. While location shooting remained standard practice for Hollywood productions, San Francisco ceased to be a hub of film and television production less than a decade after the boom began in 1967.

Throughout the three decades following World War II, Hollywood filmmakers often exploited nearby San Francisco's scenery, topography, and culture for many different narrative and aesthetic ends. Even during the city's peak years as a location (1967–1973), *Variety* observed: "There simply is no common thread running through the many films shot here in recent years.... There's never been, for example, a 'San Francisco' film style to equate with the San Francisco sound that swept the music industry in the 1960s."[1] On the surface level of film narrative, this is an accurate critique, but it fundamentally confuses subject and object. San Francisco's music scene was a product of world famous local bands; San Francisco's on-screen image was a by-product of Hollywood shooting practices. Each film shot in San Francisco reflected industry-wide changes in production economies, technology, style, and logistics that made shooting on location a favorable alternative to shooting in the soundstages, backlots, and surrounding neighborhoods of Los Angeles.

The central contradiction of this study is that San Francisco was both a unique and typical location from 1945 to 1975. The city was a privileged site for filmmaking due to its proximity to Los Angeles, its distinctive scenery, and its cultural prominence in the late 1960s. These specific qualities made San Francisco the most popular American city for Hollywood filmmaking except for Los Angeles and New York, cities with established production industries, and during its boom years in the late 1960s and early 1970s, San Francisco was nearly as prevalent on-screen. San Francisco's prominence in American culture peaked just as American films transitioned to primarily shooting on location. Filmmakers approached this exceptional city with a typical calculus, choosing sites and stylistic practices that maximized the production values of a given era under the economic and technological constraints of location shooting.

In the early 1970s, the letterhead of the San Francisco Convention and Visitors Bureau touted "Everybody's Favorite City."[2] This boast rang true in different ways in the decades following World War II. For American urbanists, San Francisco sites often served as paradigms for city form, with scenic downtown pedestrian districts seemingly immune to the threat of rundown housing and highway traffic. San Francisco was a booming tourist location, which reinforced its image as an urban playground while smoothing its economic transition to a postindustrial city. By 1967, San Francisco had gained strong utopian associations as the capital of the counterculture, a new Jerusalem for disaffected youth. While the city appeared to be building a new urban society, the old one seemed to be collapsing. Waves of race riots swept through the United States, and by the mid-1970s, major cities like New York, Chicago, and Detroit appeared on the verge of economic, physical, and cultural collapse. San Francisco quietly struggled with all of the issues that plagued other cities, although its financial problems were less severe. For the most part, however, the city's national image remained the exception to postwar urban decline and crisis—except on film.

No city experienced such a sudden and thorough destruction of its urban image than San Francisco at the hands of Hollywood location filmmakers in the early 1970s. The widening gap between the city's actual urban culture and its on-screen depiction reveals fundamental aspects of Hollywood cinema's approach to urban location shooting. First of all, a filmed city is the sum of its urban locations and studio sets. Filmmakers often chose to construct San Francisco entirely out of its tourist districts, but as in *Dirty Harry*, they could also build its image entirely out of red-light districts and blighted exurban zones. In either case, Hollywood films divorce a given location from its actual urban context and reconfigure it among other locations to build their own on-screen city.

Hollywood's depiction of San Francisco was strikingly similar to its depiction of other cities across both phases of postwar location shooting. Through the mid-1960s, whether in film noir or Cinerama travelogues, filmmakers overwhelmingly favored San Francisco's scenic views and urban landmarks. This served two purposes. First, by capturing the most distinctive sites of the city, Hollywood minimized the expense of distant location shooting. Why spend more to capture a place that was indistinguishable from Los Angeles or a studio set? Second, these images efficiently communicated an authentic San Francisco setting, a sense of real place that imbued the majority of scenes shot on the studio lot. This was not only Hollywood's standard location practice in San Francisco but in New York, Rome, and various cities around the globe.

Once location shooting became less expensive than shooting on the studio lot, filmmakers gained far greater flexibility. They could shoot anywhere in the city, although the tight budgets of the late 1960s and early 1970s forced them to move through locations at a rapid pace. Moving beyond the city's tourist districts, one might expect Hollywood films to have gained a more nuanced view of the city, but in fact the opposite was the case. Freed from the requirement to capture well-known urban sites, filmmakers sought the locations that best suited the tone of their films, which during San Francisco's location boom was remarkably bleak. In *The Conversation*, Francis Ford Coppola conveyed a gloomy city by never providing a clear view of the bay or the Golden Gate Bridge and largely avoiding popular sites; viewers unfamiliar with Union Square might forget the film was even set in San Francisco.

Despite its urban exceptionalism, Hollywood's depiction of the city said as much about public perceptions of the American city as San Francisco itself. The explosion of the urban crisis in the late 1960s prompted filmmakers to further degrade the image of San Francisco to fit the perceived reality of the American city descending into a wasteland. In three short years, the vibrant San Francisco of *Petulia* became the dystopian urban landscape of *Dirty Harry*. The felt death of the American city overwhelmed San Francisco despite its remarkable success in comparison to most major cities in the first half of the 1970s. From 1945 to 1967, San Francisco's screen image denied the actual decline of other American cities; between 1968 and 1975, on-screen San Francisco was soon overwhelmed by the prevalent imagery of the urban crisis. Off-screen, San Francisco remained a metropolitan utopia compared to most American cities, a reality that was anathema to Hollywood's new urban realism, strongly influenced by the blighted image of New York as depicted in *Midnight Cowboy* and *The French Connection*. On location in San Francisco, filmmakers sought out the darkest corners of the city, turning their backs to the city's still extant urban beauty.

San Francisco's particular attractiveness as a location for crime genre films also had a profound impact on its urban image. As a downtown-oriented alternative to Los Angeles, it was a convenient site for film noirs reliant on an earlier form of concentrated urbanism, one increasingly absent from Southern California. Numerous distinctive settings provided set pieces for violent action sequences, such as the Embarcadero Freeway in *The Lineup* and the hilly streets in *Bullitt*. San Francisco's image of a bustling urban core made it a viable stand-in for New York, a factor that prompted *Days of Wine and Roses*, *Dirty Harry*, and *The Towering Inferno* to transplant stories from New York to San Francisco for both economic and narrative reasons, such as distancing *Days* from its television original and distinguishing *Dirty Harry* from *Coogan's Bluff*. In the wake of *Bullitt*'s tremendous box office success, San Francisco boomed with gritty police films that incorporated a scenography of urban decay strongly associated with New York police films like *The French Connection* and *Serpico* (1973). Lacking the extensive physical signs of an urban crisis apparent in New York, San Francisco films often relied on graphic violence, a dim palette, and carefully chosen locations to recreate a popular image of raw urban realism that was notably absent from much of San Francisco.

END OF AN ERA

By 1975, San Francisco had passed its peak as a Hollywood location and never again approached the volume of film and television production of the boom years of 1967–1973.[3] It also became increasingly noncompetitive with North American cities offering greater financial incentives, such as Toronto and Vancouver. Like *The Towering Inferno* (1974), the vast majority of popular films and television series shot and set in San Francisco after 1975 had little or nothing to do with the actual city. As location shooting ebbed in 1974, *Variety* offered a cold assessment of the state of San Francisco production titled "Frisco Filmmaking Largely Transient." Following a six-year filmmaking boom, San Francisco still lacked key facilities, such as a professional-quality film lab, and enough key personnel, such as skilled production workers and experienced screen actors. The influx of Hollywood production had all but exhausted the novelty of San Francisco locations.[4] *Variety* suggested that the city was an attractive place for filmmakers and actors "to spend the company's money," but not an effective alternative to Los Angeles or locations with stronger financial incentives.[5] As San Francisco became an increasingly expensive city to visit, Hollywood location shooting later boomed in cheaper locations, including foreign countries like Australia and US states with tax incentives like Louisiana.

In 1976, California formed the Motion Picture Development Council, headquartered in Los Angeles, to offer assistance to filmmakers in direct response to "the pressures of growing competition from other states."[6] San Francisco, Los Angeles, and the state of California all worked to offer greater production support and streamline the bureaucratic processes that hindered location filmmaking. But California and its cities could not offer the low wages and direct financial incentives that had driven runaway production since the 1950s. Los Angeles remained essential to American filmmaking, providing a corporate center and state-of-the-art facilities to meet the technical challenges of blockbuster production, but as a location, it no longer held an unparalleled advantage. In similar fashion, San Francisco's popular appeal and cooperative government had provided an attractive environment for filmmakers to hone their location production methods in the late 1960s and early 1970s. These refined practices proved readily adaptable to other cities, states, and countries offering greater financial rewards.

By 1975, San Francisco's only major assets as a location were once again its scenic values and proximity to Los Angeles. As a result, the city resumed the ancillary role it had played in Hollywood films of the 1940s and 1950s, providing a picturesque backdrop for narratives that revealed little of its urban culture beyond the postcard tourist sites. A San Francisco setting had little bearing on hits like *Foul Play* (1978), *48 Hours* (1982), *Jagged Edge* (1985), *Basic Instinct* (1992), *Mrs. Doubtfire* (1993), *Doctor Dolittle* (1998), and *Cheaper by the Dozen* (2004). Two famous locations on the outskirts of the city, the Golden Gate Bridge and Alcatraz, are still prevalent as action set pieces, serving much the same purpose as they did in the 1950s. Like the octopus in *It Came from Beneath the Sea*, creatures continued to spectacularly destroy the landmark bridge in films like *Rise of the Planet of the Apes* (2011) and *Pacific Rim* (2013), and it remained a common site for action spectacles, including *A View to a Kill* (1985), *Hulk* (2003), and *X-Men: The Last Stand* (2006).[7] Alcatraz continued to provide a dramatic location for prison scenes in *Escape from Alcatraz* (1979) and *The Rock* (1996).

Adaptations of historical fiction and true events—including the television miniseries *Tales of the City* (1993), *The Joy Luck Club* (1993), *Zodiac* (2007), and *Milk* (2008)—were with rare exception the only productions closely engaged with San Francisco's specific urban culture, albeit one of the past.[8] After *The Streets of San Francisco* ended in 1977, two decades passed before the city returned as a major setting, this time for the crime series *Nash Bridges* (1996–2001) and *Monk* (2002–2009). Other series set in San Francisco rarely shot on location, including *Trapper John M.D.* (1979–1986), *Hotel* (1983–1988), *Too Close for Comfort* (1983–1986), *Full House* (1987–1995), and *Charmed* (1998–2006).[9]

This brief survey of the last forty years of Hollywood depictions of San Francisco suggests a rather stable and superficial image of the city, in line with changes in both Hollywood production and urban discourse. Blockbusters often involved extensive location shooting, but favored action set pieces over the exhaustive exploration of San Francisco locations prominent in early 1970s features. Once again, unique sites like the Golden Gate Bridge that instantly convey a San Francisco setting became the primary focus of location production—although, as with *The Towering Inferno*, many action sequences grew far too elaborate to stage on location. In the decade following the thirty-year period analyzed in this study (1975–1985), the rise of postmodern architecture, gentrification and Rousification, and the construction of pseudo-historical urban tourist districts redefined central city districts as realms for affluent lifestyles and urban set pieces. When San Francisco was booming as a business hub in the 1970s and a technopolis in the 1990s, the city shared more in common with other shiny new downtowns devoted to finance, tourism, and wealthy residents. It remained popular onscreen but played a far more limited role. *View to a Kill* is a telling example, because like the world cities featured in every James Bond film, San Francisco's cinematic role has been largely relegated to scenic shots and action spectacles since 1975.

The industrial tension between location shooting and studio-based production remains critical to Hollywood production strategies. Improvements in digital-effects technology over the past two decades have expanded the role of the high-tech production and post-production facilities located in and around Los Angeles and San Francisco. Just as the reliance on special effects for *The Towering Inferno* required soundstage and backlot technology, Hollywood's reliance on digitally rendered settings requires further studio-based production work, where actors perform in front of green screens and don motion-capture suits to record the movements of digitally animated characters. Bay Area companies like Pixar and Lucasfilm have thrived in this new digital production field, drawing local talent from Silicon Valley, but their films have had little if anything to do with the city itself.

The expansion of CGI effects work came at the expense of location production. A 2014 *Variety* article revealed how little time recent movies set in San Francisco spent shooting in the actual city. *San Andreas* (2015), a $100 million movie about a 10.0 earthquake hitting San Francisco, spent only six days shooting there. *Godzilla* (2014), also set in the city, spent four days in town, while the two *Planet of the Apes* sequels (2011 and 2014) grabbed establishing shots before heading to Canada.[10] As in the mid-1970s, improvements in location technology mobilized Hollywood studios to chase financial incentives without sacrificing production quality or efficiency. Weta Digital, Peter Jackson's New Zealand–based digital-effects company, developed new technology to perform motion-capture on location; this allowed *Dawn of the Planet of the Apes* (2014) to shoot cheaply in Canada and New Orleans using CGI recreations of San Francisco settings.[11] Australia devoted part of its $20 million production fund to bring *San Andreas* to Queensland.[12] As digital-effects technology grows more portable and more convincing, Hollywood will gain further independence from locations such as San Francisco and even Los Angeles. Just as in the 1960s, Hollywood union leaders have lobbied the state government to save their jobs from the eternal threat of runaway production.[13]

In 2014, San Francisco was offering a rebate of up to $600,000 to entice Hollywood producers to shoot in the city. Commenting on the current production slump, *Variety* noted the city's former prominence in Hollywood cinema: "San Francisco has a tradition as an iconic film location, with such titles as 'Bullitt,' 'Dirty Harry' and 'Vertigo.'"[14] The fact that these films, shot between 1958 and 1971, remain the most famous ever shot in the city underscores how the postwar rise of Hollywood location shooting dramatically impacted San Francisco's screen image. These definitive San Francisco films emerged out of industry conditions that promoted more extensive location work in the city. For contemporary producers, San Francisco is no longer a uniquely attractive location. Like the prewar sets that limned San Francisco on the backlot, digital reproductions of the city now provide an economic, professional-quality substitute for the difficult business of urban location shooting.

From 1945 to 1975, Hollywood re-envisioned rather than reflected the city of San Francisco, testing the limits of location filmmaking as the tools and opportunities to shoot in the city expanded. Visiting filmmakers built the city out of available locations and available assumptions about San Francisco and American cities in general. They performed urban design, not urban documentation. Location shooting is a constructive rather than a reflective process, and San Francisco's screen history affirms cinema's unique ability to construct urban space and overwhelm urban realities.

APPENDIX

Films Set and/or Shot in San Francisco between 1945 and 1975

THE FOLLOWING IS A LIST OF widely released Hollywood films (distributed by either major studios or large independents) set and/or shot in San Francisco during the thirty-year period covered by this study. It was compiled based on several different sources, including archival research, databases like the AFI catalog and IMDb (imdb.com), published guides to San Francisco movie locations, and fan sites. I cross-checked less reliable sources against more reliable ones, such as *Variety* reviews. In keeping with the focus of this book, I have omitted films depicting historic San Francisco, such as *I Remember Mama* and *How the West Was Won*. I also excluded films that had no full scenes take place in the city.

1945
The Falcon in San Francisco
Fallen Angel
Shadows Over Chinatown

1946
Shock
That Brennan Girl
The Well-Groomed Bride

1947
Born to Kill
The Chinese Ring
Dark Passage
The Lady from Shanghai
My Favorite Brunette
Night Song
Out of the Past

1948
Every Girl Should Be Married
Nora Prentiss
Race Street
The Time of Your Life
Walk a Crooked Mile

1949
Chinatown at Midnight
Impact
Johnny Stool Pigeon
Million Dollar Weekend
Mr. Soft Touch
Red Light
The Sky Dragon
Story of Molly X
Take One False Step
Thieves' Highway
The Woman on Pier 13

1950
Born to Be Bad
D.O.A.
Key to the City
The Man Who Cheated Himself
Where Danger Lives
Woman on the Run

1951
The House on Telegraph Hill
Pat and Mike
The Raging Tide
Starlift

1952
The Sniper
Sudden Fear

1953
The Bigamist
No Escape

1954
The Caine Mutiny

1955
Cinerama Holiday
Hell on Frisco Bay
Hit the Deck
How to Be Very, Very Popular
It Came from Beneath the Sea

1956
Flight to Hong Kong
Julie
The Rack
Serenade

1957
Crime of Passion
Kiss Them for Me
The Midnight Storm
Pal Joey

1958
The Gift of Love
The Lineup
Vertigo

1959
On the Beach

1960
The Facts of Life
Portrait in Black
The Subterraneans

1961
Flower Drum Song
Go Naked in the World
Man-Trap
The Pleasure of His Company
Swingin' Along

1962
Birdman of Alcatraz
Days of Wine and Roses
Experiment in Terror

1963
The Birds
A Gathering of Eagles
The Three Stooges Go Around the World in a Daze

1964
Good Neighbor Sam
Man's Favorite Sport?
Where Love Has Gone

1967
The Graduate
Guess Who's Coming to Dinner
The Love-Ins
Point Blank
Valley of the Dolls

1968
Bullitt
Head
The Love Bug
Petulia
Psych-Out
Skidoo
Yours, Mine and Ours

1969
Daddy's Gone A-Hunting
Eye of the Cat
Machine Gun McCain
The Picasso Summer

1970
Fools
The Strawberry Statement
They Call Me Mister Tibbs!

1971
Dirty Harry
Harold and Maude
The Organization
The Return of Count Yorga
Vanishing Point

1972
Butterflies Are Free
The Candidate
Play It Again, Sam

1973
The Laughing Policeman
Little Cigars
Magnum Force
Superdad
What's Up, Doc?

1974
The Conversation
Freebie and the Bean
Herbie Rides Again
The Towering Inferno

1975
The Black Bird
The Killer Elite
Mr. Ricco

Sources: American Film Institute catalog (www.afi.com); CinemaToast, "The San Francisco List" (www.cinematoast.com/sanFranciscoList.asp); Internet Movie Database (www.imdb.com); Reel SF (www.reelsf.com); San Francisco Film Museum (www.sanfranciscofilmmuseum.org/films); Joseph Alioto Papers, San Francisco History Center, San Francisco Public Library; and Jim Van Buskirk and Will Shank, *Celluloid San Francisco: The Film Lover's Guide to Bay Area Movie Locations* (Chicago: Chicago Review Press, 2006).

NOTES

INTRODUCTION

1. Daily production progress reports, October 29 –November 30, 1946, folder 1488, *Dark Passage* Production File, Warner Bros. Archive, Department of Special Collections, Doheny Library, University of Southern California (hereafter cited as WBA, USC).

2. Philip Hager, "City Helps Out: Background for Films? Often It's San Francisco," *Los Angeles Times*, December 9, 1973, F1, 31.

3. Richard Walker, "An Appetite for the City," in *Reclaiming San Francisco*, ed. James Brook, Chris Carlsson, and Nancy Peters (San Francisco: City Lights, 1998), 9.

4. Recent work, published after the initial version of this manuscript, has confronted Hollywood location shooting more directly. See R. Barton Palmer, *Shot on Location: Postwar American Cinema and the Exploration of Real Place* (New Brunswick, NJ: Rutgers University Press, 2016); and Lisa Dombrowski, "Postwar Hollywood, 1947–1967," in *Cinematography*, ed. Patrick Keating (New Brunswick, NJ: Rutgers University Press, 2014), 61–70. Palmer provides textual analysis for several films rather than a comprehensive industry history. While primarily focused on Hollywood cinematography, Dombrowski provides a useful overview of location shooting aesthetics in the 1940s and 1950s.

5. Morton Beebe and J. Bruce Hayes, "Tinseltown on the Bay," *San Francisco Sunday Examiner and Chronicle*, August 22, 1971, 10–12.

6. Geoffrey Bell, *The Golden Gate and the Silver Screen* (New York: Association of University Presses, 1984), 133–134.

7. Richard Koszarski, *Von: The Life and Films of Erich Von Stroheim* (New York: Proscenium, 2001), 143–149; Thomas Schatz, *The Genius of the System: Hollywood Filmmaking in the Studio Era* (New York: Holt and Co., 1988), 34–35.

8. General research record, May 28, 1941, folder 712, and location expense sheet, May 24, 1941, folder 1435, *Maltese Falcon* Production File, WBA, USC.

9. Steven Bingen, Stephen Sylvester, and Michael Troyan, *MGM: Hollywood's Greatest Backlot* (Solano Beach, CA: Santa Monica Press, 2011), 211–213, 298–299.

10. For the effect of wartime rationing on production practices, see Sheri Chinen Biesen, *Blackout: World War II and the Origins of Film Noir* (Baltimore: Johns Hopkins University Press, 2005), 63.

11. William Lafferty, "A Reappraisal of the Semi-Documentary in Hollywood, 1945–1948," *The Velvet Light Trap* 20 (1983): 22–26.

12. For a comprehensive analysis of the postwar rhetoric on urban decay, see Robert Beauregard, *Voices of Decline: The Postwar Fate of US Cities* (Oxford: Wiley-Blackwell, 1994).

13. Charles Jencks, *The Language of Post-Modern Architecture* (New York: Rizzoli International, 1977), 9–10.

14. Mark Shiel, "A Regional Geography of Film Noir: Urban Dystopias On- and Off-Screen," in *Noir Urbanisms: Dystopic Images of the Modern City*, ed. Gyan Prakash (Princeton, NJ: Princeton University Press, 2010), 79–80.

15. New York was the largest city between 1940 and 1970. Los Angeles had become the third largest city by 1950 and the second largest by 1970, passing Chicago. See http://www.peakbagger.com/pbgeog/histmetropop.aspx.

16. See the appendix for films set in San Francisco. For films set in Chicago, see https://www.cityofchicago.org/city/en/depts/dca/supp_info/chicago_film_office6.html. I omitted films set in the past or not set in Chicago from this tally.

17. Popular guides to San Francisco locations include Jim Van Buskirk and Will Shank, *Celluloid San Francisco* (Chicago: Chicago Review Press, 2006) and Nathaniel Rich, *San Francisco Noir: The City in Film Noir from 1940 to the Present* (New York: Little Bookroom, 2005).

18. Peter Lev, *The Fifties: Transforming the Screen, 1950–1959* (Berkeley: University of California Press, 2006), 148–155.

19. James Brook, Chris Carlsson, and Nancy Peters, *Reclaiming San Francisco: History, Politics, Culture* (San Francisco: City Lights Books, 1998), viii; Victor Gruen, *The Heart of Our Cities* (New York: Simon and Schuster, 1964), 11.

20. Brian Godfrey, "Urban Development and Redevelopment in San Francisco," *Geographical Review* 87, no. 3 (July 1997): 316–319.

21. Susan Fainstein et al., *Restructuring the City: The Political Economy of Urban Redevelopment* (New York: Longman, 1986), 202.

22. Godfrey, "Urban Development," 316–319.

23. Bingen et al., *MGM,* 297–298.

24. John Belton, *Widescreen Cinema* (Cambridge, MA: Harvard University Press, 1992), 5–14.

25. See, for example, *Screening the City*, ed. Mark Shiel and Tony Fitzmaurice (London: Verso, 2003); *Cinema and the City: Film and Urban Societies in a Global Context*, ed. Shiel and Fitzmaurice (Oxford: Blackwell, 2001); Nezar AlSayyad, *Cinematic Urbanism: A History of the Modern from Reel to Real* (London: Routledge, 2006); and *Urban Cinematics: Understanding Urban Phenomena Through the Moving Image*, ed. François Penz and Andong Lu (Bristol: Intellect, 2001).

26. See William Luhr and Peter Lehman, "*Experiment in Terror*: Dystopian Modernism, the Police Procedural, and the Space of Anxiety," in *Cinema and Modernity*, ed. Murray Pomerance (New Brunswick, NJ: Rutgers University Press, 2006), 174–193; see also Allan Siegel, "After the Sixties: Changing Paradigms in the Representation of Urban Space," in Shiel and Fitzmaurice, *Screening the City*.

27. See, for example, Edward Dimendberg, *Film Noir and the Spaces of Modernity* (Cambridge, MA: Harvard University Press, 2004); Stanley Corkin, *Starring New York: Filming the Grime and the Glamour of the Long 1970s* (New York: Oxford University Press, 2011); Mark Shiel, *Hollywood Cinema and the Real Los Angeles* (London: Reaktion, 2012); and Lawrence Webb, *The Cinema of Urban Crisis* (Amsterdam: Amsterdam University Press, 2014).

28. André Bazin, "The Myth of Total Cinema," in *What Is Cinema?*, vol. 1, trans. and ed. Hugh Gray (Berkeley: University of California Press, 2005), 17–22.

29. See the appendix for the list of films. At least sixty of these films are either film noirs, police films, or crime stories, including four comedy capers.

30. See chapters 4 and 5.

CHAPTER 1

1. As Mark Shiel notes, the 1930s through mid-1940s were overwhelmingly dominated by production on the studio lot rather than on location. See Shiel, *Hollywood Cinema and the Real Los Angeles*, 128.

2. Signal Corps filmmakers would effectively stage other scenes to supplement such documentaries and restore control over the image and narrative. See Thomas Doherty, "Documenting the 1940s," in Thomas Schatz, *Boom and Bust: The American Cinema in the 1940s* (Berkeley: University of California Press, 1999), 410–411.

3. Ezra Goodman, "Post-War Motion Pictures," *American Cinematographer* (hereafter *AC*) (May 1945): 160, 172.

4. Ibid.

5. Ibid.

6. "Studios Broaden Program of Filming Yarns in Real Locale," *Daily Variety*, October 24, 1946, 18.

7. Barry Salt, *Film Style and Technology: History and Analysis*, 2nd ed. (London: Starword, 1992), 230–231.

8. Ibid.

9. Herb Lightman, "13 Rue Madeleine," *AC* (December 1948): 88–89, 110–111.

10. Arthur Rowan, "The Steel Trap," *AC* (November 1952): 478, 496–498.

11. Frederick Foster, "Economy Lighting with Photofloods," *AC* (January 1950): 11, 20.

12. Robert Surtees, "The Story of Filming 'Act of Violence,'" *AC* (August 1948): 268, 282–284.

13. Salt, *Film Style*, 241.

14. Leigh Allen, "They Do It with Infra-Red!," *AC* (October 1949): 360, 376–378.

15. Hollis Moyse, "Latensification," *AC* (December 1948): 409, 426.

16. Herb Lightman, "Realism with a Master's Touch," *AC* (August 1950): 271, 286–288.

17. Lightman, "Old Master, New Tricks," *AC* (September 1950): 309, 318–320.

18. Leigh Allen, "New Speed for Films," *AC* (December 1949): 440, 456–457.

19. Ibid.

20. Wilfrid Cline, "Mobile Camera Lab," *AC* (December 1948): 410, 423.

21. Ralph Lawton, "Disney Unveil New Mobile Generator Unit," *AC* (February 1950): 49, 66; John del Valle, "Boom Shots Anywhere!," *AC* (August 1950): 270, 282; "What's New," *AC* (April 1953): 152.

22. Leigh Allen, "Signal System," *AC* (November 1949): 402, 417.

23. Phil Tannura, "Translucent Photo Backgrounds Cut Production Costs," *AC* (July 1949): 240–241, 259–260.

24. Lee Garmes, "Lighting Translucent Backings," *AC* (November 1949): 398–399, 417–418.

25. Herb Lightman, "Matching Location Footage With Studio Shots," *AC* (June 1950): 197, 215–216.

26. Ibid.

27. Patrick Keating, *Hollywood Lighting from the Silent Era to Film Noir* (New York: Columbia University Press, 2010), 3–7.

28. Rowan, "The Steel Trap," 478, 496–498.

29. Herb Lightman, "'The Lady From Shanghai,'" *AC* (June 1948): 200–201, 213.

30. Sheri Chinen Biesen, *Blackout: World War II and the Origins of Film Noir* (Baltimore: Johns Hopkins University Press, 2005), 63.

31. General research record, May 28, 1941, box 1, folder 712, *Maltese Falcon* Production File, WBA, USC.

32. Ibid.

33. Budget, May 24, 1941, box 1, folder 712, *Maltese Falcon* Production File, WBA, USC.

34. Ibid.

35. Daily production progress reports, June 14 and 28, 1941, box 1, folder 714, *Maltese Falcon* Production File, WBA, USC.

36. Fred Tyler to Special Effects Department, June 26, 1941, box 1, folder 714, *Maltese Falcon* Production File, WBA, USC. This often-used Los Angeles location famously appeared as the Bat Cave for the *Batman* television series and in *Invasion of the Body Snatchers* (1956).

37. Steve Trilling to Jack Warner, December 9, 1943, Story—memos and correspondence, *To Have and Have Not* Production File, WBA, USC.

38. Production and progress report, January 19, 1944–May 10, 1944, folder 1488, *To Have and Have Not* Production File, WBA, USC.

39. Jack Sullivan to Dr. Kissauer, October 5, 1943, *To Have and Have Not* research record, WBA, USC.

40. Weekly production cost, February 29, 1944, *To Have and Have Not* Production File, WBA, USC.

41. Jack Warner to Howard Hawks, March 17 and 30, 1944, *To Have and Have Not* Production File, WBA, USC.

42. "Studios Adopt Documentary Pic Format," *Daily Variety*, October 20, 1947.

43. William Lafferty, "A Reappraisal of the Semi-Documentary in Hollywood, 1945–1948," *Velvet Light Trap* 20 (1983): 22–26.

44. The American film industry worried about similar restrictions with the onset of the Korean War. See Herman Lowe, "Showbiz Scans the War Clouds," *Daily Variety*, October 18, 1950, 4.

45. "Selznick Will Shoot All Films With Real Locale," *Daily Variety*, April 30, 1946, 3.

46. "Studios Broaden Program of Filming Yarns in Real Locale," *Daily Variety*, October 24, 1946, 18; "WB Scatters Units to 4 Winds," *Daily Variety*, July 3, 1947, 3.

47. "RKO Will Shoot 3 August Films on Location," *Daily Variety*, July 22, 1947, 6.

48. "Studio is Saving Set Costs Thru Locale Lensing," *Daily Variety*, June 10, 1947, 4.

49. Production budget and cost sheet, June 4, 1947, folder 34, *The Naked City*, Gil Kurland Papers, Margaret Herrick Library, AMPAS.

50. "Studios Broaden," *Daily Variety*, October 24, 1946, 18.

51. Production budget and cost sheet, June 4, 1947, Kurland Papers, Margaret Herrick Library, AMPAS.

52. Herb Lightman, "The Naked City," *AC* (May 1948): 152–153, 178–179.

53. Ibid.

54. Ibid.

55. "Slice Film Costs 30 percent," *Daily Variety*, August 18, 1947, 1, 5.

56. "Producers' 40 percent Economy Wave," *Variety*, August 20, 1947, 5.

57. Ibid.

58. Darryl Zanuck memo, May 27, 1947, folder 144, Twentieth Century-Fox, Lloyd Bacon Papers, Margaret Herrick Library, AMPAS.

59. It is a wonder Otto Preminger made so many films at Fox.

60. Zanuck memo, May 27, 1947, Bacon Papers, Margaret Herrick Library, AMPAS.

61. Darryl Zanuck memo, December 12, 1949, folder 138, Twentieth Century-Fox, Henry King Papers, Margaret Herrick Library, AMPAS.

62. Sumiko Higashi, "Realism in Urban Art and *The Naked City*," in *Looking Past the Screen: Case Studies in American Film History and Method,* ed. Jon Lewis and Eric Smoodin (Durham, NC: Duke University Press, 2007), 368–369; Zanuck memo, December 12, 1949, King Papers, Margaret Herrick Library, AMPAS.

63. Zanuck memo, December 12, 1949, King Papers, Margaret Herrick Library, AMPAS.

64. Mark Shiel, "A Regional Geography of Film Noir: Urban Dystopias On- and Off-Screen," in *Noir Urbanisms: Dystopic Images of the Modern City*, ed. Gyan Prakash (Princeton, NJ: Princeton University Press, 2010), 79–97.

65. Mike Connolly, "Production Costs Cut 25 percent," *Variety*, January 4, 1950, 23.

66. Darryl Zanuck to Henry King, June 14, 1950, King Papers, Margaret Herrick Library, AMPAS.

67. Daily production progress reports, October 29–November 30, 1946, folder 1488, *Dark Passage* Production File, WBA, USC.

68. Hortense Morton, "S.F. Popular Color Town For Makers of Movies," April 6, 1952, *San Francisco Examiner*, Movies/San Francisco, clippings, SF History Center, SF Public Library.

69. The recently restored *Woman on the Run* (1950) features slightly more location work than others. Typical of an independent production, additional location work helped defray set construction and studio rental costs, which will be discussed in chapter 2.

70. Budget data were culled from the budgets in the production files for the above-listed titles in series 1, RKO Studio Records, Special Collections, Young Research Library, UCLA.

71. *Hollywood Reporter* clipping, September 3, 1947, folder 685, Publicity, *Dark Passage* Production File, WBA, USC.

72. *Film Daily* clipping, September 3, 1947, folder 685, Publicity, *Dark Passage* Production File, WBA, USC.

73. Newspaper clipping, 1947, folder 685, Publicity, *Dark Passage* Production File, WBA, USC.

74. Richard Coe, "Don't Be Reasonable–Then You'll Like 'Dark Passage,'" *Washington Post*, October 3, 1947, B10.

75. Synopsis, folder 1011, Research, *Dark Passage* Production File, WBA, USC.

76. Delmer Daves and Jerry Wald to Tenny Wright, September 9, 1946, folder 1858, Story—memos and correspondence, *Dark Passage* Production File, WBA, USC.

77. "Notes on Experimental Camera Work," October 23, 1946, *Dark Passage* Production File, WBA, USC.

78. Keating, *Hollywood Lighting*, 59–62.

79. The Steadicam proved most advantageous on location, in tight quarters (*The Shining*), and to simulate POV movement (as in myriad slasher films of the 1980s).

80. Zanuck memo, May 27, 1947, Bacon Papers, Margaret Herrick Library, AMPAS.

81. "Notes on Experimental Camera Work," October 1946, WBA, USC.

82. Ibid.

83. This biography by the American Society of Cinematographers mentions Burks's special-effects work. Stephen Pizello, "Robert Burks, ASC and Alfred Hitchcock," https://www.theasc.com/protect/nov98/collab/pg2.htm (accessed July 4, 2014).

84. Jerry Wald to Tenny Wright, September 30, 1946, folder 1858, Story—memos and correspondence, *Dark Passage* Production File, WBA, USC.

85. Research Department notes, September 20 , 1946, *Dark Passage* Production File, WBA, USC.

86. Herb Lissauer to Wald, September 1, 1946, folder 2459, Story, *Dark Passage* Production File, WBA, USC.

87. Daily production progress reports, October 29–November 30, 1946, folder 1488, *Dark Passage* Production File, WBA, USC.

88. "Capra Winds Tanforan Shots with 25G Savings," *Daily Variety*, May 2, 1949, 1.

89. Daily production progress reports, October 29–November 30, 1946, folder 1488, *Dark Passage* Production File, WBA, USC.

90. Ibid.

91. Ibid.

92. Ibid.

93. Wald to Daves, November 14, 1946, folder 1858, Story—memos and correspondence, *Dark Passage* Production File, WBA, USC.

94. Elizabeth Darling to Warners' Legal Department, October 28, 1947, folder 2459, Story, *Dark Passage* Production File, WBA, USC.

95. Herb Caen clippings, folder 685B, Publicity, *Dark Passage* Production File, WBA, USC.

96. *Dark Passage* pressbook, WBA, USC.

97. Daily production progress reports, October 29–November 30, 1946, folder 1488, *Dark Passage* Production File, WBA, USC.

98. Wald to Daves, November 21, 1946, folder 1858, Story—memos and correspondence, *Dark Passage* Production File, WBA, USC.

99. Daily production progress reports, October 29–November 30, 1946, folder 1488, *Dark Passage* Production File, WBA, USC.

100. Wald to Daves, November 18, 1946, folder 1858, Story—memos and correspondence, *Dark Passage* Production File, WBA, USC.

101. Wald to Humphrey Bogart and Lauren Bacall, November 8, 1946, *Dark Passage* Production File, WBA, USC.

102. Vincent Farrar, "Tough Assignment," *AC* (February 1950): 48, 62–63; William Mellor, "No Time for Weather," *AC* (May 1951): 178–179, 199.

103. Wald to Daves, November 8, 1946, folder 1858, Story—memos and correspondence, *Dark Passage* Production File, WBA, USC.

104. Wald to Daves, November 19, 1946, *Dark Passage* Production File, WBA, USC.

105. Wald to Fred Koenkamp, November 26, 1946, *Dark Passage* Production File, WBA, USC.

106. Wald to Daves, November 21, 1946, *Dark Passage* Production File, WBA, USC.

107. David Bordwell, Janet Staiger, and Kristen Thompson, *The Classical Hollywood Cinema: Film Style and Mode of Production to 1960* (New York: Columbia University Press, 1985), 59.

108. Ibid., 63.

109. *Daily Mirror*, August 30, 1947, folder 685, Publicity, *Dark Passage* Production File, WBA, USC.

110. James Brook, Chris Carlsson, and Nancy Peters, eds., *Reclaiming San Francisco* (San Francisco: City Lights, 1998), vii–viii.

111. Samuel Wallace, "San Francisco Enjoying Real Cool Climate," *Chicago Daily Tribune*, August 24, 1947, F11.

112. Thalia, "Visitor Extols Beauties of San Francisco," *Chicago Daily Tribune*, May 29, 1949, F1.

113. Peter Geoffrey Hall, *Cities of Tomorrow: An Intellectual History of Urban Planning and Design in the Twentieth Century*, 3rd ed. (Oxford: Blackwell, 2002), 192–193. Burnham proposed a similar plan for post-earthquake San Francisco.

114. Edward Dimendberg, *Film Noir and the Spaces of Modernity* (Cambridge, MA: Harvard University Press, 2004), 114.

115. Ibid., 119–121.

116. Coe, "Don't Be Reasonable," *Washington Post*, October 3, 1947, B10.

117. "Inside Hollywood," *Daily Variety*, August 7, 1950, 2.

118. Herb Lightman, "House on Telegraph Hill," *AC* (July 1951): 260–261, 274–275.

119. Ibid.

120. Ibid.

121. Ibid.

122. "Inside Hollywood," *Daily Variety*, August 7, 1950, 2.

CHAPTER 2

1. The film was only released on DVD in 2009 and is not available on VHS.

2. Patrick McGilligan, *Alfred Hitchcock: A Life in Darkness and Light* (New York: Regan Books, New York, 2004), 555.

3. Thomas Patrick Doherty, *Cold War, Cool Medium: Television, McCarthyism, and American Culture* (New York: Columbia University Press, 2003), 165–166.

4. *Cinerama Holiday* shot-by-shot continuity, folder 29, Technicolor Collection, Margaret Herrick Library, AMPAS.

5. For the decline of retail shopping in downtown Los Angeles, see Richard Longstreth, *City Center to Regional Mall: Architecture, the Automobile, and Retailing in Los Angeles, 1920–1950* (Cambridge, MA: MIT Press, 1997).

6. Edward Dimendberg, *Film Noir and the Spaces of Modernity* (Cambridge, MA: Harvard University Press, 2004), 166–170.

7. Richard Walker, "Landscape and City Life: Four Ecologies of Residence in the San Francisco Bay Area," *Ecumene* 2, no. 1 (1995): 39.

8. William Issel, "'Land Values, Human Values, and the Preservation of the City's Treasured Appearance': Environmentalism, Politics, and the San Francisco Freeway Revolt," *Pacific Historical Review* 68, no. 4 (November 1999): 624; for the impact of the Blyth-Zellerbach Committee, see Chester Hartman (with Sarah Carnochan), *City for Sale: The Transformation of San Francisco* (Berkeley: University of California Press, 2002), 8–10.

9. "Welcome to San Francisco" brochure, San Francisco Convention and Visitors Bureau, Ephemera, SF History Center, SF Public Library.

10. "The Top 50 Greatest Films of All Time," http://www.bfi.org.uk/news/50-greatest-films-all-time (accessed August 6, 2014).

11. "Film Reviews: Vertigo," *Variety*, May 14, 1958, 6.

12. Douglas Cunningham, ed., *The San Francisco of Alfred Hitchcock's Vertigo: Place, Pilgrimage, and Commemoration* (Lanham, MD: Scarecrow, 2012).

13. *To Catch A Thief* earned \$4.5 million in 1955, and *The Man Who Knew Too Much* earned \$4.1 million in 1956. *Vertigo* earned \$3.2 million in 1958. See "1955's Top Film Grossers," *Variety*, January 25, 1956, 1, 15; "109 Top Money Films of

1956," *Variety*, January 2, 1957, 1, 4; "Top Grossers of 1958," *Variety*, January 7, 1959, 48.

14. Thomas Guback, "Hollywood's International Market," in *The American Film Industry*, ed. Tino Balio (Madison: University of Wisconsin Press, 1976), 394–398.

15. Robert R. Shandley, *Runaway Romances: Hollywood's Postwar Tour of Europe* (Philadelphia: Temple University Press, 2009), 20–42.

16. "Hollywood Bigness on the Wane: 'Runaway' Fears All Too Real," *Variety*, October 10, 1956, 3.

17. Shandley, *Runaway Romances*, 80.

18. "'Runaway' Overseas Pix Prod. May Be Probed by 2 Coast Union Groups," *Variety*, June 24, 1953, 4.

19. "85 percent IATSE Jobs Highest Since '48; Cheap Pix Rapped," *Variety*, September 1, 1954, 4, 85.

20. "Cameramen Growl When Left at Home," *Variety*, March 26, 1958, 7.

21. Peter Lev, *The Fifties: Transforming the Screen, 1950–1959* (Berkeley: University of California Press, 2006), 151–152, 201.

22. "Hollywood Bigness on the Wane," *Variety*, October 10, 1956, 3.

23. "RKO, Newly Buzzing, Electing Authentic Locales Over Studio," *Variety*, October 31, 1956, 17.

24. "Salvage 'Ben-Hur' Production Assets," *Variety*, November 19, 1958, 24.

25. "Producers: Can They Beat Overhead?," *Variety*, May 30, 1956, 5.

26. Mike Kaplan, "Pictures: N.Y. Payola on Location?," *Variety*, September 11, 1957, 3, 12.

27. "Rain Big Factor on Thumbs-Down Shooting in NY," *Variety*, May 21, 1958, 30.

28. "N.Y. Mayor's Aide to Meet with FPA On Vidpix 'Relief,'" *Variety*, April 30, 1958, 27; "Kazan to Vidfilm Producers: 'Gotta Fight City Hall' on N.Y. Treatment," *Variety*, July 3, 1957, 27.

29. William Boddy, *Fifties Television: The Industry and Its Critics* (Urbana: University of Illinois Press, 1990), 187–213.

30. "Syndicated Break-Even $1,725,000," *Variety*, April 30, 1958, 27, 66.

31. Lev, *The Fifties*, 202.

32. *Vertigo* shooting schedule, September 26, 1957, folder 13, Schedules, *Vertigo* Production File, Paramount Pictures Production Papers, Margaret Herrick Library, AMPAS.

33. Abel Green, "Show Biz: Pain-in-the-Brain," *Variety*, January 8, 1958, 50; "Sam Spiegel Attacks High Ratio Of Distribution Costs to Grosses," *Variety*, August 8, 1956, 7, 12.

34. "RKO, Newly Buzzing," *Variety*, October 31, 1956, 17.

35. “Lots of Indie Lots for Sale As Vidpic Boom Cues New Interest,” *Variety*, December 10, 1952, 23, 39.

36. Lev, *The Fifties*, 200.

37. Lots of Indie Lots,” *Variety*, December 10, 1952, 23, 39; “Pictures: Fooling Around With All Those Millions May Hurt Somebody–Yates,” *Variety*, February 9, 1955, 5.

38. “Producers: Can They Beat the Overhead?,” *Variety*, May 30, 1956, 5.

39. “Rent M-G Studio Stages To Indies, Vogel Plan; May Sell Some of Land,” *Variety*, February 5, 1958, 18.

40. Gene Arneel, “20th-WB: Studio Co-Tenancy?,” *Variety*, October 3, 1956, 3, 22.

41. Fred Hift, “Pix Catch Wall Street Fever,” *Variety*, November 19, 1958, 1, 22.

42. Bob Chandler, “WB Shows the Way as Major Studios Embrace TV in One Form or Another to Help Pay the Rent,” *Variety*, November 26, 1958, 27, 52. For the collapse, see Christopher Anderson, *Hollywood TV: The Studio System in the Fifties* (Austin: University of Texas Press, 1994), 255–287.

43. Bob Chandler, “WB Shows the Way as Major Studios Embrace TV in One Form or Another to Help Pay the Rent,” *Variety*, November 26 1958, 27, 52.

44. “Green-Newman Plan for Splitting Loew’s Stirs Wall Street; Would Spin Off Studio, Retain Theatres,” *Variety*, September 10, 1958, 3, 149.

45. John Belton, *Widescreen Cinema* (Cambridge, MA: Harvard University Press, 1992), 14.

46. Ibid., 78–97.

47. Ibid., 94.

48. Ibid., 123, 140.

49. Ibid., 145–146.

50. R. A. Klune memo, February 26, 1954, folder 138, Twentieth Century-Fox, Henry King Papers, Margaret Herrick Library, AMPAS.

51. Frank Daugherty, “The Cinematographer and the Independent,” *AC* (June 1955): 344–345, 356–357.

52. “Hollywood Bigness on the Wane,” *Variety*, October 10, 1956, 3.

53. Julie Turnock, “The Screen on the Set: The Problem of Classical-Studio Rear Projection,” *Cinema Journal* 51, no. 2 (Winter 2012): 157–162.

54. Charles Loring, “Techniques for Filming Exteriors,” *AC* (January 1953): 19, 42–44.

55. Brad Chisholm, “Red, Blue, and Lots of Green: The Impact of Color Television on Feature Film Production,” in *Hollywood in the Age of Television*, ed. Tino Balio (Boston: Unwin Hyman, 1990), 221–224.

56. Ibid.

57. "Paramount Buys 50 percent Interest in Sol Lesser's Vistascope," *Variety*, April 14, 1952, 3.

58. "Academy Awards Database," http://awardsdatabase.oscars.org/ampas_awards/.

59. Alfred Hitchcock and Robert Burks location survey notes, September 20, 1957, folder 994, *Vertigo* (Locations), Alfred Hitchcock Papers, Margaret Herrick Library, AMPAS.

60. Ray Kellogg and L. B. Abbott, "Special Photographic Effects in Motion Pictures," *AC* (October 1957): 662–665, 672–677.

61. Joe Henry, "The Science of Process Photography," *AC* (January 1958): 36–37, 56.

62. Arthur Gavin, "Location-shooting in Paris for 'Gigi,'" *AC* (July 1958): 424–425, 440–442.

63. Joe Henry, "The Science of Process Photography," *AC* (January 1958): 36–37, 56.

64. Gavin, "Location Filming," 424–425, 440–442.

65. George Howard, "Design Improvements in High-wattage Filament Lamps Respond to Studio Needs," *AC* (April 1958): 228–229, 233–234.

66. Walter Strenge, "Realism in Real Sets and Locations," *AC* (October 1957): 650–651, 678–680.

67. Emery Huse, "Tri-X—New Eastman High-speed Negative Motion Picture Film," *AC* (July 1954): 335, 364.

68. Barry Salt, *Film Style and Technology: History and Analysis*, 2nd ed. (London: Starword, 1992), 244.

69. Stanley Cortez, "Tri-X in Feature Film Production," *AC* (January 1955): 33, 44–47.

70. Daugherty, "The Cinematographer and the Independent," 344–345, 356–357; Fred Woodress, "Location Photography Their Specialty," *AC* (October 1957): 654, 680–682.

71. Chisholm, "Red, Blue," 222–226; Gorham Kindem, "Hollywood's Conversion to Color: The Technological, Economic and Aesthetic Factors," *Journal of the University Film Association* 31, no. 2 (Spring 1979): 29–36.

72. "Script Starting Point to Save," *Variety*, February 15, 1956, 10; "Stones, Married Producers, Beat Overhead, Never Build a Set," May 21, 1958, 5, 20.

73. Strenge, "Realism in Real Sets and Locations," 650–651, 678–680.

74. Herb Lightman, "Filming 'Blackboard Jungle,'" *AC* (June 1955): 334–335, 358.

75. "Inside Hollywood," *Variety*, August 7, 1950, 2.

76. Darryl Zanuck to Henry King, August 1, 1953, folder 138, Twentieth Century-Fox, King Papers, Margaret Herrick Library, AMPAS.

77. Merrill Schleier, "Fatal Attractions: 'Place,' the Korean War, and Gender in Niagara," *Cinema Journal* 51, no. 4 (Summer 2012): 26–43.

78. Geoffrey Nowell-Smith, "Cities: Real and Imagined," in *Cinema and the City: Film and Urban Societies in a Global Context*, ed. Mark Shiel and Tony Fitzmaurice (Chichester: John Wiley and Sons, 2008), 99–108.

79. Charles Affron and Mirella Jona Affron, *Sets in Motion: Art Direction and Film Narrative* (New Brunswick, NJ: Rutgers University Press, 1995), 44–45.

80. Philip Scheuer, "'Vertigo' Induces Same in Watcher: Hitchcock's Latest Hinges on Complex Twist of Plot," *Los Angeles Times*, May 29, 1958, 21.

81. Carl Milliken to Sidney Boehm, December 6, 1954, box 9, folder 8540–405, 1–2, *Hell on Frisco Bay* Production File, WBA, USC; "Chicago Local Sues, Says 'Waterfront' (NJ) Libels Longshoreman's Repute," *Variety*, March 23, 1955, 5.

82. "Film Reviews: Hell on Frisco Bay," *Variety*, December 28, 1955, 6.

83. McGilligan, *Alfred Hitchcock*, 545.

84. Victor Gruen, *The Heart of Our Cities* (New York: Simon and Schuster, 1964), 11.

85. Dean MacCannell, *The Tourist: A New Theory of the Leisure Class* (Berkeley: University of California Press, 1999), 111.

86. MacCannell, *The Tourist*, 14.

87. *Vertigo* shooting schedule, September 26, 1957, Hitchcock Papers, Margaret Herrick Library, AMPAS.

88. *Vertigo* daily production reports, October 18, 1956–February 25, 1958, folder 12, Paramount Pictures Production Records, Margaret Herrick Library, AMPAS.

89. *Vertigo* storyboards, "Exterior Cypress Point," file 997, Hitchcock Papers, Margaret Herrick Library, AMPAS.

90. Hitchcock-Burks location survey notes for *Vertigo*, September 20, 1957, Hitchcock Papers, Margaret Herrick Library, AMPAS.

91. Ibid.

92. Ibid.

93. Morrie Reardon's screen credits appear in the American Film Institute catalog, http://www.afi.com/members/catalog/ (accessed August 6, 2014).

94. "Delights for Delegates," *Life*, August 20, 1956, 44–49.

95. Doc Erickson oral history, 196, Margaret Herrick Library, AMPAS.

96. Ibid., 194.

97. Unit Production Managers' Credit Bulletin and "Operations Worldwide" on Foreign Locations 1952–1957, October 1, 1957, Unit Production Managers File, WBA, USC.

98. "Scenic Telegraph Hill Roped Off Easter for 'Pal Joey' and Taxpayers Squawk," *Variety*, May 1, 1957, 2.

99. "Frisco Station Airs 20 'Editorials' Against 20th Filming 'Kiss' On Nob Hill," *Variety*, May 10, 1957, 10.

100. "Location Crews and Casts Good Hollywood Ambassadors Barring Tactlessness or Turpitude," *Variety*, January 25, 1956, 3, 20.

101. Rev. Michael Sullivan correspondence, October 15, 1956–February 19, 1957, folder 1002, *Vertigo* (Sets), Hitchcock Papers, Margaret Herrick Library, AMPAS.

102. "Scenic Telegraph Hill Roped Off Easter For 'Pal Joey' and Taxpayers Squawk," *Variety*, May 1, 1957, 2.

103. Daily production reports, October 18, 1956–February 25, 1958, *Vertigo*, Paramount Pictures Production Records, Margaret Herrick Library, AMPAS.

104. Ibid.

105. Scott Curtis, "The Last Word: Images in Hitchcock's Working Method," in *Casting a Shadow: Creating the Alfred Hitchcock Film*, ed. Will Schmenner and Corinne Granof (Chicago: Northwestern University Press, 2007), 15–17.

106. MacCannell, *The Tourist*, 32.

107. Rebecca Solnit, "Cinema City: Muybridge Inventing Movies, Hitchcock Making Vertigo," in *Infinite City: A San Francisco City Atlas*, ed. Rebecca Solnit (Berkeley: University of California Press, 2010), map 3.

108. William Whyte, "Introduction," and Daniel Seligman, "The Enduring Slums," in *The Exploding Metropolis* (Garden City, NY: Doubleday, 1958), 8, 111.

109. Cover image, "Life's Party: San Francisco Opera Opening," *Life*, October 6, 1952, 152–158; "Elegance for an Opening," *Life*, October 1, 1956, 167–169.

110. "Surge in 20th Shares to 30 Reflects Added Low-Cost Films Plus Oil (to Come) Under Studio," *Variety*, June 12, 1957, 22.

111. The temporary loss of about a thousand movie theaters in 1954 helps explain the year's drop in production. See Lev, *The Fifties*, 303–305.

112. Newspaper clipping, 1952, *The Sniper*, col. 161, Stanley Kramer Papers, Special Collections, UCLA Library. Martin Scorsese provides the introduction for *The Sniper* on DVD (Sony Pictures, 2009) and lauds the film's distinctive use of real locations and semi-documentary style.

113. Shooting schedule, September 24–October 23, 1951, *The Sniper*, Kramer Papers, Special Collections, UCLA Library.

114. Bernard Dick, ed., *Columbia Pictures* (Lexington: University Press of Kentucky, 1992), 15.

115. Tim Brooks and Earle Marsh, *The Complete Directory to Prime Time Network TV Shows: 1946–Present*, 5th ed. (New York: Ballantine, 1992), 1095.

116. Musuraca may have held this claim before starting on *The Lineup*. He shot five films for RKO set entirely or partially in San Francisco, including *I Remember Mama* (1948), for which he won the Academy Award for Cinematography.

117. Clifford Harrington, "Rain, Fog Nor Wind Ever Slows Location Shooting for 'The Lineup,'" *AC* (June 1958): 362–363, 378–379.

118. Ibid.

119. Ibid.

120. Ibid.

121. *San Francisco Beat* ad, *Variety*, September 7, 1955, 28–29.

122. Don Siegel, *A Siegel Film: An Autobiography* (London: Faber and Faber, 1993), 211.

123. Ibid.

124. Incredibly, it would remain unfinished until the 1989 earthquake facilitated and necessitated its demolition.

125. William H. Lathrop, Jr., "San Francisco Freeway Revolt," *Transportation Engineering Journal* 97, no. TE1 (February 1971): 137.

126. Ibid.

127. Ibid., 136.

128. Ibid., 137.

129. Joseph A. Rodriguez, *City Against Suburb: The Culture Wars in an American Metropolis* (Westport, CT: Praeger, 1999), 26.

130. Ibid., 36.

131. Gruen, *Heart of Our Cities*, 136.

132. Siegel, *A Siegel Film*, 212.

CHAPTER 3

1. Robert Landry, "Sick Tales of a Healthy Land," *Variety*, March 1, 1961, 1, 21.

2. Whitney Williams, "Hollywood's Self-Diagnosis," *Variety*, April 3, 1963, 19, 20.

3. Ibid.

4. Ibid.

5. Robert Landry, "Film Myths Not to Live By," *Variety*, January 4, 1961, 15.

6. Dick Williams, "Parade of Downbeat Pictures Continues," *LA Times*, January 20, 1962, newspaper clipping, *Days of Wine and Roses* Production File, WBA, USC.

7. Ibid.

8. "Feds Veto Alcatraz Film," *Variety*, October 29, 1958, 3.

9. "'Lolita' as U.S. Choice for Venice Fest; It's a Switch from Previous 'Niceness,'" *Variety*, August 15, 1972, 4, 20.

10. "Seven Arts Forecast Re 'Lolita,'" *Variety*, August 15, 1962, 4, 20.

11. "Names that Rode High in 1958," *Variety*, January 7, 1959.

12. Thomas Doherty, *Hollywood's Censor: Joseph I. Breen and the Production Code Administration* (New York: Columbia University Press), 322–325.

13. Peter Lev, *The Fifties: Transforming the Screen, 1950–1959* (Berkeley: University of California Press, 2006), 93–94.

14. Landry, "Film Myths Not to Live By."

15. Paul Monaco, *The Sixties, 1960–1969* (Berkeley: University of California Press, 2001), 24.

16. "How Producers Minds Work Today: Inducements Go By Private Likes," *Variety*, June 10, 1959, 3, 28.

17. "At Home to 'New' Slants 'n Ideas: Kramer Re UA," *Variety*, June 24, 1959, 12.

18. Ibid.

19. "Major Film Companies: 1955–1960," *Variety*, May 18, 1960, 4.

20. Monaco, *The Sixties*, 58.

21. "Metro's Six From Overseas: Hedge Coast Shutdown," *Variety*, March 9, 1960, 3.

22. Dora Albert, "Foreign Press in New Hard Look," February 21, 1962, 11.

23. "Films of Mayhem from Many Lands Unreel at Cannes," *Variety*, May 8, 1963, 1, 172.

24. Doherty, *Hollywood's Censor*, 327–330.

25. R. Barton Palmer and William Bray, *Hollywood's Tennessee* (Austin: University of Texas Press, 2009), 151–163.

26. Landry, "Film Myths Not to Live By."

27. Monaco, *The Sixties*, 58.

28. McEwen to Roy Obringer, December 1, 1961, *Days of Wine and Roses* Production File, WBA, USC.

29. Horace Sutton, "Frisky Life in San Francisco," *Washington Post*, January 14, 1962, K1; Richard Joseph, "A Look into San Francisco's Wacky Nightclub Kick," *Chicago Tribune*, October 20, 1963, G7.

30. Whitney Williams, "Hollywood's Self-Diagnosis," *Variety*, April 3, 1963, 19–20.

31. "Studio Backlotters' Unemployment Down," *Variety*, July 31, 1957, 20.

32. "Studios Unload of Assets," *Variety*, June 3, 1959, 5, 13.

33. "Sold Its Acreage, Now 20th May Need Rental Space for Production," *Variety*, May 3, 1961, 2.

34. "Studios Unload of Assets," *Variety*, June 3, 1959, 5

35. "Layoffs Multiply: Warner's 'This May Be Permanent,'" *Variety*, March, 2, 1960, 3–22.

36. "Studio's Bloodshot Dawn," *Variety*, March 9, 1960, 3, 26.

37. Ibid.

38. "Economy Axings Hit Paramount," *Variety*, May 18, 1960, 4.

39. Ibid.

40. "Many Omens Write a Warranty That 'Worst is Over' for Pictures," *Variety*, March 1, 1961, 1, 93.

41. Gene Arneel, "Home is Where You Shoot: But O'Seas No Longer Cheap," *Variety*, June 15, 1960, 3, 16.

42. Jack Pitman, "New York Production: Helping & Hurting," *Variety*, November 1, 1961, 17.

43. "H'wood Job Mart Hit Hard By Over-the-Hill Pix, Video Hours," *Variety*, April 11, 1962, 3, 19.

44. Ibid.

45. Robert Landry, "'Runaway': What They Say and Do," *Variety*, November 2, 1960, 4.

46. "Fume again on 'Runaway' Films," *Variety*, June 1, 1960, 3, 6.

47. "Cameramen Ask 'Dislocation' Benefits; New Moves Hit Runaway Trend," *Variety*, October 5, 1960, 17.

48. Tom Pryor, "Competition & 'Runaway' as Twins in Hollywood, Once a 'Company Town,'" *Variety*, January 10, 1962, 5, 50.

49. Matthew Bernstein, *Walter Wanger, Hollywood Independent* (Berkeley: University of California Press, 1994), 352.

50. "H'Wood—O'Seas Row Boils Up," *Variety*, August 24, 1960, 7, 20.

51. Ibid.

52. "Says Bill Wyler: 'Runaway as Term Makes Li'l Sense,'" *Variety*, December 14, 1960, 5.

53. "U.S. To Rein 'Runaway' Prod.?," *Variety*, September 13, 1961, 5.

54. Arneel, "Home is Where You Shoot," *Variety*, June 15, 1960, 3, 16.

55. Abel Green, "Talent Agencies Virtually Film Producers; Wm. Morris' Recent 35 Packages; Lastfogel Re 'Runaway,'" *Variety*, November 14, 1962, 3, 11.

56. Pryor, "Competition & 'Runaway,'" *Variety*, January 10, 1962, 5, 50.

57. Monaco, *The Sixties*, 13–14.

58. "Coast Kids Self; European Film Production Is Still Third Cheaper; Preminger Raps U.S. 'Standbys,'" *Variety*, January 30, 1963, 5, 24.

59. Pitman, "New York Production," *Variety*, November 11, 1961, 17.

60. "America's Film Industry Too Big for H'wood Alone: Charles Schneer," *Variety*, November 22, 1961, 5, 21.

61. William Ornstein, "Hollywood Versus Other Places," *Variety*, January 10, 1962, 7.

62. William Ornstein, "Fox Filming in Many Lands," *Variety*, June 7, 1961, 5, 20.

63. "Proposes MGM Adopt Decision To Stay in U.S.," *Variety*, February 27, 1963, 13.

64. "Screen Actors Guild Favors Kennedy's Plan to End Star O'Seas Tax Shelter," *Variety*, June 7, 1961, 16.

65. "U.S. To Rein 'Runaway' Prod.?," *Variety*, September 13, 1961, 5.

66. "Dent Subcommittee Gone, Unmourned," *Variety*, April 18, 1962, 7.

67. "Screen Actors Asking No Pay Hike; Realism in Light of 'Runaway,'" *Variety*, November 14, 1962, 1, 18.

68. "IATSE Dickering While Crafts Fret as Features Shy From Hollywood," *Variety*, October 19, 1960, 13.

69. "Kiss Ones that Don't Goodbye," *Variety*, November 23, 1960, 7.

70. Thomas Pryor, "Action on 'Runaway' at Last," *Variety*, May 16, 1962; Pryor, "Competition & 'Runaway,'" *Variety*, January 10, 1962, 5, 50.

71. Pryor, "Competition & 'Runaway,'" *Variety*, January 10, 1962, 5, 50.

72. Pryor, "Action on Runaway"; *Variety* further towed the industry line by always placing "runaway" in quotations, leaving a trace of doubt on union accusations.

73. "Runaway Prod. Trend Quickens 25 Out of 36 Pix," August 15, 1962, 2, 52.

74. Mike Fessier, "Runaways, Please Come Home," *Variety*, May 1, 1963, 5, 82.

75. "Proposes MGM Adopt Decision To Stay in U.S.," *Variety*, February 27, 1963, 13; "Crafts Hear Zanuck Assurances of 20th Resumption in Hollywood: Costs No Longer Favor Overseas," *Variety*, January 30, 1963, 5.

76. Fessier, "Runaways," *Variety*, May 1, 1963, 5, 82.

77. Charles Greenlaw to Arthur Schaefer, July 11, 1963, Grievance and Arbitration Decisions, folder 1031A, Arbitrations Regulation, WBA, USC.

78. William Ornstein, "Hollywood Versus Other Places," *Variety*, January 10, 1962, 7.

79. "5-Day Week Contributed to 'Runaway"—Skouras," *Variety*, December 13, 1961, 1; Gene Arneel, "Don't Film to Please Unions,'" *Variety*, October 17, 1962, 1, 13.

80. "Howard Koch Says Runaway Prod. Is Here to Stay, 'H'wood is Dead,'" *Variety*, December 26, 1962, 2, 47.

81. "Hollywood's Everywhere But in Calif.," *Variety*, August 15, 1962, 4.

82. Pitman, "New York Production," *Variety*, November 11, 1961, 17.

83. Ibid.

84. "Make-Way-For-Tomorrow Thought 'Guides' Foreman in New 'Young' Emphasis," *Variety*, July 15, 1959, 30.

85. Mervyn LeRoy, "Make Way for Youth," *AC* (February 1963): 92, 112.

86. Abel Green, "Goldenson: 'Back to Sanity,'" *Variety*, February 27, 1963, 3, 18.

87. "Pros and Cons Re Runaway," *Variety*, December 7, 1960, 11.

88. "The Pit and the Pendulum"—A Study in Horror Film Photography," *AC* (October 1961): 612–613, 623–624.

89. "Says Bill Wyler: 'Runaway as Term Makes Li'l Sense,'" *Variety*, December 14, 1960, 5.

90. "No 'Runaway' for Vidpix Prod. Which Likes H'wood," *Variety*, December 20, 1961, 1.

91. "Vidpix Yen for 'Location,'" *Variety*, February 18, 1959, 20.

92. "Sock Pix Payoff: 3 Brokers Touting U-Decca Shares," *Variety*, March 2, 1960, 3, 22.

93. "Universal Pace Better 'n Double 1961; Audit Date to Match That of Decca," *Variety*, September 26, 1962, 3; "MCA Recontruct'g Old Universal City," September 26, 1962, 3.

94. "Revue Lot Really Jumpin' With Telepix Employment at Peak," *Variety*, December 25, 1963, 31.

95. "Stop One 'Runaway,'" *Variety*, April 11, 1962, 3.

96. "Harold Hecht: 'France on Universal Backlot Saves 'Cognac' $500,000,'" *Variety*, April 24, 1963, 7. "Cognac" was released as *Wild and Wonderful.*

97. Steven Bingen, Stephen X. Sylvester, and Michael Troyan, *MGM: Hollywood's Greatest Backlot* (Solano Beach, CA: Santa Monica Press, 2011), 297–298.

98. *Birdman of Alcatraz*, despite its title, largely takes place in Kansas's Leavenworth Penitentiary. San Francisco appears only in the film's final scene on the boat dock facing the island, briefly but notably shot on location.

99. Vaughn Shaner, "New Double-X Pan Twice As Fast as Plus-X," *AC*, August 1960, 484–485, 493–494.

100. Arthur Gavin, "'Experiment in Terror," *AC* (May 1962): 288–289, 318, 320–321.

101. "'Sunlight Dims as Hollywood's Trump'—Garfein," *Variety*, October 5, 1960, 17.

102. Don Hyndman, "Steady Progress in Film Improvement," *AC* (May 1961): 299, 316, 318.

103. Vaughn Shaner, "New Double-X Pan Twice As Fast as Plus-X," *AC* (August 1960): 484–485, 493–494.

104. Ibid. Quote refers to *The Adventures of Huckleberry Finn* (1960).

105. Ibid.

106. Shaner, "New Double-X"; Robert Allen Mitchell, "Color in Motion Pictures and TV, Part III: Natural Color for Television," *AC* (November 1959): 672, 699–700.

107. Hyndman, "Steady Progress," *AC* (May 1961): 299, 316, 318.

108. Arthur Rowan, "We Travel Light and We Travel Fast," *AC* (August 1959): 490, 506.

109. "Gerry O'Hara, British Asst. Director, Touts Value of Shooting Outside Studio," *Variety*, February 27, 1963, 17.

110. Jack Pitman, "Real Things Vs. Studio Mockups" *Variety*, July 20, 1960, 23.

111. Fred Foster, "The Sun Gun Photo Light," *AC* (May 1962): 292–293, 314–318.

112. Walter Beyer, "Travelling Matte Photography and the Blue-Screen System: Part II: Specifications for Equipment and Photography," *AC* (January 1964): 34–44.

113. Barry Salt, *Film Style and Technology: History and Analysis*, 2nd ed. (London: Starword, 1992), 241–242.

114. Dr. Norwood Simmons, "The New Eastman Color Negative and Color Print Films," *AC* (June 1962): 362–363, 385; Salt, *Film Style*, 241–242.

115. Frederick Foster, "A Faster Color Negative," *AC* (June 1959): 364–365, 369–370.

116. Darrin Scot, "Panavision's Progress,"*AC* (May 1960): 302, 304, 320–324. This put color filmmaking even below the threshold of Columbia's latensified 50 foot-candle features of the 1940s, described in chapter 1.

117. Hyndman, "Steady Progress," 299, 316, 318.

118. Herb Lightman, "Shooting Black and White in Color," *AC* (August 1959): 486–487, 499–500.

119. Ibid.

120. Arthur Gavin, "Not an Interior in the Picture!," *AC* (March 1959): 166–167, 191–192.

121. Arthur Gavin, "Filming 'The F.B.I. Story,'" *AC* (May 1959): 286–287, 305–307.

122. Arthur Gavin, "'The Defiant Ones'—Ultimate in Mood Photography," *AC* (August 1958): 484–485, 500, 502.

123. Ibid.

124. Darrin Scot, "Filming the Impossible for 'The World, The Flesh and The Devil,'" *AC* (June 1959): 346–347, 378–380; Joseph Brun, "Odds Against Tomorrow," *AC* (August 1959): 487–488, 510.

125. Gavin, "Experiment in Terror," *AC* (May 1962): 288–289, 318, 320–321.

126. Sam Leavitt, "Filming 'Anatomy of a Murder' in the Story's Actual Locale," *AC* (July 1959): 416–417, 443.

127. "Detroit Preems 'Anatomy'; Preminger Edited Film on Location as Shot," *Variety*; May 13, 1959, 15; Robert Landry, "Bureau of Missing Business," *Variety*, June 10, 1959, 7.

128. Leavitt, "Filming 'Anatomy of a Murder,'" 417, 443.

129. "Tout Value of Filming Off-Lot Under Full 'Field Headquarters' Plan," *Variety*, May 20, 1959, 1, 78.

130. Leavitt, "Filming 'Anatomy of a Murder,'" 417, 443.

131. Denise Mann places *Sweet Smell of Success* on the margins of Hollywood production as a threat to mainstream features and a predecessor to the Hollywood

Renaissance of the late 1960s. However placed within the context of subsequent films of the late 1950s and early 1960s, this 1957 film appears as an early example of a wave of dark, independently produced films that kept theaters running between mainstream blockbusters. Denise Mann, *Hollywood Independents: The Postwar Talent Takeover* (Minneapolis: University of Minnesota Press, 2008), 243–239, 249.

132. Herb Lightman, "Hazardous Assignment in an Asphalt Jungle," *AC* (July 1961): 408–409, 435–437.

133. Ellsworth Fredricks, "'Seven Days in May,'" *AC* (October 1963): 586–587, 609–611.

134. Bob Allen, "Shooting Under Cover with Available Light," *AC* (August 1963): 466–467, 483–484.

135. Lightman, "Hazardous Assignment."

136. "Racial Outbreaks at Frisco Firstruns," *Variety*, August 31, 1960, 3, 21.

137. "Radio Review: The Line-up," *Variety*, November 22, 1950, 31.

138. Jeff Smith, *The Sounds of Commerce: Marketing Popular Film Music* (New York: Columbia University Press, 1998), 74–76; Sam Wasson, *A Splurch in the Kisser: The Movies of Blake Edwards* (Middletown, CT: Wesleyan University Press, 2009), 135.

139. "Television Reviews: Peter Gunn," *Variety*, September 24, 1958, 27.

140. Art Woodstone, "NBC Do-Good Image Gets Major Billing at Web-Affiliate Powwow: Durgin's Derring-Do a Big Click," *Variety*, November 8, 1959, 28.

141. Ibid.

142. Bill Greeley, "Only 9 Client-Agency Controlled Shows Set for Network Airing—On Other Madison Ave. Fronts," *Variety*, June 15, 1960, 30; "Bristol-Myers to Drop 'Peter Gunn,'" *Variety*, March 22, 1961, 26.

143. Peter Gunn ad, *Variety*, July 19, 1961, 39; "O.F.'s Sale-a-Day on 'Peter Gunn,'" *Variety*, August 16, 1961, 30.

144. "Crime-Suspense Shows (No Matter How You Splice 'Em It's Violence) on the Upswing as TV Staple," *Variety*, July 6, 1960, 27, 46.

145. Ibid.

146. William Whyte, "Introduction," in *The Exploding Metropolis* (Garden City, NY: Doubleday, 1958), 8; Lewis Mumford, *The City in History* (San Diego: Harcourt, 1961), 486.

147. Bob Chandler, "Ascendancy of Writer-Producer in Telefilm Arena; 17 Such Entries Helming Major Network Shows," *Variety*, August 12, 1959, 31.

148. Art Woodstone, "Wanted: Production Execs," *Variety*, August 12, 1959, 31; "Another Producer in 20th-to-WB Shuffle," *Variety*, November 1, 1961, 4.

149. At the time, the lesser-known partners in this new venture, Project 111, were Freddie Fields and David Begelman. After founding CMA in 1960, they rose to become mega-agents in 1960s and 1970s Hollywood. Begelman became

production head of Columbia in 1973. Fields represented directors such as Francis Ford Coppola, Steven Spielberg, and George Lucas. See Richard Natale, "Fields Fielded Top Client List," *Daily Variety*, December 13, 2007, 1, 20.

150. He would eventually make the feature version, *Gunn*, in 1967.

151. "Edwards-Fields-Begelman Move on Many Fronts as Project III Rolls," *Variety*, July 19, 1961, 24.

152. "Keeping Clear of Bankers: Goal for A&P Bunch," *Variety*, October 25, 1961, 3.

153. Gavin, "Experiment in Terror," *AC* (May 1962): 288–289, 318, 320–321.

154. As a point of reference, this was the same meager illumination used for Columbia's late 1940s B-films. The resulting image quality was inferior and required the latensification process to boost a viable exposure.

155. Gavin, "Experiment in Terror," *AC* (May 1962): 288–289, 318, 320–321.

156. Ibid.

157. Ibid.

158. Ibid.

159. "Film Reviews: Experiment in Terror," *Variety*, March 21, 1962, 6.

160. Lathrop likely used a motorized zoom lens, which appeared in late 1960 as a alternative to the cumbersome hand-cranked zoom lens. See John Forbes, "Product Report: Motor-driven Zoom Lens," *AC* (December 1960): 746.

161. Gavin, "Experiment in Terror," *AC* (May 1962): 288–289, 318, 320–321.

162. Metty shot *Touch of Evil* (1958), and *Experiment in Terror* employs a similar "kitchen sink" approach to film noir cinematography. Both films rely on extremely high contrast lighting, night-for-night photography, jarring camera angles, and creative camerawork.

163. Gavin, "Experiment in Terror," *AC* (May 1962): 288–289, 318, 320–321.

164. "Showman's Reviews," *Motion Picture Herald*, March 28, 1962, 491.

165. "Film Reviews: Experiment in Terror," *Variety*, March 21, 1962, 6.

166. Final script, January 10, 1962, *Days of Wine and Roses* Production File, WBA, USC.

167. Jack McEdwards to Martin Manulis, January 8, 1962, San Francisco location survey, Correspondence, *Days of Wine and Roses* Production File, WBA, USC.

168. Ibid.

169. Budget, February 8, 1962, Budgets, *Days of Wine and Roses* Production File, WBA, USC.

170. Bob Holden to Jack McEdwards, January 16, 1962; Lawrence Schiller to Mort Lichter, February 11, 1962; Correspondence, *Days of Wine and Roses* Production File, WBA, USC.

171. Jack McEdward and Chief Cahill, January 9 and 11, 1962; McEdward to Martin Manulis, January 8, 1962; Correspondence, *Days of Wine and Roses* Production File, WBA, USC.

172. Schiller to Lichter, February 18, 1962, Correspondence, *Days of Wine and Roses* Production File, WBA, USC.

173. Daily production reports, February 9–May 29, 1962, Production Reports, *Days of Wine and Roses* Production File, WBA, USC.

174. R. A. Pease to Charles Greenlaw, January 11, 1962; Rear Adm. Allen Winbeck to Warner Bros., March 7, 1962; Gordon Bau to Charles Greenlaw, January 17, 1962; all in Correspondence, *Days of Wine and Roses* Production File, WBA, USC; budget, February 8, 1962, *Days of Wine and Roses* Production File, WBA, USC.

175. Daily production reports, February 9–May 29, 1962, Production Reports, *Days of Wine and Roses* Production File, WBA, USC.

176. "Film Review: Days of Wine and Roses," *Variety*, December 5, 1962, 11.

177. "Top Rental Films of 1963," *Variety*, January 8, 1964, 37, 71; production budget, *Days of Wine and Roses* Production File,WBA, USC.

178. Victor Gruen, *The Heart of Our Cities*, (New York: Simon and Schuster, 1964), 175.

179. Kevin Lynch, *Image of the City* (Cambridge, MA: MIT Press, 1964), 10.

180. Ibid.

181. Gladwin Hill, "West Coast Rivals: Los Angeles and San Francisco Have Attractions That Defy Comparison," *New York Times*, November 1, 1959, section XX, 33.

182. Edward Dimendberg, *Film Noir and the Spaces of Modernity* (Cambridge, MA: Harvard University Press, 2004), 148–149.

183. William Luhr and Peter Lehman describe the omnipresence of police surveillance but argue that Red Lynch's invasion of Kelly's space questions the power of police surveillance. Yet the distinction between public and private space is vital to the plot. Lynch disguises his public appearance to avoid detection from the near-omniscient FBI. Eventually, he enters a public space, but even among a crowd, he is spotted and eliminated by the FBI, who seamlessly police public space. See William Luhr and Peter Lehman, "*Experiment in Terror*: Dystopian Modernism, the Police Procedural, and the Space of Anxiety," in *Cinema and Modernity*, ed. Murray Pomerance (Piscataway, NJ: Rutgers University Press, 2006), 180–187.

184. Luhr and Lehman note the similarity between the ending of *Experiment in Terror* and Harry's (Clint Eastwood) encounter with Scorpio (Andy Robinson) in *Dirty Harry* (1971). As I discuss in chapter 5, the similar scenes both include ascending helicopter shots but also have key differences offering disparate visions of San Francisco. See Luhr and Lehman, "*Experiment in Terror*," 188.

185. Ibid., 185–187.

186. Frankenheimer and Edwards recall this in later interviews and commentaries for each version of *Days of Wine and Roses*. See John Frankenheimer interview on the DVD *The Golden Age of Television* (New York: Criterion, 2009); Blake

Edwards commentary, *Days of Wine and Roses* DVD (Burbank, CA: Warner Home Video, 2010).

187. Pamela Wojcik, *The Apartment Plot: Urban Living in American Film and Popular Culture, 1945 to 1975* (Durham, NC: Duke University Press, 2010), 39.

188. Jane Jacobs, "Downtown Is for People," in *The Exploding Metropolis* (Garden City, NY: Doubleday, 1958), 161–162.

189. "Film Review: Days of Wine and Roses," *Variety*, December 5, 1962, 11.

190. *Days of Wine and Roses* ads, *Variety*, January 9, 1963, 34–35.

191. *Experiment in Terror* trailer script, February 7, 1962, fol. 135, Jack Atlas Papers, Margaret Herrick Library, AMPAS.

192. Jane Jacobs, *The Death and Life of Great American Cities* (New York: Random House, 1961), 585.

CHAPTER 4

1. "Big Rental Films of 1968," *Variety*, January 8, 1969, 15; "Big Rental Films of 1969," *Variety*, January 7, 1970, 15.

2. Art Seidenbaum, "Spectator, 1964: Film Mogul Dips Toe in Bay Area," *Los Angeles Times*, July 8, 1964, D1.

3. Robert Joseph, "Tapping S.F.'s Film Potential," *Los Angeles Times*, April 30, 1967, C16.

4. Ibid.

5. Ibid.

6. Rick Setlowe, "California's Camelot: 'Where Everything is Happening,'" *Daily Variety*, October 29, 1968, 22–23, 94.

7. Ibid.

8. Rick Setlowe, "Miscellany: Frisco Is Psychedelphia; So Many Happenings You Can't Tell Hippies From the Interrelated Tourists," *Variety*, April 12, 1967, 2.

9. Ibid.

10. Setlowe, "California's Camelot," *Daily Variety*, October 29, 1968, 22–23, 94.

11. "MGM Lot: Sell, Cut or Rent," *Variety*, September 11, 1968, 3; 21; "Film Biz Okay in 1965: Exhibition and Production," *Variety*, January 1, 1966, 67.

12. Steven Bingen et al., *MGM: Hollywood's Greatest Back Lot* (Solano Beach, CA: Santa Monica Press, 2011), 219.

13. "MGM Orders Review Re Culver City Site: Stay or Go Conejo Way?," *Variety*, June 7, 1967, 1, 71.

14. Bingen et al., *MGM: Hollywood's Greatest Back Lot,* 268.

15. Robert Landry, "Hollywood-Beyond-the-Smog: Malibu Tract's New Frontyard," *Variety*, May 29, 1963, 1, 18.

16. "U Dictum: The Hills Must Go," *Variety*, October 7, 1964, 7; Bernard Dick, *City of Dreams: The Making and Remaking of Universal Pictures* (Lexington: University of Kentucky Press, 1997), 165.

17. "Universal Building to Stagger Reality," *Variety*, January 1, 1964, 4.

18. See chapter 2.

19. Landry, "Hollywood-Beyond-the-Smog," *Variety*, May 29, 1963, 1, 18.

20. Ibid.

21. "Schneider, O'Brien, Zanuck Meeting," *Variety*, October 30, 1963, 3.

22. "Hollywood Studios at SRO: Rentals Boom; 'Runaway' Fade," *Variety*, August 11, 1965, 7; "Finish Goldwyn Backlot," *Variety*, October 7, 1964, 7.

23. "Metro Joining Other Studios in Rental Hike," *Variety*, February 1956, 3; Dave Kaufman, "Employment So Bullish in H'wood, Unions Foresee Labor Shortage," *Variety*, June 29, 1966, 24.

24. Thomas Pryor, "Hollywood and 'Runaway,'" *Variety*, April 26, 1967, 41.

25. "Hollywood's Runaway Boom: U.S. Production Holds Steady," *Variety*, September 2, 1964, 1, 62.

26. "Film Biz Okay in 1965: Exhibition and Production," *Variety*, January 1, 1966, 67.

27. Pryor, "Hollywood and Runaway," *Variety*, April 26, 1967, 41.

28. "'Camelot' Home to Cal; Tricky Logistics Involve Use of Spanish Castles," *Variety*, October 19, 1966, 16.

29. Mark Harris, *Pictures at a Revolution: Five Movies and the Birth of New Hollywood* (New York: Penguin, 2009), 258.

30. "D.C. Eyes Runaway Pix and TV—Again," *Variety*, August 31, 1966, 2.

31. Dave Kaufman, "Hollywood All-Out Anew to Halt 'Runaway' Theatrical & TV Filming," *Variety*, December 6, 1967.

32. "31 percent of Hollywood Crafts 24,000 Pool Idle; Press to End 'Inventory' Slowdown," *Variety*, March 27, 1968, 16.

33. Thomas Pryor, "Hollywood Unions Fight 'Runaway' But Waving U.S. Flag Not Enough," *Variety*, May 8, 1968, 35.

34. Ibid.

35. Herb Lightman, "Portable Lightweight Equipment Keeps Production Costs Down," *AC* (July 1964): 374–375, 403–404.

36. "Unions Started 'Runaway' Trend But Fairbanks Back in L.A. and Jolly," *Variety*, October 12, 1966, 4.

37. Peter Bart, "Where the Action Isn't," *New York Times*, July 31, 1966, D7.

38. "With Studio City Operating, Count 27 Picture Producers in Miami," *Variety*, February 9, 1966, 22.

39. Stuart Byron, "Second Try for Studio City, Miami; Call It Ideal Midpoint for Budget Pics Between L.A. and Mexico," *Variety*, October 18, 1967, 5, 22.

40. Stanley Corkin, *Starring New York: Filming the Grime and the Glamour of the Long 1970s* (New York: Oxford University Press, 2011), 6.

41. "L.A. Labor Laments to Lindsay Lure; New York Seeks No 'War of Cities,'" *Variety*, February 15, 1967, 11.

42. Ibid.

43. "Mayor's Campaign to Make Frisco Hollywood's 'Backlot' Succeeding," *Daily Variety*, August 21, 1968, 1, 4.

44. Ibid.

45. Hank Stockert, "Is Filming Technology Losing Ground?," *AC* (April 1965): 226–228.

46. Ibid.

47. Walter Beyer, "Travelling Matte Photography and the Blue Screen System," *AC* (October 1964): 564–565, 568, 592, 598; Stockert, "Is Filming Technology Losing Ground?," *AC* (April 1965): 226–228.

48. Don Norwood, "The Camera of the Future," *AC* (June 1966): 390–392.

49. "Motion Picture Lighting Past, Present and Future," *AC* (July 1967): 480–483, 500–501, 510, 512–513.

50. Arthur Miller, "'Natural Lighting' For Interior Sets," *AC* (September 1966): 618–621.

51. Fenton Hamilton, "Studio Set Lighting—Present and Future," *AC* (April 1964): 248–249.

52. "New Tungsten-Halogen High-Wattage Lamps," *AC* (May 1968): 342–344, 370–371.

53. Ray Fernstrom, "Low Budget Color Photography of *A Swingin' Summer*," *AC* (May 1965): 293–295.

54. Andrew Laszlo, "Recent Trends in Location Lighting," *AC* (September 1968): 666–668, 696–697.

55. Barry Salt, *Film Style and Technology: History and Analysis*, 2nd ed. (London: Starword, 1992), 258; Mike Waddell, "*Cinema Verite* and the Documentary Film," *AC* (October 1968): 789, 796–798.

56. "The Boston Location Filming of 'The Thomas Crown Affair,'" *AC* (October 1968): 740–743, 786–787, 793–795.

57. Behrend's, Inc., ad, *AC* (April 1965): 212.

58. Arriflex ad, *AC* (April 1968): 255.

59. Herb Lightman, "Cinematographer with a 'Split Personality,'" *AC* (February 1968): 104–107, 132–134, 138–139, 142–144.

60. Éclair ad, *AC* (August 1967): 563.

61. Éclair ad, *AC* (February 1969): 223.

62. "The Academy Award-winning Nagra Recorder," *AC* (June 1966): 409–411, 432.

63. “Product Report: The Colortran Hydraulic Crab Dolly,” *AC* (September 1966): 522–525.

64. Brad Chisholm, “Red, Blue, and Lots of Green: The Impact of Color Television on Feature Film Production,” in *Hollywood in the Age of Television*, ed. Tino Balio (Boston: Unwin Hyman, 1990), 227–229; Gorham Kindem, “Hollywood’s Conversion to Color: The Technological, Economic and Aesthetic Factors,” *Journal of the University Film Association* 31, no. 2 (Spring 1979): 29–36.

65. Ted Fogelman, “Extended Development of Eastman 5251 Color Negative,” *AC* (June 1967): 412–413.

66. “Eastman Introduces Three Revolutionary New Films,” *AC* (June 1968): 424–426, 449, 466–467.

67. Ibid.

68. “Product Report: The Lowell Quartz System,” *AC* (May 1968): 360–262, 382.

69. Andrew Laszlo, “Recent Trends in Location Lighting,” *AC* (September 1968): 666–668, 696–697.

70. For a detailed exploration of this ethos, see Patrick Keating, *Hollywood Lighting from the Silent Era to Film Noir* (New York: Columbia University Press, 2010).

71. Laszlo, “Recent Trends in Location Lighting,” *AC* (September 1968): 666–668, 696–697.

72. Herb Lightman, “Hitchcock Talks About Lights, Camera, Action,” *AC* (May 1967): 332–335, 350–351.

73. Miller, “‘Natural Lighting,’” *AC* (September 1966): 618–621.

74. Ibid.

75. Morton Beebe and J. Bruce Hayes, “Tinseltown on the Bay,” *San Francisco Sunday Examiner and Chronicle*, August 22, 1971, 10–12; “Locations-CA, San Francisco,” clippings file, Margaret Herrick Library, AMPAS.

76. “Eastman Introduces Three Revolutionary New Films,” *AC* (June 1968): 424–426, 449, 466–467.

77. Scott Higgins, *Harnessing the Technicolor Rainbow: Color Design in the 1930s* (Austin: University of Texas Press, 2009), 212. The 1967 Academy Awards merged black-and-white and color cinematography back into a single category, indicative of the growing rarity of black-and-white features.

78. Burnett Guffey, “The Photography of *King Rat*,” *AC* (December 1965): 777–781.

79. Harris, *Pictures at a Revolution*, 386; Paul Monaco, *The Sixties, 1960–1969* (Berkeley: University of California Press, 2001), 69.

80. Higgins, *Harnessing the Technicolor Rainbow,* 217.

81. Lightman, “Hitchcock Talks About Lights, Camera, Action,” interview by Herb Lightman, *AC* (May 1967), 332–335, 350–351.

82. Charles Loring, "Filming 'Torn Curtain' By Reflected Light," *AC* (October 1966): 680–683, 706–707.

83. Ibid.

84. Lightman, "Cinematographer with a 'Split Personality,'" *AC* (February 1968): 104–107, 132–134, 138–139, 142–144.

85. Herb Lightman, "Raw Cinematic Realism in the Photography of 'Bonnie and Clyde,'" *AC* (April 1967): 254–257.

86. Gillo Pontecorvo, "'The Battle of Algiers'; An Adventure in Filming," *AC* (April 1967): 266–269.

87. Dave Saunders, *Direct Cinema* (New York: Wallflower, 2007), 82–83; Robert Allen and Douglas Gomery, *Film History: Theory and Practice* (New York: Knopf, 1985), 237.

88. Waddell, "*Cinema Verite* and the Documentary Film," *AC* (October 1968): 789, 796–798.

89. "The Director-Cameraman Relationship," *AC* (May 1968): 52–53, 64–66, 338–389, 364–365.

90. "Motion Picture Lighting," *AC* (July 1967): 480–483, 500–501, 510, 512–513.

91. Ibid.

92. "The Boston Location Filming of 'The Thomas Crown Affair,'" *AC* (October 1968): 740–743, 786–787, 793–795.

93. "Motion Picture Lighting," *AC* (July 1967): 480–483, 500–501, 510, 512–513.

94. "The Boston Location Filming of 'The Thomas Crown Affair,'" *AC* (October 1968): 740–743, 786–787, 793–795.

95. Kevin Thomas, "Chartoff and Winkler: Entrepreneurs of the Offbeat Film," *Los Angeles Times*, January 16, 1968, D1.

96. Ibid.

97. "Britons See Irony in Choice of 'Petulia' as U.S. Entry at Cannes," *Variety*, May 15, 1968, 17.

98. Ron Wise, "True 'Runaway': Film Costs," *Variety*, July 27, 1966, 15.

99. "Hollywood Unions Greater 'Threat' to Yank Pix Biz Than Runaways: Prem," *Variety*, November 9, 1966, 1.

100. "Third Case in Hollywood Brands IATSE Cameramen's Local as Job Monopoly," *Variety*, February 15, 1967, 11.

101. Thomas Pryor, "$100-Mil. in 'Runaway' Pix," *Variety*, August 17, 1966, 3.

102. Bart, "Where the Action Isn't," *New York Times*, July 31, 1966, D7.

103. Harris, *Pictures at a Revolution*, 136–137.

104. David Talbot, *Season of the Witch: Enchantment, Terror, and Deliverance in the City of Love* (New York: Simon and Schuster, 2012), 90.

105. Joseph, "Tapping S.F.'s Film Potential," *Los Angeles Times*, April 30, 1967, C16.

106. A key factor in these competing aesthetics that deserves further scholarly attention is a widening aesthetic gap between genres in the 1960s. While crime thrillers had to develop a new color aesthetic, many comedies remained comfortable in a slightly more subdued Technicolor gloss. Even in 1972, the candy-colored 1950s palette of *What's Up, Doc?* did not limit the box office success or youth appeal of the San Francisco screwball comedy.

107. Rick Setlowe, "Barbary Coast's New 'Frisco Sound' Phasing-out Hashbury Hippies?," *Variety*, August 23, 1967, 1, 62.

108. "Television Reviews: Ironside," *Variety*, March 29, 1967, 46.

109. "Television Reviews: Ironside," *Variety*, September 20, 1967, 33.

110. Aniko Bodroghkozy, *Groove Tube: Sixties Television and the Youth Rebellion* (Durham, NC: Duke University Press, 2001), 75–85.

111. Herb Lightman, "Voyage on a Soundstage," *AC* (January 1965): 28–29, 68. Kramer shot on location when needed for the plot, such as the action chase through the woods in *The Defiant Ones* (1958), although this was limited to Southern California. See Arthur Gavin, "'The Defiant Ones'—Ultimate in Mood Photography," *AC* (August 1958): 484–485, 500, 502.

112. Harris, *Pictures at a Revolution*, 296–299.

113. Ibid., 373.

114. Setlowe, "California's Camelot," *Daily Variety*, October 29, 1968, 22–23, 94.

115. Peter Hartlaub, "Memorable Goofs in Movies About San Francisco," http://www.sfgate.com/movies/article/Memorable-goofs-in-movies-about-S-F-5355388.php (accessed July 8, 2014).

116. Harris, *Pictures at a Revolution*, 315–316.

117. Lightman, "Cinematographer with a 'Split Personality,'" *AC* (February 1968): 104–107, 132–134, 138–139, 142–144.

118. Ibid.

119. Beebe and Hayes, "Tinseltown on the Bay," *San Francisco Sunday Examiner and Chronicle*, August 22, 1971, 10–12. The company shot in Tijuana after wrapping in San Francisco. See daily production reports, April 3–June 12, 1967, Budget and Production Reports, *Petulia* Production File, WBA, USC.

120. Joseph, "Tapping S.F.'s Film Potential," *Los Angeles Times*, April 30, 1967, C16.

121. "Julie Christie–Dick Lester Combo for 'Kook' Film; Seek Distrib Support," *Variety*, March 9, 1966, 5.

122. Tino Balio, *United Artists: The Company That Changed the Film Industry* (Madison: University of Wisconsin Press, 1987), 248–252.

123. Ibid.

124. "Julie Christie–Dick Lester Combo," *Variety*, March 9, 1966, 5.

125. Ibid.

126. "Lester Forecasts San Francisco Pic," *Variety*, July 6, 1966, 17; "Britons See Irony," *Variety*, May 15, 1968, 17. The financial implications of this classification are murky and further complicated by Seven Arts' purchase of Warner Bros. before *Petulia* was released.

127. "Julie Christie–Dick Lester Combo," *Variety*, March 9, 1966, 5; "Lester Forecasts," *Variety*, July 6, 1966, 17.

128. "The New Rock," *Life*, June 28, 1968, 45–62.

129. Setlowe, "Barbary Coast's New Frisco Sound," *Variety*, August 23, 1967, 1, 62.

130. Ralph Rosenblum and Robert Karen, *When the Shooting Stops . . .*, (New York: DeCapo, 1986), 12–13.

131. Setlowe, "Miscellany: Frisco Is Psychedelphia," *Variety*, April 12, 1967, 2, 78.

132. Bob Solo to Dutch Meyer, December 23, 1966, folder 2019, Production Correspondence, *Petulia* Production File, WBA, USC.

133. Walter McEwen to Jack Warner, April 20, 1967, folder 2019, Production Correspondence, *Petulia* Production File, WBA, USC.

134. McEwen to Warner, May 10, 1967, folder 2019, Production Correspondence, *Petulia* Production File, WBA, USC.

135. Ibid.

136. Daily production reports, April 3–June 12, 1967, Budget and Production Reports, *Petulia* Production File, WBA, USC.

137. McEwen to Warner, May 10, 1967, folder 2019, Production Correspondence, *Petulia* Production File, WBA, USC. Lester did not make another film until *The Three Musketeers* (1973).

138. See Steven Bach, *Final Cut: Art, Money, and Ego in the Making of Heaven's Gate, the Film That Sank United Artists* (New York: Newmarket, 1999).

139. Rick Setlowe, "Lester 'Adopts' Rains for 'Petulia,'" *Variety*, May 10, 1967, 11.

140. Ibid.

141. Roeg proved his value as a filmmaker and landscape cinematographer far from San Francisco with his extraordinary footage of the Australian Outback in *Walkabout* (1971).

142. Beebe and Hayes, "Tinseltown on the Bay," *San Francisco Sunday Examiner and Chronicle*, August 22, 1971, 12.

143. Albert Morch, "Elite in the Act," *San Francisco Examiner and Chronicle*, March 10, 1968, Movies/San Francisco, *San Francisco Examiner* clippings file, SF History Center, SF Public Library.

144. Setlowe, "Miscellany: Frisco Is Psychedelphia," *Variety*, April 12, 1967, 2, 78; "Reel SF: Petulia-Topless Club," http://reelsf.com/reelsf/petulia-topless-bar (accessed July 20, 2017).

145. Ibid.

146. Kathleen Carroll, "Julie Christie Charms in Mod Film," *New York Daily News*, June 11, 1968, folder 2019, Production Correspondence, *Petulia* Production File, WBA, USC.

147. Colin Rowe and Fred Koetter, *Collage City* (Cambridge, MA: MIT Press, 1984), 149.

148. Joseph, "Tapping S.F.'s Film Potential," *Los Angeles Times*, April 30, 1967, C16.

149. Ibid.

150. Abe Greenberg, "Frisco Quietly Raids Film Biz!," *Citizen News*, April 4, 1967, "Locations-CA, San Francisco," clippings file, Margaret Herrick Library, AMPAS.

151. "Big Rental Films of 1968," *Variety*, January 8, 1969, 15; "'Petulia,' Out-Take At Cannes, Opens At Gotham's Plaza," *Variety*, May 29, 1968, 5.

152. "Big Rental Films of 1969," *Variety*, January 7, 1970, 15; Marc Eliot, *Steve McQueen: A Biography* (New York: Random House, 2011), 212. *Variety* placed *Bullitt* as the third highest earner of 1969, just behind *Funny Girl* ($16.5 million) and *The Love Bug* ($17 million). Eliot cites other sources that estimate *Bullitt*'s domestic gross at upward of $35 to $80 million.

153. Kevin Thomas, "Chartoff and Winkler, " *Los Angeles Times*, January 16, 1968, D1.

154. "Big Rental Films of 1968," *Variety*, January 8, 1969, 15; "Film Reviews: Point Blank," *Variety*, September 6, 1967.

155. Stanley Eichelbaum, "Steve McQueen Film Seeks 'Feel of City,'" *San Francisco Examiner*, February 22, 1968, in *San Francisco Examiner* clippings, Filmmakers/San Francisco, SF History Center, SF Public Library.

156. "MGM Renting Alcatraz for Film Scenes," *Los Angeles Times*, March 6, 1967, "Locations-CA, San Francisco," clippings file, Margaret Herrick Library, AMPAS.

157. Michael Ciment, *John Boorman* (London: Faber, 1986), 73; quoted in Peter Wilshire, "The Art of Dying: *Point Blank*," *Offscreen.com*, 17, no. 4, www.offscreen.com/index.php/pages/essays/art_of_dying/ (accessed February 18, 2014).

158. Allan Siegel, "After the Sixties: Changing Paradigms in the Representation of Urban Space," in *Screening the City*, ed. Shiel and Fitzmaurice (London: Verso, 2003), 147–153.

159. Eichelbaum "Steve McQueen Film," February 22, 1968, Filmmakers/San Francisco, SF History Center, SF Public Library.

160. Rick Setlowe, "Frisco's Slant on 'Runaway,'" *Variety*, March 27, 1968, 7, 20.

161. Setlowe, "Miscellany: Frisco Is Psychedelphia," *Variety*, April 12, 1967, 2, 78.

162. Eichelbaum, "Steve McQueen Film," February 22, 1968, Filmmakers/San Francisco, SF History Center, SF Public Library.

163. William Fraker oral history, 144–146, Margaret Herrick Library, AMPAS.

164. Morch, "Elite in the Act," March 10, 1968, Filmmakers/San Francisco, SF History Center, SF Public Library.

165. "Alioto Pushes 'Bullitt' Benefit," November 8, 1968, Filmmakers/San Francisco, SF History Center, SF Public Library.

166. Fraker oral history, 145–146, Margaret Herrick Library, AMPAS.

167. Setlowe, "Frisco's Slant," *Variety*, March 27, 1968, 7, 20.

168. Ibid.

169. Rosenblum and Karen, *When the Shooting Stops*, 3–4.

170. Jim Van Buskirk and Will Shank, *Celluloid San Francisco* (Chicago: Chicago Review Press, 2006), 33.

171. Monaco, *The Sixties*, 98–99.

172. The 50 × 20 foot room was a luxury for Keller compared to the typical 12 × 15 studio editing room. Frank Keller Papers, Margaret Herrick Library, AMPAS.

173. Keller notes, Keller Papers, Margaret Herrick Library, AMPAS.

174. Fraker oral history, 149–150, Margaret Herrick Library, AMPAS.

175. Ibid., 144, 153.

176. See chapter 2.

177. Fraker oral history, 142, Margaret Herrick Library, AMPAS.

178. Setlowe, "Frisco's Slant," *Variety*, March 27, 1968, 7, 20.

179. Fraker oral history, 158, Margaret Herrick Library, AMPAS.

180. Ibid., 159.

181. Ibid., 156.

182. Ibid., 144–145.

183. Walter MacEwan to Raymond Wagner, June 8, 1967, folder 2019, Production Correspondence, *Petulia* Production File, WBA, USC.

CHAPTER 5

1. "Alioto Pushes 'Bullitt' Benefit," *San Francisco Examiner*, November 8, 1968, clippings file, Filmmakers/SF, SF History Center, SF Public Library.

2. David Talbot, *Season of the Witch: Enchantment, Terror, and Deliverance in the City of Love* (New York: Simon and Schuster, 2012), 33.

3. "Frisco Mayor Cools Ghetto by Getting Militants Jobs in Pix There; Extras Guild 'Furious,'" *Daily Variety*, December 18, 1968.

4. Cover image, *Life*, August 27, 1965.

5. Robert Beauregard, *Voices of Decline: The Postwar Fate of U.S. Cities* (Oxford: Wiley-Blackwell, 1994), 160, 175–176.

6. Ibid., 153, 166, 196.

7. Ibid., 176.

8. Stanley Corkin, *Starring New York: Filming the Grime and the Glamour of the Long 1970s* (New York: Oxford University Press, 2011), 6–7.

9. Kenneth B. Clark, *Dark Ghetto: Dilemmas of Social Power* (New York: Harper and Row, 1967), 25.

10. Abel Green, "Show Biz Hurt by Violence," *Variety*, January 8, 1969, 3, 56, 58, 60; Rick Perlstein, *Nixonland: The Rise of a President and the Fracturing of America* (New York: Scribner, 2008), 383–386.

11. Perlstein, *Nixonland,* 186.

12. Talbot, *Season of the Witch*, 150–151, 208. Talbot suggests the Zebra murders of late 1973 were the first great threat to San Francisco's 1960s and 1970s self-image of racial tolerance.

13. Brian Godfrey, "Urban Development and Redevelopment in San Francisco," *Geographical Review* 87, no. 3 (July 1997): 316–319.

14. Alfred Borcover, "'Everybody's Favorite' San Francisco Changes, Yet Stays the Same," *Chicago Tribune*, February 28, 1971, F1.

15. "Cinema '72: A Matter of Survival," *AC* (June 1972): 636–637, 689–694.

16. "Notes for a Film Survival Kit; University of So. Calif Panels Avoid Dogmatic and Simplistic Formulas," *Variety*, April 12, 1972, 3–20; "Cinema '72," 636–637, 689–694.

17. A. D. Murphy, "Film Trade Sanity Asserts Itself; Inventory Down From Crazy Highs," *Variety*, April 12, 1972, 3, 20.

18. Green, "Show Biz," *Variety*, January 8, 1969, 3, 56, 58, 60.

19. Ibid.

20. H. P. Koenig, "San Francisco: Cool, Exciting," *Chicago Tribune*, January 19, 1969, G9.

21. Green, "Show Biz," *Variety*, January 8, 1969, 3, 56, 58, 60.

22. Stuart Byron, "Big Budgets' Big Bust-Up," *Variety*, July 23, 1969, 3, 20.

23. Murphy, "Film Trade Sanity," *Variety*, April 12, 1972, 3–20. David Cook also describes Murphy's assessment, omitting the effect of interest rates, in *Lost Illusions: American Cinema in the Shadow of Watergate and Vietnam, 1970–1979* (Berkeley: University of California Press, 2000), 11.

24. Cook, *Lost Illusions*, 11–14.

25. "Par to Unload Cahuenga Stage," *Variety*, January 15, 1969, 5.

26. "Exodus at Par: Runs Above 150," *Variety*, September 3, 1969, 3, 29.

27. "Universal Adds 2 for 34 Stages," *Variety*, January 29, 1969, 4; "U Slashing Overhead," *Variety*, November 26, 1969, 6.

28. "Despite Big B.O. Costs Drag Fox," *Variety*, September 2, 1970, 3, 76.

29. Steven Bingen, Stephen X. Sylvester, and Michael Troyan, *MGM: Hollywood's Greatest Back Lot* (Solano Beach, CA: Santa Monica Press, 2011), 268–277.

30. Ibid., 219.

31. Ibid., 268–277.

32. Thomas Pryor, "Film Backlots: Survival Key," *Variety*, December 23, 1970, 1, 48.

33. A. D. Murphy, "Columbia to Co-Tenant WB Studio; First Case of Long-In-Gab Coast Idea," *Variety*, June 9, 1971, 3, 24.

34. Ibid.

35. Bernard Dick, *City of Dreams: The Making and Remaking of Universal Pictures* (Lexington: University of Kentucky Press, 1997), 165.

36. David Kaufman, "Survey of H'wood Craft Unions Finds Unemployment for Most; Sex Pic Processing Helps Some," *Variety*, October 15, 1969, 3, 22.

37. Kaufman, "Coast Unemployment Gloom," *Variety*, October 15, 1969, 7, 20.

38. Robert Hawkins, "Yanks 'Runaway' to H'wood," *Variety*, August 14, 1968, 1, 10.

39. "Reverse 'Runaway' Continues; U.K.'s Winner to Roll 'Lawman' in Mexico," *Variety*, February 3, 1970, 31.

40. "Yorty's Good Intentions, Wrong Facts," *Variety*, March 24, 1971, 6.

41. Byron, "Big Budgets' Big Bust-Up," *Variety*, July 23, 1969, 3, 20.

42. "Yorty's Good Intentions, Wrong Facts," *Variety*, March 24, 1971, 6.

43. "IATSE Gets 22 percent (By 4th Year) in Studio Pact; Showmen Reject Vidpic Residuals, Runaway Balm," *Variety*, February 12, 1969, 5, 25.

44. "Their Defeat Only 'Paper Victory' for Cinemobile, Is View of Teamsters," *Variety*, December 9, 1970, 6.

45. Kaufman, "Coast Unemployment Gloom," *Variety*, October 15, 1969, 7, 20.

46. Peter Biskind, *Easy Riders, Raging Bulls: How the Sex-Drugs-and-Rock-n-Roll Generation Saved Hollywood* (New York: Simon and Schuster, 1999), 52–80.

47. Ibid., 75–76.

48. "Four Kept in Hollywood; Producers Appreciate Nickel & Dime Savings," *Variety*, March 18, 1970, 6.

49. "BBS & Hollywood Unions," *Variety*, November 8, 1972, 3, 20. Almendros gained support from a stunning list of filmmakers, including Mike Nichols, Peter Bogdanovich, Francis Ford Coppola, Haskell Wexler, and Laszlo Kovacs. Fouad Said, inventor and president of Cinemobile, was another advocate. Other foreign cinematographers, like Kovacs and Vilmos Zsigmond, were long consigned to low-budget pictures while barred from joining the union. See *No Subtitles: Lazslo and Vilmos* (Los Angeles: Cinema Libre Studio, 2012), DVD. See also Cook, *Lost Illusions*, 356–357.

50. "H'wood's New Breed of 'Personal' Films Has Corporate Angle: Modest Budgets," *Variety*, June 25, 1969, 3, 29.

51. Addison Verrill, "Engineered WB Turnaround," *Variety*, December 8, 1971, 5, 22.

52. Ibid.

53. Lee Beaupre, "Despite 'The Revolution' in Film Biz, Lag Between Production and Release Remains Constant; MGM a Speedster," *Variety*, September 27, 1972, 3, 20.

54. "'French Connection' to Cash Flow and Precedent of 'Bullitt': Contrasting Cost," *Variety*, November 24, 1971, 5.

55. Herb Lightman, "The Filming of *Medium Cool*," *AC* (January 1970): 22–25, 58–59, 75, 80.

56. Ibid.

57. Herb Lightman, "Photographing Without Arc Light," *AC* (April 1970): 306–311, 344–345, 371.

58. *The Molly Maguires* grossed $1 million domestically on an $11 million budget (Cook, *Lost Illusions*, 496).

59. Lightman, "Photographing Without Arc Light," *AC* (April 1970): 306–311, 344–345, 371. Glenn Farr, "An Evaluation of Quartz Set-lighting Equipment Versus Conventional Incandescent and Brute Arc Set-Lighting Equipment," *AC* (April 1970): 352–353.

60. "The Evolution of a New Macro-Zoom Lens System," *AC* (1971): 580–583.

61. Charles Loring, "Arriflex 35BL Makes Production Debut in Across 110th Street," *AC* (August 1972): 876–878, 913–914.

62. Sydney Samuelson, "Technology: Survival of the Fastest," *Variety*, January 5, 1972, 40; Barry Salt, *Film Style and Technology: History and Analysis*, 2nd ed. (London: Starword, 1992), 276.

63. Lee Beaupre, "Malpaso Credo: Costs Must Shot On Screen, Not Expense Account: Location Is Best for 'Morale,'" *Variety*, November 14, 1973, 5, 20; Patrick McGilligan, *Clint: The Life and Legend* (New York: St. Martin's, 2002), 198.

64. "The New Nagra SN Miniature Professional Tape Recorder," *AC* (December 1970): 1178–1179, 1234

65. Jim Songer, "New Video West Instant Replay System is Reflex and Wireless," *AC* (July 1971): 716–719.

66. Milton Forman and Fenton Hamilton, "'Air Bubble' Location Stage," *AC* (January 1970): 49–50, 63.

67. Richard Whitehall, "A Step Forward for the Film Technology of the Seventies," *AC* (March 1970): 242–245, 259.

68. Rand Layton, "Filming 'The Candidate' on Location Calls For Some Fast 'Natural Habitat' Decisions," *AC* (September 1972): 1022–1023, 1048–1050.

69. "Multi-gadget Movie Van Rolls Into Hollywood," *AC* (June 1969): 541–544.

70. Ibid.; "Saga of the Cine Mobile," *AC* (November 1969): 1068–1071, 1123.

71. Cinemobile ad, *AC* (April 1971): 310–311; *The Godfather* Cinemobile ad, *AC* (September 1971): 866.

72. Jan Dawson, "Midnight Cowboy," *Sight and Sound* (Fall 1969): 4, 38, 211–212.

73. Ibid.

74. Gregg Steele, "On Location with 'The Godfather,'" *AC* (June 1971): 568–571.

75. "THX 1138: Made in San Francisco," *AC* (October 1971): 993–994, 1018–1019, 1031, 1058–1059, 1062.

76. "Photographing the 'French Connection,'" *AC* (February 1972): 158–161, 184–185, 211–219.

77. Ralph Woolsey, "The Photography of 'The New Centurions,'" *AC* (September 1972): 1028–1031, 1067–1069.

78. "Photographing the 'French Connection,'" *AC* (February 1972): 158–161, 184–185, 211–219.

79. "THX 1138," *AC* (October 1971): 993–994, 1018–1019, 1031, 1058–1059, 1062.

80. Steele, "On Location with 'The Godfather,'" *AC* (June 1971): 568–571.

81. "Photographing the 'French Connection,'" *AC* (February 1972): 158–161, 184–185, 211–219.

82. "THX 1138," *AC* (October 1971): 993–994, 1018–1019, 1031, 1058–1059, 1062.

83. Paul Ramaeker, "Realism, Revisionism and Visual Style: *The French Connection* and the New Hollywood *Policier*," *New Review of Film and Television Studies* 8, no. 2 (June 2010): 144–163.

84. "Photographing the 'French Connection,'" *AC* (February 1972): 158–161, 184–185, 211–219.

85. Gene Polito, "Photographing 'Prime Cut,'" *AC* (June 1972): 654–657, 672–673, 705–709.

86. Woolsey, "Photography of 'The New Centurions,'" *AC* (September 1972): 1028–1031, 1067–1069.

87. Loring, "Arriflex 35BL," *AC* (August 1972): 876–878, 913–914.

88. Ibid.

89. Layton, "Filming 'The Candidate,'" *AC* (September 1972): 1022–1023, 1048–1050.

90. For multicamera shooting, see Layton, "Filming 'The Candidate,'" *AC* (September 1972): 1022–1023, 1048–1050; for faster editing, see Polito, "Photographing 'Prime Cut,'" *AC* (June 1972): 654–657, 672–673, 705–709.

91. Corkin, *Starring New York*, 6–7.

92. "Lindsay Signs New Film Pact," undated clipping, , "Committee on Filmmaking, 1971–1974," Mayor Joseph Alioto Papers, file no. SFH52A, SF History Center, SF Public Library.

93. Abel Green, "Seek B'Way Riff Raff Curbs," *Variety*, March 11, 1971, 1, 74.

94. Corkin, *Starring New York*, 33–45.

95. "Frisco's Good Clean Fun; 'Your Kids Can Bring You' Motto; Laff Goal," *Variety*, March 10, 1970, 1, 74.

96. Corkin, *Starring New York*, 6–7.

97. Rick Setlowe, "Hit March Inventory Tax," *Variety*, April 24, 1968, 5, 28.

98. Corkin, *Starring New York*, 6.

99. "L.A. Sets up One Stop Film Permits," *Back Stage*, December 24, 1971, clipping, "Committee" folder, Alioto Papers, SF History Center, SF Public Library.

100. Filmmaking committee meeting notes, June 2, 1972, and June 29, 1972; Robert Dolan to Wallace Wortman, July 6, 1972; all in "Committee" folder, Alioto Papers, SF History Center, SF Public Library.

101. See chapter 2.

102. "N.Y. Asks Teamsters, Cameramen Start Flexibility, Eat Same Time, Fight Street-Shoot Art Director," *Variety*, December 15, 1971.

103. Abel Green, "N.Y. Too Expensive For Par," *Variety*, September 8, 1971, 5, 24; "'Poorly Planned' Prods. Always Up Costs Photogs," *Variety*, September 8, 1971, 5, 24.

104. "Come to N.Y. With Open Mind, and Filming No 'Sweat': Mark Carliner," *Variety*, September 22, 1971.

105. Ann Brebner to Alioto, June 19, 1972, "Committee" folder, Alioto Papers, SF History Center, SF Public Library.

106. Chester Hartman, *City for Sale: The Transformation of San Francisco* (Berkeley: University of California Press, 2002), 65–68.

107. Lance Williams and Larry Hatfield, "Joseph Alioto, 1916–1998," *SF Gate*, January 30, 1998, http://www.sfgate.com/news/article/JOSEPH-ALIOTO-1916-1998-3237990.php#src=fb (accessed April 17, 2014); Godfrey, *Urban Development*.

108. Hubert Bernhard, "'Bullitt' Made San Francisco a Movie Star," *San Francisco Examiner*, December 25, 1973, 8–9, Filmmakers/SF, *San Francisco Examiner* clippings file, SF History Center, SF Public Library.

109. Rick Setlowe, "Mayor's Campaign to Make Frisco Hollywood's 'Backlot' Succeeding," *Daily Variety*, August 21, 1968, 1, 4.

110. Not coincidentally, *Take the Money and Run* was an early adopter of the Cinemobile, which allowed the production to shoot in ninety-two different locations around San Francisco. See "Saga of the Cinemobile," *AC* (November 1969): 1068–1071, 1123.

111. Setlowe, "Mayor's Campaign."

112. Morton Beebe and J. Bruce Hayes, "Tinseltown on the Bay," *San Francisco Sunday Examiner and Chronicle*, August 22, 1971, 10–12; "Locations-CA, San Francisco," clippings file, Margaret Herrick Library, AMPAS.

113. Jim Harwood, "San Francisco," *Daily Variety*, October 27, 1970, 36.

114. "Ponti Antonioni in N.Y.; Seek Negro 'Expert on Riots' for 'Zabriskie Point,'" *Variety*, May 1, 1968, 1, 78.

115. Rick Setlowe, "Campus 'Revolution' Themes Coming; First-to-Market Angle at Columbia," *Variety*, January 14, 1970, 6.

116. "City's Lure to Movie Producers," January 24, 1969, Filmmakers/SF, SF History Center, SF Public Library.

117. Edward Powell to Alioto, May 7, 1970, "Filmmaking, 1968–1971" folder, Alioto Papers, SF History Center, SF Public Library.

118. Donald Tayer to Alioto, June 9, 1970, file no. SFH52A, Alioto Papers, SF History Center, SF Public Library.

119. Kathy Ryan to John DeLuca, December 4, 1974, "Committee" folder, Alioto Papers, SF History Center, SF Public Library.

120. Cook, *Lost Illusions*, 410–413.

121. Television movie producers continued to beg for exceptions throughout the 1970s due to their shoestring budgets. See Will Tusher, "Radio-Television: Extra Union Pressures on H. Movies," *Variety*, June 15, 1977, 47, 56.

122. "WB Vidpix Prod'n Outlay," *Daily Variety*, December 8, 1970, 1, 11; "The Making of Fools," *San Francisco Examiner*, May 10, 1970, Filmmakers/SF, SF History Center, SF Public Library; Stanley Eichelbaum, "Getting Located Here," *San Francisco Examiner*, October 10, 1971, Filmmakers/SF, SF History Center, SF Public Library.

123. "Location: San Francisco," 1961–1972, file no. SFH52A, Alioto Papers; "4th-Generation TV Star," *San Francisco Chronicle*, July 23, 1969, Filmmakers/SF; both in SF History Center, SF Public Library.

124. "WB Vidpix," *Daily Variety*, December 8, 1970, 1, 11.

125. Gene Phillips, *Godfather: The Intimate Francis Ford Coppola* (Lexington: University of Kentucky Press, 2013), 64–70.

126. Christopher Pearce, "San Francisco's Own American Zoetrope," *AC* (November 1971): 1001–1004, 1050–1051, 1063.

127. Stanley Eichelbaum, "Debut of a Personal Film-Making Plant," *San Francisco Examiner*, December 12, 1969, Filmmakers/SF, SF History Center, SF Public Library.

128. "THX 1138," *AC* (October 1971): 993–994, 1018–1019, 1031, 1058–1059, 1062.

129. Thomas Pryor, "Frisco Mayor New Aggressive Ally of H'wood Labor," *Daily Variety*, October 2, 1968, 2. This diplomatic stance toward Los Angeles also supported Alioto's larger aspirations as a potential Democratic vice-presidential candidate in 1968 and a candidate for California governor in 1974.

130. Herb Caen, "Ballad of Dirty Harry," *San Francisco Chronicle*, January 9, 1972; Bernhard, "'Bullitt,'" *San Francisco Examiner*, December 25, 1973, 8–9, clippings file; both in Filmmakers/SF, SF History Center, SF Public Library.

131. Raymond Syufy to John DeLuca, September 6, 1972, "Film Festival, 1971–1974" folder, Alioto Papers; *San Francisco Examiner*, December 25, 1973, 8–9, clippings file, Filmmakers/SF; both in SF History Center, SF Public Library.

132. Stanley Eichelbaum, "Love Scenes in the Crowd," *San Francisco Examiner*, August 22, 1971, Filmmakers/SF, SF History Center, SF Public Library.

133. "Outrage at Alta Plaza," November 17, 1971, Filmmakers/SF, SF History Center, SF Public Library.

134. Jerry Burns, "Previewing the Use of S.F. for the Movies," *San Francisco Chronicle*, November 22, 1971, 42, Filmmakers/SF, SF History Center, SF Public Library.

135. Talbot, *Season of the Witch*, 82–89.

136. Herb Caen, "Hello Out There," *San Francisco Chronicle*, November 23, 1971, Filmmakers/SF, SF History Center, SF Public Library.

137. Jim Harwood, "Frisco Has Some Second Thoughts On Wooing Film Productions," *Daily Variety*, December 10, 1971, 1, 32.

138. Harwood, "Mayor Alioto Assures Filmmakers He Wants To Keep Prod'n in Frisco," *Daily Variety*, December 23, 1971, 1, 13.

139. Gerald Smith to Robert Mendelsohn, December 2, 1971, "Committee" folder, Alioto Papers, SF History Center, SF Public Library.

140. Sam Yorty to Snazelle Films, December 16, 1971, "Committee" folder, Alioto Papers, SF History Center, SF Public Library.

141. Art Blum to Alioto, October 3, 1972, "Committee" folder, Alioto Papers, SF History Center, SF Public Library.

142. See *AC* (October 1971).

143. Film committee meeting notes, June 2, 1972, "Committee" folder, Alioto Papers, SF History Center, SF Public Library.

144. "Bay Area Lures Film-Makers—A Place to Work and Live," September 19, 1971, Filmmakers/SF, SF History Center, SF Public Library.

145. Film committee meeting notes, June 2, 1972, "Committee" folder, Alioto Papers, SF History Center, SF Public Library.

146. "'Dirty Harry' Premiere," *Variety*, November 24, 1971, 6; McGilligan, *Clint*, 211.

147. Peter Lev, *American Films of the 70s* (Austin: University of Texas Press, 2000), 34–39.

148. Gordon Gow, "Dirty Harry," *Films and Filming* (June 1972): 55, 58; Richard Combs, "8 Degrees of Separation," *Film Comment* 38, no. 4 (July/August 2002): 50–53; Ramaeker, "Realism, Revision," 151.

149. McGilligan, *Clint*, 205–206; Stanley Eichelbaum, "Rooftop Drama North Beach," *San Francisco Examiner*, Filmmakers/SF, SF History Center, SF Public Library.

150. Don Siegel, *A Siegel Film: An Autobiography* (London: Faber, 1993), 358–359; McGilligan, *Clint*, 168–169, 206.

151. L. H. Whittemore, "A Hard Cop and His Patient Partner on a Menacing Beat," *Life*, June 20, 1969, 52–63; "Letters to the Editor," *Life*, July 11, 1969, 16A.

152. Gerald Moore, "We've Always Wanted to Be Cops," *Life*, November 13, 1970, 32–37.

153. Nancy Ford, "Bagdad-by-the Bay: San Francisco: All a Tourist Could Want," March 8, 1970, G7.

154. Beaupre, "Malpaso Credo," *Variety*, November 14, 1973, 5, 20

155. McGilligan, *Clint*, 171; 197–198; Beaupre, "Malpaso Credo," *Variety*, November 14, 1973, 5, 20.

156. McGilligan, *Clint*, 198.

157. Tentative schedule and city facilities request, May 29, 1971, "Filmmaking" folder, Alioto Papers, SF History Center, SF Public Library.

158. Philip Hager, "City Helps Out: Background for Films? Often It's San Francisco," *Los Angeles Times*, December 9, 1973, F1, F31.

159. Jack Rosenblum, "Scene Shifting," May 4, 1971, *San Francisco Examiner*, Filmmakers/SF, SF History Center, SF Public Library.

160. Eichelbaum, "Rooftop Drama in North Beach," Filmmakers/SF, SF History Center, SF Public Library.

161. Siegel, *A Siegel Film*, 370–371.

162. Claude Jarman to Chief Alfred Nedler, Alioto Papers, SF History Center, SF Public Library.

163. McGilligan, *Clint*, 210–212.

164. "Film Reviews: Dirty Harry," *Variety*, December 22, 1971, 6, 20.

165. Verrill Addison, "Biggest WB Week & Half-Year," Variety, August 16, 1972, 3, 24.

166. Eichelbaum, "Rooftop Drama in North Beach," Filmmakers/SF, SF History Center, SF Public Library.

167. McGilligan, *Clint*, 166.

168. Richard Slotkin, *Gunfighter Nation: The Myth of the Frontier in Twentieth-Century America* (New York: HarperPerennial, 1993), 1–21.

169. Slotkin, *Gunfighter Nation*, 588–589.

170. Ibid., 556–558.

171. Abel Green, "Street Crime Clips Show Biz," *Variety*, January 1972, 1, 50.

172. André Bazin, "The Western: Or the American Film Par Excellence," in *What Is Cinema?*, vol. 2, trans./ed. Hugh Gray (Berkeley: University of California Press, 2005), 140–148.

173. Siegel, *A Siegel Film*, 365–367, 375.

174. Richard Combs describes these voyeuristic moments as peculiar, perverse directorial flourishes ("8 Degrees of Separation," *Film Comment* 38, no. 4 [July/August 2002]: 50–53).

175. Caen, "Ballad of Dirty Harry," *San Francisco Chronicle*, January 9, 1972, Filmmakers/SF, SF History Center, SF Public Library.

176. Paul Virilio, *War and Cinema: The Logistics of Perception* (London: Verso, 1989), 2–3.

177. Perlstein, *Nixonland*, 3–4.

178. Virilio, *War and Cinema*, 24–25.

179. Warren Maitland, "The Sky Is Not the Limit," *AC* (February 1966): 102–105.

180. Luhr and Lehman note this similarity but not the differences. See Luhr and Lehman, "*Experiment in Terror*: Dystopian Modernism, the Police Procedural, and the Space of Anxiety," in *Cinema and Modernity*, ed. Murray Pomerance (Piscataway, NJ: Rutgers University Press, 2006), 180–187. See also chapter 3, n184.

181. "TV Costs: Dough-Re-Mi-Farther," *Variety*, September 12, 1973, 47; "WB Vidpix," *Daily Variety*, December 8, 1970, 1, 11.

182. "Location: San Francisco," 1961–1972, "Committee" folder; Alioto to Quinn Martin, undated, "Festival" folder; both in Alioto Papers, SF History Center, SF Public Library.

183. Miller to Alioto, June 7, 1973, "Festival" folder, Alioto Papers, SF History Center, SF Public Library.

184. Karl Malden oral history, 370, Margaret Herrick Library, AMPAS.

185. Rob Knight, "New TV Season—What Is It?," *Variety*, September 27, 1972, 27, 43.

186. "Location: San Francisco," 1961–1972, Alioto Papers, SF History Center, SF Public Library.

187. "Short Takes on Returning Shows," *Daily Variety*, September 19, 1973, 32.

188. Tim Brooks and Earle Marsh, *The Complete Directory to Prime Time Network TV Shows: 1946–Present*, 5th ed. (New York: Ballantine, 1992), 1101–1102.

189. Malden oral history, 368, Margaret Herrick Library, AMPAS.

190. Cinemobile ad, *Daily Variety*, January 3, 1974, 2.

191. "Television Reviews: Streets of San Francisco," *Variety*, September 20, 1972, 34.

192. Jean Hughes to Chet Rhodes, April 9, 1973, "Committee" folder, Alioto Papers, SF History Center, SF Public Library.

193. Donald Rogers oral history, 233, Margaret Herrick Library, AMPAS.

194. Joelle Yuna, "Television in the Streets," *San Francisco Sunday Examiner and Chronicle, California Living Magazine*, September 2, 1973, 20–24, Filmmakers/SF, SF History Center, SF Public Library.

195. Ibid.

196. Ibid.

197. Ibid.

198. Jacques Marquette, "Streets of San Francisco Truly a Moving Experience," *AC* (August 1975): 908–909.

199. "Runaway Kids," *Life*, November 3, 1967, 18, 29; Aniko Bodroghkozy, *Groove Tube: Sixties Television and the Youth Rebellion* (Durham, NC: Duke University Press, 2001), 75–86.

200. Marquette, "Streets," *AC* (August 1975): 908–909.

201. See column from October 10, 1972; and Jack Rosenblum, "A Movie Plot," *San Francisco Examiner*, August 29, 1973; Filmmakers/SF, SF History Center, SF Public Library.

CHAPTER 6

1. David Cook, *Lost Illusions: American Cinema in the Shadow of Watergate and Vietnam, 1970–1979* (Berkeley: University of California Press, 2000), 498–500.

2. "All-Time Film Rental Champs," *Variety*, January 5, 1977, 16.

3. In a detailed case study of *The Conversation*, Lawrence Webb directly ties San Francisco's urban redevelopment to the film's narrative. I see a more tenuous connection between *The Conversation* and broader conceptions of the American city, resonant with Webb's larger argument on the impact of the urban crisis on 1970s filmmaking. See Lawrence Webb, *The Cinema of Urban Crisis* (Amsterdam: Amsterdam University Press, 2014), 138–144.

4. Charles Champlin, "Oscar Race '75: Blockbusters Versus Gems," *Los Angeles Times*, January 12, 1975, clippings file, "Locations-CA, San Francisco," Margaret Herrick Library, AMPAS.

5. Herb Caen, "It Takes All Kinds," *San Francisco Chronicle*, February 4, 1974, 35.

6. Clipping from March 14, 1973, Filmmakers/SF, *San Francisco Examiner* clippings file, SF History Center, SF Public Library.

7. Judy Warrenfeltz, "A Day at The Movies," *Sunday Examiner and Chronicle*, June 10, 1973; Jack Rosenblum, "A Star is Born," *Sunday Examiner and Chronicle*, April 25, 1973; both in Filmmakers/SF, SF History Center, SF Public Library.

8. Clipping from *San Francisco Examiner*, January 5, 1975, Filmmakers/SF, SF History Center, SF Public Library.

9. Clipping from *San Francisco Examiner*, February 23, 1975, Filmmakers/SF, SF History Center, SF Public Library.

10. Philip Hager, "City Helps Out: Background for Films? Often It's San Francisco," *Los Angeles Times*, December 9, 1973, F1, 31; "Film in San Francisco, 1973"; Filmmakers/SF, SF History Center, SF Public Library.

11. Dick Alexander, "On Location in San Francisco," *San Francisco Examiner*, February 27, 1973, Filmmakers/SF, SF History Center, SF Public Library.

12. List of locations for *The Laughing Policeman* (1973), "Committee on Filmmaking, 1971–1974," Alioto Papers, file no. SFH52A, SF History Center, SF Public Library.

13. Caen, "It Takes All Kinds," *San Francisco Chronicle*, February 4, 1974, 35.

14. Duffy Jennings, "Movies Giving S.F. a Bad Name," *San Francisco Chronicle*, April 26, 1974, Filmmakers/SF, SF History Center, SF Public Library.

15. David Talbot, *Season of the Witch: Enchantment, Terror, and Deliverance in the City of Love* (New York: Simon and Schuster, 2012), 169, 206–215.

16. Caen, "It Takes All Kinds," *San Francisco Chronicle*, February 4, 1974, 35; clipping from *San Francisco Examiner*, August 8, 1974; Filmmakers/SF, SF History Center, SF Public Library.

17. Jim Harwood, "Frisco Cops Reflecting Screen Image, or Are Films Mirroring Real-Life Men in Blue?," *Daily Variety*, January 10, 1974.

18. Jennings, "Movies 'Giving S.F. a Bad Name,'" *San Francisco Chronicle*, April 26, 1974.

19. Hager, "City Helps Out," *Los Angeles Times*, December 9, 1973, F1, 31.

20. Anthony Ray to Donald Scott, January 18, 1973, "Committee" folder, Alioto Papers, SF History Center, SF Public Library.

21. Ibid.

22. Hager, "City Helps Out," *Los Angeles Times*, December 9, 1973, F1, 31.

23. Ibid.

24. Caen, "That's Me All Over," *San Francisco Chronicle*, March 12, 1973, Filmmakers/SF, SF History Center, SF Public Library.

25. Ibid.

26. Donald Tayer to John DeLuca, May 29, 1973, "Committee" folder, Alioto Papers, SF History Center, SF Public Library.

27. Jeanne Miller, "Next, He'll Set Fire to an S.F. Skyscraper," *San Francisco Examiner*, September 21, 1973, Filmmakers/SF, SF History Center, SF Public Library.

28. Production notes from location scouting trip to San Francisco, December 10–14, 1974, *Killer Elite* locations, folder 507, Sam Peckinpah Papers, Margaret Herrick Library, AMPAS.

29. Miller, "Next, He'll Set Fire to an S.F. Skyscraper," *San Francisco Examiner*, September 21, 1973, Filmmakers/SF, SF History Center, SF Public Library.

30. "Frisco Fest Name-Drop," *Variety*, October 22, 1975.

31. Production notes, December 10–14, 1974, Peckinpah Papers, Margaret Herrick Library, AMPAS.

32. K. Connie Kang, "Too Tough to Tumble," *San Francisco Examiner*, April 28, 1975, Filmmakers/SF, SF History Center, SF Public Library.

33. Moder to DeLuca, November 29 and December 19, 1972, "Committee" folder, Alioto Papers, SF History Center, SF Public Library.

34. "Filming to Close Freeway," *San Francisco Examiner*, April 7, 1973, Filmmakers/SF, SF History Center, SF Public Library.

35. "Tout Frisco Location," *Variety*, July 31, 1974.

36. "Location: San Francisco," *Killer Elite* locations, folder 507, Peckinpah Papers, Margaret Herrick Library, AMPAS.

37. "Not 'One-Stop' for S.F. Permits," *Hollywood Reporter*, July 21, 1976, clippings file, "Locations-CA, San Francisco," Peckinpah Papers, Margaret Herrick Library, AMPAS.

38. "McG to JAD [John DeLuca]," March 16, 1973, "Committee" folder, Alioto Papers, SF History Center, SF Public Library.

39. Ann Hanley, "San Francisco's Film, Video Industry Awakening," *Hollywood Reporter*, March 11, 1976, clippings file; "Locations-CA, San Francisco," Peckinpah Papers, Margaret Herrick Library, AMPAS.

40. Clipping from *San Francisco Chronicle*, January 8, 1970, Filmmakers/SF, SF History Center, SF Public Library.

41. Production notes, December 10–14, 1974, Peckinpah Papers, Margaret Herrick Library, AMPAS.

42. Ad, *Variety*, July 31, 1974, 29.

43. Several articles on Florida filmmaking appear in the June 1973 issue of *AC*.

44. George Williamson, "The Anonymous Actors of S.F.," December 16, 1974, *San Francisco Chronicle*, Filmmakers/SF, SF History Center, SF Public Library.

45. Ibid.

46. Marian Zailian, "For Frustrated S.F. Actors, the Times Are Changing," *San Francisco Chronicle*, July 4, 1976, Filmmakers/SF, SF History Center, SF Public Library.

47. Herb Caen, "That's Me All Over," *San Francisco Chronicle*, October 19, 1971, 17.

48. Army Archerd, "Hollywood Cross-Cuts," *Variety*, January 29, 1969, 26.

49. Gene Phillips, *Godfather: The Intimate Francis Ford Coppola* (Lexington: University Press of Kentucky, 2013), 67–72.

50. "Pictures: Moderate Fees in Directors Co.; Payoff Later With Stock Issue," *Variety*, September 6, 1972, 3, 13.

51. Phillips, *Godfather,* 72–75.

52. Ibid., 65.

53. Herb Lightman, "Photokina 74," *AC* (December 1974): 1407–1408, 1466.

54. Mona Skager to Mike Medavoy, January 3, 1974, Production-*Killer Elite*, folder 415, Peckinpah Papers, Margaret Herrick Library, AMPAS.

55. "'THX 1138': Made in San Francisco," *AC* (October 1971): 993–994, 1018–1019, 1031, 1058–1059, 1062.

56. Stanley Eichelbaum, "Debut of a Personal Filmmaking Plant," *San Francisco Examiner*, December 12, 1969, Filmmakers/SF, SF History Center, SF Public Library.

57. Haskell Wexler oral history, 390, Margaret Herrick Library, AMPAS; Phillips, *Godfather,* 75.

58. Phillips, *Godfather,* 75–76.

59. Wexler oral history, 387, Margaret Herrick Library, AMPAS.

60. Ibid., 387, 393.

61. Ibid., 390.

62. Phillips, *Godfather,* 75.

63. Michael Ondaatje, *The Conversations: Walter Murch and the Art of Editing Film* (New York: Knopf, 2002), 157, 161–162.

64. Phillips, *Godfather,* 80.

65. David Bordwell, Janet Staiger, and Kristen Thompson, *The Classical Hollywood Cinema: Film Style and Mode of Production to 1960* (New York: Columbia University Press, 1985), 376–377.

66. "Charge Coppola Roughed TV Man," *Variety*, December 26, 1973, 5; "Coppola Act Is Out of 'The Godfather,'" *San Francisco Examiner*, February 22, 1973, Filmmakers/SF, SF History Center, SF Public Library.

67. Phillips, *Godfather,* 76, 80.

68. "Film Reviews: The Conversation," *Variety*, April 3, 1974, 14.

69. Phillips, *Godfather,* 83.

70. John Dorr, "Movie Review: Towering Inferno," *Hollywood Reporter*, December 16, 1974, "Locations-CA, San Francisco," clippings file, Margaret Herrick Library, AMPAS.

71. "Stirling Silliphant: Just One 'Disaster' After Another," December 18, 1974, publicity clippings, folder 9, box 20, Stirling Silliphant Papers, Special Collections, Young Research Library, UCLA.

72. Rick Setlowe, "Days of Extensive Location Shooting Numbered: Robson," *Daily Variety*, October 2, 1968, 8.

73. Charles Loring, "The Towering Inferno and How It Was Filmed," *AC* (February 1975): 158–161.

74. "Locations on the Wane, More Films Roll in Studios: Burbank's Hagel," *Variety*, October 10, 1973, 5.

75. *Towering Inferno* shooting schedule, 1974, folder 13, box 49, Silliphant Papers, Special Collections, Young Research Library, UCLA.

76. Addison Verrill, "U.S. Antihero Films Flop Overseas, Decry 'Default of Sentiment,'" *Variety*, April 24, 1974, 3, 24.

77. John Campbell, "The Upside-Down Filming of 'The Poseidon Adventure,'" *AC* (September 1972): 990–993, 1026–1027, 1070–1071.

78. Loring, "The Towering Inferno," *AC* (February 1975): 158–161.

79. Dick Atkins, ed., *Method to the Madness (Hollywood Explained)* (Livingston, NJ: Prince, 1975), 175–179.

80. "The Towering Inferno," *IATSE Bulletin*, Joseph Biroc Papers, Margaret Herrick Library, AMPAS.

81. "Stirling Silliphant," December 18, 1974, Silliphant Papers, Special Collections, Young Research Library, UCLA.

82. Dorr, "Movie Review: Towering Inferno," *Hollywood Reporter*, December 16, 1974, Margaret Herrick Library, AMPAS.

83. "The Towering Inferno," *IATSE Bulletin*, Biroc Papers, Margaret Herrick Library, AMPAS.

84. Herb Lightman, "The Production Design," *AC* (November 1974): 1326–1329, 1342.

85. Dorr, "Movie Review: Towering Inferno," *Hollywood Reporter*, December 16, 1974, Margaret Herrick Library, AMPAS.

86. Atkins, *Method to the Madness*, 176.

87. Miller, "Next, He'll Set Fire," *San Francisco Examiner*, September, 21, 1973, Filmmakers/SF, SF History Center, SF Public Library.

88. Atkins, *Method to the Madness*, 176.

89. "Film Reviews: The Towering Inferno," *Variety*, December 18, 1974, 13.

90. Marc Eliot, *Steve McQueen: A Biography* (New York: Random House, 2011), 276–278; "Stirling Silliphant," December 18, 1974, folder 9, Silliphant Papers, UCLA-SC.

91. Biskind, *Easy Riders, Raging Bulls: How the Sex-Drugs-and-Rock-n-Roll Generation Saved Hollywood* (New York: Simon and Schuster, 1999), 279.

92. Atkins, *Method to the Madness*, 177; Campbell, "The Upside-Down Filming," *AC* (September 1972): 990–993, 1026–1027, 1070–1071.

93. Loring, "The Towering Inferno," *AC* (February 1975): 158–161.

94. "The Towering Inferno," *IATSE Bulletin*, Biroc Papers, Margaret Herrick Library, AMPAS.

95. Bob Fisher, "Photographing the Dramatic Sequences for 'The Towering Inferno,'" *AC* (February 1975): 162–165.

96. David Hammond, "'Action Unit' Lives Up to Its Name While Shooting 'The Towering Inferno,'" *AC* (February 1975): 166–169, 228–229.

97. "Film Reviews: The Towering Inferno," *Variety*, December 18, 1974, 13.

98. Meeting notes, July 20, 1973, folder 3, box 64, file 1079, Silliphant Papers, Margaret Herrick Library, AMPAS.

99. "The Towering Inferno," June 13, 1974, folder 456, *The Towering Inferno*, Linwood Dunn Papers, Margaret Herrick Library, AMPAS.

100. Hammond, "Action Unit," *AC* (February 1975): 166–169, 228–229.

101. *Towering Inferno* shooting schedule, 1974, folder 13, box 49, Silliphant Papers, Margaret Herrick Library, AMPAS.

102. Susan Berman, "They Moaned, They Groaned; Paul Newman Didn't Show," *San Francisco Examiner*, July 22, 1974, Filmmakers/SF, SF History Center, SF Public Library.

103. Clipping from unknown newspaper, July 15, 1974, publicity clippings, folder 9, box 20, Silliphant Papers, Margaret Herrick Library, AMPAS.

104. Hammond, "Action Unit," *AC* (February 1975): 166–169, 228–229.

105. Fisher, "Photographing the Dramatic Sequences," *AC* (February 1975): 162–165.

106. Hammond, "Action Unit," *AC* (February 1975): 166–169, 228–229.

107. Notes from battalion chief Jack Cavallero, San Francisco Fire Department, meeting notes, folder 3, box 64, file 1079, Silliphant Papers; "The Towering Inferno," *IATSE Bulletin*, Biroc Papers; both at Margaret Herrick Library, AMPAS.

108. "Firemen Switch, Aid 'Inferno' Film," *San Francisco Examiner*, November 1, 1974, Filmmakers/SF, SF History Center, SF Public Library.

109. *Towering Inferno* ad, *Variety*, January 8, 1975, publicity clippings, folder 9, box 20, Silliphant Papers, Margaret Herrick Library, AMPAS.

110. Hammond, "Action Unit," 166–169, 228–229.

111. Cook, *Lost Illusions*, 255.

112. Biskind, *Easy Riders, Raging Bulls*, 266–267.

113. Ibid., 263.

114. Ibid., 276.

115. Ibid., 277.

116. Cook, *Lost Illusions*, 47–51.

117. Cook, *Lost Illusions*, Appendix 6, 492.

118. Clipping from *San Francisco Examiner*, May 30, 1976, Filmmakers/SF, SF History Center, SF Public Library.

119. Cook, *Lost Illusions*, 40–50.

CONCLUSION

1. Jim Harwood, "Frisco Filmmaking Largely Transient," *Daily Variety*, October 29, 1974, 98.

2. Kathy Ryan to John DeLuca, December 4, 1974, "Committee" folder, Alioto Papers, SF History Center, SF Public Library.

3. Harwood, "Frisco Filmmaking," *Daily Variety*, October 29, 1974, 98.

4. Ibid.

5. Ibid.

6. Liz Brady, "California's New Motion Picture Development Council," *AC* (June 1976): 678, 695–697.

7. A YouTube compilation highlights how frequently the Golden Gate Bridge appears under assault in Hollywood cinema: http://www.youtube.com/watch?v=jw7K6zg3fhI (accessed July 23, 2014).

8. Much of *Zodiac* and *Milk* took place during San Francisco's location shooting boom of the 1960s and 1970s, and reproduce certain film aesthetics of the period, including low-key night cinematography in *Zodiac* and desaturated color in *Milk*.

9. All of the series listed ran at least 100 episodes.

10. Dave McNary, "Set in California, but Shot Where It Is Cheap," *Variety*, March 15, 2014, 33–34.

11. Michele Manelis, "How Weta Digital Conquered 'Planet of the Apes' Again," *Queensland Times*, July 18, 2014, http://www.qt.com.au/news/how-weta-digital-conquered-planet-apes-again/2315993/ (accessed July 25, 2014).

12. McNary, "Set in California," *Variety*, March 15, 2014, 33–34.

13. Ibid.

14. Ibid.

BIBLIOGRAPHY

ARCHIVAL SOURCES

Alioto, Joseph. Papers. San Francisco History Center, San Francisco Public Library.

Bacon, Lloyd. Papers. Margaret Herrick Library, Academy of Motion Picture Arts and Sciences (AMPAS).

Biroc, Joseph. Papers. Margaret Herrick Library, AMPAS.

Dunn, Linwood. Papers. Margaret Herrick Library, AMPAS.

Erickson, Doc. Oral History. Margaret Herrick Library, AMPAS.

Fraker, William. Oral History. Margaret Herrick Library, AMPAS.

Hitchcock, Alfred. Papers. Margaret Herrick Library, AMPAS.

Keller, Frank. Papers. Margaret Herrick Library, AMPAS.

King, Henry. Papers. Margaret Herrick Library, AMPAS.

Kramer, Stanley. Papers. Special Collections, Charles E. Young Research Library, University of California, Los Angeles (UCLA).

Kurland, Gil. Papers. Margaret Herrick Library, AMPAS.

Malden, Karl. Oral History. Margaret Herrick Library, AMPAS.

Paramount Production Records. Margaret Herrick Library, AMPAS.

Peckinpah, Sam. Papers. Margaret Herrick Library, AMPAS.

RKO Production Records. Special Collections, Charles E. Young Research Library, UCLA.

Rogers, Donald, Oral History. Margaret Herrick Library, AMPAS.

San Francisco Examiner. Movies/SF, clippings file. San Francisco History Center, San Francisco Public Library.

Silliphant, Stirling. Papers. Special Collections, Charles E. Young Research Library, UCLA. Technicolor Collection. Margaret Herrick Library, AMPAS.

Warner Bros. Archives. UCLA.

Wexler, Haskell. Oral History. Margaret Herrick Library, AMPAS.

BIBLIOGRAPHY

Affron, Charles, and Mirella Jona Affron. *Sets in Motion: Art Direction and Film Narrative*. New Brunswick, NJ: Rutgers University Press, 1995.

Allen, Robert, and Douglas Gomery. *Film History: Theory and Practice*. New York: Knopf, 1985.

Anderson, Christopher. *Hollywood TV: The Studio System in the Fifties*. Austin: University of Texas Press, 1994.

Atkins, Dick, ed. *Method to the Madness (Hollywood Explained)*. Livingston, NJ: Prince, 1975.

Bach, Steven. *Final Cut: Art, Money, and Ego in the Making of Heaven's Gate, the Film That Sank United Artists*. New York: Newmarket, 1999.

Balio, Tino. *United Artists: The Company That Changed the Film Industry*. Madison: University of Wisconsin Press, 1987.

Bazin, André. *What is Cinema?*. 2 vols. Edited and translated by Hugh Gray. Berkeley: University of California Press, 2005.

Beauregard, Robert. *Voices of Decline: The Postwar Fate of U.S. Cities*. Oxford: Wiley-Blackwell, 1994.

Bell, Geoffrey. *The Golden Gate and the Silver Screen*. New York: AAUP, 1984.

Belton, John. *Widescreen Cinema*. Cambridge, MA: Harvard University Press, 1992.

Bernstein, Matthew. *Walter Wanger: Hollywood Independent*. Minneapolis: University of Minnesota Press, 2000.

Biesen, Sheri Chinen. *Blackout: World War II and the Origins of Film Noir*. Baltimore: Johns Hopkins University Press, 2005.

Bingen, Steven, Stephen X. Sylvester, and Michael Troyan. *MGM: Hollywood's Greatest Backlot*. Solano Beach, CA: Santa Monica Press, 2011.

Biskind, Peter. *Easy Riders, Raging Bulls: How the Sex-Drugs-And-Rock 'n' Roll Generation Saved Hollywood*. New York: Simon and Schuster, 1998.

Boddy, William. *Fifties Television: The Industry and Its Critics*. Urbana: University of Illinois Press, 1990.

Bodroghkozy, Aniko. *Groove Tube: Sixties Television and the Youth Rebellion*. Durham, NC: Duke University Press, 2001.

Bordwell, David, Janet Staiger, and Kristen Thompson. *The Classical Hollywood Cinema: Film Style and Mode of Production to 1960*. New York: Columbia University Press, 1985.

Brook, James, Chris Carlsson, and Nancy Peters. *Reclaiming San Francisco: History, Politics, Culture*. San Francisco: City Lights, 1998.

Brooks, Tim, and Earle Marsh. *The Complete Directory to Prime Time Network TV Shows: 1946–Present*. 5th ed. New York: Ballantine, 1992.

Chisholm, Brad. "Red, Blue, and Lots of Green: The Impact of Color Television on Feature Film Production." In *Hollywood in the Age of Television*, edited by Tino Balio, 213–234. Boston: Unwin Hyman, 1990.

Ciment, Michael. *John Boorman*. London: Faber, 1986.

Clark, Kenneth B. *Dark Ghetto: Dilemmas of Social Power*. New York: Harper and Row, 1967.

Cook, David. *Lost Illusions: American Cinema in the Shadow of Watergate and Vietnam, 1970–1979*. Berkeley: University of California Press, 2000.

Corkin, Stanley. *Starring New York: Filming the Grime and the Glamour of the Long 1970s*. New York: Oxford University Press, 2011.

Cunningham, Douglas, ed. *The San Francisco of Alfred Hitchcock's Vertigo: Place, Pilgrimage, and Commemoration*. Lanham, MD: Scarecrow, 2012.

Curtis, Scott. "The Last Word: Images in Hitchcock's Working Method." In *Casting a Shadow: Creating the Alfred Hitchcock Film*, edited by Will Schmenner and Corinne Granof, 14–26. Chicago: Northwestern University Press, 2007.

Dick, Bernard. *City of Dreams: The Making and Remaking of Universal Pictures*. Lexington: University of Kentucky Press, 1997.

———, ed. *Columbia Pictures*. Lexington: University Press of Kentucky, 1992.

Dimendberg, Edward. *Film Noir and the Spaces of Modernity*. Cambridge, MA: Harvard University Press, 2004.

Doherty, Thomas. *Cold War, Cool Medium: Television, McCarthyism, and American Culture*. New York: Columbia University Press, 2003.

Dombrowski, Lisa. "Postwar Hollywood, 1947–1967." In *Cinematography*, edited by Patrick Keating, 60–83. New Brunswick, NJ: Rutgers University Press, 2014.

Eliot, Marc. *Steve McQueen: A Biography*. New York: Random House, 2011.

Fainstein, Susan, Norman Fainstein, Richard Child Hill, Dennis R. Judd, and Michael Peter Smith. *Restructuring the City: The Political Economy of Urban Redevelopment*. New York: Longman, 1986.

Godfrey, Brian. "Urban Development and Redevelopment in San Francisco." *Geographical Review* 87, no. 3 (July 1997): 316–319.

Gruen, Victor. *The Heart of Our Cities*. New York: Simon and Schuster, 1964.

Guback, Thomas. "Hollywood's International Market." In *The American Film Industry*, edited by Tino Balio, 387–409. Madison: University of Wisconsin Press, 1976.

Hall, Peter Geoffrey. *Cities of Tomorrow: An Intellectual History of Urban Planning and Design in the Twentieth Century*. 3rd ed. Oxford, UK: Blackwell, 2002.

Harris, Mark. *Pictures at a Revolution: Five Movies and the Birth of New Hollywood.* New York: Penguin, 2009.

Hartman, Chester, with Sarah Carnochan. *City for Sale: The Transformation of San Francisco.* Berkeley: University of California Press, 2002.

Higashi, Sumiko. "Realism in Urban Art and The Naked City." In *Looking Past the Screen: Case Studies in American Film History and Method,* edited by Jon Lewis and Eric Smoodin, 353–380. Durham, NC: Duke University Press, 2007.

Higgins, Scott. *Harnessing the Technicolor Rainbow: Color Design in the 1930s.* Austin: University of Texas Press, 2009.

Issel, William. "'Land Values, Human Values, and the Preservation of the City's Treasured Appearance': Environmentalism, Politics, and the San Francisco Freeway Revolt." *Pacific Historical Review* 68, no. 4 (November 1999): 611–644.

Jacobs, Jane. *The Death and Life of Great American Cities.* New York: Random House, 1961.

———. "Downtown Is for People." In *The Exploding Metropolis,* edited by *Fortune,* 157–184. Garden City, NY: Doubleday, 1958.

Jencks, Charles. *The Language of Post-Modern Architecture.* Revised and enlarged edition. London: Rizzoli, 1977.

Keating, Patrick. *Hollywood Lighting from the Silent Era to Film Noir.* New York: Columbia University Press, 2010.

Kindem, Gorham. "Hollywood's Conversion to Color: The Technological, Economic and Aesthetic Factors." *Journal of the University Film Association* 31, no. 2 (Spring 1979): 29–36.

Koszarski, Richard. *Von: The Life and Films of Erich Von Stroheim.* New York: Proscenium, 2001.

Lafferty, William. "A Reappraisal of the Semi-Documentary in Hollywood, 1945–1948." *Velvet Light Trap* 20 (1983): 22–26.

Lathrop, William H., Jr. "San Francisco Freeway Revolt." *Transportation Engineering Journal* 97, no. TE1 (February 1971): 133–144.

Lev, Peter. *The Fifties: Transforming the Screen, 1950–1959.* Berkeley: University of California Press, 2006.

Longstreth, Richard. *City Center to Regional Mall: Architecture, the Automobile, and Retailing in Los Angeles, 1920–1950.* Cambridge, MA: MIT Press, 1997.

Luhr, William, and Peter Lehman. "Experiment in Terror: Dystopian Modernism, the Police Procedural, and the Space of Anxiety." In *Cinema and Modernity,* edited by Murray Pomerance, 174–193. New Brunswick, NJ: Rutgers University Press, 2006.

Lynch, Kevin. *Image of the City.* Cambridge, MA: MIT Press, 1964.

Mann, Denise. *Hollywood Independents: The Postwar Talent Takeover.* Minneapolis: University of Minnesota Press, 2008.

MacCannell, Dean. *The Tourist: A New Theory of the Leisure Class*. Berkeley: University of California Press, 1999.

McGilligan, Patrick. *Alfred Hitchcock: A Life in Darkness and Light*. New York: Regan Books, 2004.

———. *Clint: The Life and Legend*. New York: St. Martin's, 2002.

Monaco, Paul. *The Sixties, 1960–1969*. Berkeley: University of California Press, 2001.

Mumford, Lewis. *The City in History*. San Diego: Harcourt, 1961.

Naremore, James. *More Than Night: Film Noir in Its Contexts*. Berkeley: University of California Press, 1998.

Nowell-Smith, Geoffrey. "Cities: Real and Imagined." In *Cinema and the City: Film and Urban Societies in a Global Context*, edited by Mark Shiel and Tony Fitzmaurice, 99–108. Chichester: John Wiley and Sons, 2008.

Ondaatje, Michael. *The Conversations: Walter Murch and the Art of Editing Film*. New York: Knopf, 2002.

Palmer, R. Barton. *Shot on Location: Postwar American Cinema and the Exploration of Real Place*. New Brunswick, NJ: Rutgers University Press, 2016.

Palmer, R. Barton, and William Bray. *Hollywood's Tennessee*. Austin: University of Texas Press, 2009.

Perlstein, Rick. *Nixonland: The Rise of a President and the Fracturing of America*. New York: Scribner, 2008.

Phillips, Gene. *Godfather: The Intimate Francis Ford Coppola*. Lexington: University of Kentucky Press, 2013.

Ramaeker, Paul. "Realism, Revisionism and Visual Style: The French Connection and the New Hollywood Policier." *New Review of Film and Television Studies* 8, no. 2 (June 2010): 144–163.

Rodriguez, Joseph A. *City Against Suburb: The Culture Wars in an American Metropolis*. Westport, CT: Praeger, 1999.

Rosenblum, Ralph, and Robert Karen. *When the Shooting Stops . . .* New York: DeCapo, 1986.

Rowe, Colin, and Fred Koetter. *Collage City*. Cambridge, MA: MIT Press, 1984.

Salt, Barry. *Film Style and Technology: History and Analysis*. 2nd ed. London: Starwood, 1992.

Saunders, Dave. *Direct Cinema*. New York: Wallflower, 2007.

Schatz, Thomas. *Boom and Bust: The American Cinema in the 1940s*. Berkeley: University of California Press, 1999.

———. *The Genius of the System: Hollywood Filmmaking in the Studio Era*. New York: Holt, 1988.

Schleier, Merrill. "Fatal Attractions: 'Place,' the Korean War, and Gender in Niagara." *Cinema Journal* 51, no. 4 (Summer 2012): 26–43.

Shandley, Robert. *Runaway Romances: Hollywood's Postwar Tour of Europe*. Philadelphia: Temple University Press, 2009.

Shiel, Mark. *Hollywood Cinema and the Real Los Angeles*. London: Reaktion, 2012.

———. "A Regional Geography of Film Noir: Urban Dystopias On-and Off-Screen." In *Noir Urbanisms: Dystopic Images of the Modern City*, edited by Gyan Prakash, 75–103. Princeton, NJ: Princeton University Press, 2010.

Siegel, Allan. "After the Sixties: Changing Paradigms in the Representation of Urban Space." In *Screening the City*, edited by Mark Shiel and Tony Fitzmaurice, 137–159. London: Verso, 2003.

Siegel, Don. *A Siegel Film: An Autobiography*. London: Faber and Faber, 1993.

Slotkin, Richard. *Gunfighter Nation: The Myth of the Frontier in Twentieth-Century America*. New York: HarperPerennial, 1993.

Smith, Jeff. *The Sounds of Commerce: Marketing Popular Film Music*. New York: Columbia University Press, 1998.

Solnit, Rebecca. "Cinema City: Muybridge Inventing Movies, Hitchcock Making Vertigo." In *Infinite City: A San Francisco City Atlas*, map 3. Berkeley: University of California Press, 2010.

Talbot, David. *Season of the Witch: Enchantment, Terror, and Deliverance in the City of Love*. New York: Simon and Schuster, 2012.

Turnock, Julie. "The Screen on the Set: The Problem of Classical-Studio Rear Projection." *Cinema Journal* 51, no. 2 (Winter 2012): 157–162.

Van Buskirk, Jim, and Will Shank. *Celluloid San Francisco*. Chicago: Chicago Review Press, 2006.

Virilio, Paul. *War and Cinema: The Logistics of Perception*. London: Verso, 1989.

Walker, Richard. "An Appetite for the City." In *Reclaiming San Francisco*, edited by James Brook, Chris Carlsson, and Nancy Peters, 1–19. San Francisco: City Lights, 1998.

———. "Landscape and City Life: Four Ecologies of Residence in the San Francisco Bay Area." *Ecumene* 2, no. 1 (1995): 33–64.

Wasson, Sam. *A Splurch in the Kisser: The Movies of Blake Edwards*. Middletown, CT: Wesleyan University Press, 2009.

Webb, Lawrence. *The Cinema of Urban Crisis*. Amsterdam: Amsterdam University Press, 2014.

Whyte, William. "Introduction." In *The Exploding Metropolis*, edited by *Fortune*, 7–22. Garden City, NY: Doubleday, 1958.

Wilshire, Peter. "The Art of Dying: Point Blank." Offscreen.com 17, no. 4, http://www.offscreen.com/index.php/pages/essays/art_of_dying/.

Wojcik, Pamela. *The Apartment Plot: Urban Living in American Film and Popular Culture, 1945 to 1975*. Durham, NC: Duke University Press, 2010.

INDEX

Page numbers in italics refer to figures.